W9-COZ-700

DISCARDED

THE
UNIVERSITY OF WINNIPEG
PORTAGE & BALMORAL
WINNIPEG 2. MAN.   CANADA

A LIFE OF ROBERT CECIL

Donald Macbeth photo

Lord Burghley and his Son Robert, 1st Earl of Salisbury

from the picture by an unknown Painter at Hatfield House

DA
358
.S2C4
1971

A LIFE OF
ROBERT CECIL

FIRST EARL OF SALISBURY

By ALGERNON CECIL

AUTHOR OF "SIX OXFORD THINKERS" ETC.

WITH ILLUSTRATIONS

GREENWOOD PRESS, PUBLISHERS
WESTPORT, CONNECTICUT

Originally published in 1915
by John Murray, London

First Greenwood Reprinting 1971

Library of Congress Catalogue Card Number 71-109717

SBN 8371-4207-5

Printed in the United States of America

TO

MY FATHER·

THE OLDEST LIVING OF ROBERT CECIL'S DESCENDANTS

THIS BOOK

IS VERY AFFECTIONATELY DEDICATED

PREFACE

THIS book, like all books of the kind, has put me under very heavy obligations. To Lord Salisbury I am especially indebted for permission to see and to make use of the vast collection of MSS. at Hatfield, of which even a larger number bear upon the life of Robert Cecil than upon that of his father. Part of these are now accessible to the public through the *Calendar* published by the Historical Manuscripts Commission ; but several volumes of the *Calendar* are not as yet in print, and I am very much more than grateful to the Historical Manuscripts Commissioners for allowing me to read through these in the rough, and particularly to Sir Edward Fry and Mr. R. A. Roberts for promoting my application to do so. Permission was granted to me on the understanding that I should only transcribe passages for citation from the original documents, and I have tried faithfully to carry out this regulation.

Apart from the Papers themselves and the *Calendars* made of them, my obligations at Hatfield are still very large. From my cousins, Lord and Lady Salisbury and Lady Gwendolen Cecil, I have received much kindness, which I could not attempt to particularise, but which I shall never forget. And to Lady Gwendolen I owe also one or more valuable suggestions about the subject-matter. But my debt at Hatfield would remain still in great part unacknowledged if I were to omit to thank Mr. R. T. Gunton for his unfailing and invaluable assistance, the outcome of a long familiarity with the family records and an immense knowledge of the family history. The private memoranda regarding Robert Cecil, which he has compiled, were placed at my disposal, and have been a most valuable source of information. I am sure I speak not for myself alone, but on behalf of all members of the Cecil family, when I thank him most unfeignedly for the infinite care and unflagging research which he has devoted to the study of Hatfield and its inhabitants.

It is not, of course, at Hatfield alone that Robert Cecil has to be sought. The Record Office contains much of the most interesting information about him ; and from Mr. Hubert Hall and Mr. A. E. Stamp I have received the kindest assistance and advice. To them, as to others at the Record Office, I tender my warmest thanks.

At various times and in various manners I have contracted lesser but not less real obligations. The Master of St. John's College, Cambridge, very kindly supplied me with all the available information about Cecil's connection with that place. My friends, Dr. Norman Moore and Mr. Geoffrey Gathorne-Hardy, gave me some interesting help—the one of a medical, the other of a legal character—for which I am greatly obliged. To Lord Spencer, the Duke of Westminster, Maud, Lady Calthorpe, and Mr. John Audley Harvey I owe much gratitude for the permission, most kindly accorded, to read and use manuscripts belonging to them. To Lord Winchilsea and Nottingham I desire to express my thanks for his letter regarding a MS. once in the Hatton Collection. To Mr. Warwicke Bond I am grateful for a letter of advice in regard to a special point of which he had knowledge. To Admiral the Hon. Sir Hedworth Meux I am obliged for a permission to visit the scanty remains of the old palace at Theobalds ; and to his agent, Mr. Pryce Harrison, for showing me over them. And I must not forget to thank Mr. R. Merriman of Sempringham, near Marlborough, for the generous and kindly assistance he gave me, an entire stranger to him, in tracing the locality of Salisbury's death.

To Don Juan Montéro of the Archivo General de Simancas I am greatly indebted for the researches he has been kind enough to make on my account in regard to the question of Salisbury's Spanish pension. And I am also much obliged to MM. Jaimé de Ceniga and R. Martinez for the very careful translations which they made for me of documents relating to that affair. I cannot conclude my list of acknowledgments without adding one other name. Mr. Herbert Fisher has been in no way connected with the making of this volume. But everyone who has tried to write a book must be aware that a statement of his immediate obligations represents but a mere fraction of his real debts. And my con-

science and my affection would remain alike un-
satisfied if I made no allusion here to one of the
best of tutors and most generous of friends.

*   *   *

It seems proper to add a word in regard to a
matter which, as a friend has pointed out to me, might
attract criticism or provoke misunderstanding. I
have from time to time used the term ' Catholic '
where most members of the English Church would
now write ' Roman Catholic.' I have not done this
with any militant intention ; nor must I be supposed
to associate myself in this place with either party
in the controversy which rages around the word.
At the time of which I am writing the expression
would have been generally accepted as implying an
adherent of the Papacy, and it is in this sense that,
for convenience' sake, I use it. If I were compelled
further to defend myself I should do so by pointing
out that this is the meaning which so accomplished
a theologian as James I. is content to give to it within
a year or so of his becoming Defender of the Faith,
and in a letter where he makes a profession of High
Church doctrine.

A. C.

September 28th, 1914.

CONTENTS

LIST OF ILLUSTRATIONS

[I have to thank Lord Salisbury for kindly permitting the reproduction
of the pictures mentioned above as being at Hatfield.]

A LIFE OF ROBERT CECIL

FIRST EARL OF SALISBURY

CHAPTER I

THE STAGE AND THE ACTOR

" Weep not, my wanton, smile upon my knee ;
When thou art old, there's grief enough for thee.''
Sephestia's Song to her Child in GREENE's " Menaphon.''

" FOR my own part," says Gibbon,[1] in a familiar
passage, " could I draw my pedigree from a general,
a statesman, or a celebrated author, I should study
their lives with the diligence of filial love." To many
to whom Gibbon's studies are a care and Gibbon's
memory a cult, those words have doubtless come home
both as a charge and as an inspiration. More fortunately situated than he was, they have found at hand
a pious duty to perform, and have entered upon it
in some, perhaps vain, perhaps presumptuous, hope
that out of the very accident of their descent they
may bring to bear upon their subject a keener insight
and a firmer grasp. And Robert Cecil, as it happens,
has never found, in any adequate sense of the term,
a biographer. Though he was for fourteen years to
all intents and purposes Prime Minister of England,
though his premiership chanced to cover almost
exactly the duration of those momentous years in
which Shakespeare was giving to the world the
supreme glories of the English race, yet he has met

[1] *Memoirs*, p. 3.

with the scantiest attention ; and in the long procession of English statesmen, his figure, naturally
pathetic, seems to have acquired all the added pathos
of neglect. Beside the splendid gifts of his contemporaries, beside the reckless valour of Essex,
the splendid vitality of Ralegh, the far-shining
wisdom of Bacon, his own patient labour has
passed unperceived, just as amid that crowd of
splendid gallants, among whom his lot was cast,
his own insignificant person passed unnoticed or
despised. Statesmanship is commonly impatient
of heroics, and Robert Cecil was not a hero. He
carried on the tradition of a cautious policy, under
which his country had grown great, and in no
contemptible sense he was his father's son: Placed
between two epochs of momentous revolution
—between the close of the great Protestant up-
heaval and the bursting of the greater Puritan
storm—the administration of the Cecils possesses
of necessity rather the tentative character of a
provisional government than the strong repose of a
national spirit perfectly at one with itself. The
country was passing through a hundred and fifty
years of unrest, the inevitable consequence of the
tremendous mental and spiritual shock of the
Renaissance and the Reformation. The time was
not ripe for a settlement, and the merit of the Cecils
is that they made no attempt to hurry it. But this
is perhaps of all merits the least alluring. Also, in a
measure, it is true that Robert Cecil has been his own
worst enemy. He made no bids for popularity ; he
was usually indifferent to the opinion of the mob ;
and he left little record of that inner life of thought
and being which might have won him the sympathy
or the interest of more penetrating critics. Careful
only of that which was his care, well-beloved only
of those who knew him well, he moves across the
page of history, a dim figure picking his way across

untravelled country, beneath uncertain lights, towards a goal which no man clearly saw.

We need not labour his pedigree. It was enough
distinction for him then, and is still, to have been
born his father's son ; and we may leave ambiguous
that dim descent from the princes of Wales which
Camden was at some pains to establish for Lord
Burghley. He was born on 1st June 1563,[1] perhaps at
his father's house in Cannon Row.[2] The Fates, with
delicate irony, twisted the slender thread of the infant's
life into the web of those larger destinies with which
the man was some day to struggle. The year of his
birth was that in which a Puritan Parliament first urged
the problem of the succession upon its Sovereign's
notice. Four years earlier the House of Commons
had pressed the Queen to marry, and had received
an ambiguous reply, which they took for a modest
assent, and the Queen intended for a gracious refusal.
From that time, for close on twenty-five years, Elizabeth prostituted the noblest of human passions to
the manifold exigencies of her diplomacy. The detail
of her policy became of design an endless mystification, incomprehensible to her enemies, her people,
sometimes to her ministers, perhaps sometimes to
herself. She was the most unabashed of opportunists.
To-morrow and to-morrow and to-morrow crept in
with petty pace for thirty years, whilst the Queen
groped her way amidst her perils, saving herself again
and again by costly sacrifices of honour and decency,
being saved again and again by her own good fortune,
by the allies, to whom she dealt out her parsimonious
subsidies, and by those greater allies to whom she
gave no subsidies at all—wind and wave and the
stout hearts of her English people. It may be true

[1] *Hatfield Calendar*, pt. v. p. 69 ; see also the inscription on Lady
Burghley's tomb in Westminster Abbey.

[2] The registry at St. Margaret's, Westminster, does not, however,
show any entry respecting his baptism.

that a more straightforward policy offered a poorer
chance of success, though either a consistent adhesion
to the Protestant policy of Leicester and Walsingham,
or the Flemish policy of Burghley, would have been
infinitely more creditable than that irregular mixture
of the two which the Queen preferred. It may be—
for the opinion is in effect Burghley's own [1]—that
Elizabeth did in fact realise the conception of her
famous portrait at Hatfield, and was the possessor of a
thousand eyes and ears and of that serpentine sagacity
which even the Bible does not hesitate to commend.
But if this be so—and good judges have doubted
it—it is still true that these are not the dominant
emblems in the picture. " Non sine sole iris " :—in
the rainbow-lights that play about her hand lies
quivering the genius of Elizabeth. She was possessed
of that radiant patriotism, that abiding confidence
that God would not fail her people, that indefinable
property of making men realise that their country
is the embodiment of a spiritual life deeper and
truer than their own, which is not of necessity in-
compatible with great personal selfishness.

That very selfishness had, besides, as we know,
its patriotic limitations. She never gratified herself
at the expense of the nation at large. Whatever
personal injustices she may have perpetrated, she
had at heart, and was felt to have, the integrity and
security of her people. She thought no sacrifice
too great for this. *Salus populi* was for her *suprema
lex* ; and she knew no other. By this law, therefore,
she has been judged, and will be judged while Time
lasts.

What is true of her is true also of the men who
worked for her. If, under the influence of the cos-
mopolitan and individualist spirit of the eighteenth
and nineteenth centuries, we have insensibly grown
accustomed to judge men's lives and work by widely

[1] Peck, *Desid. Cur.*, p. 46.

NON SINE SOLE
IRIS

QUEEN ELIZABETH. THE "RAINBOW" PICTURE

(Painted by Zucharo. Hatfield House)

[*To face p.* 4

different standards, we need the more carefully to adjust our criterion as we cross the threshold of the sixteenth. Devotion to country was at the heart of some of the best actions of that age, as of some of the worst. Dislodged from their ancient anchorage in the past, from that Christendom whence the Church had moved into action like a majestic fleet flying a common flag and inspired by a common hope, not yet inclined to entrust their salvation to the isolated effort of the human soul, the heirs of the English Reformation consecrated their loftiest emotion to the service of the State. They sought in their country the unity, the singleness of purpose which they could no longer find elsewhere ; they hedged their Sovereign in with a new divinity ; they required of their fellow-citizens a faith hardly less absolute and a fidelity something more stringent than had been asked before ; and they constructed a code of geographical morality which left them free to plunder and assault their foes out of season as well as in it. Those wonderful Elizabethan seamen, whom we hardly know whether to call heroes or freebooters, but from whom we cannot withhold our admiration, were at worst no more than the complement of the statesmen of their time. Everywhere the principles of Machiavelli were shamelessly practised, and, beside the profound and passionate sense of spiritual things which may be found even in the dying prayer of Machiavelli's earliest pupil,[1] we find the most unblushing deceit, the most insidious guile, the most pitiless cruelty. These things, no doubt, appeared to be almost part and parcel of public life, and men accepted them, just as we accept some of the more revolting practices of our own time, without too close inquiry. Public morality, even at its best, is relative to time and circumstance;

[1] Thomas Cromwell's last prayer is printed in Froude's *Hist. of Engl.*, chap. xvii.

only when we cross the threshold of the individual
conscience do we touch the absolute and perfectible.
A generation after Robert Cecil was laid in his grave,
the moral horror of the spy-system struck Falkland
in its fulness,[1] but even that lofty spirit could see
no way of escape, and only satisfied his scruples at
the expense of another man's integrity ; nor has the
world to this day found any more complete solution
of the problem than to avert its eyes. Burghley
and Cecil, if they had given the matter a thought,
would have said that they could not afford the
luxurious moralities of a settled government. They
used spies as they used the torture-chamber—in
their time at the climax of its employment [2]—because
these seemed the only practicable means of securing
the Sovereign's life. It is difficult to say a word in
their defence : it is almost as difficult to pronounce
their condemnation. We have to pass such things by,
remembering that the human mind is ' hospitable ' and
very patient of conflicting purposes, remembering that
from among these brutalities men emerged whose hearts
beat as high as our own, whose conduct sometimes
seems to glow with a larger and more radiant meaning.

Elizabeth, as she was the embodiment of many of
the qualities of her people—of their patriotism, their
courage, their patience, their sense of perspective, and
their masculine resolve—became also the cynosure
of their gallantry and the object of their trust. In
the ship of State (to use the ancient metaphor which
in regard to that age at least is no artificial one)
her part was that of the sail. She knew how to
catch every favouring breeze that blew, how to tack
and trim before every gale. Beside her, Burghley
seems like a mast, solid, serviceable, always in its

---

[1] Clarendon, *Great Rebellion*, vii. 226.

[2] " If we may draw our conclusions from the entries in the Council-
books there is no period of our history at which this instrument
(torture) was used more frequently and mercilessly than during the
latter years of Elizabeth's reign " (Jardine, *On the Use of Torture*, p. 26).

place, always steady. His function was, in fact, different, but not less necessary to the safe sailing of the vessel ; nor was Elizabeth ever in any real doubt of his importance to her success. The great historian of the period has borne an eloquent witness to the range and depth of Burghley's judgment, to his mastery of principle and detail. " From the great duel with Rome to the terraces and orange groves at Burleigh, nothing was too large for his intellect to grasp, nothing too small for his attention to condescend to consider."[1] But, for all that, the figure of the Lord Treasurer has rebelled obstinately against biographical treatment. It may be the fault of the biographers. Or it may be that in his case success was so even, so steady, that we lose interest in a career which seems mathematically assured. In all his long life there is but one record of an impulsive action—his early improvident marriage with the penniless Mary Cheke. Thenceforward he became a model of sedate and prudent conduct, a repertory of wise saws and solemn purposes. Shakespeare made fun of him in the character of Polonius ; and the world has accepted him ever since as the mirror of a complete statesman.

Robert Cecil was not the son of Mary Cheke. That unfortunate lady died within a year of her marriage, leaving a boy whose gay young blood was to be the plague of his father's slow pulses. Burghley married again some three years later. He appears to have preferred alliances which smacked of Greek scholarship and an Essex soil. Mary Cheke had been the sister of one of the finest Greek scholars of the time ; Mildred Cooke was the daughter of another. But Sir Anthony Cooke, besides being a noted Grecian, was a man of substance and counsel, tutor to Edward vi., and father of daughters, two of whom, at least—Lady Burghley and Lady Bacon

[1] Froude, *Hist. of Engl.*, vii. p. 462.

—were remarkably clever, and gave birth to remarkably clever sons. Mildred, the eldest, as the inscription on her tomb records, received her education at the hands of her father and at his hands alone. She won herself a name for wisdom, piety, domestic virtue, and unobtrusive benevolence, and was perhaps as admirable a disciple of the virtuous woman in the Proverbs as the world has seen. Timothe Bright, who knew her in her home, went so far as to compare the *domus Ceciliana* to a university.[1] From her the boy received his religious education— that " true knowledge and worship of his Creator and Redeemer " of which his father speaks, " without which all other things are vain and miserable." The complexion of Lady Burghley's Protestantism can hardly be doubtful. Sir Anthony Cooke had been one of those Englishmen who, like Bishop Jewel, had followed Peter Martyr to Strasburg during the Marian persecution ; and Jewel's *Apology*, which had been submitted to Burghley for approval before publication, may be taken to represent the ecclesiastical position of the Cookes and the Cecils. The main features of that position were the appeal to the faith and practice of the Primitive Church and the plain teaching of Scripture,[2] the identification of the Church of Rome with the Harlot of the Apocalypse,[3] and the assertion of a present fundamental unity of belief and of a future external concord between the Reformed Churches.[4]

Burghley no doubt gave to these things the limited measure of assent of which a man is capable who has not found it impossible to accommodate his devotions, as the times required, to three or four different codes of belief. He had neither the mind of a theologian nor the body of a martyr. But of those sound practical moralities which take the just

---

[1] W. J. Carlton, *Timothe Bright*, p. 28.
[2] Jewel, *Apology*, c. 6 and 4.   [3] *Ibid.*, c. 6.   [4] *Ibid.*, c. 3.

measure of success in the world we inhabit, his
conscience was a repertory. The Ten Precepts
which he addressed to his son Robert as a supple-
ment to the Ten Commandments will keep anyone
prosperous to the end of his days and the world
laughing till the end of time :—

" When it shall please God to bring thee to man's
estate, use great providence and circumspection in
choosing thy wife. For from thence will spring all
thy future good or evil. And it is an action of life,
like unto a stratagem of war : wherein a man can
err but once. If thy estate be good, match near
home and at leisure ; if weak, far off and quickly.
Enquire diligently of her disposition and how her
parents have been inclined in their youth. Let her
not be poor, how generous soever. For a man can
buy nothing in the market with gentility. Nor choose
a base and uncomely creature altogether for wealth ;
for it will cause contempt in others and loathing in
thee. Neither make choice of a dwarf, or a fool ;
for by the one thou shalt beget a race of pigmies ;
the other will be thy continual disgrace, and it will irk
thee to hear her talk. For thou shalt find it, to thy
great grief, that there is nothing more fulsome than a
she-fool. And touching the guiding of thy house,
let thy hospitality be moderate ; and, according to
the means of thy estate, rather plentiful than sparing,
but not costly. For I never knew any man grow
poor by keeping an orderly table. But some consume
themselves with secret vices, and their hospitality
bears the blame. . . . Beware thou spend not above
three or four parts of thy revenues ; nor above a
third part of that in thy house. For the other two
parts will do more than defray thy extraordinaries,
which always surmount the ordinary by much ;
otherwise thou shalt live like a rich beggar, in continual want. And the needy man can never live
happily nor contentedly. For every disaster makes

him ready to mortgage or sell. And that gentleman who sells an acre of land, sells an ounce of credit. For gentility is nothing else but ancient riches.

" Bring thy children up in learning and obedience, yet without outward austerity. Praise them openly, reprehend them secretly. Give them good countenance and convenient maintenance according to thy ability ; otherwise thy life will seem their bondage, and what portion thou shalt leave them at thy death, they will thank death for it and not thee. . . .

" Marry thy daughters in time, lest they marry themselves. And suffer not thy sons to pass the Alps. For they shall learn nothing there but pride, blasphemy and atheism. And if by travel they get a few broken languages, that shall profit them nothing more than to have one meat served in divers dishes. Neither, by my consent, shalt thou train them up in wars. For he that sets up his rest to live by that profession can hardly be an honest man or a good Christian. Besides, it is a science no longer in request than use. For soldiers in peace are like chimneys in summer. . . .

" Be not served with kinsmen or friends, or men intreated to stay ; for they expect much and do little : nor with such as are amorous, for their heads are intoxicated. And keep rather two too few, than one too many. Feed them well and pay them with the most : and then thou mayest boldly require service at their hands. Let thy kindred and allies be welcome to thy house and table. Grace them with thy countenance, and father them in all honest actions. For by this means thou shalt so double the band of nature, as thou shalt find them so many advocates to plead an apology for thee behind thy back. . . . Beware of suretyship for thy best friends. He that payeth another man's debts seeketh his own decay. . . . Neither borrow money of a neighbour or a friend, but of a stranger ; where paying for it thou shalt hear no more of it. Otherwise thou shalt eclipse thy credit, lose thy freedom, and yet pay as dear as to another. But in borrowing of money, be precious of thy word. For he that hath care of keeping days of payment is lord of another man's purse.

" Undertake no suit against a poor man with receiving much wrong. For, besides (that) thou makest him thy compeer, it is a base conquest to triumph where there is small resistance. Neither attempt law against any man before thou be fully resolved that thou hast right on thy side, and then spare not for either money or pains ; for a cause or two, so followed and obtained, will free thee from suits a great part of thy life.

" Be sure to keep some great man thy friend, but trouble him not for trifles. Compliment him often with many, yet small, gifts, and of little charge. And if thou hast cause to bestow any great gratuity, let it be something which may be daily in sight. Otherwise, in this ambitious age, thou shalt remain like a hop without a pole, live in obscurity, and be made a football for every insulting companion to spurn at.

" Toward thy superiors be humble, yet generous, with thine equals familiar, yet respective. Towards thine inferiors show much humanity and some familiarity ; as to bow the body, stretch forth the hand, and uncover the head ; with such-like popular compliments. The first prepares thy way by advancement. The second makes thee known for a man well-bred. The third gains a good report ; which, once got, is easily kept. For right humanity takes such deep root in the minds of the multitude, as they are easilier gained by unprofitable courtesies than by churlish benefits. Yet I advise thee not to affect, or neglect popularity too much. Seek not to be Essex ; shun to be Rawleigh. Trust not any man with thy life, credit or estate. For it is mere folly for a man to enthrall himself to his friend, as though, occasion being offered, he should not dare to become the enemy.

" Be not scurrilous in conversation, nor satirical in thy jests. The one will make thee unwelcome to all company, the other pull on quarrels and get thee hatred of thy best friends. For suspicious jests (when any of them favour the truth) leave a bitterness in the minds of those which are touched. And, albeit I have already pointed at this inclusively ; yet I think it necessary to leave it to thee as a special caution. Because I have seen many so prone to quip and gird, as they would rather leave their friend than their jest. And if perchance their boiling brain yield a quaint scoff, they will travel to be delivered of it as a woman with child. These nimble fancies are but the froth of wit." [1]

The precepts were compiled some time in the early 'eighties,[2] when Essex was beginning to make his way at Court, and Cecil not yet come to man's estate. Between 1563 and 1580 there is a gap in the boy's history which we cannot fill ; and just as we have to guess the course of his moral and religious development from the opinions of his parents, so we have to imagine the progress of his mental and physical culture from the scheme arranged by Burghley, perhaps in the very year of Robert Cecil's birth, for the education of his ward, Lord Oxford :—

" Morning. To be ready at 7. French and Breakfast to 8. Latin to 9. Dancing and walking to 10. Writing and Drawing and Prayers till 11.

" Afternoon. Cosmography from 1 to 2. French to 3. Latin to 4. Writing, walking till prayers." [3]

Cecil's life at Cambridge lies in scarcely less

[1] Stowe MSS., 143, f. 100.   [2] 1582.
[3] S. P. Dom., Eliz., 26/50.

obscurity. He went up at the age of sixteen, carrying " his virtuous mother's will and free gift of £30 given yearly to a college in Cambridge." [1] But at St. John's nothing is remembered of him. He must have passed under the beautiful gateway of that most beautiful College, where Lady Margaret's particular white Daisies are displayed beside the Portcullis of the Beauforts and the Tudor Rose, and he must have known the First Court in its pristine and uninjured splendour. But his brief academic career did not fall at an interesting moment in the life of the place. Its intellectual glories were no longer at their height. That pre-Reformation efficiency, which had attracted the praise of Erasmus, when the students spoke (or were expected to speak) either Greek, Latin, or Hebrew at meals, was long gone by ; [2] and the subsequent reactionary wave of Puritan enthusiasm, which passed over the College at the beginning of the reign and disturbed the equanimity of Burghley, had waned with the exile of Cartwright. For the rest, Greene probably and Nashe possibly were hanging about the college, which the latter afterwards affirmed to be " the sweetest nurse of knowledge in all that University " ; [3] but Robert Cecil probably never ran across either of them, and would not have been the better for it if he had. Nor was the College at this time adding to its outward magnificence ; that ' statlie new building '—the Second Court—in which Robert Cecil's son was one day to be lodged, and which is now the most satisfying architectural feature of the place, was not yet born.

One glimpse and one glimpse only of Cecil's undergraduate days is to be seen upon the mirror of Time. Dr. Perne, the Vice-Chancellor, writes to Burghley in 1581 to thank him for sending amongst

---

[1] *Life and Death of the Earl of Salisbury*, p. x.
[2] Mullinger, *St. John's College, Cambridge*, p. 22.
[3] Nashe, *Lenten Stuffe*, v. 241.

other tokens of his favour toward the University
that "worthy and godly monument of his Lordship's
goodwill toward the advancement of learning . . .
his loving son, Mr. Robert, who hath shewed such
an example of godly diligence both at sermons and
disputations . . . that he gave just occasion to
allure many other to the imitation of his diligence
in hearing and carrying good profit from the same ;
as did well appear in him after every of the said
exercise, at dinner or supper, not only to me but
also to others, for the which I could have wished
him to have been made a Master of Art with my
Lord of Essex if it had been your pleasure, without
the knowledge whereof neither he nor we durst
attempt anything at this time."[1] Dr. Perne concludes by expressing a hope that this paragon of
prudence and industry may be allowed to remain at
the University. What fate that suggestion met with
is not clear. In the next year Howland, the Master
of St. John's, is found recommending a Mr. Wilkinson,
a man, "quiet, staid, honest and of a good nature,
which . . . is a very hard thing to promise for any
man," for the post of private tutor to Mr. Robert.[2]
But in spite of one contemporary assertion to the
contrary,[3] Cecil does not appear to have taken his
M.A. degree.[4]

Another Wilkinson[5] records how at this time the
neighbourhood of the Strand was beset at night by
riotous young law-students, who grew to be the
terror of the honest folk of the neighbourhood. A
competent watch was, therefore, set, hard by the
church, in the hope of dealing effectively with the
rascals and restoring tranquillity to the neighbour-

---

[1] S. P. Dom., Eliz., 149/65.   [2] Hatfield MSS., 162/84.
[3] *Life and Death of the Earl of Salisbury*, p. x.
[4] See Harl. MSS., 7046, f. 63. "A grace for Robert Cecil, Earl of
Salisbury, to be M.A. without observing the usual ceremonial."
[5] Wilkinson, *Londina Illustrata*, under St. Clement Dane's, 19th
July 1605.

hood. What came of it we do not know, unless, as
is probable, the principal malefactors were those two
' tyrannical youths ' to whom the Recorder meted
out sharp sentences, because, as he wrote to Burghley,
he supposed them ' descended of the blood of Nero.' [1]
But about seven at night, continues Wilkinson, the
watch " saw young Mr. Robert Cecil, the Lord
Treasurer's son, pass by the church, and, as he
passed, give them a civil salute, at which they said,
' Lo ! you may see how a nobleman's son can use
himself and how he putteth off his cap to poor men.
Our Lord bless him.' This passage," adds Wilkinson, " the Recorder wrote in a letter to his father,
adding, ' Your Lordship hath cause to thank God for
so virtuous a child.' "

A name for virtue was clearly to be had rather
cheaply by noblemen's sons ; but, at any rate, it
is plain that Robert Cecil had no facility in the
cultivation of wild oats. He was probably at this
time a student at Gray's Inn, where his name is
entered as ' specially admitted ' in the year 1580.
Several years later, on the eve of his departure for
Flanders, he declares his intention of reading law
with his cousin, Spencer, if the latter be in his
company.[2]

Strange as it seems, there is some reason to think
that he was already a Member of Parliament. In
his maiden speech in 1592 he claims to have sat in
five parliaments, and as infancy was in those days
no more than a theoretical disqualification, we may
take it that Burghley found him a seat in the Parliament of 1580,[3] although no record of it remains
in the imperfect parliamentary annals of the time.
If it was so, we need not greatly commiserate him.
Parliament was then a body which sat merely to
transact business, and which carried out its work in

---

[1] Lansdowne MSS., 37/5.　　　[2] S. P. Dom., Eliz., 208/69.
[3] That is, the third session of the Parliament of 1572.

a business-like way. The constituencies on their part were very ready to accept advice from the Government as to who were fit and proper persons to sit in the great council of the realm. No one was obliged to speak in order to let his supporters know that he was alive and kicking ; and the prizes of place and power, as Bacon discovered, were as likely to fall to those who held their tongues as to those who used them. The consequence was that sessions were short, few, and to the point ; that politics were a duty and not a trade ; and that statesmen had time to attend to affairs of State.

Robert Cecil doubtless attended carefully, as he always did, to what was going on, heard Mildmay's speech foreshadowing the penal laws against the Catholics, and gave his vote with a due sense of the gathering perils of his country. But he made no attempt to address the House until in his fifth parliament he came before it as a minister of the Crown. His education was, in fact, proceeding with that absence of haste which characterised all that he and his father undertook. His health, besides, was not of the best, and Burghley did not want to lay any tax upon it before the time. Not until the early summer of 1584 did he go abroad, and then only to France,[1] where Sir Edward Stafford, his kinsman,[2] was the English ambassador. Burghley, as we know, distrusted a trans-Alpine tour ; it may be doubted whether a Gallic one was less dangerous or more improving. France was at this time drinking the lowest dregs of the cup of wrath. Faction had rent the country into two. Bribery had eaten away all sense of public honour. Religion, or rather the form

---

[1] There does not seem to be the slightest foundation for the idea (Life of Cecil in *Cabinet Cyclop.*, p. 3) that he visited Italy. His knowledge of Italian, such as it was, was derived from a teacher he had in England, and Burghley disapproved of trans-Alpine journeys.

[2] See the letter from Stafford to Burghley. Cotton MSS., Galba, E. vi. 232.

of it, was propagated by the assassin's dagger ; and the utter moral depravity of the upper classes was too notorious for denial.   But the most captivating element in a political situation, at least from an observer's point of view, one would not have supposed to be wanting.   If any concurrence of forces could have provided excitement, the personalities of Catherine de' Medici, Henry iii., the Guises, and the King of Navarre (just become, by the death of Anjou, heir to the crown), appeared nicely calculated to supply it.   Yet it is precisely of dulness that the traveller complains in this August of 1584. Paris, he says, was never so dead, in all men's opinion, as it is now.   But he likes the country very well indeed, and is very well content with his reception. He wishes to stay abroad as long as his father will allow him.   He revels in the warmth.   He will not willingly " hold his face to the cold northern coast with the seat of the warm sun at his back."   He would see Orleans, Tours, Blois, and Angers before his recall ; but for the moment attends disputations at the Sorbonne, without feeling any inclination to change his religion.   " I continue," he concludes, " an English settled Huguenot." [1]

How long he remained in France we do not know. He wrote to Walsingham in the end of September, giving a report of the state of parties and apologising for the inadequacy of " these unripe gathered fruits of my two months' travel." [2]   And as he liked the country so well, he may have been tempted to prolong his time there.   But he was probably back for the meeting of Parliament in the autumn of that same year.   After this the fog again settles down, and we can learn nothing of him until in 1586 he is returned as member for Westminster,[3] to the Parliament

[1] S. P. Dom., Eliz., 172/118.
[2] Cotton MSS., Galba, E. vi. 252.
[3] Members of Parliament, Official Return, pt. i.

which sealed, so far as any Parliament could do so, the doom of the Queen of Scots—the Parliament to which Hatton in his opening speech addressed the memorable words, " Ne pereat Israel, pereat Absolon."

CHAPTER II

FROM THE LOW COUNTRIES

" Travel in the younger sort is a part of education. . .
things to be seen and observed are : the courts of p
especially when they give audience to ambassado
the walls and fortifications of cities and towns an
the havens and harbours . . . shipping and navie
armories, arsenals, magazines, exchanges, burses,
houses. . . . As for the acquaintance which is to be s
in travel, that which is most of all profitable is acquain
with the secretaries and employed men of ambassa
for in so travelling in one country, he shall suck th
perience of many."—BACON's *Essays, On Travels*.

THE foreign policy of Elizabeth ran, more or l
according to the caprice or wisdom of that inc
culable woman, in two different and increasing
divergent channels. In desire, perhaps, the Que
adhered to the old English tradition, which h
descended from Wolsey and from before Wolsey,
an understanding, though perhaps seldom exactl
a cordial one, with Burgundy—with ' the wateris
Burgundy,'[1] that is, or Netherlands, which ha
passed into the hands of Philip of Spain, but whic
still retained a character, a destiny, and an interest
of its own. This was the policy to which Burghley's
cautious and conservative disposition naturally inclined, for it was a policy essentially peaceful and
diplomatic, was clear of religious fanaticism, and
rested on that even balance of power in north-

[1] The expression is drawn from *King Lear*. See Seeley's *Growth of
British Policy*, i. p. 45.

western Europe, which sentiment, security, and commercial advantage alike dictated. With France and Scotland on the one side, England and Burgundy on the other, the scales were evenly dressed ; and in the marriage between Philip and Mary, and the faint suggestion of marriage between Philip and Elizabeth, we see the ancient forces still plainly at work.

Over against this policy lay one infinitely more congenial to the spirit of the age, because infinitely more daring and infinitely more religious. Almost all the names which have made the Elizabethan age remembered can be cited in its support. Leicester and Walsingham, Essex and Ralegh, Drake and all the host of seamen who followed in his train, were from their several standpoints for a policy that was Protestant, bellicose, imperial, productive of spoils and honours, quick in results and boundless in possibilities. The Cecils held back, doubting whether England was yet strong enough, or enough at one with herself, to seize an empire which two hundred years later she was able to conquer ' in a fit of absence of mind.'

Each year that Elizabeth reigned caused Burghley's policy to appear less necessary and the other more alluring. The fall of Mary Stuart, the massacre of St. Bartholomew, the gathering flood in the Netherlands, the tardiness of Philip, the theological affinities of James, tempted Elizabeth little by little to bolder and more definite courses, which culminated in Drake's ever-memorable attack on Cadiz in April 1587. Burghley, however, who had been in real or affected disgrace since the execution of the Queen of Scots in the February of that same year, had recovered his ascendancy over the Queen so soon as Leicester retired to Buxton to be treated for the gout. He was indeed too late to stop Drake from starting, but from that moment the country which had been

sailing merrily into conflict returned to its normal path of equivocal negotiation. For a few months it seemed possible that his counsels might once again avail to leash the dogs of war, though he himself cherished no illusions as to the grave state of public affairs. In a striking, if tedious, treatise,[1] which he drew up in the autumn of 1587, he says that it is inconceivable that Philip will be content with anything short of battle. The situation, as he pointed out, had been profoundly modified by two acts, the wisdom of which he considered very doubtful. Mary's execution had provoked her son to adopt an attitude of dangerous hostility ; whilst in the attack on Cadiz the King of Spain had suffered an insult which even a lesser monarch could not have afforded to leave unavenged. There lay a fearful peril in the possibility of an alliance between Spain and Scotland. The Queen ought therefore to abandon her temporising policy in respect of James and give him that assurance of the English succession which alone could make him her loyal supporter. On the other hand, she must avoid all appearance of soliciting peace from Philip, who would regard her offer as a proof of conscious weakness and press forward his attack the more confidently.

The proposals for a conference came, in fact, if we may trust Robert Cecil's information,[2] from the Flemish merchants, who were utterly tired of a ruinous war. It suited the other parties concerned to smile upon this pretence of peace. Philip was never sorry for delay : Elizabeth had become alive to the gravity of her danger; Burghley had to set the national defences in order and to placate the King of Scots ; and Alexander of Parma was neither anxious to prolong a war, the miseries of which he deeply regretted, nor to promote another, the difficulties of

[1] S. P. Dom., Eliz., 203/62.
[2] S. P. For., Flanders, 2/86 ; cf. *ibid.*, 88.

which he clearly perceived.[1] The English Government, indeed, at one moment cherished the hope that Parma might be provoked by resentment or interest to disown Philip and receive the sovereignty of the Netherlands at the hands of England and France; and it was proposed to give a secret commission to Herbert or Paulet to work in this sense behind the backs of the other Commissioners.[2] But this plan was ultimately dropped,[3] as well it might be, for Parma, however much he might kick against the pricks, was accustomed to keep his allegiance stainless. The Commissioners, therefore, were sent over to Ostend without any secret instructions ; the Queen doubtless hoping that time would extricate her from her embarrassments, as it had done so often before.

The *personnel* of the Commission was designedly distinguished. The head of the house of Stanley, a man of rather neutral tint in politics and religion, but reputed a follower of Leicester,[4] lent the dignity of a great name ; and with him was joined Lord Cobham, whose daughter Robert Cecil afterwards married. The commoners were Sir Amyas Paulet,[5] Sir James Crofts, and Dr. Valentine Dale. Paulet's name, as that of the gaoler of Mary Stuart, is too familiar to require comment. Crofts, the Comptroller of the Queen's Household, is presented to us alternatively as a knave and as a fool ; and it is not of the first importance to determine which opinion is correct. Dale, the Master of Requests, was probably the most interesting member of the Commission. He had pretty nearly boxed the compass of the liberal professions and had seen public life in most of its aspects.

---

[1] Cal. of State Papers, Spain, 1587–1603, pp. 236–8.   Hatf. MSS., ii. p. 301 (for date of Memorandum see Pollard, *Pol. Hist. of England, 1547–1603*, p. 403).

[2] Cal. of State Papers, Spain, 1587–1603, pp. 140–89.

[3] *Ibid.*, p. 214.   [4] *Ibid.*, p. 184.

[5] I am not satisfied that in the end Paulet accompanied the expedition, but he is credited with having done so in the *Dict. of Nat. Biog.*

He had been a lawyer, a Member of Parliament, a diplomatist, and a dean ; had discharged on commission the duties of the Lord High Admiral, and had assisted at the trial of the Queen of Scots. Testimony still remains to the readiness of his wit, for it was he who, when the Spanish Ambassador suggested sarcastically that negotiations should be carried on in French, since Elizabeth styled herself Queen of France, made answer, " Nay, then let us treat in Hebrew, since your Master calls himself King of Jerusalem." [1]

The proposal that Robert Cecil should accompany the expedition had come from Derby,[2] who took a great fancy to him as time went on. Cecil required no pressing and applied at once to his father for leave to go. Lady Burghley, he says, had been a little anxious on account of his delicate health and ' the unpleasantness of the country,' but had raised no serious opposition to the journey. " I doubt not," he adds in the fashion of the time, " but God (if He be so pleased) will prosper me in it, seeing I trust in Him and mean to apply myself to no evil course, but only to see and hear something that may make me wiser and yield me the satisfaction that the being present at such a matter, however it succeed, may afford my young years." [3]

The next letters come from Dover. Derby writes to Burghley a civil note to thank him for giving the desired permission to his son ; " whose continual presence," he adds, " I have so good liking of for those rare parts which I daily find in him, that we almost be never asunder but at bedtime. I have entreated him to ride with me in my coach, both because I would shroud him from the cold blasts which some time we taste of, riding through this bleak and champaign country, as also to make the

---

[1] Howell, *Familiar Letters* (ed. 1705), iv. 433.
[2] Lansdowne MSS., 55/42.   [3] S. P. Dom., Eliz., 208/69.

way seem shorter by our sundry conferences. I
have sent your Lordship here inclosed the copy of
Mr. Secretary's letter, whereby you shall perceive
what care he hath of your son ; and in my opinion
he shall do her Majesty good service and stand me
and the rest in good stead."[1]

Robert Cecil writes to his father himself a few
days later :—

"DOVER, 16th Feb.

" . . . I received the 10th of this present your Lordship's
letter of the 8th containing your fatherly counsel both concerning
my duty to God and your direction for my behaviour in particular
to the honourable Earl of whom in this journey I am a poor
follower. The first I so regard as it shall be my chiefest care
with God's assistance sincerely and truly to observe it for *nam
sola salus servire Deo*. The second I hold so due a debt as I
will study not willingly to break it. . . . My health I thank
God is very good, especially when I take my mornings in the
top of the castle. The hungry air of the sea-side . . . though
it be cold, yet by its dryness agrees well enough with my constitution. Of any passage in haste as I can conceive no hope,
so will I not complain of the wind, which being contrary yet is
not partial ; my fortune being no worse than (that of) my
betters. By the benefit of my admittance to their conference
the time spent seems much the shorter, for . . . the arguments
that fall out upon the commission and instructions between the
two civilians, where the maturity of the one's knowledge, who
hath joined reading with his travel, is tempered by the other's
deep learning, who is both slow and sure . . . minister many
things not unworthy of remembrance. I received from her
Majesty by Mr. Crofts a gracious message under her sporting
name of Pigmy, adding unto it her care of my health and looking
to hear of me ; whereof I have not so taken hold as that she
might conceive I thought it became me to presume to write
unto herself, not being desirous of the office, because either must
I write of nothing vainly or else must I enter into that which is
both subject here to suspicion and there to misconstruction.
I have here written to my cousin Stanhope as I know he will
show her Majesty wherein. Though I may not find fault with
the name she gives me, yet seem I only not to mislike it because
she gives it. It was interlaced with many fairer words than I
am worthy of. . . ."[2]

---

[1] Lansdowne MSS., 55/42.   [2] S. P. Dom., Eliz., Add., 30/80.

On the 25th he is able to write from Ostend :—

" The passage was so good as I need not write that I was not
sick, for I assure your Lordship, being embarked in the *Merlyn*
about six o'clock we lay at anchor hard by the Lord Admiral,
who had forty sail in his fleet, himself aboard in the *Ark Rawleigh*,
till ten o'clock at night when the Earl of Derby weighed anchor,
with whom we were to go. And then hoisting up sail I lay me
down aloft the hatches and never waked till the cock crew in
our ship, wherewith we, waking, within one hour found Dunkirk
on our broad-side. By ten o'clock we arrived at Ostend." [1]

To his father's secretary, Michael Hicks—one of
those naturally tactful and deservedly popular people
whose mission it is to guide the footsteps of great
persons through the tedious mazes of social diplomacy
—Cecil writes the first letter that brings us face to
face with the peculiar humour of the man himself.

" Mr. Hicks, lest you might think Ostend hath altered my disposition, though it may chance to change my complexion, I have
written these few lines. You live, and so doth Mr. Arundell too,
in safety and pleasure ; both which I never wanted till now. The
soldiers (are) every day disposed to mutiny; nothing (is) to be had
but what we brought with us, and that spoiled with lying shipped
a month for want of wind and waftage. My cousin Spencer is
gone toward Brussels to the Duke. When you hear I have been
there, believe it. The governor of the next town, hearing that
we had greyhounds and setters in our company, for hares and
partridges (are) as plentiful by the waste of the land as crows in
England, sent this day a drummer, which was led in blindfold,
. . . for leave that he might with his dogs in safety hunt under
the town, and sent us a passport to do the like at Odenborch
which is two Dutch miles from us. We need not fear him in
these trifles for such is the weakness of this place as in ten days
he may have it, if he will sit down before it ; which, assure you,
this treaty once broken, he will not be long about. If there be
cessation of arms, as I hope there will, we shall to Bruges, and
then I will go to all the brave towns about. . . . My health
was never so good, I praise God. Honesty is a goodly jewel.
Many things I could be merry with in my letters to you both,
but *literæ scriptæ manent* and *vivat* the good Earl of Derby
whose muttons die, his hens starve, and we are fain nevertheless

---

[1] S. P. Dom., Eliz., Add., 30/80.

to eat them. My house is all my riches with which I trust you.
From Ostend, where I shall learn what becomes a soldier, though
I must say *Cedant arma togæ*. This 29th of February, leap-
year. Your nose would drop i' faith, don Michael, if you were
as cold as we have been. Not a fair woman nor an honest.

" To Mr. Michael Hycks, my friend by the fire-side, I believe." [1]

If Robert Cecil was tempted to make fun of his
chief in private, he successfully concealed his inclinations in public. " I cannot omit," writes Derby to
Burghley, " but let your Lordship know that your son,
Mr. Cecil, doth still so orderly carry himself as is specially well liked both of me and the rest." [2] And again
later : " I . . . assure your Lordship that, finding many
good parts in the young gentleman which do much
content me, I will not fail but be in your Lordship's
stead to him, so far as resteth in my power, until
our return." [3] Cecil was, in fact, eminently prudent
and industrious and of that kind of carefulness
which, though often peculiarly provoking to contemporaries of fuller blood, secures the confidence and
approval of older men. " I have," he writes to his
father, " written to divers of my friends, but neither
have nor mean to touch the cause in hand otherwise
than as an ordinary advertisement of things known
to everybody and not subject to mistaking, and yet
shall mine own office of a friend unto them not be
evil accepted." Then he goes on to speak of Crofts,
whose journey to Dunkirk, which was held by the
Spaniards, excited very natural comment. " I think
Mr. Comptroller's being at Dunkirk and his treatment
there will not be unscanned though, truly Sir, I
think his meaning be most direct. He is in his
health but crazy,[4] though not sick, this having
proved a cold journey for his old years. Mr. Dale
hath lent me some of his books of Treaties, which
help me to spend my time not altogether idly." [5]

---

[1] Lansdowne MSS., 107/42.   [2] S. P. For., Flanders, 2/53.
[3] *Ibid.*, 74.   [4] ' Shaky ' (?).   [5] S. P. For., Flanders, 29th Feb. 1588.

But Robert Cecil had still an eye for other things besides the improvement of his mind and the achievement of his work. A letter to his father about this time shows a taste for sport, or at least for the fruits of it :—

" The territory about this town for six miles about is as full of pheasants and partridges as may possibly be. They daily both fly into the town and are brought in by the soldiers. A gentleman in our company has a setting-dog and a net, so as I doubt not to eat partridges this Lent of mine own taking though I ask no leave of the lord of the soil for conscience's sake. If my lady of Oxford [1] were here her beauty would be quickly marred, for when we sit in our poor lodging by the fire we look all as pale and wan as ashes by the smoke of our turfs which makes me envy your Lordship's porter that sits all day by a sweet fire of sea-coal in your lodge. *Sed ferre ignem fortem patiuntur ; nemo recuset.*" [2]

In spite of the unkindly fuel Cecil kept his health. " My friend Mr. Cecil is well," writes Cobham to Burghley, " and doth agree with the air." [3]

There were other wild animals about of a less tractable disposition than pheasants and partridges. " The land all about," writes Cecil in that graceful Italian hand of his which is so refreshing to read after the crabbed Gothic of his companions, " is so devastated that where the flat country was wont to be covered with kine and sheep it is now fuller of wild swine and wolves, whereof many come so nigh the town that the sentinels that watch every night . . . upon a sandhill on the east side . . . have had them in a dark night upon them or they were ware." [4]

The preliminaries of a treaty in the sixteenth and seventeenth centuries were as important or at least as controversial as the treaty itself. In the present instance the meeting-place of the rival commissioners,

<hr />

[1] His sister.   [2] S. P. For., Holland, 21st Feb. 1588.
[3] S. P. For., Flanders, 3rd Mar. 1588.   [4] *Ibid.*, 4th Mar. 1588.

a matter involving the nicest questions of etiquette, was as yet unsettled; and Dale, doubtless as the ablest diplomatist on the Commission, was deputed to confer with the Duke of Parma with a view to its determination. Cecil had no mind to loiter in Ostend whilst the negotiations were going forward elsewhere. He had come over to see something of the world, even though the world in those days could only be seen with a certain amount of discomfort. The journey to Ghent, Dale declares, was both painful and costly. " Mr. Cecil and I supped one night both of us with an orange saving that I treated [1] him with half a red herring. It was two days before we had a couple of eggs apiece, and then we thought we fared like princes, and yet truly we had great entertainment for the season. Mr. Cecil sat nine hours upon his horse . . . yet he is very well and very honourably used by the Duke." [2]

Cecil was apparently too busy with all he saw to bother much about the hard fare ; his own account at least says little or nothing of it. But he notices the inconvenience caused them by the deep dikes, in order to avoid which they had to alight from their horses. At Odenborch the governor gave them an escort of forty or fifty men, who conveyed them to Bruges. There they supped with a M. La Motte, whose wife found favour with Cecil, being " a fair gentlewoman of discreet and modest behaviour and yet not unwilling sometimes to hear herself speak." On the Friday following they started at seven a.m. for Ghent, which they reached at five p.m., after a most miserable passage through foul lanes and woods, where, but for the convoy, the freebooters of Zealand would have certainly picked their purses.

---

[1] I am not at all satisfied with this reading, but I can think of no other, and this seems to approximate to the sense.

[2] S. P. For., Flanders, 2/91 [14th Mar. 1588].

" . . . Of the town of Bruges," continues the correspondence,
"I need not write, for though now it be very great and fair yet
your Lordship knew it when it was rich and at the best, as I
perceive by the finding of your Lordship's name written in a
chimney in the chamber where I was lodged.   Two miles from
Ghent Monsieur Grenier met his Lordship and conveyed him to
his lodging where after one hour's stay the President Richardotte,
a tall gentleman, came from his Altesse to welcome him, and to
appoint him audience the next morning.   There he supped with
him and after left him to his rest.   There is in all their mouths
nothing but desire and hope of peace, as well in their speeches
that are counsellors as especially (and that I think from the
bottom of their hearts) in their minds that are natives in the
country, whose misery is incredible both without the town,
where all things are wasted, houses spoiled, and grounds
unbelaboured, and also even in these great cities where they
are for the most part poor beggars, even in the fairest houses.
The burgomasters of the town, with weeping eyes, came to his
Lordship and expressing their great desire to have quiet and
their joy that it began thus far to be thought on, would needs
present him certain pots of wine according to the manner of
the country, which could not be refused, being but such a trifle.
To whom was answered that true it was for the great compassion had of their estates by her most excellent Majesty (upon
notice given that the Duke was desirous to hear of a peace)
she had vouchsafed to make this overture, which, if it took
not the desired effect yet was not her Majesty to be thought
behind therein, but those that had already been cause of the
contrary, whereto they all agreed and prayed for her Majesty.
According to the appointed time on Saturday morning the
President and Monsieur Grenier accompanied his Lordship to
the Duke's Court where he was brought first into a dining
chamber, after into a second chamber, and next into a
chamber where his Altesse was accompanied with the Marquis
of Guasta, the Marquis of Renti, the Prince of Arenberg, the
Count Nicolas, the Duke of Nageret's son, a Spaniard, Signor
Cosmo, Le President Richardotte and two persons besides
these named.   Small and mean was the furniture of his
chamber, which though they attribute to his private living
here, yet is it a sign that peace is the mother of all honour
and state, as may best be perceived by the Court of England,
which her Majesty's royal presence doth so adorn, as it
exceedeth this as far as the sun surpasseth in light the other
stars of the firmament.

" After Mr. Dale's message delivered, which the Duke heard
with great attention, the Duke replied sometime in French,

sometime in Italian, alleging that his French tongue was imperfect, as indeed it is. And that done those gentlemen that were there being presented by Mr. Dale unto him, among the rest it pleased him more particularly to question with me of her Majesty's good health and estate, assuring me that there was not a Prince in the world (reserving always the question between her Majesty and the King) whom he desired more to do service unto than to her Majesty ; of whose perfection he had heard so much that he wished that all things might so fall out as that with conveniency it might be his fortune to see her before his return into his own country, which he desired not to do as a servant to him that was not able still to maintain war, or as one that feared any harm that might befall him therein, for as touching any such matter his account was made long ago to endure whatever God should send, but only because [1] he grew weary to behold the miserable estate of these people fallen upon them through their own folly. Wherein he thought whosoever could do the best offices should do *pium et sanctissimum opus,* being right glad that the Queen my mistress was not behind him in the zeal thereof, and adding thus far more that for mine own particular (in respect he understood I was son to him who had always served his sovereign with unfeigned sincerity, and that he saw he was appointed chiefly to deal in this cause of importance by her Majesty) he would leave no courtesy unperformed that I should have need of here or otherwise. I answered him that where his Altesse expressed his good affection, particularly to her Majesty and chiefly to this cause in hand, I knew her Majesty esteemed of him as a prince of great honour and virtue, and that for this good work begun no man should ever have cause but to think her Majesty most zealously affected to bring all things to a perfect peace and quiet in this afflicted country, affirming that for mine own particular I would be glad to do him service in anything I could, reserving the integrity of my loyal duty to my most Gracious Sovereign.

" He likewise saluted Mr. Crofts, Mr. Spencer, and Mr. Pyne. And so for the present Mr. Dale was carried home by the President Richardotte ; and after followed the Prince of Arenberg who dined with him, all of the Duke's charges.

" The next morning being Sunday the Duke sent for him again and heard him with all courtesy that may be, himself debating the points stood upon very earnestly, though he had before in the afternoon sent the President unto him to inform him what his resolution was. The particularities of all this

---

[1] In the original, ' that.'

negotiation I leave as is fit to Dr. Dale's relation, who truly in my poor and weak judgment discharged the matter discreetly, considering that without resolution from England he could not decline from his instructions ; earnestly specifying Ostend, which it seemeth the Duke never appointed of as a place of colloquy more than for a port to land in, holding it as he said . . . most dishonourable . . . for him to send his deputies to a town of the King's ' occupée par vos autres messieurs.' But for a place neutral, wheresoever her Majesty pleased, he could have been content, seeing her Majesty had done him the honour to send so far and such persons. Likewise for the commission he hoped no man thought that either they would meet without one from him, or that he would give any but such as he had ample power and authority for from the King, as upon the meeting should plainly appear, till which time he desired not sight of theirs.

" Monsieur Richardotte in his conference with Dr. Dale wished above all things expedition, both, saith he, to prevent any accident out of Spain or in England to hinder it, saying it had served his Majesty well if it had been begun two months since.

" I do still desire your Lordship to pardon my scribbled letters, and yet again what with the inconveniency of the place to write in and the haste I make to bed in respect of Mr. Doctor Dale's early departure to-morrow morning I am constrained *in eandem foveam incidere* which I beseech your Lordship to hold excused as an error but far from negligence or presumption. And so with my most humble and hearty prayers to God for your Lordship's long life and health, to the advancement of her Majesty's service and the support of your children, whereof I am the meanest though most bound, I humbly crave your Lordship's and my lady my mother's daily blessing. From Gant this 10th of March 1587 being Sunday at night. . . . Your Lordship's most obedient son humbly

" ROBT. CECILL." [1]

Such, then, according to his private letters, was Cecil's part in the diplomatic mission of 1588. Fifteen years later, when he had risen to be all-powerful, his youthful exploits had grown to mythical proportions, and the defeat of the Spanish Armada came to be regarded as the first-fruits of his dexterous cunning. " At the very height of the Spanish pre-

[1] S. P. For., Flanders, 2/82.

parations against England in 1588," so the Venetian Secretary of Legation informed his Government in 1603, " Queen Elizabeth, of her own initiative, despatched into Flanders Robert Cecil, a little hunchback, and then in private life, but very wise ; and he, in simple traveller's garb but with credentials from her, whispered to the ear of Alexander Farnese that the Queen would give Arabella as wife to his son Ranuccio, and with her the succession to the throne. The whole world has seen the results of that step."[1]   How excellent are the tapestries with which the historic imagination hangs the halls of Clio !

Early the next morning Dale started as arranged. But, two miles from Ghent, Cecil left him in order to see Bergen-op-Zoom and Antwerp, ' the best city in all these parts.' And here a biographer may venture to abridge and very slightly to adapt Cecil's account of his travels, for, as the reader is by now aware, sixteenth-century prose is not always the best vehicle for carrying narrative.

"The way," says the traveller, "was exceedingly fair and straight, the villages well-inhabited, and the ground very diligently laboured, having only been saved from the general spoliation by the provident care of the Bailiff of the ' Pays de Bays ' (or, as we call it, the Land of Waste). He levies a tax on the inhabitants for every cow and beast, and thus is able to maintain certain soldiers who, so soon as they have intelligence of any freebooters pursue them and incontinently hang them up on the spot. In our thirty miles' ride we found a dozen places where justice had been done to such persons. I had the Duke's passport to come and see this town (Antwerp), which is one of the pleasantest cities I ever saw for situation and building but utterly abandoned by those rich merchants who used to frequent it, saving some Italians, one of whom—and a very rich one—fell into my company and must needs lodge me in his house, affirming that his Altesse had so appointed him. When they knew I was attached to the Commission, I had all favour and freedom to see all places in the town worth remark, of which I found very many especial and singular. The Burgomaster of the town

---

[1] Venet. Cal., x, p. 41.

was born in England and christened by King Edward, whose
name he carries, being son to the Imperial Ambassador in King
Edward's time. His name in whose house I lie is Carolo Lan-
franchy, in good favour with the Duke and very inward with
Mons. Champigny, at whose motion he (by a letter to M. Andreas
de Loo) first set this matter on foot. Thus it is confessed that
the first overture came from their parts [1] whereof they make
no scruple, holding it so good a work as they think him happiest
that most can further it. For it is most certain that only those
Spanish captains and they that have no other living but by the
king's pay alone hinder as much as may be the good success
thereof, wherein none are more maliciously disposed than those
of our own nation who have fallen from their true obedience to
their sovereign. These have already caused it to be bruited
that now that her Majesty hath kept the Duke from any enterprise at Ostend, she hath no meaning further to proceed but to
take advantage of some circumstance of place or time even by
naming such a place for the colloquy as is well known was neither
thought of before nor any time to be yielded unto.

" All the gentlemen of the country and men of living are
utterly spoiled, and receive no penny almost of their living ;
in which point I hear Mons. Champigny is shrewdly nipped,
who hath gotten great seigneuries that yield him not a tenth
penny that he received before. What the Duke's mind may be
herein I have nothing but some outward appearances to inform
me beside his own solemn protestations. First his own estate
is such, that, if the war utterly cease and he retire himself home
his own patrimony is so great that he hath sufficient to maintain
the dignity of a Prince and that beyond his father, having
(as the Spaniards under-hand will speak) not a little enriched
himself in these wars. If by an accord the state of these countries
come to repose and the trade begin again to be set open for
merchants, such is the industry of the people and so great will
be the traffic, that (if the ground be tilled and the towns frequented from England and the Esterlings) he that shall peaceably
command here for the King shall live in greater happiness than
the King of Spain himself with all his riches, which are now
not a little exhausted. To maintain these forces the King
spendeth, as I have been informed by this Italian merchant,
who is an officer under the *pagador*, more than 400,000
crowns a month. Besides as they all confess they know well
enough how hard his fortune shall be that best speedeth in
a war with so mighty a nation. . . . Their preparations,
if they were ten times greater than they are, would be no

---

[1] Cf. S. P. For., Flanders, 2/88.

greater than they desire you should suppose them: of which I
will more particularly advertise you in my next letter, for I mean
to go from here to Bergen-op-Zoom by water so as to see the
shipping better. . . . The counsellors that most govern his
Altesse's resolutions are all Burgundians or Italians, his partiality
to whom makes all the Spaniards very greatly repine. . . .
Montdragon, who is governor of the citadel here, would have
quickly laid his authority upon me, if I had not had a direct
passport from his Altesse, for all my copy of the safe-conduct
of the Commissioners and their train.   The Duke, as I have
heard, keeps a hard hand on him, the rather because one of his
people [1] is suspected of a libel to the effect that the King has now
discovered his own folly and weakness in suffering his affairs to
be governed by one that for his private glory and desire of
repose was content to disgrace all the King's old servants to
make great instead his own compatriots, and to correspond
with the Queen of England, whose meaning was nothing less
than to suffer the King quietly to enjoy his own as might well
be perceived by her countenance of Mr. Drake in all his actions,
to which they maliciously give a worse name.   I was promised
a copy of this libel but have it not yet.   There are two or three
imprisoned that were suspected of making it. . . . By the means
of the Italian, I have seen the citadel which is counted the
goodliest and strongest place of all Europe." [2] . . . "From
Antwerp on Thursday last in the afternoon as the tide fell out
I came in a skiff down the river which is blocked on both sides
with sconces.[3]   After I had passed the place where the relics
yet remain of the *steciada* at the siege of Antwerp, I was to pass
close by the fort of Ordam . . . where being hailed by the
Governor I was forced to land and, after showing my passport,
was both suffered to pass quietly and offered wine and beer. . . .
I could not go any further than Lyllo Sconce that night, where
I passed the fleet of Count Maurice,[4] and, having cast anchor
as near him as I could get my poor skipper, who was afraid to
go too near, to carry me (meaning to have tarried aboard all
night), I was sent to from Lyllo, and, being known to be an
Englishman, the governor of the fort gave me leave to rest in
his Sergeant-Major's cabin till morning that the tide might
serve me for Bergen.   He that commandeth is called Colonel
Michael. . . .   Having sent the day before for leave to come to
Bergen, the Governor in the morning sent to Lyllo Captain
Baskerville, who came to Lyllo and finding me there went with
me to Bergen.   He is a proper gentleman, akin to me by your

---

[1] In the original, ' one that was toward him.'
[2] S. P. For., Flanders, 2/86.   [3] *i.e.* forts.   [4] ' Morrys.'

Lordship whose house hath often matched with his in which respect he thought no pleasure he could do me too much. There is not a more serviceable gentleman in all the garrison and there are there as many brave men, both captains and soldiers, in the town as I saw in any garrison of the enemies or other companies whatsoever that I passed through, which hath been . . . above seven or eight thousand that lie in the quarters between Bruges and Antwerp. Beside the continual garrisons he (*i.e.* Parma) hath above thirty thousand men in those parts with those he hath sent with the P. Chymay toward Bonn. There is no day that he baketh not fifty thousand loaves. They are relieved every week with lendings but now they are in hope of some pay for the day I came to Antwerp there arrived a ton of gold whereof there was great joy, for the safe coming of it to the town which they greatly suspected. Money is as scant with them as in other places, and for their shipping upon the river of Antwerp it will prove but a scarecrow : in all that river I saw not, with hoys, scutes and all, above twenty-one—three of them of the burden of three hundred tons and upwards ; one, which is the Admiral, is about four hundred ; the fifth, called the *Gallyon*, is a great ship well furnished with brass pieces to the number of five hundred, little lower than the cannon, but it is a common received opinion that she hath such an imperfection that she will never be able to brook the sea before she be new made. The rest are ordinary poor things. They report that there is more lying at Dunkirk and Sluys, which I know nothing of; but this I assure your Lordship when at my first coming over to Antwerp I asked if these were all the shipping, they answered I should see more if I went down the river ; but it proved otherwise.

" Of the Armada of Spain the talk is great insomuch as news being brought of the Marquis de Santa Croce's death, the Duke said only this, ' Eh l bien, Dieu lui pardonne ! ' 'For he hath been,' saith he, ' the stay of our coming onward in which I hope his successor will not be so much to blame for the having crossed all our counsels.' And this was all the thought he took for him.

" To return to the garrison of Bergen. . . . Arriving there on Friday by three o'clock in the afternoon I stayed there all night being invited to supper by Sir William Reade. The next day Sir John Wingfield, brother-in-law to my Lord Willoughby, invited me to dinner. His wife, the Countess of Kent, lieth in, being newly brought to bed of a son, which Sir William Drury came from the Hague to christen, as my Lord's Deputy, three days ago.[1] There be many tall gentlemen especially Captain

---

[1] In the original, ' before.'

Francis Vere,[1] that was in Sluse, who is a very proper man and was as ready to have showed me any courtesy as I could have desired. . . . On Saturday after dinner I went with Sir W. Drury to Dordrecht, but I did not arrive till Sunday morning for the wind fell out contrary so as we were fain to lie at anchor even before Steenberg all night. On Monday morning my Lord Willoughby went to the Hague, on whom I attended. His Lordship dined at Rotterdam by the way and after passed by Delft, which is the finest built town that ever I saw. I mean to return by Brill which is but twelve English miles hence and from thence by God's grace to Flushing, where I will only attend a good wind for Ostend that I may not be absent from the treaty; which, as I would be sorry to miss, so am I not a little glad that God hath been pleased to grant me good and perfect health to see so many places . . . worth the seeing—and that in a time so short.

"The towns of this country are much divided and like thereby to give advantage to the enemy who will be glad to nourish faction to set them a fire. Dort hath newly confirmed their oath publicly to her Majesty and at my Lord Willoughby's passage through Rotterdam they there promised all conformity. . . . My Lord Willoughby met to-day with Count Maurice, in whom there is neither outward appearance of any noble mind, nor inward virtue; in my life I never saw a worse behaviour except it were one that lately came from school. . . . At Antwerp as I was at supper news was brought to certain Italian merchants of a great booty that the garrison of Bergen had taken as high as Brussels, and of a boat that went that morning from Antwerp, wherein they reported there were sixty thousand florins besides prisoners a dozen. It struck them in a dump and made me wish myself out of the town. They forthwith sent to lay the country for them in their return, whereof when I gave advertisement the next day to the garrison of Bergen they likewise made out certain horse and foot to meet them and succour them in their coming homeward; which took good effect, for this night word came to my Lord Willoughby that they were come home with all the spoil, whereof they are well worthy, considering how far they go for it."[2]

"On Wednesday the 20th March I went from the Hague to Brill, my Lord Willoughby having occasion to see Truxis, the late Bishop and Elector of Cologne.[3] I took it in my way to Masland Sluse and, attending his Lordship thither saw him and spake with him. He is a very goodly gentleman, well-fashioned and of good speech for which I must rather praise him than

---

[1] 'Veare.'   [2] S. P. For., Flanders, 2/98 [19th Mar. 1588].
[3] 'Collen.'

for loving a wife better than so great a fortune as he lost by
her occasion.   The house he lives in is called the Castle of
Hounsdick being of right the Comte of Arenberg's inheritance.
My Lord Willoughby returning back to the Hague, I went that
night over from Masland Sluse by water to Brill, which I
desired to see the rather for that my brother once commanded
in it for her Majesty.   The good opinion he left behind him
was such as, in respect I was known to be his brother, most
of the burghers and officers in the town strove to offer me one
more courtesy than another with many kind protestations of
their affections towards him.   From whence (I) being fully
determined to have gone toward Flushing the next morning over
the Islands, the wind came south-west and that so exceeding
tempestuous that I was stayed for three days and could not get
any man that would venture to go over the Flack which is but
four Dutch miles from Helvoetsluys to Bomeny in the Island
of Zierickzee, where I likewise was one day wind-bound. . . .
On Sunday last the stormy weather ceased and Sir W. Drury
went back to the Hague and I took my journey toward Flushing
first to Bomeny by water and then in a cart called here a ' wagen '
to Zierickzee to bed.   The waters are often very rough between
the islands, and yet are there none but little scutes to pass in,
which with a small gale of wind are ready to turn their keel
upwards ; which made me stay for settled weather. . . . Sir W.
Russell hath used me kindly for your Lordship's sake and hath
let me have twenty musqueteers to man my hoy, though I hope
my passport from the Duke will be a sufficient security." [1]

The more valuable part of his observations—
those relating principally to the shipping in the
Scheldt—Cecil conveyed in a letter to Walsingham
of March 30th. The reader, however, who has had
the patience to peruse what has gone before, will have
little use for them ; and one or two curiosities at the
end of the letter are all that is worth quoting here.

" In Antwerp," says the traveller, " I had means made unto
me by one Wiseman, an Essex gentleman, that hath long served
the King of Spain, that by my mediation, his leave might be
procured to come home, upon assurance of some good service to
redeem his lost and mis-spent years.   To your honour I thought
good so much to impart as (to) one that is best able to direct by

---

[1] S. P. For., Flanders, 2/3.

answer (me) who as yet seemed little moved with his desire. Tressam would have spoken with me but it fitted not my poor fortune to deal with persons so disloyal without warrant. Of the Peace those who understand it I know will best inform your honour, whose honourable place challengeth all such advertisements. For mine own part I see it not begun yet, and therefore believe it cannot so soon receive any perfect end. If it do, either may we thank the King of Spain's weakness or fear the consequence. I beseech you, Sir . . . for the substance of my letter value it at that favourable rate (at) which you have always esteemed my devotion to serve you, as your many favours have often assured me. I have presumed to send you two boxes of Italian conserved plums, especially good to cool thirst in any distemper by pain or fever, from both which God keep you still : but, when it shall so happen, I dare be bold to affirm they shall do no harm, if they do not much the contrary. And so, it being now too late to crave pardon, I commit myself humbly to your favourable protection." [1]

About ten days later he writes to his father in the usual respectful style.

" May it please your Lordship the last letter I wrote by my servant Roger Houghton was scarce begun when contrary to my expectation the Captain of the *Charles*, one of her Majesty's pinnaces, hastily sent to have my man aboard by reason the wind blew so stiff. . . . Whereupon I scribbled off my letter and sent away the bearer thereof to the pinnace . . . for which I beseech your Lordship to pardon me—both for the disordered writing and undigested matter. Which errors though your Lordship sometimes dispenses with, yet may the continuance thereof give your Lordship suspicion of negligence which I would be loth to incur by any means. . . . The Duke himself willed Richardotte to speak unto me for a fine hound and a brace of English greyhounds Your Lordship would wonder how fond he is of English dogs. I could not but in good manners promise him to provide them . . . especially since it proceeded [2] from his own particular motion, insomuch as at Ghent he begged a dog of Pyne, which he gave him though he was little worth. I know full well some friends I have will quickly furnish me from England with them, which I hope if I bestow them upon him cannot be evil taken, being thereto desired. Mons. la Motte sent me a cast of hawks when he sent my Lord Cobham his

---

[1] S. P. For., Flanders, 2/118.
[2] In the original, ' proceeding.'

THE
UNIVERSITY OF WINNIPEG
PORTAGE & BALMORAL
WINNIPEG 2, MAN.   CANADA

three hawks. There is no five days but I receive a courteous message from one or other with sometimes a pheasant or a hare. We can requite them no way more to their contentment at Bruges than with five or six hundred oysters which since their Lordships' arrival are daily to be bought in the town.

" My Lord of Derby's two chaplains have seasoned this town better with sermons than it had been before with prayers of a year's space, whereby the gentlemen here are benefited, to whom they also minister a general communion amongst us that live this good time here in a town of garrison where all sin is rifest.

" My Lord Derby hath had a sore touch of the stone, whose keeping his chamber makes me often go a-begging to my Lord Cobham's table." [1]

The last letter which we have is dated on the 9th of April.

" . . . There hath been care taken that the place of the second meeting may be as near as the other side may possibly assent to, chiefly for the more honour to her Majesty by the nearness to the town she holds. . . . La Motte is minded to be here to see the tents pitched, which is appointed shall be within a mile of the town in (as) fair a green plot [2] as ever I saw. . . . My Lord of Derby is meetly well recovered and will,[3] I hope, be able to be present at the meeting for the more honour of the cause. On their side Mons. Champigny is so loth to fail that he means to have his bed in his coach to ease his infirmity, wherewith he is very shrewdly travailed."

Here the correspondence closes, for Cecil returned to England a few days later.[4] His letters are, of course, of no commanding importance, though Burghley thought some of them worth sending on to Walsingham. We read them for their freshness, their gaiety, their glimpses of a world of which we can never hear too much, perhaps also for the subtler glimpses of character and the making of character

---

[1] S. P. For., Flanders, 3/134.
[2] ' Platt.'   [3] ' Shall.'
[4] S. P. For., Flanders, 3. Cobham to Burghley [16th April]. Cecil arrived in England on 26th April (Cal. of S. P., Span., p. 274). The Commissioners did not return till 4th August (S. P. Dom., Eliz., 214/23).

which they afford, for Cecil was peculiarly tractable, peculiarly responsive to the counsel of older men. Such counsel, such training was to be had, as it always is, for the asking. With the sands visibly running lower, the sky darkening towards dusk, there was nothing left to the Elizabethans to desire more ardently than that men should be found to carry on their work when they themselves had crossed the bar and bourne of Time. " I would wish Mr. Cecil to have somewhat that may serve him in time to come," writes Dr. Dale to Burghley a few days after the young diplomatist had returned home, " that [1] the observation of things past, and the reasons of the actions of former times may serve them that are now in action. For I see but some that are furnished like to serve in such things hereafter. I would there were more such now as have been—as Mr. Wotton, Mr. Peters (?), the Bishop of Durham, and such others. Sed virtutem præsentem contemnimus, absentem desideramus." [2]

[1] In the original, 'as.'
[2] S. P. For., Flanders, 3. Dale to Burghley [22nd April 1588].

CHAPTER III

MARS, CUPID, AND ST. ANTHONY

" And when he saddest sits in homely cell,
　　He'll teach his swains this carol for a song—
　' Blest be the hearts that wish my sovereign well :
　　Curst be the souls that think her any wrong.'
　Goddess, allow this aged man his right
　To be your headsman now that was your knight."
　　　　　　　　PEELE, " A Farewell to Arms."

CECIL did well to return to England. The shifting
weights in the balance were now driving the needle
once again in the direction of war, and there can have
been few English gentlemen of so poor a spirit as to
be willingly absent from their native land in her hour
of crisis. Cecil was no soldier ; his disposition, his
training, his grave infirmities made him a man of peace.
But, just as men, not naturally wise or eloquent, will
covet a place in a historic debate, counting it a
memorable privilege merely to have taken part in
it, so the young Englishmen of 1588 vied with each
other in seeking some share in the coming encounter,
where, as their chronicler says, " immortal fame and
glory was to be attained and faithful service to be performed unto their prince and country."　And Hakluyt
generously reckons Robert Cecil among those ' great
and honourable personages ' who flocked to the
standard at the silver trumpet-call of duty.　For
the rest we know that he was at one time on Winter's
ship [1]—under the command of that captain to whom

---

[1] Hatf. Cal., xi. p. 144.

Burghley nearly thirty years before had declared there was no need to give a character because all men spoke well of him.[1] We know, too, that he was a spectator of the great fight off Calais on 29th July, for he himself relates how much more terrible it appeared from the land than it really was,[2] but whether he merely saw what he could of it from the cliffs of Dover, or whether, as he had in mind, he contrived to put out a little way to sea, we cannot be sure.[3] At any rate he was at Dover the following day (the 30th), trying to learn something of the unfortunate Derby, whose diplomatic negotiation had been left high and dry by the outbreak of war.[4] A few months later, in the October of 1588, we find him making some endeavour to possess himself of a trophy of the Armada in the shape of a silver bell, belonging to Lady Gorge and once the property of Don Pedro (de Valdez).[5]

There is a picturesque though improbable story which makes him something more than a spectator of the Spanish defeat. Sometime in the earlier part of the year a stray packet of Spanish letters, greatly defaced by the action of the sea-water, was brought to the Council. The writing was beyond the power of anyone present to decipher. Cecil, who was there, recollected that among his acquaintance he numbered one, Richard Percival, a perfect scholar in the Greek, the Latin, and the Spanish tongues ; and to Percival, accordingly, application was made. The man did not

---

[1] Quoted by Froude, *Hist. of Engl.*, pt. ii. c. 3.

[2] S. P. Dom., Eliz., 213/66.

[3] H.M. C. Reports, Rutland MSS., 25th July 1588. Robert Cecil to ——— Manners: "This night we shall hear from my Lord Admiral, I hope. But for any hot fight, there is not like to be any till they be come so low as between Dunkirk and Margate ; to which coast I mean to ride and see if in any rivall (my arrival ?) we can go forth a little way into the sea without danger, as many gentlemen did upon the western coast."

[4] S. P. Dom., Eliz., 213/66.   [5] Lansdowne MSS., 58/39.

fall short of his recommendations. In a brief time
he had accomplished what was asked of him, and
the Council read the contents of the papers in an
English translation. These proved to be of the first
importance, disclosing, so our chronicler avers, ' the
whole design of that invasion.' [1] It is a pity that
so pretty a story bears an *imprimatur* too late by
half a century to allow of credence.

Mildred, Lady Burghley, died on the 5th April 1589,[2]
to the inconsolable regret of her husband, whose
burdens she had helped to bear for more than forty-
two years. She lived long enough to know of her son's
engagement to Lord Cobham's daughter, Elizabeth
Brooke (at one time, it would seem, the affianced
bride of Sir George Carey [3]), but not long enough to
see them married, for the marriage was celebrated
on 31st August. Burghley's advice upon the choosing
of a wife has already been quoted. If the attribution
to his son of a letter in the British Museum be correct,
it appears that Cecil did not think well to follow it.
" The object to mine eye yesternight at supper,"
the young man wrote to his sister-in-law in words
which recall something of the pathos of *Cyrano*,
" hath taken so deep impression in my heart that
every trifling thought increaseth my affection. I know
your inwardness with all parties to be such, as only it
lieth in your power to draw from them whether the
mislike of my person be such as it may not be qualified
by any other circumstances. Which, if it be so, as
of likelihood it is, I will then lay hand on my mouth,
though I cannot govern my heart, and, saving my
duty to God, exclaim on Nature, which hath

---

[1] H.M. C. Reports, Egmont MSS., i., ii., 20th Feb. 1649, "History
of Richard Percival." The improbability of the story is increased by
the fact that Cecil was not at this time a Councillor.

[2] Hatf. Cal., v. p. 71.

[3] Hatf. Cal., iv. p. 346. Sir George Carey to Sir Robert Cecil, in
1593 : " That honourable lady of great worth that was my wife before
yours."

yielded me a personage to hinder me all other good fortune." [1]

Elizabeth Brooke had the wit to judge by another standard than the common, and she had her reward. The marriage, so far as we know, was ideally happy. Cecil had not that fault which a learned student of the age [2] has seized upon as its cardinal failing—the inability to reverence woman. It was not for him that *Romeo and Juliet* needed to be written. His reserved nature found in his wife's society the natural outlet for his deeper feelings ; and when she died the happiest of him died with her.

It is to the first two or three years of joyous, unaffected married life, before the cares of State began to fall upon his shoulders, that we may, with some probability, assign a few trivial letters that have come down to us among the vast Hicks Collection at the British Museum. One or two extracts from these will not be, perhaps, altogether unacceptable :—

"Mr. Hycks, your letters are welcome because they be not short : let mine be not unwelcome because they be not long, for the good will is all one. Sir W. Rawley and I dining together in London we went to your brother's shop where your brother desired me to write to my wife in any wise not to let anybody know that she paid under 3s. 1od. a yard for her cloth of silver. I marvel she is so simple as to tell anybody what she pays for everything." [3]

"Mr. Michael, I have not leisure to answer the fruits of your f . . dle bald pate, which hath been read by those you left together, till our bellies almost burst with laughing, for more cogging descriptions, more knavish constructions, more wicked interpretations or ungrateful acceptations of our honest, gentle-

---

[1] Lansdowne MSS., 101/128. The letter is not in Cecil's hand, and is merely signed, " R. C.," nor has it date or address. The attribution to Cecil depends on the correctness of an anonymous guess on the back of the document : " This letter was probably sent to the lady of Sir Thomas Cecil, elder brother of Sir Robert."

[2] Brewer, *English Studies*, p. 293.

[3] Lansdowne MSS., 107/35.

manly, and friendly entertainment could no pen express. Your mother hath sent me a suit of hangings which she sends me word withal that she hath kept for Michael these thirty-two years, and if he will not marry—and that I do know so much—she will then make me a conveyance of her house and her stuff. This I swear to you I received from her this day and I believe you will swear that I am not like to refuse such an offer for foolish baby kindness to you my friend, neither is there any here that doth advise me to reject the kindness. . . . Mrs. MackWylliams commends her to the Clerk of Kitchen which commonly carries the badge of a white crown, and poor Bess Cecil will know you, she saith, for a cozener in leaving her your poll-pate instead of a French crown." [1]

" . . . Your cogging letter I have shewed and of the word 'cony' straight was made such an argument as the phrase was by them held not so bald as your bald crown. The whoreson Papists they would fain change for your Puritan's company and I can assure you that we are merry and would be the better if you were here. All this I write you may take for a favour, for I have well supped and am almost asleep. And if this weather had not broke up, good Michael, after my first sleep . . . I would have tried whether there be either capon or cony, which would have made one of them thank you for giving cause by your argument." [2]

The chaff, of course, is cheap enough, turning, as it does, on such matters as Hicks' bald head ; but its very cheapness is evidence of the writer's lightness of heart. Melancholy men seldom crack a joke unless it be a good one.

How Cecil employed himself when he was not carousing with Michael Hicks we do not precisely know. He had his duties, such as they were, as Member of Parliament ; [3] and he was, besides, Sheriff of Hertfordshire. [4] For the rest, he probably hung about the Court, like other young men of fashion, waiting for favours, which in the case of the Lord Treasurer's son were likely enough to fall. The

---

[1] Lansdowne MSS., 107/37.   [2] *Ibid.*, 107/43.

[3] Tressler (*Sir Robert Cecil*, p. 15) states that Cecil administered all his father's offices in Hertfordshire. I am unable to find any authority for this statement, and Tressler's own reference does not appear to justify it.

[4] Birch, *Mems. of Queen Eliz.*, i. p. 57.

Queen laughed at and liked him, and his prospects were the more secure because they were utterly detached from his mistress's susceptibilities.

In May 1591 Elizabeth visited the Lord Treasurer at Theobalds. That famous house has long gone the way of less stable structures, but its name is handed down among the most sumptuous palaces of a sumptuous age. Begun soon after Robert Cecil's birth, and intended originally as the modest appanage of a younger son, it had grown under Burghley's hand and at Elizabeth's instigation until its adornments became some of the wonders of the land and its design served as a model for the yet more memorable pile erected by Hatton at Holmby.[1] Hentzner, who saw it some years after the visit presently to be described, has recorded his impressions with all the business-like brevity of a modern guide-book ; and with the aid of Thorpe's plans and Savile's chronicle we are able to reach some conception of the charm and splendour of the place. The merchant-princes of the city had already begun to carry their wayside villas towards Waltham, but Theobalds was set back from the road and approached by a broad causeway running across the grass for some two hundred yards between avenues of ash and elm. The building itself lay in three courts, built with sides of unequal height, so that there were walks along the leads on the east and west. The great hall still formed the centre, not the entrance, of a house ; and it was there that in this instance at least the decoration was liveliest, for there were trees so cunningly fashioned with fruit and leaves that the birds flew in to enjoy their advantages.[2] But Burghley's taste for arboreal ornamentation was not satisfied even with this, and the walls of the Green Gallery were covered with genealogical trees displaying the pedigrees of the

---

[1] Gotch, *Early Renaissance Architecture in England*, p. 77.
[2] *Ibid.*, p. 146.

Tudors and their predecessors and the heraldic devices of the various county families throughout the kingdom. It may have been this room which Harington says [1] brought to his mind the lines in *Orlando Furioso* [2]—

> " But, which was strange, where erst I left a wood
> A wondrous stately palace now there stood."

The staircase too was calculated to strike the eye of a visitor. It was—

> "a large and lightsome stair
> Without the which no room is truly fair." [3]

But the most alluring feature of the place lay without rather than within. The gardens, if they might not in loyalty or logic rival those of the royal palace at Nonesuch, were at least sufficiently splendid, and may, for all we know, have suggested some of the reflections in Bacon's famous essay. They were planted with a great variety of trees and shrubs, intersected with particularly puzzling mazes, and sown with curious columns and pyramids of wood. There were other agreeable accessories : a fountain ; a summer-house with marble figures of the twelve Cæsars inside it ; and leaden cisterns commonly inhabited by fish but large enough to allow human beings to cool themselves in in hot weather. Round the garden ran a moat sufficiently broad and deep to carry a boat. All this lay on the south side of the house. And on the north side, too, there was a garden, which was perhaps the more used of the two, since one of the physicians of the day declares that the south wind ' corrupts and makes evil vapours.' [4]

Such was Theobalds, so far as we can learn anything about it ; a very pleasant estate for a younger

---

[1] Hatf. Cal., xii. p. 188.   [2] *Orl. Fur.*, bk. xliii. 124.

[3] *Ibid.*, bk. xlii. 69.

[4] Boorde, " Compendyous Regyment," quoted by Gotch, *Early Ren. Arch. in England*, p. 57.

son, looking perhaps from a distance, with its towers and lanthorn, something like Hatfield. And it is Theobalds, rather than Hatfield, that we have to think of as Robert Cecil's home.

The honour of receiving the Queen was one which had to be paid for. A hundred pounds a day in the current coinage was the price of entertaining Elizabeth ; and that sum required to be multiplied by ten before she was out of the house,[1] and then, perhaps, trebled again before it conveys to our minds any adequate notion of the real cost. The Lord Treasurer's welcome took the usual fantastic form in which Elizabeth delighted. George Peele had been employed to write a suitable address, and Robert Cecil, arrayed in the dress of an anchoret, came forward at the Queen's arrival to deliver it. The " Hermit's Oration " is no masterpiece of poetry, but it claims a place in Cecil's biography both as a curious illustration of the times he lived in and because of certain events in his family history, not in themselves of much importance, but which may as well be intimated by this means as by any other :—

" My sovereign Lady and most gracious Queen,
Be not displeas'd that one so meanly clad
Presumes to stand thus boldly in the way
That leads into this house accounted yours ;
But mild, and full of pity as you are,
Hear and respect my lamentable tale.

I am a hermit that this ten years' space
Have led a solitary and retired life
Here in my cell, not past a furlong hence,
Till by my Founder,[2] he that built this house,
Forgetful of his writing and his word,
Full sore against my will I was remov'd ;
For he, o'ertaken with excessive grief,
Betook him to my silly hermitage,
And there hath liv'd two years and some few months,
By reason of these most bitter accidents ;

[1] S. P. Dom., Eliz., 238/157, 158.   [2] Lord Burghley.

As first of all, his agèd mother's death
Who liv'd a fifth and saw her four descents
Of those that lineally have sprung from her;
His daughter's death, a Countess of this land,[1]
Lost in the prime and morning of her youth;
And last of all, his dear and loving wife.
These brought him to this solitary abode,
Where now he keeps, and hath enjoinèd me
To govern this his house and family,
A place unfit for one of my profession;
And therefore have I oft desir'd with tears
That I might be restorèd to my cell,
Because I vow'd a life contemplative;
But all in vain; for though to serve your Majesty,
He often quits the place and comes to Court,
Yet thither he repairs, and there will live.
Which I perceiving, sought by holy prayers
To change his mind and ease my troubled cares;
Then, having many days with sacred rites
Prepar'd myself to entertain good thoughts,
I went up to the lantern of this hall,
The better to behold God's works above;
And, suddenly, when my devotion 'gan
To pierce the heavens, there did appear to me
A lady clad in white, who clos'd my eyes
And, casting me into a slumbering trance,
' I am,' said she, ' that holy prophetess
Who sung the birth of Christ ere He appear'd;
Sibylla is my name; and I have heard
The moan thou mak'st for thy unquiet life,
Take thou this table, note the verses well;
Every first golden letter of these lines
Being put together signify her name
That can and will relieve thy misery,
And therefore presently go search her out,
A princely paragon, a maiden Queen
For such a one there is and only one: '
And therewithal she vanish'd once again.
After this vision, coming down from thence,
The brute [2] was that your Majesty would come,
But yet my Founder kept his hermitage
And gave me warrant to provide for all,
A task unfitting one so base as I,
Whom neither sons nor servants would obey;

---

[1] **Lady Oxford.**   [2] **Bruit.**

The younger [1] like to scorn my poor advice,
Because that he hereafter in this place
Was to become the guardian of this house
And so the same to settle in his blood,
By that young babe, whom I have heard of late
By your appointment bears my Founder's name ;
Therefore I wish for my good Founder's sake,
That he may live with this his first-born son,
Long time to serve your sacred Majesty,
As his grandfather faithfully hath done.

Now since you know my most distressed plight,
My guardian carelessness which came by care,
I humbly crave these verses may be read,
Whose capital letters make Elizabeth,
By you, my noble Lord High Admiral ;
The rather for (that) this great prophetess
Seem'd unto me as if she had foretold
Your famous victory o'er that Spanish navy,
Which by themselves was term'd Invincible.
Seeing in these lines your princely name is writ,
The miracle of time and nature's glory,
And you are she of whom Sibylla spake,
Vouchsafe to pity this your beadman's plaint,
And call my Founder home unto his house
That he may entertain your Majesty,
And see these walks, wherein he little joys,
Delightful for your Highness and your train ;
Wherein likewise his two sons that be present
Will be both dutiful and diligent,
And this young Lady Vere,[2] that's held so dear
Of my best Founder, her good grandfather.
And lastly for myself, most gracious Queen,
May it please you to restore me to my cell,
And at your Highness' absolute command,
My Lord High Chancellor may award a writ
For peaceable possession of the same ;
And that your Majesty's Lord Chamberlain
May from your Highness have the like command
To cause my Founder, now the Guardian
Of this (fair) house, increas'd for your delight,
To take the charge thereof this present night.
Which being done, I'll to my hermitage,

---

[1] Cecil himself.   [2] Lady Oxford's daughter.

And for your Highness pray continually
That God may pour upon you all his blessings,
And that the hour-glass of your happy reign
May run at full and never be at wane.
Thus, having nought of value or of worth,
Fit to present to such a peerless Queen,
I offer to your Highness, here, this bell,
A bell which hermits call St. Anthony,
Given me by my noble Lord and Founder,
And I'll betake me to this brazen bell
Which better me beseems ten thousand fold
Than any one of silver or of gold."

The Queen took the Hermit's advice. She drew up, or caused to be drawn up, a letter from " Elizabetha Anglorum, id est, a nitore Angelorum Regina formosissima et felicissima to the disconsolate and retired Sprite, the Hermit of Tybole."

" Where(as)," said this singular document, " in our High Court of Chancery it is given to understand that you, Sir Hermit, the abandonate of Nature's fair works and servant to Heaven's wonders have for the space of two years and two months possessed yourself of fair Tybollet, with her sweet rosary the same time, the recreation of our right trusty and well-beloved Sir William Sitsilt, Knight ; leaving to him the old rude repose, wherein . . . your contemplate life was relieved ; . . . suffering your solitary eye to bring into his house desolation and mourning . . . whereby Paradise is grown wilderness and for green grass are come grey hairs, We, upon advised consideration, have commanded you to your old cave, too good for the forsaken, too bad for our worthily beloved Councillor. And . . . we have given power to our Chancellor to make out such and so many writs as to him shall be thought good, to abjure desolations and mourning (the consumer of sweetness) to the frozen seas and deserts of Arabia Petrosa, upon pain of 500 despights to their terror and contempt of their torments if they attempt any part of your house again." [1]

Melancholy, more obedient than the Ocean, retreated, we may presume, at the royal command,

[1] Strype's *Annals*, vol. iv. p. 108.

but of the Hermit we shall hear something again presently.

At the close of the festivities on 20th May, Cecil was knighted, and more than two months later (on 2nd August) sworn of the Privy Council at Nonesuch.[1] By special favour to his father no other appointment detracted from the lustre of his own.[2] He was not more than twenty-eight, but from this time until his death, twenty-one years later, his history becomes in an increasing measure the history of his country.

In the early part of 1592 he received his first important trust. He was appointed to sit on the Commission which tried Sir John Perrot. The ex-Lord-Deputy of Ireland was one of those hot-tempered soldiers to whose hasty expressions no considerate person would attach any grave import-ance. Burghley, who took his true measure, knew him for a faithful servant,[3] and in our time the great historian[4] of the distressful country has singled him as one of the most humane of the Elizabethan rulers. But in that age men had often to give a temporal account of their idle words. Informers were never wanting to repeat and magnify ; and Perrot, on his own admission, had said more than he ought to have done — had suggested that the Queen might some day need from him that very military assistance which it was his grievance that she did not render him in sufficiently ample measure. The Commission found themselves obliged to convict, and the Queen exacted her pound of flesh. Perrot went to the Tower under sentence of death, which he might probably have suffered at the hands of the executioner, if Nature had not intervened to remove the occasion. Burghley and Cecil had done what they could to reverse his imprisonment. The world imputed their

---

[1] Hatf. Cal., v. p. 71.
[2] Cotton MSS., Calig., E. viii/120.
[3] Camden's *Ann.*
[4] Lecky.

efforts to bribery. On his death-bed Perrot was at pains to declare with the most solemn asseveration that no money had ever passed between him and them ; except as he said that which Burghley had supplied to relieve his more pressing wants in gaol.[1] The first charge, at any rate, against Robert Cecil does not bear examination.

[1] Hatf. Cal., iv. pp. 195-6.

CHAPTER IV

PUBLIC AFFAIRS

" . . . He that commands the sea is at great liberty, and may take as much and as little of the war as he will. . . . Surely, at this day, with us of Europe, the vantage of strength at sea, which is one of the principal dowries of Great Britain, is great: both because most of the kingdoms of Europe are not merely inland, but girt with the sea most part of their compass, and because the wealth of both Indies seems in great part but an accessory to the command of the seas."—BACON'S *Essays, Of Kingdoms.*

SIR FRANCIS WALSINGHAM died in April 1590, and Burghley, in spite of his age, took over the direction of foreign policy. This course, indeed, was probably agreeable to the aims of the two persons mainly concerned in it, for the Queen had no wish to restore the disgraced Davison, and the Lord Treasurer no doubt intended to secure the place for his son[1] so soon as Cecil had received the necessary training.

Walsingham's work fell, according to our modern notions, under two heads. There was, on the one hand, the conduct of the English relations with foreign countries, and on the other the management of the famous spy-service, which, humanly speaking, did more than anything else to preserve Elizabeth's life. In practice the two were nearly connected, for the persons over whom watch had mostly to be kept were either themselves foreigners or in close dependence upon foreign influences. The general conduct of foreign affairs Burghley kept in his own

[1] See S. P. Dom., Eliz., Add., 12th March 1591.

hands ; the particular discovery of plots and treasons he had already begun to confide to his most intimate relative about the very time when the Queen visited Theobalds.

On 18th May 1591, Michael Moody writes to him to say that he can " obtain for Mr. Robert Cecil, his Lordship's son, more intelligence from abroad than Queen or Council have, without charge."[1] The language used by the spy suggests, what was possibly the case, that Cecil carried on his work at first in an unofficial manner. There seem to have been few better methods of obtaining credit at Court, outside the obvious ones afforded by war on sea or land, than the possession of reliable knowledge about the plans and machinations of the enemy. And when the whole future of the country, its religion, its independence, the relative stability of its government, might be said to hang upon the slender thread of the Queen's life, the importance of that kind of information could hardly be exaggerated. Essex set up a secret-service of his own, under the direction of Anthony Bacon, Cecil's first cousin ; and Thomas Phelippes, the decipherer, apparently carried on for a time extensive investigations on his own account. It may well have been that Burghley thought Cecil would recommend himself for the Secretariate by showing that he was already possessed of the ability to discharge its duties. But probably no exact lines can be drawn between his public and his private business. Once he was a Privy Councillor he must have been the principal channel of information. And as Burghley grew more bent and his steps feebler, the burden of work was shifted, no doubt almost insensibly, from the father to the son.

There is honour among spies. Nothing is more striking than the strict limitations which Snowden, perhaps the ablest of Cecil's instruments, sets upon

[1] S. P. Dom., Eliz., 238/155.

his labour. " I cannot," he told his employer, " in
conscience accuse a Catholic *in quanta* a Catholic,
or a priest *in quanta* a priest, unless he should on
the other leg be a lame member and evil subject to
his prince and country. If this be expected I will
neither see nor hear nor come near any Catholic, but
of that little money I have I will live poorly to
myself. . . ."[1] Such views consorted well enough
with those in which Cecil had been brought up.
Burghley was a moderate man, and there is reason
to think that he realised and appreciated the great
sum of ill-requited and ill-remembered loyalty that
existed among the moderate English Catholics of
the time. It is noted, says Snowden in 1591, by
Catholic gentlemen who are great adversaries of the
Spanish practices, that since the causes of Catholics
came to his Lordship's arbitrament, things have
gone on with wonderful suavity.[2] But in an age
when a man's standard and conception of religious
truth were vital elements in his citizenship, when, for
better or worse, ' a religious opinion was a political
event,' the privileges of toleration were of necessity
tightly drawn. Burghley endeavoured to knot them
precisely at the point where he himself had found
them hang sufficiently loose for tolerable comfort.
He had gone to Mass in Mary's reign ; he required
his fellow-countrymen to go to Church in Elizabeth's.
This, at any rate, was the rule incorporated in the
Act of Uniformity, and Burghley had not been
unwilling to see it honoured as well in the breach as
in the observance. But Time, or rather the Pope
and Cardinal Allen, had played havoc with his
benevolent intentions, and tighter cords had had to
be knotted to hold in the seminary priests and drive
out the importers of papal bulls. Still, in a really
admirable spirit of conciliation, considering the
intense and constant provocation to which he was

[1] S. P. Dom., Eliz., 239/2.   [2] *Ibid.*, 239/26.

subject, he clung to his old test ; and in some instructions given in this very year of 1591 we find the old principle coupled with the old injunction not to press supposed recusants in other matters of conscience.[1] But the world was running furiously against moderation. No view is more mistaken than that which regards the years after the defeat of the Armada as the calm which follows the storm. The Puritans, assured of safety, broke into most scurrilous pamphleteering, directed against the Anglican Episcopate. Whitgift, led on by a laudable affection for order and discipline, and supported in the Council by Cecil's father-in-law, Lord Cobham, set in motion the inquisitorial machinery of his new Court of High Commission to bring about a factitious uniformity among Protestants. The seminary priests, tormented by failure, redoubled their efforts to persuade the King of Spain that the English were utterly disaffected. And the Queen and her courtiers, stimulated by victory, embarked with greater zest and confidence on that buccaneering policy which diverted a substantial fragment of the wealth of the Indies to their own manifold and often wasteful uses. No war, perhaps, has ever been so nearly reduced to the forms of commercial speculation as this last long conflict with Spain. Each enterprise was financed and planned exactly as a company of merchants might plan and finance a scheme of trade. Money was invested in shares, and those who took the largest risks had the chance of taking the largest profits. It is in connection with the greatest of these ventures that Cecil's name again comes to the front.

On the 17th August 1592, Sir John Borough wrote to announce that he had taken a carrack, or treasure-ship, " by which he hoped that Her Majesty should receive more profit than by any ship that ever came into England." [2] The *Madre de Dios* carried, in

[1] S. P. Dom., Eliz., 240/43.   [2] Lansdowne MSS., 70/27.

fact, merchandise which was valued in contemporary coin at £150,000 sterling.[1] The conception of the enterprise lay with Ralegh ; the credit of the capture with Borough and Crosse, acting respectively as agents for the two principals, Ralegh and Cumberland ; but the lion's share of the profit—a share out of all proportion to her actual interest in the venture—was claimed by the Queen. But, sharp as Elizabeth was, the birds of prey were sharper, and before the Royal Commissioners could appropriate the treasure, a great quantity of it had been spirited away with a dexterity proportionate to the value at stake. The Commissioners seem to have been poor creatures, and the Privy Council were obliged to send Cecil down to wake them up, which he appears to have done in a literal as well as a metaphorical sense.[2] His visitation has indeed something of a Napoleonic rigour and rapidity about it ; but the Commissioners were very well satisfied to shift their responsibilities, and begged that he might not be permitted to fulfil his intention of making an early departure.[2] His own account of his proceedings is sufficiently amusing :—

"May it please your Lordship," he writes to his father, "whomsoever I met by the way within seven miles that either had anything in cloak, bag, or malle, which did but smell of the prizes, either at Dartmouth or Plymouth (for I assure your Lordship I could well smell them almost, such hath been the spoils of amber and musk amongst them). I did . . . return him with me to the town of Exeter. . . . I stayed any which should carry news to Dartmouth or Plymouth at the gates of the town. I compelled them also to tell me where any trunks or malles were. . . . Finding the people stubborn . . . I . . . remitted two innkeepers to prison ; which example would have won the Queen £20,000, a week past. I have lit upon a Londoner's shop, in whose house we have found a bag of seed pearls, divers pairs of damasks, cypresses and calicos with a very great pot of musk, certain tassels of pearls and divers other things. . . . And by

---

[1] Hakluyt; and Hatf. Cal., iv. p. 234.
[2] Lansdowne MSS., 70/44.

my rough dealing I have left an impression with (the Mayor) and the rest. . . . My Lord, there never was such spoil. I have intercepted letters wherein I find who have written to London to their friends to come down and wherein they have promised what they will do for them. I . . . keep the letters to charge the parties at Dartmouth. And this party who had all those things is gone this day back again for more booty. I will take him by the way and make as much benefit of him and of his knowledge as I can. . . . I will suppress the confluence of those buyers of which there are above two thousand. The name of Commissioners is common in this country and in these causes. But my sending down hath made many stagger. Fouler weather, more desperate [1] ways, more obstinate people did I never meet with. I will stay four or five days at Dartmouth and Plymouth but no longer." [2]

Fear was not the only weapon in the hands of the Government. Ralegh was at this time under one of those clouds in which his rash nature constantly involved him, but his great popularity with sailors made it worth while to send him down to Dartmouth under custody in order to bring this milder influence to bear upon the situation. Cecil was aboard the carrack when he appeared ' with his keeper,' and is responsible for a lively vignette of the spectacle :—

"I assure you," he writes to Heneage, "his poor servants, to the number of one hundred and forty, goodly men, and all the mariners came to him with such shouts and joy that I never saw a man more troubled to quiet them in my life. But his heart is broken, for he is very pensive longer than he is busied, in which he can toil terribly. But if you heard him rage at the spoils finding all the short wares utterly diminished, you would laugh as I cannot choose but do.[3] . . . He . . ., finding that it is known that he hath a keeper, wheresoever he is saluted with congratulation for liberty, doth answer, ' No, I am still the Queen of England's poor captive.' I wished him to conceal it, because here it diminisheth his credit which I do vow to you before God is greater among the mariners than I thought for. I do grace him as much as I may, for I do find him marvellous greedy to do anything to recover the conceit of his brutish offence."

---

[1] In the original, ' desperater.'　　　[2] S. P. Dom., Eliz., 243/16.
[3] In the original, ' as I do which I cannot choose.'

Cecil passes on to other matters, which show us that " England's Forgotten Worthies " were not always held in so high esteem as we hold them now :—

" I have examined Sir John Gilbert by oath and all his, who I find clear, I protest to you in most men's opinions. . . . I assure you on my faith I think him wronged in this, howsoever in others he may have done like a Devonshire man. . . . We have rats white and black, drink like smoke in taste, and, God help me, I brought so little provision for long staying that I pray God I come home without quick cattle. Give me leave to be merry with you for, if I were whipped, I must be bold with my friends, in which number I account you. But if you retain me not in the good thoughts of her mind, whose angelical quality works strange influences in the hearts of a couple of her servants according to their several moulds, *actum est de amicitia.*" [1]

Persons of angelical quality do not, however, live wholly upon air, and Cecil was too skilful a courtier to omit to furnish the proper supplies of nectar and ambrosia :—

" It is the property of the Creator," he writes to the Queen, " to accept the labour of men, from the abundance of their affection, without measure of their abilities to perform any action acceptable to divine worthiness. Herein I am most blessed that I am a vassal to His celestial Creature, who pleaseth out of angelic grace, to pardon and allow my careful and zealous desires. My services are attended with envy. I must be offensive to the multitude and to others that may be revengeful who also have many and great friends. I can please none because I thirst only to please one, and malice is no less wakeful in itself than fearful to others, were not my trust in her divine justice which never suffereth her Creatures to complain. The comfort I receive of those sacred lines is best expressed in silence, but I have written them anew in my heart and adjoined them unto the rest of my admiring thoughts, which always travailing from wonder to wonder spend themselves in contemplation, being absent and present in reading secretly the story of marvels in that more than human perfection. I hope the end of this my travail shall be accepted with no less than the beginning is vouchsafed, for I have no other purpose of living but to witness what I would perform if I

---

[1] S. P. Dom., Eliz., 243/17.

had power. If I could do more than any man it were less than
nothing balanced with my desires ; if I could do as much as all
the world, it were neither praise nor thanks worthy in respect of
the duty I owe and the princess whom I serve." [1]

The business of the carrack hung on into the
following year. In the end the Queen appears to
have made the very substantial sum of £80,000,[2]
whilst the remainder of the treasure was divided
by Cecil and his colleagues into six equal parts, of
which three were allotted to Cumberland, two to
Ralegh, and one to the City of London, these being
the other contributories. Cecil's eneigy and skill was
praised in an unlooked-for quarter. " I dare give
the Queen £10,000," wrote Ralegh, " for that which
is gained by Sir Robert Cecil coming down, which
I speak without all affection or partiality, for he hath
more rifled my ship than all the rest." [3]

Robert Cecil is, perhaps, the only man of whom
it may be said that he found himself virtual leader of
the House of Commons without ever previously having
taken part in its debates. When he rose on the 26th
of February 1593 to introduce the work of the session
he gave the best possible explanation of his previous
silence ; he had never before had anything that in
good conscience he wanted to say.[4] Whether this
circumstance was matter for praise or blame, Cecil
left his hearers to decide, closing his modest reference
to himself with the old maxim, " Nec te collaudes,
nec te vituperes ipse."

He passed on to treat of public affairs. His
natural good sense led him to preface his remarks
with a few happily turned sentences about Queen
and country—that Queen who, he said, had " made
this little land a sanctuary for all the persecuted
Saints of God " ; that country which from want of

[1] Hatf. Cal., v. p. 632.   [2] S. P. Dom., Eliz., 244/75.
[3] Stebbing, Sir Walter Ralegh, p. 98.
[4] D'Ewes' Journals, and throughout.

making adequate provision had run so near a risk four years before. Philip, he pointed out, was still spreading his toils around them. In Lorraine and Brittany his arms were meeting with success ; and Brittany was admirably situated for striking at the extensive English trade with La Rochelle and Bordeaux, or more directly at England herself. Another point of attack was also open to him : " Seeing it to be but a folly to make wooden bridges to pass into Ireland he hath found out a safer and stronger passage by land, and that by Scotland ; which though it be not talked of on the Exchange nor preached at Paul's Cross, yet it is most true and in Scotland as common as the high-way." And Cecil ended warningly : " The King of Spain's malice daily increaseth against us ; the number of Papists daily increaseth or at leastwise becomes more manifest. . . . Consult how to withstand such imminent dangers which the greater they be the sooner they should be looked into and remembered."

The language, though not exaggerated, was calculated for effect. To consult for the commonweal meant in the sixteenth century little more than to determine what amount and manner of taxation should be levied. A committee was accordingly appointed to consider the matter, and reported a day or so later in favour of a grant double the usual one, this is two subsidies and four-fifteenths and tenths. The product of an ordinary vote was on an average £45,000 a year ;[1] in the present instance, therefore, the Government might have reckoned on obtaining £90,000. But this was manifestly insufficient, for upon the maintenance of the revolt in the Low Countries alone Elizabeth was spending £120,000.[2] Burghley adopted a procedure which looks strange to-day. The Lords threw out the Finance Bill, not

[1] Prothero, *Statutes and Constitutional Documents*, p. lxxxii.
[2] S. P. Dom., Eliz., 244/69.

because the proposed taxation was too heavy, but because it was too light. The representatives of the Commons were then sent for, and informed by the Lord Treasurer that their Lordships would assent to nothing less than a grant of three entire subsidies, to be paid during the next three years. And Burghley suggested, not obscurely, that many rich men's incomes, particularly in the City of London, were assessed too low. It fell to Cecil to report his father's speech to the Lower House, together with an intimation that the Lords desired a conference with the Commons on the question ; and this he did with proper modesty. Everyone concluded that the Lords proposed to confer upon the amount of the subsidy, and Bacon and others took exception to this course as unconstitutional. The Government were probably without instructions, were, anyway, embarrassed, and suffered defeat by 89.

By the time the House met again the following week the Queen had in all probability been consulted.[1] Cecil, anyhow, came down prepared to travel along the line of least resistance, and made a speech which by reason of its incisiveness and its dexterous evasion might—so far as we can judge from the scanty report—have been delivered to-day. Unton had attacked him bitterly,[2] complaining that the names of those who were opposed to the conference had been reported to the Queen as if hostile to the subsidy, and, further, that a conference upon finance ran counter to precedent and privilege ; and Cecil, provoked possibly at having to make what looked, at any rate, like a graceless concession, provoked too, perhaps, at finding himself in conflict with an old friend,[3] replied with some asperity. " The third man's (*i.e.* Unton's) motion," he said, " consisted of three points. The first

[1] Spedding, *Letters and Life of Francis Bacon*, i. pp. 219, 220.
[2] Hatf. Cal., iv. p. 452.
[3] Cotton MSS., Calig., E. viii. 124.

was News, the second was History, and the third . . . a Motion. His News was that men's names were given up to the Queen. This was news ; for I heard it not before. The History was a large report of the progress of the matter. His Motion was, that we should confer with the Lords about a subsidy with them, but not conclude a subsidy with them. His matter seems contrary to his meaning, or else is more than ever was meant ; for it was never desired of us by the Lords that we should confer with them about a subsidy."

It may have been so. At this distance of time and with fragmentary reports we are not really in a position to doubt Cecil's word.[1] But it was clearly unfortunate that feeling had been allowed to run so high, when there was no more occasion for it than a misunderstanding.

A long road had still to be traversed, even when the stone of stumbling had been removed, and the conference had passed off well. Cecil hated talk. " I am glad to see the willingness of the House and readiness to yield aid ; and having a feeling of the necessity requiring it, my desire is, that the sentence which has had so many parentheses, might now be brought to a period, and the bear's whelp that hath so many times been licked over might now be made somewhat. For that is always the most honourable conclusion which having received many contradictions, is in the end concluded."

It was all in vain. The κακόηθες of speech was not yet exhausted, and the contest began to rage again over the time to be allowed for the levy of the full subsidy. Cecil rose at last, deprecating the endless discussion, and proposed that a subsidy and two-fifteenths and tenths be paid in each of the first two years, and the same amount distributed in two parts over the third and fourth years. This was agreed

---

[1] As Spedding in effect does.

to, and the Queen made free of Parliaments for four years to come.

The financial difficulty was not the only one by which Cecil was taught the inconveniences of public life. The name of Morrice still figures in text-books on the Constitution as that of a lesser martyr in the cause of liberty. He was Attorney of the Court of Wards, and probably in that capacity he had become intimate[1] with Burghley and his son. Presuming, perhaps, on this circumstance, he introduced two Bills to restrain Whitgift's new inquisition. In the debate which followed, Cecil, as representing the Government, felt himself at length obliged to take part. He rose without preparation and suggested that the Bill should be entrusted to him to commend to the Queen, and, if she approved it, to *re*commend to the House. This was probably the best chance of extricating the ' wise and learned ' Morrice from the net which he had spread for himself, but Coke, who was Speaker, interposed and carried off the Bills for consideration. Elizabeth was extremely angry when she heard what had happened, gave Coke the strictest orders to allow no bill touching matters ecclesiastical to be read, and, to make assurance sure, put Morrice in prison and deprived him of his office and his status as a barrister.

But the Parliament of 1593 is better remembered for other things than its finance or the case of Morrice. It passed the last Act—for many years to come— against Roman Catholics, and the first against Dissenters. Persons of all religious complexions over the age of sixteen were now required to attend church, or, in default, to be hanged or banished. Only wealthy Papists could any longer escape by paying a fine of £20 a month.

Robert Cecil had no hand in promoting these draconic statutes. He had perhaps some faint

[1] Hatf. Cal., 1st March 1593.

glimmering of the truth that the course and conduct
of the human spirit can never be a matter of human
commandment ; at all events he confined his activities
to the less interesting but more profitable region of
bodily well-being. The Social-Problem weighed upon
his age, as it weighs upon our own, as we have the
highest authority for supposing it will weigh more
or less upon every generation while Time is. In
this very Parliament of 1593, Fulke Greville had
drawn attention in some impressive words to the
wealth of the country manifest in " the sumptuous-
ness in apparel, in plate, and in all things," and to
the discontent which any further taxation of the
poorer classes might occasion. And, in language
which might conveniently be used when power was
not under popular control, he urged the wealthy
knights and burgesses sitting around him to increase
their own burdens, " for otherwise the weak feet will
complain of too heavy a body. . . . If the feet knew
their strength as we know their oppression, they
would not bear as they do." Cecil was not content
to leave the matter there. On the 12th March he
moved " for some course of necessary relief to be
had and devised for the great number of poor people
pressing everywhere to beg," who fell, as he declared,
into three classes : the maimed soldiery, who deserved
relief ; the sick and aged, who needed charity ; and
the stout, idle rogues, who wanted work and whipping.

Some days later Heneage, the Vice-Chamberlain,
took up the cause of the first division—the soldiery,
returned from the wars, broken in limb and fortune,
whose distress was (so Ralegh affirmed) the principal
fountain of the prevailing destitution. Heneage's
remedy was one which, *mutatis mutandis*, should be
commended to benevolent legislators in every age.
He proposed that of those sitting in the House every
Privy - Councillor should subscribe thirty shillings,
every knight and every knight of the shire ten

shillings, and every burgess five shillings to the
relief of distress. This self-taxing ordinance was
carried, and the collection enforced ; any attempt
at evasion being met with the penalty of a double
charge. Cecil followed with a proposal for a bill
embodying a continual contribution. This was
referred to a committee. On the 28th he reports
that the Committee could reach no conclusion, and
the Bill had to be recommitted. On the 5th April
it passed its third reading. The Act provided that
every parish should be rated at not less than 1d.
or more than 6d. weekly. The sum, whatever it
came to, was to be collected by the Churchwardens
and paid over to the High-Constable, through whose
hands it passed into those of the Justices at Quarter
Sessions. To them necessitous soldiers, who had
resided in the county for the greater part of the
three years preceding their service, and who came
provided with certificates from their commanding
officers, were entitled to appeal, and, on the appeal
being allowed, to receive in the case of a private
not more than £10, of a non-commissioned officer
not more than £15, and of a lieutenant not more
than £20 a year. A register of the pensioners was to
be kept, and any who begged were to be disqualified
and treated as vagabonds.

Cecil's name is connected with one other discussion in this Parliament of 1593. The City of
London was promoting a proposal to check aliens
from selling foreign commodities by retail. On the
one side it was argued that the English retail traders
were being undersold ; on the other hand, that in
charity England could not refuse foreigners the
means of earning their livelihood. Cecil spoke at
the end of the debate. He disclaimed all skill in
economics. His mind, he said, had only reached a
conclusion by reason of the length of the argument.
He did all honour to the charitable dispositions which

had made England the refuge of distressed peoples,
though charity to them ought not to be allowed
to hinder or injure Englishmen. But his quarrel
with the Bill was rather that it would do no good,
unless it were drawn wider so as to cover selling in
gross. He proposed it should be recommitted and,
the House agreeing, his name and Ralegh's were
added to the Committee appointed to consider it.

CHAPTER V

THE CASE OF DR. LOPEZ

> " *Machiavel* . . . . . . I come not, I
> To read a lecture here in Britain,
> But to present the tragedy of a Jew
> Who smiles to see how full his bags are crammed,
> Which money was not got without my means."
> MARLOWE, *The Jew of Malta*. Prologue.

BURGHLEY was far from well during 1593,[1] but his
sense of duty at the Council board did not slacken,
and at the close of the year he divided the honours
of regular attendance with Howard of Effingham.[2]
Still the mantle was visibly falling from his shoulders,
and, as the last and wisest of Elizabeth's old servants
began to fail, the question whether or not Robert
Cecil should succeed his father became only second
in importance to that of the succession of the throne.
Place and power were as alluring as ever ; but the
Queen was still capricious, uncertain, fond with
baffling alternation now of a handsome presence,
now of a prudent counsellor. The old foes had new
faces, but their recommendations and their policies
were still the same. Where Leicester had stood
once, Essex—his stepson—stood now ; a nobler and
an abler man, but marked by a like affection for
bold, aggressive measures and finding favour with
the Queen by the grace and spirit of his carriage.
And Cecil, as his father had done before him, was

---

[1] Hatf. Cal., 1593, *passim*.
[2] Both attended eighty-nine meetings, the maximum (Acts of the
Privy Council).

building up a reputation for industry and caution—
virtues in which his brilliant rival was conspicuously
lacking, and which gather their harvest late but
abundantly. Only he was deficient in demeanour,
in that massive dignity of bearing which added so
much appearance of weight and power to Burghley's
counsels.

The first passes of the duel were fought over the
famous conspiracy of Dr. Lopez ; and it is natural
to ask at the outset of such a life as Cecil's, in which
treason and plot play so large a part, whether these
ugly stories are really entitled to the notice which
chroniclers accord them. To the philosophic historian, indeed, they appear to be of the slightest
consequence ; scarcely distinguishable in kind from
the murder trials whose process and detail the news-
boys of to-day press upon us at the street corners.
The constitutional historian, again, regards them
coldly, making but little account of one name more
or less in a catalogue of conspiracies. But in the
less rarefied atmosphere in which the biographer and
the annalist live and move and have their being,
such matters are of a vast importance. All the
temper of the times is latent in their folds. To
study those things by which men were greatly moved,
to interrogate the sources of common hopes and fears,
is to find the key to the practical statesmanship of
the age. The tragedies of Shakespeare, revolving, as
they so constantly do, around the subject of treachery,
are a lasting reminder of the part which treason and
plot played in the life of the sixteenth century.
They disclose imaginatively what the plots of Lopez
and Squire and Essex and Catesby reveal actually—
the extreme instability of government. The Sovereign
was bound to have a lively expectation of meeting
death by the cup or the dagger ; the statesman was
bound to regard the block as a likely conclusion to
all his labours. And a change of rulers in the then

condition of men's minds commonly meant a fresh
and a far-reaching dislocation of habits and ideas,
of all that fabric of creed and custom in which the
foundations of a state are really laid.   To a nation
which had passed from the hands of Henry into the
hands of Somerset, from the hands of Somerset into
the hands of Northumberland, from these again into
those of Mary, and then once more into those of
Elizabeth, continuity of government had become the
cardinal necessity, the true measure of statesmanship.   We shall never understand the conditions or
the character of Cecil's work unless we constantly
remember that conspiracies and intrigues threatened
not merely the Sovereign's life or his own tenure of
power, but the unseen foundations of society itself.   The
thrust and parry of the assassin's dagger or the courtier's
tongue are as vital an element in the politics of that
century as the thrust and parry of parliamentary debate
in our own.   Fortunately for the historian, they have
also a swiftness and poignancy of which parliamentary
proceedings are not now commonly possessed.

And the Lopez Conspiracy is no exception to the
general rule.   Its dramatic quality appealed to the
tone and temper of the time ; and not the master-hand
of the age alone has preserved its memory in immortal
pages.   It stirred men's imagination even in a century when imagination was richly fed ; it revolted
men's conscience even when treason was commonplace incident ; and it provoked a trial in which the
jury, even to Cecil's unimpressionable eye, seemed
' the most substantial ' he had ever seen.   But,
apart from all this, a biography of Cecil cannot pass
it by, for the first of the many insinuations made
against him is that he deserted Lopez when Lopez
began to fall.[1]

---

[1] Hume, *Treason and Plot*: " It was the Cecil method never to
champion an unpopular cause " (p. 146). . . . " Cecil was as eager as Essex
now to wash his hands of sympathy with the fallen wretch " (p. 150).

The story, of course, like most stories of the kind, flows from tainted sources ; neither Lopez nor his accusers were men of honour. But it was carefully sifted by the best experts of the day, and there is no reason to think they were deceived. The exact order of the events is more easy to call in question than the events themselves, but it must have run substantially as in the account which follows.

Lopez was a Portuguese Jew who had settled in England. He had the dominant qualities, rightly or wrongly, attributed to his race—ability and avarice. He was, besides, plausible and unscrupulous. He climbed the ladder of his profession with success, passed from the post of house-physician at St. Bartholomew's Hospital into the service of Leicester and finally into that of the Queen. His foreign connections enabled him to be of political use to Walsingham, though, if his accuser is to be believed, he overreached himself and was put in the Tower ;[1] a lesson which he never forgot. He was, anyhow, too valuable a man to be altogether spared to medicine, at a time when the fortunes of England and Portugal were closely interlaced ; and Essex, eager to spread wide his nets, impressed him as a spy-master, with the Queen's knowledge indeed, but without more than her grudging assent.[2] The principal pawn at this time on the diplomatic chess-board was a certain Don Antonio, who possessed a shadowy and discreditable claim to the throne of Portugal. It had, however, suited Elizabeth to give him countenance and grant him asylum, and it had been in his interest that, after the destruction of the Armada, she had dispatched the ill-starred expedition to Lisbon, in which Essex took part contrary to her express commands. This expedition Lopez had certainly promoted and possibly betrayed.[3] After its failure some

---

[1] Harleian MSS., 871.   [2] Goodman, *Court of James I.*, p. 150.

[3] So Dimock, *Engl. Hist. Rev.*, July 1894, "Conspiracy of Dr. Lopez."

of the Portuguese suitors who had hung upon its success transferred their affections, or at least their services, to Philip of Spain; and a negotiation, of which Lopez had knowledge, sprang up with Fuentes and Ibarra, the Spanish Ministers in the Netherlands. The first agent in the affair was a certain Manuel d'Andrada, who had been liberated by the English Government at Lopez's instigation in the idea that he would make a traitor of double dye, and under the pretence of betraying England to Spain betray Spain to England. Lopez had the paying of him; and up to December 1593 secret-service money was still passing.[1]

But Andrada was only a decoy-duck, and in due course, when he had lured Lopez far enough, the conduct of the transaction was taken over by another Portuguese gentleman named Ferrera; [2] a man once of great fortune but grown so needy that he was willing to sell all that a gentleman counts precious for a little gain. The talk of peace, which had been the alleged purpose of the negotiation, was now dropped, and instead there was talk of killing Don Antonio, seducing his son and remaining adherents, and at last of compassing the Queen's death. Lopez's mind was one of those which oscillate with the prospects of advantage, and we shall never know at what moment he changed his allegiance and passed from the attitude of fishing inquiry on behalf of the English Government to that of murderous servility to the Spanish. He himself, indeed, denied to the end that, in respect at least to the Queen's death, he had ever been seduced into treason; but it is certain that during the summer of 1593, and at his dictation, Ferrera wrote letters, which, whatever their motive, were of a highly compromising and mysterious char-

---

[1] Harl. MSS., 871, p. 59 (i).
[2] Ferrera was in a position to negotiate a rich marriage for Lopez's daughter (Hatf. Cal., vii. p. 253).

acter. This was not known until later, but in
October, probably by the advice of Essex, Ferrera
was arrested on a general charge of tampering with
the loyalty of the Portuguese attached to Don
Antonio. Some letters designed for him which came
over in the Flemish mail increased the sphere of
suspicion; and Ferrera, who saw in what quarter
danger lay, made some imprudent efforts from prison
to get a message through to Lopez so as to check
the treasonable correspondence, or at least waylay
the contents of the post-bag. But Essex was too
quick for him. Two messengers, one coming, the
other departing, were taken at Dover, and with them
a whole budget of papers. As Essex said, he had
made a great draught and he doubted not that some
good fish would be taken amongst the fry.[1]

The fish were not wanting in flavour. There was
a letter from Lopez to Ferrera, which suggested that
he had been over-free in his communications about
the Court. There were letters from Christofero Moro
and Ibarra, Philip's ministers, promising favour and
reward; and the correspondence contained, besides,
mysterious talk of musk and amber and pearls and
costly merchandise, " so sorted and matched as it
might safely appear these did serve for cipher to
colour great matters." [1]

But beyond all this was a letter from one, Manuel
Louys, to Ferrera, by which it appeared there was
some important and secret matter, which required
a decisive answer from the Court of Spain. The
following passage in it especially excited suspicion :
" The Bearer hereof will tell your Worship the price
in which your pearls are held. I will advise you
perfectly of the uttermost penny that will be given
for them and crave what order you will have set down
for the conveyance of the money and wherein you
would have it employed. Also this Bearer shall tell

[1] Harl. MSS., 871.

you in what resolution we rested about a little musk
and amber the which I am determined to buy.   But
before I resolve myself I will advise of the price
thereof.   And if it please your Worship to be
my partner I am persuaded we shall make good
profit."

Pearls and musk and amber and good profit !
Elizabeth's counsellors scented a rank conspiracy and
set to work to disinter it from the roots.   By good
fortune the Manuel Louys who had written the
letter applied at this very time to the English Consul
at Calais for a safe-conduct into England.   The
Clerk of the Council was instructed to send him what
he wanted, but to word it in such a manner that it
should be no real protection.   Louys, or Tinoco (for,
after the manner of spies, he had an alias), came over,
all unsuspecting, and was quietly secured.

When the news of this capture reached him,
Lopez could no longer remain in doubt as to his own
peril.   He burnt those of his papers which were at
Hampton Court, where the Queen was residing, and
then rushed up to London to do as much for the rest.
He was none too soon.   The Queen had been slow
to think harm of him, and Burghley, in the first
blush of the affair, had even employed him to look
through Ferrera's post-bag.   But the weak joints
in his harness did not escape the vigilant eyes that
play about a Court.   He had replied to Ferrera's
note that he would spend three hundred pounds,
if it were necessary, to stay or stop the Flemish
packets.   He had changed countenance when he
was informed that Ferrera had been arrested.
He had dropped some cryptic and uneasy words
about cozening the King of Spain before the Queen,
who resented them as she resented anything
like insolence in regard to her fellow-sovereigns.
Ferrera's charges, besides, constituted a formidable
indictment against him.   Essex, not perhaps alto-

gether free of personal animus,[1] already believed in his complicity. It was decided to examine him, though the Queen and the Cecils believed he would satisfactorily clear himself. He was brought to Burghley's house in the Strand, and interrogated by the three Privy Councillors. He gave so good an account of himself, that Cecil posted back to Hampton Court to reassure the Queen. Elizabeth took occasion to give Essex a lesson, and to his great chagrin called him ' a rash and temerarious youth.' [2] But, for perhaps the only time in the course of their mutual relations, Essex was right and the Queen and Cecil wrong. When Lopez was confronted with Ferrera his explanations gave way ; and the great oaths with which he tried to establish his innocence probably invited his examiners to a contrary opinion. Ferrera, on the other hand, impressed them by one of those natural and spontaneous touches which commonly defy invention and sometimes offer the simplest way of deciding whether or not a man is speaking the truth. Being asked if Lopez ever wrote any compromising letters himself, he replied, " answering on the sudden, ' No, he will not write, for walking by the Tower one day I remember how he said he was once in that place for the like matter and therefore would take heed to come there again.' " [3]

There was another witness available. Cecil had been appointed to receive the depositions of Tinoco, and that wretched man was constantly examined. He took what, in the view of a spy, commonly appeared the royal road to freedom. He offered to transfer his allegiance to the English Government, and declared

---

[1] Goodman (*Court of James I.*, pp. 150, 152-3) says that Lopez had been in the habit of giving his informations directly to the Queen, so that Essex lost the credit of supplying them ; and further that he had revealed to Don Antonio and Perez certain confidential matters about Essex, which as a doctor he had no right to betray.

[2] Birch, *Mems. of the Reign of Eliz.*, i. p. 151.

[3] Harl. MSS., 871.

he could do it good service if he might see Lopez
and get the necessary credentials. This latter
proposal was an obvious device to get speech of the
doctor. Cecil saw through it and presently dragged
from Tinoco two letters which had been entrusted to
him by Fuentes and Ibarra. They were referred to
Elizabeth. She picked out one or two phrases—
" the benefit of the world," " those shadows you
speak of "—which seemed to point to some matter
greater than the affairs of Don Antonio. Tinoco
was again interrogated, and in the end declared that
what was required of the Court Physician was " a
thing horrible to be named," but which he named,
none the less, forsooth, the poisoning of the Queen. It
remained to search his clothes. While he was in
bed at the gatehouse at Westminister these were
examined, and two letters for unlimited credit were
found upon them.

Such letters do not lightly drop into the pockets
of needy adventurers. The game was fully up.
The evidence, verbal and circumstantial, hung
together, and the two spies, who were separately
examined, told the same story. It had been a
tedious affair to worry out the truth, but the end was
reached at last. " The business," says an anonymous
examiner who was possibly Coke,[1] " was like a round
circle, and, when anything was gotten of any of
them, the rest were presently dealt with upon these
points and did sometimes confess the same, sometimes enlarge and give more matter to work upon, as
it had been the expungation of a fortress with trenches
and defences so that it seemed invincible. But, by
continual labour, sapping, mining and hewing out of
hard rock and approaching by little and little, all
these defences were taken away, and breach was
made." [2]

Tinoco and Ferrera were slow to speak, but what

[1] M. Hume, *Treason and Plot*.   [2] Harl. MSS., 871.

they said they apparently stuck to. With Lopez
it was otherwise. He began with denial, and then
passed to confession and avoidance. At first he knew
nothing of the plot ; ultimately he acknowledged it,
but declared he had participated in it innocently,
hoping to do the Queen service. When the gravity
of his conduct was ascertained, his lodging was
shifted from Essex House to the Tower, and there,
on the 30th January, Essex and Cecil met to examine
him. It was as they drove away that there occurred
an incident which serves conveniently to bring Francis
Bacon upon our narrow stage.

The Bacons were Burghley's nephews by marriage,
and, whatever may have been the case with Anthony,
the elder brother, Francis, never forgot the claim which
he had upon that powerful connection. He was very
poor, very brilliant, very ambitious ; the last partly,
no doubt, from an honest desire to use his great talents,
but partly also from a lower and less creditable
motive. One of the austerest as well as one of the
most scrupulous of judges [1] has picked out eye-service
—men-pleasing—as his dominant and besetting sin.
At all events neither pride nor modesty ever tied his
lips. He asked, or his friends asked on his behalf,
persistently and without hesitation ; and that for
which he asked was sometimes more than others had
the right or the power to give him. It has been the
fashion to regard the Cecils as his secret and inveterate
opponents, but neither their letters nor their acts are
proof of it. There is no warrant at all for thinking
that they regarded him with particular dislike. No
doubt all that was best in him, all that has come
down to us, filtered and consecrated by Time, was
hidden from them, at least at the moment we are
speaking of, as it was hidden from most, perhaps all,
of his contemporaries. Nor, even if they could have
known it, were they the kind of men to appreciate the

[1] Dean Church.

really noble and single-hearted endeavour with which, through good report and ill, he pursued that new philosophy of nature which had early captured his fancy. Busy and practical, they doubtless thought of him chiefly as a poor relation and one who was hard to satisfy. But this is not to call their repeated professions of goodwill insincere.[1] What Burghley wrote to Lady Bacon was probably quite true—that he was of less power to do his friends service than the world was pleased to fancy.[2] And had Bacon taken the rather unpalatable advice his relatives gave him—not to fly at too high game—it is possible he would have attained his end more quickly than he did. As it was, without any exact breach with them, he attached himself to Essex—Essex, whose sympathies were so much wider, whose generosity was so much more expansive than theirs, who, perhaps, alone among his contemporaries, had some idea of what Bacon was really worth. Bacon's fortunes became Essex's care ; Bacon's success a matter personal to his friend. When, in the course of 1593, the Attorney-Generalship fell vacant, Essex resolved to spare no pains to secure it for his follower. But he overrated his influence with Elizabeth, who was still incensed at Bacon's speech on the subsidies at the beginning of the year. The Queen procrastinated, as she loved to do on every occasion. There was, indeed, beyond all dispute, another claim to be considered. Coke was an older man, a more learned lawyer, a more approved servant than Bacon. What we call ' jobs ' were not unknown, but it is clear Elizabeth would have been open to criticism if she had selected Bacon at the instance of her favourite. Burghley behaved quite straightforwardly. He had promised Bacon to do

[1] " I do assure you that I have no kinsman living (my brother excepted) whom I hold so dear " (Cecil to Egerton, 27th March 1594, Hatf. Cal.).

[2] Lambeth MSS., 649/80; quoted by Spedding, *Life and Letters of Francis Bacon*, i. p. 255.

what he could for him, and he stood by Essex in maintaining his fitness against the rest of the Council.[1] But he made no pretence to the Queen of thinking him better qualified than Coke; and his impartial judgment told him that Bacon ought to be satisfied with the place of Solicitor-General which Coke would vacate.[2] This lukewarmness Essex could not forgive; and as he and Cecil drove away from the Tower, after the examination of Lopez, his fiery, overbearing temper broke loose. Cecil, it is true, was responsible for the occasion. Presumably in the hope that Essex might be brought to abandon the impossible, but certainly with great absence of tact, he remarked that the Queen was intending to fill the vacant office before five days were out, and then went on to inquire whose candidature his companion favoured. Essex replied very naturally that his wishes had long been known, and that he was pledged to Bacon. " Good Lord," said Cecil, " I wonder your Lordship should go about to spend your strength in so unlikely a matter. Give me a single precedent," he continued, " for the appointment of so raw a youth to a place of such moment." Essex saw his chance. " I can produce no example of that," he said, " for I have made no search, but I could name a younger man than Francis, of less learning and no greater experience, who is suing and shoving with all his might to get an office of far greater weight than the Attorneyship." Cecil had the wisdom to keep his temper. " I know well," he replied, " that your Lordship means me, but if my years and experience are small, I have studied in a school where the schoolmaster's wisdom and learning are great." Then he went on to speak of his father's long and painful travail on behalf of the State, sufficient to merit some recognition in the person of his son. As to Bacon, he prayed Essex to reconsider

[1] Spedding, *Life and Letters of Francis Bacon*, i. p. 289.
[2] *Ibid.*, p. 258.

his demand. "'If at least your Lordship had spoken of the Solicitorship,' quoth good, gentle Sir Robert," —so runs the speech in Anthony Standen's rather malicious report,—"'that might be of easier digestion to Her Majesty.' 'Digest me no digestions,' saith the Earl, ' for the Attorneyship for Francis is that I must have, and in that will I spend all my power, might, authority and amity, and with tooth and nail defend and procure the same for him against whomsoever ; and whosoever getteth this office out of my hands for any other before he have it, it shall cost him the coming-by. And this be you assured, Sir Robert, for now do I fully declare myself. And for your own part, Sir Robert, I think strange both of my Lord Treasurer and you that can have the mind to seek the preferment of a stranger before so near a kinsman . . . [1] For if you weigh in a balance the parts every way of his competitor and him, only excepting five poor years of admitting to a House of Court before Francis, you shall find in all other respects whatever no comparison between them.' And that," concludes Standen, " was the end of their speeches," as indeed it well might be.[2]

Essex might storm as he pleased at the Cecils, the decision lay in fact, as well as in law, with Elizabeth. And Elizabeth was slow and obdurate, and, as is thought,[3] ever mindful of Bacon's speech on the subsidies. Presently she appointed Coke to be Attorney, and then the struggle began again over the Solicitorship. It was said once more that Cecil was doing his best to thwart his relatives. But Bacon's biographer has affirmed [4] that he can find no evidence to justify such a belief ; and Bacon himself in letters [5] to his uncle and his cousin has left it on record that he had been far too ready to credit idle

---

[1] There is a word here which I cannot read. Birch, in his transcript, omits it altogether.

[2] Bacon MSS., Lambeth, 650/50.

[3] Spedding, *Life and Letters of Francis Bacon*, i. p. 361.

[4] *Ibid.*, p. 355.   [5] *Ibid.*, pp. 356, 358.

gossip of the kind.   In the end, all his expectations
were defeated.   Fleming got the coveted place ; and
Essex, for all his boasting, was obliged to console
his friend with an estate.

Years afterwards, when Essex lay in his grave
and former things had passed away, Cecil told Bodley
how sharp and persistent had been Essex's pro-
vocations at this time of his life.   Small passions
provoke great events, and the world in general and
the University of Oxford in particular has no great
cause to regret that arrogant acerbity.   For Bodley's
Library was the outcome of the sharp contention.
Bodley himself, as is well known, had all the claim
upon the vacant Secretariate which diplomatic services
could confer; and it had, in fact, been Burghley's intention that he should share the post with Robert Cecil.
But in an ill-advised moment he allowed himself to
be drawn into an intimacy with Essex.   Every recommendation that Essex made to the Queen in Bodley's
favour was accompanied with words disparaging the
merits of Cecil.   Elizabeth, already tiring of her
favourite, was none the better pleased by these
exhibitions of jealousy.   And Burghley and Cecil, on
their part, came to regard Bodley in the light of one
who had preferred another's countenance to their
own.   But Bodley moved on a higher plane of being
than any with which they were familiar.   Finding
that his political career had become a new apple
of discord in an old dispute, he resolved to work for
his country in fields which excite no envy because
the fruits are gathered too late for ambition.   From
that resolution nothing could ever draw him.   In
vain Cecil pressed him at a later date to become his
colleague as Secretary, in vain he offered him a seat
at the Council-board, in vain he gave him the opportunity of fulfilling the most distinguished diplomatic
missions.   The good man was not to be moved.   He
had, as he tells us, " concluded to set up his staff at

the library-door in Oxon " ;[1] and there it remained.
When we compare it with those of his diplomatic
contemporaries, we find that it alone has budded.

Sharp as the contention between the protagonists
had been, Cecil was too diplomatic to allow it to
expand into an open breach. Within a few months
we find him writing to Essex with every appearance
of goodwill : " My good Lord, you shall not need so
much ceremony with me for opening of any letters,
public or private. If public they be matters wherein
your Lordship hath a great partage. If private I
dare trust you, seeing I am no lover, which humour
indeed affords nɔ company."[2]

We have still to wind up the miserable story of
Lopez. When the plot had been unfolded in all its
detail, Essex, Cecil, and Howard of Effingham saw
the wretched man for the last time and brought him
literally to his knees. Lifting his face to heaven he
prayed God to take vengeance on him if he had
purposed any such thing as he was accused of. His
interlocutors were inexorable. Then he admitted
that he had indeed spoken with Ferrera about the
Queen's death, though he declared he had never
intended to execute the deed. We cannot be absolutely sure it was not so. Where such a defence is
set up, it is hardly possible to say there is no shade
of doubt. But the doubt was not one of which Lopez
could look to have the benefit. As Bacon says in
his admirable review of the case,[3] there were three
reasons why such a plea could not stand. The first
was that Lopez had never opened the matter to the
Queen or her Councillors ; unaccountable conduct in
an age when, as Lopez at his time of life must have
known well enough, men were often brought quick

[1] The authority for this and the preceding statements is Bodley's
Autobiography.

[2] S. P. Dom., Eliz., 249/3.

[3] Printed among the minor works in Spedding's *Life and Letters
of Francis Bacon*, vol. i.

into judgment for their idle words. Then ' he came too late to this shift.' He set up two defences, which were not agreeable to each other. He began by blank denial ; he passed to confession and avoidance, and at last tried denial again. It was impossible to decide when he was telling the truth, and there was very little reason to suppose he told the truth at all. And lastly he would not have the blood-money sent over to England. It was to be paid in Antwerp. Had he been faithful to Elizabeth, had he merely intended to despoil Philip, had he purposed to continue his residence in England, it is difficult to explain this stipulation. On the unfavourable hypothesis it falls into line well enough.

On such grounds, then, we may conclude that the imposing Commission which tried him at the Guildhall found him guilty. We have no report of the trial ; we know that judicial methods then were different from ours ; and we know, too, that the age, living as it did under the shadow of a great fear, had a short way with suspected traitors. But though justice fell with a heavy hand, men like Essex, Cecil, Howard of Effingham, and Buckhurst were not fiends ; and we do our ancestors a wrong if, of set purpose, we seek to reverse their verdicts. The Queen showed by her conduct both before and after the trial that she felt a natural tenderness for her physician, and, if her servants could have found it in their consciences, we may assume they would have acquitted him. Cecil, who had been slow to believe the worst, had no doubt of it at the end. After sentence was passed, he returned to his father's house in the Strand and dashed off a few lines to Winwood, which, brief as they are, contain our only record of what must have been a memorable scene.

" . . . Never," he said, speaking first of Ferrera and Tinoco, " was prince's cause so trimly handled by such a couple of servants as gave the evidence."

Then of Lopez. " The villain confessed all the day that he had indeed spoken of this matter, and promised it, but all forsooth to cozen the King of Spain. But when he saw both his intent and overt fact were apparent, the vile Jew said that he did confess indeed to us that he had talk of it, but now he must tell true, he did belie himself and did it only to save himself from racking ; which the Lord knoweth our souls witness to be most untrue, and so was he told home. And the most substantial jury that I have seen have found him guilty in the highest degree of all treasons, and judgment (was) passed against him with applause of all the world." [1]

Lopez was taken back to the Tower. So long as he remained there, the sentence could not be executed without a royal warrant. Elizabeth, as before in Mary's case, as afterwards in Essex's, suffered all the pangs of hesitation. Lopez had of necessity been in the closest relations with her, and she could not bring herself to sign. Then Essex, seeing how things were, resorted to a legal subterfuge.[2] By Chief Justice Popham's connivance Lopez was removed from the Tower to the King's Bench Prison at Southwark. This brought him under the ordinary jurisdiction of the Courts, and the royal signature to a death-warrant was no longer required. He was taken before a judge, asked if he had any reason to give why sentence should not be carried out, and then ordered for immediate execution. There we may take leave of him ; not sorry, perhaps, to be free from any obligation to view the last appalling scene at Tyburn. During the three months' delay, whilst his life was hanging in the balance, there is every reason to think that the image of Shylock had begun to haunt the mind of Shakespeare.

[1] S. P. Dom., Eliz., 247/97.
[2] The story is told by Goodman (*Court of James I.*), i. pp. 154-5.

CHAPTER VI

LABOUR AND SORROW

" Thyself hast loved ; and I have heard thee say
No grief did ever come so near thy heart
As when thy lady and thy true love died,
Upon whose grave thou vow'dst pure chastity."
Two Gentlemen of Verona, Act IV. Sc. iii.

OF Cecil's private life between 1593 and 1596 information is as usual scanty. His children were
healthy, and his son William—that same ' simple
Lord Salisbury,' whom Pepys was to see seventy
years after, seated in the gallery of Hatfield Church [1]—
a remarkably fine boy.[2]   But Cecil did not escape the
trials of a nursery. The wet-nurse of little Frances,
not content to flirt with the steward's boy, sub-
sidised the diet of pottage and posset-ale, which her
master had prescribed for her, with copious draughts
of beer, and ' waxed blear - eyed ' in consequence.
It was thought necessary to report her doings, and
among Cecil's correspondence her iniquities still
present a little oasis where every tired student of
those tedious files will halt to read how when my
my lord's steward cut short her intimacy with
young Jennings, she ' howled like a stark Bedlam and
swooned withal, or rather counterfeited a swooning.' [3]
    Cecil himself must have been hard put to it to
find time to compose such domestic agitations. In
addition to his police-work he had become what we
should call Minister-in-attendance, and was con-

---

[1] Pepys' *Diary*, 16th October 1664.
[2] Hatf. Cal., iv. p. 526.   [3] *Ibid.*, p. 445.

stantly with the Queen. " Her Majesty," writes Wolley, even in May 1593, to Burghley, " looks for his counsel by himself or Sir Robert." [1] Whilst the father still directed the foreign policy of the country, it was to the son that the French Ambassador would apply to procure him audiences. And suitors of all kinds increased and multiplied. Those who had got into prison and wanted to get out ; those who were out of prison and afraid of getting in ; those who were suffering from the law's delays ; those who were suffering from the law's activities ; those who were in exile and sought permission to come home ; those who were at home and sought permission to go abroad ; those who were in feeble health and wanted a butcher licensed to provide meat for them during Lent ; [2] those who had inventions or informations to sell ; those who had sighted desirable places for themselves or their friends to fill ; a prisoner who fancied a little more fresh air in his cell ; [3] a pilot who had unwittingly evaded the Customs and been heavily fined in consequence ; [4] a bore with a burden of litigation [5]—Cecil had now to deal with all the motley and importunate crowd which throngs the steps of public men in every age and country. He met them very differently from his easy-going rival. " I am the bolder to fly to your Lordship in these occasions," writes a suitor to Essex, " for that my good patron Sir Robert is somewhat reserved, punctual and precise, so as not to seem partial in my cause that am so bounden and beholding unto him." [6] For Cecil, if he failed in large-hearted expansive generosity, was rich in that steady discriminating affection, which seldom fails to meet with a reward. " I cannot be found disloyal to him," says the same writer—a spy—" or any of that family, without

[1] S. P. Dom., Eliz., 245/11.   [2] Hatf. Cal., v. p. 151.

[3] *Ibid.*, p. 236.   [4] *Ibid.*, p. 231.

[5] *Ibid.*, vi. pp. 208, 291, 404.   [6] S. P. Dom., Eliz., 248/52.

perpetual note of infamy and ingratitude, and in
truth (before God I speak it !) I made choice rather
to make hazard of my life and liberty in the last
voyage I made, than that he in dealing with me
should lose the least point of his honour, conceipt
abroad of his wisdom, or his estimation." [1]

It was at a request from Cecil, prompted by
Archbishop Hutton, that the Queen spared the life
of, and provided a maintenance for Lady Margaret
Neville, who had fallen into the company and convictions of recusant Papists. Some of the letters
most comforting to the eye of the biographer in that
year of 1595, are Lady Margaret's grateful thanks
and Hutton's praise of the Minister's ' godly actions '
and ' charitable pains.' [2] But Cecil did not always
present this admirable appearance to his ghostly
fathers. The misappropriation of ecclesiastical revenues was carried on by the Queen with the same
diligence of which the Reformers had once accused
in the Pope ; and Fletcher takes the opportunity of
his translation from Worcester to London [3] to write
Cecil a strong denunciation of that atrocious system
of plunder. But the Minister was himself nearly concerned in the traffic. Elizabeth, moved by the goodwill she had borne to Lady Cobham, was set upon
procuring a lease for George Brooke, Cecil's younger
brother-in-law, out of the properties of the see
of York.[4] The Archbishop was persecuted with
pertinacity, and the consequent worry assisted his
decline. When Hutton succeeded him, the suit was
renewed. " Episcopi in Anglia semper pavidi," says
the well-tried adage. Hutton promised to be an
honourable exception to the rule. " Surely if I
should yield . . . " he wrote to Cecil and Wolley,
" I think verily it would be a mean to bring my
hoary hairs with grief unto my grave. I did never

---

[1] S. P. Dom., Eliz., 248/52.   [2] Hatf. Cal., v. pp. 176, 220, 226.
[3] *Ibid.*, p. 31.   [4] *Ibid.*, p. 35.

hurt any ecclesiastical living in my life ; I think it not lawful ; and I am persuaded in conscience that I ought not to leave any living in worse case to my successor than my predecessor did leave it unto me." [1] But it is not quite clear that this position was maintained. Brooke appears to have got some sort of lease, though Hutton also appears to have retained some sort of conscience.[2] Anyhow, the Archbishop was not delivered from further importunity ; and we find him later on resisting Mr. Brooke's solicitations for an archdeaconry.[3]

Cecil's letter-bag, as has indeed been already shown, was not without its humours. The Governor of Wisbeach Castle lets a couple of captive priests escape, and writes to Cecil in great distress to excuse himself. He was away when the fugitives absconded ; the deed was done at dead of night, ' when quiet rest is due to every man ' ; above all, he stands this Lent upon the conclusion of a marriage with a Warwickshire lady of very sufficient means—one Mrs. Boughton —who may take an aversion to him if Cecil should deal hardly with him on account of the evasion.[4]

The Bishop of St. David's has composed an indiscreet prayer for the Queen to offer up, in which she is made to say that " she has now entered a good way into the climacterical year of her age." This unblushing revelation of the fact that she is over sixty-three has been more than Elizabeth could stomach. The prelate has been put in confinement, and writes to Cecil to obtain his release.[5]

Thomas Arundell has been fool enough to offend the Queen by accepting a title from the Emperor. His father writes to assure Cecil of his dislike to the whole affair, but chiefly of the fact that his descendants for all time must be counts and countesses—

[1] Hatf. Cal., v. p. 50.
[2] *Ibid.*, viii. p. 414.
[3] Hatf. Cal., vi. p. 139.
[4] *Ibid.*, p. 174.
[5] S. P. Dom., Eliz., 262/42.

' a matter . . . peevish, hard and absurd to my understanding.' [1]

Lord North has received an anonymous copy ' of the most heavenly prayer ' he has ever read. He begs Cecil, as a Privy-Councillor, to take steps ' to bolt ' the author of it, so that he may know ' where the Saint is shrined and go and join him.' [2]

We may as well wind up, here and now, these eccentricities of correspondence. Anne, Lady Herbert, at a much later date, favours him with ' the first-fruits ' of her son Edward's Latin.[3] And Sir A. Gorges sends him in 1609 an account of what he justly describes as the ' rare and very pitiful case ' of Sir John and Lady Kennedy. " I have thought good," writes the worthy knight, " to let your Lordship understand that this morning about the break of day there came to my gates the Lady Kennedy in very strange and wretched manner, bare-legged, in her petticoat and an old cloak and her night-gear ; in great fright and almost starved for cold. She desired house-room and fire of my wife, her cousin, being, as she said, driven out of her house by Sir John Kennedy that in great violence break in upon her. . . . I know these things in particular do no whit concern your Lordship . . . but as to a great magistrate of the State . . . give the knowledge because the case is rare and very pitiful." [4]

Sometimes historic faces—other than the familiar ones—peer through the papers. Lyly, the Euphuist, who lives now by nothing more substantial than the title of his book, writes to implore Cecil to take pity on his abject destitution. He would call in person, but is troubled with the Court-cough — ' that is, to gape so long for a suit and cough without it.' He has waited twelve years for the fulfilment of the Queen's promises. He hopes he shall not be used

[1] Hatf. Cal., vii. p. 36. [2] *Ibid.*, vi. p. 211.
[3] S. P. Dom., Jas. I., 68/36. [4] S. P. Dom., Jas. I., 48/7.

worse than an old horse, which, after service done, has his shoes pulled off and is turned to grass, not suffered to starve in the stable.   Then he adds with a bitterness which many a starveling playwright has had occasion to echo : " I will cast my wits in a new mould . . . for I find it folly that, one foot being in the grave, I should have the other on the stage." [1]

Beside this piteous vision of Fame in rags is one of Liberty in chains.   Peter Wentworth, accounted one of the first martyrs for freedom of speech, was buying posthumous glory in his cell in the Tower. " I have been here four years and twenty-four weeks," writes the unhappy man, who had done no more than desire to have the Protestant Succession assured ; " this three months I am troubled with sickness, only for want of air, exercise and liberty.   Here I cannot expect any health.   It would pity your heart to see my oftener than weekly sickness, who am above seventy-three years of age." [2]   Cecil was ready to relegate the old man on surety to the houses of some friends ; [3] but we have every reason to think that death was too quick for him, and that only the broken spirit, not the enfeebled body, escaped the confines of the Tower.

For to touch politics in any form or shape was in those days to walk with the lightnings playing about one's feet.   One can hardly follow the course of sixteenth-century biography without growing to expect that sooner or later the blow will fall, the life be blasted and end in wretchedness and disgrace, if not actually on the scaffold.   Obscurity is no safeguard ; politics are the accursed thing.   Among Cecil's letters is one from Thomas Phelippes, whose name, little known to the casual reader, is familiar to every student of the period.   Half the dark secrets of the time lay buried within the com-

[1] S. P. Dom., Eliz., 265/61 (22nd December 1597).
[2] Hatf. Cal., vii. p. 325.   [3] *Ibid.*, pp. 286, 303.

pass of that strange man's knowledge. He worked
for Walsingham, for Burghley, for Cecil ; an invaluable auxiliary, deciphering, perhaps counterfeiting,
the crabbed allusive script in which men stowed
their plots. But the secret of his own life has never
been read, and we feel him only as an obscure, yet
powerful presence, not as we feel the touch of human
flesh and blood. A letter [1] to Cecil remains to tell
us that the griefs and disappointments of age shook
his passionless frame at last ; that he fell into
some disfavour with the Queen, perhaps only because his failing powers gave slower results ; more
probably because, for good reason or bad, he was
no longer trusted as before.

If Phelippes was the brain of the great system
of espionage over which Cecil presided, Richard
Topcliffe, the gaoler of the Gate-House Prison,
was its hand. Our record of national biography
invites us to think of him as a remorseless mastiff,
delighting himself in the tracking and tearing of
human flesh, particularly the flesh of seminary
priests. It may have been so. But Topcliffe himself, it is fair to notice, foresaw and repudiated the
picture. . . . " You cannot believe," he writes to
Cecil in regard to the Catholics it was his duty to
examine, " that disloyalty we simple commissioners
do see by their fury expressed, being put to trial.
And that is our grief, and mine especially, that we
are often taken to be cruel. But God is the witness
of all." [2] The truth is no doubt that there were
two sort of Catholics, some of them simple-hearted
Christians, others of them ravenous wolves in sheep's
clothing.[3] Unfortunately for Topcliffe, in a celebrated case, he mistook one kind for the other. Father
Southwell was one of the choicest spirits of the

---

[1] Hatf. Cal., vii. p. 96.   [2] *Ibid.*, v. p. 91.
[3] Contrast, *e.g.*, S. P. Dom., Eliz., 262/28 with Hatf. Cal., vii.
p. 364.

age, harmless as a dove, inspired with an exquisite
gift of song, utterly loyal to what he thought the
truth.   This man Topcliffe, to his great contentment,[1]
took.   What occurred during the three years that
followed we do not know for certain.   Southwell's
plaintive poems, all of them probably composed in
prison,[2] are proof at least that it was distressing.
Topcliffe, on his own showing, was ready to stand
the heroic priest against the wall with his hands
fastened above his head until he supplied the information which the Queen required.[3]   But this
discovered no extraordinary brutality at a time
when among the Acts of the Privy Council we find
an instruction that in case of need certain persons
are to be ' pinched with the torture as in such cases
is accustomed.'[4]   The records of the Society of
Jesus, however, enlarge the story and report some
words of Burghley, which—and this is the point
that touches us—have been wrongly ascribed[5] to
Robert Cecil.   The passage runs thus : " Southwell
had long before imposed upon himself a strict rule
of silence if he should be put to the question.
This he observed with such constancy that the
commissioners declared that he seemed to be rather
a stock than a human being, and Cecil, the chief
among the Queen's Councillors at that time, when
the talk had fallen on the examinations of Southwell,
is said to have burst out with the following speech :
' Antiquity may boast its Roman heroes, and the
patience of prisoners when tortured ; our age is in
no way inferior, nor does English courage yield to
Roman.   We have now in our hands a certain Southwell, who though put to the question thirteen times,
cannot be induced to confess anything, not even the

---

[1] " I never did take so weighty a man " (Strype, *Ann.*, iv. No. 89).
[2] Grosart's edition, p. lxxxviii.   [3] Strype, *Ann.*, iv. No. 89.
[4] Acts of the P. C., 8th February 1592.
[5] Porroz, *Vie du Père Robert Southwell*, p. 140.

colour of the horse he rode on a particular day, for
fear his enemies should conjecture from that indication where he had lodged, or with what Catholics
he had been consorting on this occasion.' "[1]   The
Cecil who spoke was certainly Burghley, for Southwell
suffered the extreme and frightful penalties of the
law three years before the Lord Treasurer died.   But
we may hope that Robert Cecil shared the ineffective sentiment, if it was ever uttered, and cursed an
age when Justice was driven to strike so blindly and
Mercy seldom dared to show her face.

One other fragment of his correspondence holds
the eye for an instant — ' Pembroke's Mother,'
writing to thank the powerful Minister for ' his
great kindness to her son,' just about to enter upon
life at Court, and for his ' favourable remembrance
of herself.' [2]   But it is only a fragment, hardly
worth the mention, if any word of thanks from Mary
Sidney had not unfading charm.

This chase of scented paper has brought us by
shady and sequestered bypaths to the close of
the year 1597. We have now to retrace our steps
and travel to the same point by the Queen's
highway.

In the summer of 1594 Elizabeth had come again
to Theobalds, and the old joke about the Hermit
had been resumed. Cecil, doubtless arrayed in a
suitable disguise, had presented himself before the
Queen in the character of the vanished sprite and
delivered the following curious address, which he
himself is said to have penned [3] :—

" MOST GRACIOUS SOVEREIGN,—I humbly beseech you not to
impute this my approaching so near to your sacred presence so
rudely at your coming to this house to be a presumption of a
beggar ; for I hope when your Majesty shall be remembered by

---

[1] Morris, *Hist. Prov. Anglic. Soc. Jesu*, lib. v. p. 193.
[2] Hatf. Cal., vii. p. 375.   [3] Rawl. MSS., D. 692, f. 106.

me who I am and how graciously you have heretofore on the like occasion relieved my necessity, your Majesty will be pleased to receive my thanks upon my knees with all humility.

"I am the poor Hermit, your Majesty's Beadman, who at your last coming hither (where God grant you may come many years) upon my complaint, by your princely favour, was restored to my hermitage by an injunction when my Founder, upon a strange conceit to feed his own humour, had placed me contrary to my profession in his house amongst a number of worldlings, and retired himself in my poor cell, where I have ever since by your only goodness (Most Peerless and Powerful Queen!) lived in all happiness, spending three parts of the day in repentance, the fourth in praying for your Majesty, that as your virtues have been the world's wonder, so your days may see the world's end.

"And surely I am of opinion I shall not flatter myself, if I think my prayers have not been fruitless (though millions have joined in the like); in that, since my restitution, not only all your actions have miraculously prospered, and all your enemies been defeated, but that which most amazeth me, to whose long experience nothing can seem strange, with these same eyes do I behold you the self-same Queen, in the same estate of person, strength and beauty, in which so many years past I beheld you, finding no alteration but in admiration, in so much as I am persuaded, when I look about me on your train, that Time, which catcheth everybody, leaves only you untouched.

"And now, most gracious Lady, as I have most humbly thanked you for that which is past, so being constrained to trouble your Majesty with another petition, not much differing from the former, I have presumed to prepare for you an offering, only as a token of my devotion, though meter for an Hermit to present, as a badge of his solitary life, than for so great a Monarch to receive ; but my poverty cannot amend it.

"I am (as your Majesty seeth) an old aged man, apt to be full of doubts, and experience hath taught me that many men's promises are no charters ; yet is not my Founder to be mistrusted, whose word is a scale to others, and I hear it commonly reported he had no disposition to put out tenants, so am I most sure he will never remove me whom your Majesty hath placed.   Only this perplexeth my soul and causeth cold blood in every vein, to see the life of my Founder so often in peril ; nay, his desire as hasty as his age to inherit his tomb, being nature's tenant. But this I hear (which is his greatest comfort and none of your least virtues) that when his body being laden with years, oppressed with sickness, having spent his strength for public service, desireth to be rid of worldly cares, by ending his days ; your

Majesty with a band of princely kindness, even when he is most grievously sick and lowest brought holds him back and ransometh him.   In this my anxiety have I addressed myself to your sacred person, whom I beseech to consider (it is not rare) that sons are not ever of their father's conditions ; and it may be, that when my young Master shall possess this, which now under my Founder I enjoy (whereof I hope there shall be no haste) he may be catched with such liking of my dwelling, as he will rather use it for a place of recreation than of meditation ; and then of a Beadman shall I become a Pilgrim.   And therefore, seeing I hear it of all the country folk I meet with, that your Majesty doth use him in your service as in former time you have done his Father, my Founder, and that although his expense and judgment be no way comparable, yet, as the report goeth, he hath something in him like the child of such a parent, I beseech your Majesty to take order, that his grey hairs may be assurances for my abode, that, howsoever I live obscure, I may be quiet and secure not to be driven to seek my grave, which though it may be everywhere, yet I desire it to be here.   This may be done, if you will enjoin him for your pleasure, whose will is to him a law, not to deny me the favour formerly procured of his Father at the motion of that goddess of whom he holds himself a second creature.

"And now a little further to acquaint your Majesty with my hap (though I must arm myself with patience); my Founder, to leave all force for you and your train, hath committed to my nest all his unfledged birds, being the comfort of his age, and his precious jewels, being to some of them grandfather, to others more, all derived from his good opinion of me.   But such a wanton charge for a poor old man, as now they hear of the arrival of such an admirable work of Nature, a man must pluck their quills, or else they will daily fly out to see your Majesty ; such is the working of the grandfather's affection in them, and your virtue and beauty.

"To this charge I will hie me, seeing it is my destiny.   And for all your Majesty's favour I can but continue my vowed prayers for you, and, in token of my poor affection, present you on my knees these poor trifles agreeable to my profession, by use whereof and by constant faith I live free from all temptation.   The first is a bell, not big, but of gold ; the second is a book of good prayers, garnished with the same metal ; the third is a candle of virgin's wax, meet for a virgin queen.   With this book, bell, and candle, being hallowed in my cell with good prayers, I assure myself, by whomsoever they shall be kept, endued with a constant faith, there shall never come so much as an imagination of my spirit to offend them ; the like whereof I will still retain in my cell, for my daily use, in ringing the bell, in singing of my prayers, and giving me light in the night for the increase of my devotion, whereby I may be free to my meditation and prayers for your Majesty's continuance in your prosperity, in health and princely comfort." [1]

The Queen left Theobalds on 21st June. Three weeks later she visited Robert Cecil at his house in the Strand ; an honour which his proud father duly records in the chronicle of family history.[2]

Biography has its laws as well as more exact sciences. The reader will not complain if, at the close of a chapter which has been so largely devoted to scattered personal incident, the chronological succession of events be broken, and the domestic allowed to outrun the public narrative.

Lady Cecil has never been more than a dim figure in the background of this story. Of her life we have in fact only the faint glimpses which have been set down as they presented themselves. But her death makes it evident what manner of affection she had inspired in those who knew her. It was in giving birth to her second daughter, Catharine, that she passed away at the close of 1596. She had lived, as we shall learn, to see her husband appointed Secretary of State ; and in the latter months of her life, husband and wife had been planning to inhabit a house in Chelsea which the widowed Lady Dacre had left to Lord Burghley, and Lord Burghley had resigned to his son.[3] The blow fell, as such blows can fall, with an appalling suddenness, scattering all the hopes and dreams of early life and carrying the man on swiftly from youth to age. In the examination which Mayerne made of him in his last illness, the doctor notices that he turned grey in his thirtieth year.[4] The figure is probably approximate. We

---

[1] Rawl. MSS., D. 692, f. 106.   [2] Hatf. Cal., v. p. 71.
[3] R. Davies, *The Greatest House in Chelsey*, pp. 43, 44.
[4] Ellis, *Orig. Lett.*, ser. ii. vol. iii. p. 246: "Canities cœpit anno xxx°."

can hardly be wrong in attributing to this consummate grief the first waning of his physical strength.   He was, we know, completely overwhelmed,[1] so completely as to alarm his friends.   Ralegh sent him a letter which for beauty and high emotion deserves to be placed among the noblest memorials of the age.

" Sir," wrote that intrepid student of mortal things, " because I know not how you dispose of yourself I forbear to visit you, preferring your pleasing before mine own desire.   I had rather be with you now than at any other time if I could thereby either take off from you the burden of your sorrows or lay the greatest part thereof on mine own heart.   In the meantime I would but mind you of this, that you should not overshadow your wisdom with passion, but look aright into things as they are.   There is no man sorry for death itself, but only for the time of death, everyone knowing that it is a bond never forfeited to God.   If then we know the same to be certain and inevitable, we ought withal to take the time of his arrival in as good part as the knowledge, and not to lament at the instant of every seeming adversity which we are assured have been on their way toward us from the beginning.   It appertaineth to every man of a wise and worthy spirit to draw together unto sufferance the unknown future to the known present looking no less with the eyes of the mind than those of the body, the one beholding afar off and the other at hand, that those things of this world in which we live be not strange unto us when they approach as to feebleness which is moved with novelties, but that, like true men participating immortality and knowing our destinies to be of God, we do then make our estates and wishes, our fortunes and desires all one.

" It is true that you have lost a good and virtuous wife and myself an honourable friend and kinswoman ; but there was a time when she was unknown to you ; for whom you then lamented not.   She is now no more yours nor of your acquaintance, but immortal and not needing or knowing your love or sorrow.   Therefore you shall not grieve for that which now is as then it was when not yours, only bettered by the difference in this that she hath passed the wearisome journey of this dark

---

[1] " Mr. Secretary went upon Saturday to Blackfriars to see my Lord Cobham, which was the first day they met since my Lady Cecil's death.   It was long ere that they speak [sic] one to another ; there appeared the fulness of grief and passion in them " (Sidney Papers, ii. p. 18).

world and hath possession of her inheritance. She hath left behind her the font of her love, for whose sakes you ought to care for yourself that you leave them not without a guide and not by grieving to repine at His will that gave them you, or by sorrowing to dry up your own times that ought to establish them.

" Sir, believe it, that sorrows are dangerous companions, converting bad into evil and evil into worse, and do no other service than multiply harms. They are the treasures of weak hearts and of the foolish. The mind that entertaineth them is as the earth and dust whereon sorrows and adversities of the world do us, the beasts of the field, trend, trample and defile. The mind of man is that part of God which is in us, which by how much it is subject to passion by so much it is farther from Him that gave it us. Sorrows draw not the dead to life but the living to death, and if I were myself to advise myself in the like, I would never forget my patience till I saw all and the worst of evils and so grieve for all at once, lest, lamenting for some one, another might yet remain in the power of destiny of greater discomfort.

" Yours ever beyond the power of words to utter.
" W. RALEGH."

Ralegh wrote in the fulness of his generous heart ; Lady Russell,[1] Cecil's grim Puritan aunt, and Lord Burgh,[2] with the more limited range of wisdom and feeling that pertained to them, yet to the same effect. They besought him not to give way to his grief, but to bury it beneath the cares of his high office. In due time he learnt to do so ; but the monument which he set up to his wife in the St. Nicholas Chapel at Westminster still repeats in the hearing of each successive generation his intense and passionate regret. He had applied to George Goodwin to draw up a suitable inscription ; and from the thirty-six epitaphs which that industrious scholar had forthwith composed he selected some lines expressive of the new relation which had arisen between himself and his wife—between her, gone indeed to her rest, yet tied to earth by love and troth and fondest memories, and himself with a

[1] Hatf. Cal., vii. p. 281.   [2] *Ibid.*, p. 56.

weary vale of years still to travel, even though a
vale lit by an ever-brightening star :—

UXOR

" Reginæ a cameris, Baronis Filia cari
    Fida Equitis conjux Elizabetha fui.
Unus amor nobis, una indivulsa voluntas,
    Cor unum, una Fides inviolata fuit.
Ille mei si quando potest deponere curam
    Ille potest animæ non memor esse suæ."

MARITUS

" Si lacrimis constaret amor (carissima conjux)
    Prosequerer lacrimis funera sæpe tua
Nam mihi quam fueris redamata, tuum (Pia sponsa)
    Testabor meritum, conscius ipse mihi.
Sed nec amor patitur (socia regnante) dolere
    Et Christi major te sibi strinxit amor.
Ergo tuo (dilecta) bono cum pace fruare (*sic*)
    Spero, mihi tecum portio pacis erit."

" A Brooke by name, the Baron Cobham's child,
A Newton was she by her Mother's side.
Cecil her husband this for her did build
To prove his love did after death abide,
Which tells unto the Worlds that after come
The World's concept whilst here she held a room;
How Nature made her wise, and well-beseeming
Wit and condition, silent, true and chaste.
Her virtues rare won her much esteeming
In Court with Sovereign still with favour graced.
Earth could not yield more pleasing earthly bliss,
Blest with two babes, the third brought her to this."

Cecil never married again. The Queen, indeed,
believed that he had taken a vow of perpetual
celibacy, but he himself affirmed that his promise
did not extend beyond three years.[1] Towards the
end of 1599 he was alleged to be engaged to one of
Lord Shrewsbury's daughters,[2] but nothing came of
the rumour, which was very possibly without founda-

[1] Collins, Sidney Papers, ii. p. 40, 13th November 1599.
[2] S. P. Dom., Eliz., 273/12.

tion. The world, however, did not rest content ;
and his name was presently coupled with those of a
Mrs. Bridges,[1] of Barbara Ruthven,[2] and again, very
absurdly, of Arabella Stuart.[3] Whatever value we
set upon these rumours we should do him wrong if
we thought they caused him to forget his first and
great affection. As late as 1603 we know that it
still seemed to him ' the dearest bond that ever I
was tied in.'[4]

[1] S. P. Dom., Eliz., 279/77.   [2] Hatf. MSS., 187/8.
[3] S. P. Dom., Eliz., 287/50.   [4] Hatf. Cal., xii. p. 631.

CHAPTER VII

ESSEX

" *York*. Be that thou hopest to be, or what thou art
Resign to death ; it is not worth the enjoying.
Let pale-faced fear keep with the mean-born man
And find no harbour in a royal heart.
Faster than springtime showers comes thought on thought,
And not a thought but thinks on dignity."
Henry VI., Part ii. Act iii. Sc. i.

THE period of years through which we have now
to thread our way revolves around the person of
Essex. The spirited, attractive boy, whose grace
of speech and bearing had early captured Elizabeth's
attention, had by this time grown to be a political
force of the first magnitude. And with the consciousness of merit and success his character had
passed into that later deplorable phase, which
could brook no opposition, and avenged defeat and
disappointment by peevishness and violence. He
gradually lost sight of the distinction between what
he might do in a private and what he might do in a
public capacity ; and Elizabeth was to blame for it,
since, in his case, she allowed herself to treat grave
disobedience to her will, grave resistance to her
authority, as if it could be forgotten and forgiven
like a lover's quarrel.

Francis Bacon's keen eye saw only too clearly
the road his friend and patron was going. " How
is it now ? " he wrote, boldly enough, to Essex in 1596,
" A man of a nature not to be ruled : that hath
the advantage of my affection and knoweth it ; of

an estate not grounded to his greatness ; of a popular
reputation ; of a military dependence ! I demand
whether there can be a more dangerous image than
this represented to any monarch living, much more to
a lady and of Her Majesty's apprehension."[1]

Essex, he saw, was already walking amongst
precipices. Do the one thing needful, he exhorts ;
' win the Queen '—win her by showing that your
past conduct came of dissatisfaction, not of disposition ; by taking Leicester and Hatton for your
models, than which there is no readier mean to make
Elizabeth think you are in the right way ; by giving
at least the appearance of sincerity to your adulation ;
by submitting to petty defeats with a good grace ;
by seeking a civil not a military influence, so as to be
released from the suspicion of martial greatness ;
by making no show of liking popularity ; by a
careful economy in your domestic concerns which
may relieve the Queen from any necessity to enrich
you.

It was wise, if in some points worldly advice ;
but Essex was too far gone in ambition to take it.
With a reckless disregard of every interest but his
own, a reckless determination to achieve fame at
any cost, he threw the dice again and again, staking
more highly each time, until at last he found himself a dishonoured bankrupt, paying forfeit with his
life. In 1595 he launches his unworthy intrigue
against the peace-policy of the Cecils. In 1596 he
scores at Cadiz the signal triumph of his career. In
1597 he tries to double his fame, but suffers a disastrous
failure, which he expiates by some months of morti-
fication. Then come the three last bids for fortune,
each wilder and more impulsive than the last :
in 1599 the Irish folly ; then the unauthorised
desertion of his command ; finally, in 1601, the de-

[1] Spedding, *Life and Letters of Francis Bacon*, ii. c. 2, 4th October
1596.

liberate attempt to raise the metropolis against the Government. And at last, blasted in all his high hopes and noble impulses, he meets with a traitor's death upon the scaffold. There is a great psychological tragedy lurking behind the political drama—a tragedy as poignant and forcible as any History offers. But it is not this that we are called to look at. Rather we have to watch the episode develop through the eyes of a prudent and sagacious statesmanship.

A keen critic has said that the British Empire was acquired in a fit of absence of mind. It was not so that Essex wished to see it won. He desired a deliberate policy of aggression, with all the opportunities of service and distinction which such a policy would give. He desired to smite the Spaniards hip and thigh, to strike at them not only by sea but at home, to outdo Drake and Leicester, to make of Cadiz a Spanish Calais, to draw the new power of France—new because it was now in the hands of Henri Quatre and the *Politiques*—into a vigorous offensive alliance against the ultra-Catholic forces directed by Philip of Spain. It was a brilliant policy, and one well calculated to appeal to the young England of the Armada. But it was also costlier, more risky, more prodigal in human life than that of never bringing matters to an issue, of stopping just short of decisive measures, by means of which, for thirty years, Burghley had played upon Philip's natural indecision and kept the power of Spain at bay. And it is characteristic of Elizabeth that all her love of and pride in Essex never led her to countenance unreservedly the measures which he proposed. Yet he spared no pains to recommend them. He sent Antonio Perez, that master of intrigue, who had once been Philip's and was now his own jackal, to write alarmist despatches from France, and stir the Queen, if possible, into more vigorous

action. And later he tampered with Sir Henry
Unton's instructions with the same intention. Perez
and the English Ambassador were to suggest that,
without more generous assistance from England,
Henry would conclude a peace with Spain behind
Elizabeth's back.[1]

Essex may have coloured the course of events ; he
could hardly discolour the character of the man who
was making them. The King of France, with the adop-
tion of a new set of religious convictions, had pretty
nearly abandoned every shred of private honour.
He who had bought civil peace with a lie in the soul
would hardly hesitate to buy foreign peace with a
lie on the tongue. And peace was imperative, for
the land was worn bare with fighting. The desired
end might be attained either by treating with Spain
for a cessation of hostilities, or with England and
Holland for an effective continuance of them. Henry
tried both methods simultaneously. He solicited
the hand of the Infanta, and negotiated with Elizabeth and the United Provinces for an offensive
alliance against Philip. When the former project
fell through he fell back upon the latter. So it came
about that, having failed in one year to secure the
King of Spain for a father-in-law, he made in the next
a formal declaration of war, in which he denounced
him as the most infamous of assassins. Treachery
was, of course, the commonplace, even the essence
of the diplomacy of the Renaissance, but it had the
effect of making co-operation extremely difficult.
Elizabeth, Henry, and the Dutch burghers were,
besides, no longer a well-assorted trio. The bond of
religious sympathy between King and Queen, whatever it had been worth, was snapped for ever ; the
bond of interest was bound to disappear so soon
as France could get an advantage by dissociating
herself from her allies. And no personal regard

[1] Hume (M.), *Treason and Plot*, pp. 169, 191.

could have survived the incredible meanness of
Elizabeth about Calais. Then, between Holland
and England there lay the greatest of all solvents—
a debt. The Queen was for ever requiring her loans
to be repaid, and the Dutch for ever evading the
demand. The alliance subsisted chiefly on bygone
habit and immediate necessity.

The year 1595, notable as it was for Mondragon's
last campaign, does not concern us here, but the
events of its successor strained the combination
to the splitting. De Rosnes, a Frenchman who had
passed from the service of the League into the service
of Philip of Spain, effected the capture of Rysbank,
the fort which commanded Calais harbour. The
city fell without serious resistance, and the governor
retired into the citadel, expecting assistance. It
was this moment that Elizabeth chose to drive a
bargain. She would help Henry, but she would
help him at a price, and that price was the transfer
of the city to herself. Her fleet hung idle at Dover
whilst Sidney crossed to Boulogne to propose the
Jew's contract. In the meanwhile the Spaniards,
bearing for once some resemblance to Dame Justice
in the fable, took the substance of the oyster and
left the shell to the disputants. Elizabeth herself
must bear the full blame for what had occurred. The
differences of her councillors had been composed in
face of clear obligation. Essex had written to Cecil to
tell him how Howard was champing and chafing at
the enforced inaction,[1] whilst Burghley in less passionate language told his son how grave an error the
Queen had committed.[2]

The mischief, however, was done, and could not
immediately be undone. But it was still possible
to singe the King of Spain's beard, and Howard and
Essex sailed off to Cadiz. Before they left, Cecil
transmitted to Essex, with some fulsome words of

[1] S. P. Dom., Eliz., 257/30.   [2] Hatf. Cal., vi. p. 141.

commendation,[1] the lofty prayer which Elizabeth had composed for the success of the expedition. The Queen was not disappointed of her desire. In the course of the summer, the expedition returned, covered with glory and having looted the famous seaport without any undue barbarities. Cecil in the meanwhile had secured less evanescent if less scintillating honour. On Monday, the 5th of July 1596, as the Acts of the Privy Council record, " Sir Robert Cecil, Knight, second son to the Lord Treasurer, was sworn Principal Secretary to Her Majesty." He had got it at last—the place which public expectation had long ago given him—and he was to make it in the years which were coming the hub and pivot of public business. Even nine months later Rowland Whyte does not scruple to call him " the greatest counsellor of England in all matters of despatches." [2] But beyond a merry reference to his new dignity in a letter to Michael Hicks,[3] he shows no sign of elation ; his appointment was, after all, only a recognition of facts. If Essex was jealous his anger passed away like the morning cloud. Iu the twelve months that followed the Cadiz expedition their relations, through the good offices of Ralegh, became those of a cordial regard which might in better conditions have ripened into something more. Their correspondence abounds in expressions of goop feeling. They are Ἔρος and Ἀντέρος to one another.[4] Whyte in his letters to Sidney notices the ' exceeding great kindness ' that exists between them.[5] In the bitter disappointment which attended the first attempt to start on the Islands Voyage, it is Cecil to whom Essex communicates his griefs.[6] And Cecil on his part seeks to cheer the anxieties of his friend by

[1] The letter and prayer are printed in Birch's *Memoirs of Queen Elizabeth*, ii. 18.
[2] Collins, Sidney Papers, ii. p. 25.   [3] Lansdowne MSS., 107/48.
[4] S. P. Dom., Eliz., 264/13.   [5] Collins, Sidney Papers, ii. p. 32.
[6] S. P. Dom., Eliz., 264/34 and 61.

retailing the gossip of the Court [1]—the very human nothings which are the soundest narcotic for the careworn mind. " The Queen," he is able to declare, " is so disposed now to have us all love you that she and I do every night talk like angels of you." [2]

It is in this connection that the gorgeous figure of Paul Dialyn crosses our horizon. Armed with a commission from the King of Poland, that absurd and pompous personage appeared from the East in the summer of 1597 to restore the peace of Christendom and preach a new crusade against the Turk. More especially he was to seek the restoration of the privileges of the Hanse Towns.[3] At The Hague he was received with all courtesy, though his proposals for a peace with Spain met with a firm refusal. In England he met with less agreeable treatment. Elizabeth never suffered a fool gladly. Cecil gives Essex the following delighted account of what occurred.

" My good Lord,—By a letter of yours, written on Saturday, what hour I know not, your Lordship seemeth to conceive what might be the reason that things run on by us with so great silence; wherein, that you may see the poor unfortunate Secretary will leave no scruple in you of lack of industry to yield you all satisfactions, whom it were inhumanity to neglect, the circumstances considered of your cares and affairs which have much of their dependency upon the breath of this place. . . . There arriv'd here three days since in the city an Ambassador out of Poland, a gentleman of excellent fashion, wit, discourse, language and person. The Queen was possessed by some of our new counsellors that are as cunning in intelligence as in deciphering, that his negotiation tendeth to a proposition of peace. Her Majesty, in respect his father, the Duke of Finland, had so much honoured her, besides the liking she had of this gentleman's comeliness and qualities brought to her by report, did resolve to receive him publicly in the Chamber of Presence where most of the earls and noblemen about the Court attended and made it a great day. He was brought in attired in a long

---

[1] S. P. Dom., Eliz., 264/54.   [2] *Ibid.*, 264/57.
[3] Hatf. Cal., vii. p. 320.

robe of black velvet, well jewelled and buttoned, and came to
kiss Her Majesty's hand, where she stood under the state ;
from whence he straight retired ten yards off and then began
his oration aloud in Latin with such a countenance as in my
life I never beheld.   The effect of it was this :—That the King
hath sent him to put Her Majesty in mind of the ancient con-
federacies between the Kings of Poland and England ; that never
a monarch in Europe did willingly neglect their friendship, that
he had ever friendly received her merchants and subjects of all
qualities ; that she had suffered his to be spoiled without restitution, not for lack of knowledge of the violences but of mere
injustice, not caring to minister remedy notwithstanding many
particular petitions and letters received, but to confirm her disposition to avow these courses, violating both the law of Nature
and Nations; (and that) because there was quarrels between her
and the King of Spain, she therefore took upon her by mandate
to prohibit him and his countries, assuming thereby to herself
a superiority not tolerable over other Princes.   He . . . wished
her to know that if there were no more than the ancient amity
between Spain and him it were no reason to look that his subjects
should be impeded, much less now when straight obligations of
blood had so conjoined him with the illustrious House of Austria,
concluding that if Her Majesty would not reform it he would.
To this, I swear by the Living God, that Her Majesty made one
of the best answers extempore in Latin that ever I heard, being
much moved to be so challenged in public, especially so much
against her expectation.   The words of her beginning were
these :—' Exspectavi legationem, mihi vere querelam adduxisti.
Is this the business your King hath sent you about ?   Surely I
can hardly believe that if the King himself were present he
would have used such a language for, if he should, I must have
thought that being a King not of many years and that *non
de jure sanguinis sed jure electionis, immo noviter electus*, may
haply be uninformed of that course which his father and ancestors have taken with us and which peradventure shall be
observed by those that shall live to come after us.   And as for
you,' saith she to the Ambassador, ' although I perceive you
have read many books to fortify your arguments in this case,
yet am I apt to believe that you have not lighted upon the
chapter that prescribeth the form to be used between Kings
and Princes ; but, were it not for the place you hold, to have
an imputation so publicly thrown upon our justice, which as yet
never failed, we would answer this audacity of yours in another
style.' . . .
       " I assure your Lordship though I am not apt to wonder, I
must confess before the Living Lord that I never heard her,

when I knew her spirits were in passion, speak with better moderation in my life.

"You will think it strange that I am so idle as to use another's hand. I assure you I have hurt my thumb at this hour and because the Queen told me she was sorry you heard not his Latin and hers, I promised her to make you partaker of as much as I could remember, being as I know the worst you would expect from her and yet the best (that) could come from any other. If therefore this my letter find you and that you write back before your going, I pray you take notice that you were pleased to hear of her wise and eloquent answer." [1]

Essex's pleasure was recorded in the fashionable manner. "It was happy," he said, "for Her Majesty that she was stirred and had so worthy an occasion to show herself. The heroes would be but as other men if they had not unusual and unlooked-for encounters." [2]

There was another matter to which the correspondence between the two men occasionally alluded. Parliament, that wisely infrequent assembly, was to meet again in the autumn of 1597, and Essex desired to be present. Cecil did his best to get it postponed until his colleague should be returned from the Islands Voyage. [3] When it met in November it was confronted with a demand for three entire subsidies and six fifteenths and tenths. Cecil, perhaps fearful of opposition, had intended to pack the Commons with trusted nominees, but was slow in getting to work, and the opportunity slipped by. [4] There was, however, no occasion for alarm. The members listened favourably to the 'large discourse most excellently delivered,' [5] in which he showed 'the purposes, practices, and attempts' of the King of Spain against the Queen and her lands and subjects. No one attempted to repeat Bacon's dangerous exploit

[1] S. P. Dom., Eliz., 264/51 (i). There is also a copy in the Spencer Papers (Box 31) among the memorials of Bess of Hardwick.
[2] S. P. Dom., Eliz., 264/58.   [3] *Ibid.*, 264/5 and 67.
[4] Hatf. Cal., vii. pp. 385, 482.
[5] D'Ewes' *Journals*, and throughout.

of the preceding Parliament, and the grant was not only equal in amount to the last but was to be gathered more rapidly. Cecil spoke again upon the decline of tillage in Northumberland, Cumberland, and Westmorland, and so well that the Dean of Durham wrote to commend him for his ' grave and wise ' speech.[1] This did not exhaust his activities. An absurd point of procedure had cropped up. The Lords had made an amendment to a Bill explanatory of a statute ; and their clerk had inscribed it on parchment instead of paper without endorsing it. The Commons consequently declared their inability to take notice of it, and were indignant when the Upper House accused them of levity. They had their own clerk up, and went thoroughly into the subject. It appeared that amendments ought to be set down on paper, but new matter on parchment ; and Cecil was entrusted with the duty of communicating this important circumstance to their Lordships' ears. The *Journals* wisely omit to record what they replied to him. In the debates on poverty and destitution, then as now the staple of domestic legislation, he does not appear to have taken any part. We know that he cared for the poor, but very possibly he thought that the poor had as many friends in Parliament as was good for them. Other matters, besides, in which he had more skill, were already claiming his attention.

[1] S. P. Dom., Eliz., 265/36.

CHAPTER VIII

THE EMBASSY TO FRANCE

" Dessus le Nil jadis fut la Science,
    Puis en Grèce elle alla,
Rome depuis en eut l'expérience,
    Paris maintenant l'a.
Villes et forts et royaumes périssent
    Par le temps tout exprès,
Et donnent lieu aux nouveaux qui fleurissent
    Pour remourir après."
PIERRE DE RONSARD,
" A Anthoine Chasteigner."

" All States are ungrateful and so are their ministers."—WOTTON'S
Table Talk. (Pearsall Smith's *Life and Letters of Sir H.
Wotton*, vol. ii. App. 4.)

THE fall of Calais settled nothing. Though for the
moment it had forced Henry back into the arms of his
old allies, the force of interest was sure in the end to
drive him in a contrary direction. He bound himself, indeed, with all the bonds that diplomacy could
devise not to make peace without Elizabeth's consent,
and the Queen gave a corresponding pledge. But
the very treaty was conceived in guile. A fine show
of troops, which the English undertook to supply,
was set down on paper and sufficed to ensnare the
honest Dutchmen into a similar engagement ; whilst
a secret understanding between the crowned heads,
of which the Republic had no knowledge, reduced
the English contingent by one-half, and narrowly
limited the sphere of its operations. Meanwhile
Calais and the captured towns of the north were so

many trump cards in the hands of the Spaniards.
Philip had it in his power to make the King of France
master in his own house ; to give to that distracted
country the forgotten blessings of foreign and
domestic peace ; to restore again to its coronal of
cities the long-lost jewel of the north.[1] And Philip
would do anything for hatred of Elizabeth and the
Dutch. Henry began once more to treat.

It is to his credit that he made little secret of his
intention. M. de Maisse was sent over to England
to announce that the King was intending to negotiate
with Spain and to invite the Queen's co-operation.
The proposal was not disagreeable to Elizabeth. She
was tired of the expense of war ; she had Ireland on
her hands ; and her instructions to her Ambassador
show that she was as ready to coerce the Dutch as
Henry was to coerce her.[2] We do not need, therefore,
to spend time in pitying her on account of the infidelity of her ally. She knew, besides, or ought to
have known, with whom she had to deal ; her own
mind was a perfect mirror of princes. Reason of
state in that baneful glass made fair every violation
of public truth and honour.

Cecil, who had been conversant with the tenor
of Maisse's mission, was despatched to France in the
month of February 1598. Gossip reports that he was
reluctant to go, fearing that appointments which he
could not approve would be made in his absence,
and that Essex gave him a friendly promise that
nothing of that sort should be done.[3] His associates
were John Herbert, the Master of Requests, and Sir
Thomas Wilkes, and among his suite were numbered
Southampton and Sir George Carew. The Commissioners were sent, in fact, to spy out the land

[1] Calais had been recovered by the French, January 1558, but
captured by the Spaniards in April 1596.

[2] S. P. For., France, 41/299.

[3] Sidney Papers, ii. p. 89. Whyte to Sidney.

to discover, if possible, what was really passing at Vervins,[1] where Henry's emissaries were already in conference with those of Spain. "The chiefest of our journey," writes Cecil candidly to his father, "is inquisition."[2] Instructions, however, of a more elaborate character were delivered to the envoys for their better guidance. In dealing with Henry they were advised to dwell with what effect they might upon the perfidious conduct of the Spaniards in respect of the Ostend negotiation of 1588, as well as upon the ungrateful clause in the Treaty of Câteau-Cambrésis, by which the cession of Calais to France was limited to eight years so that in the event of its being recaptured Elizabeth might fairly keep it as a set-off against the moneys owed her. Any Anglo-Spanish peace, it was further laid down, must involve the confirmation of the United Provinces in their ancient liberties, and notably in freedom of religion, and the restoration to England of those commercial advantages which she had enjoyed by the treaties with Burgundy in the time of Charles v. But there was to be no nonsense allowed on the part of the Dutch ; and, if they advanced pretensions of an unreasonable character, they were to be put in this dilemma—either England and France would make peace without them, or else they would be required to bear the whole expense of the war.[3]

The Dutch, indeed, showed a highly suspicious want of alacrity in getting their diplomatic mission under way ; and Cecil, after waiting some time for them in London, was finally obliged to start alone. He went by barge to Gravesend, and from there by coach to the sea-coast, sleeping at the postmaster's houses at Sittingbourne, where he received a jewel as a

---

[1] S. P. For., France, 41/299.   [2] *Ibid.*, 41/120.
[3] The instructions are to be found in S. P. For., France, 41/299, and in a Journal of the Embassy among the Westminster MSS. at Eaton Hall.

parting mark of the Queen's favour, and again at Canterbury.[1] An adverse wind kept him some time kicking his heels at Dover ; it was an incident with which diplomatists had always to reckon, and which might be pregnant with consequences. Henry, so he heard, was tired of waiting for him, and had reached Fontainebleau on his way to Brittany, where the latest fires of the League were still flickering. If this were so, he asked leave to follow ; the essential, as he knew, was to get speech of the King himself, who was far more friendly to England than his ministers. Other rumour which floated across the Channel was to the effect that the fair Gabrielle desired to see France ' in a long robe ' (i.e. at peace), since she was much wasted with following the camp.[2] These and like trifles Cecil employed his abundant leisure in writing to his father and Essex. To the Queen he wrote only of her charms and graces ; of his despair at being parted from her ; how this was the climax of his losses, following as it did upon the deaths of his mother, sister, and friends ; of his devotion to her Divine Presence whose pure spirit, he profanely says, created him of nothing ; and the rest of the fulsome stuff which no courtier was then ashamed to excogitate.[3] For the rest, he occupied his enforced delay by looking on at some coursing ; getting thereby, he declares, so much good ' by the sharp air that I am become a man of two meals.'[4]

A heavy storm was followed by a change in the weather, and the Commissioners made a tolerable crossing to Dieppe on the night of the 17th in the six ships told off for their transport [5]—Cecil in the *Vanguard*, Herbert in the *Answer*,[6] Wilkes in the *Quittance*. The last-named of the three envoys was already sick, and at Rouen he fell hopelessly

[1] Eaton Hall MSS.   [2] S. P. For., France, 41/136.
[3] *Ibid.*, 41/133.   [4] *Ibid.*, 41/136.
[5] *Ibid.*, 41/131 ; cp. S. P. Dom., Eliz., 266/71.   [6] Or the *Crane*.

ill. The others waited some days for his recovery,
but time pressed, and as they had little doubt how
his matter would end, they eventually left him and
posted on to Paris. Their reception in France had
lacked nothing in honour. A M. de Boderie, one
of the King's household, had met them at Dieppe
with a letter of welcome from his master : at Rouen
they had been feasted, so well as Lent would admit,
by the duc de Montpensier, and Cecil had lodged in
a bed as excellently upholstered as any in the land.[1]
Passing by Pontoise and St. Denys, where, as their
journal records, ' some time was spent before dinner
in viewing the monuments of that church,'[2] they
came to Paris, ' an insolent place ' full of rakes and
robbers.[3] Whilst he was there, Cecil saw Perez,
who gave him a useful description of the humours
of the Court. He had already gauged the political
situation. " Your Worships," he writes home, " may
assure yourselves of this one thing, that this country
(which hath endured a war of such perpetuity) both
needeth and affecteth peace universally."[4] And he
goes on to point out what every Frenchman knew,
that France had more to gain by peace than her
adversary, because her powers of recuperation were
superior to those of any country in the world. About
the King he was under no illusion. " He is one of
those princes," he had written to the Council from
Dover, " which thinks all things honest which are
profitable, I having heard that it is his ordinary word,
' Qui a le profit a l'honneur.' "[5] And this, though
he modifies it inexplicably in one despatch by credit-
ing Henry with ' great virtue and sincerity,'[6] was his
considered opinion at the close of his embassy.[7]

The King was, in fact, as Cecil saw, in the hands of

[1] S. P. For., France, 41/182.
[2] Eaton Hall MSS., Journal of Cecil's Embassy.
[3] S. P. For., France, 41/204.
[4] Ibid., 41/204. Also given in the Eaton Hall MSS.
[5] Ibid., 41/149.   [6] Ibid., 41/204.   [7] Ibid., 42/60.

his ministers and his people. " When the match is to be played between the Council, the Nobility, and the Populace of France on the one side and the King only on the other, the odds is to be laid rather on the plurality than the unity."[1] The only chance of accomplishing anything lay in getting speech of the Sovereign apart from his councillors. Among these, Villeroy stood out as the genius of the peace with Spain. " A very wise man," so Cecil describes him, at the close of his embassy, " of person very low but finely timbered, fair-spoken, affects to show temper, leads the King, and holds the States deputies to the wall, but runs all another course with me because they stoop to him, but we do a little *faire le ménage* with them all, and so had we need, for your Lordship best knows our power."[2]

The point, therefore, from the first was to get speech of Henry, who was at least more frank than his minister, and with this intent the Commissioners went on from Paris to Angers, passing through Chartres and Orleans, Blois and Amboise and Tours, and visiting with curious eyes, as so many other of us have done since, the scene of Guise's assassination.[3]

Elizabeth was not best pleased when she discovered how quickly her Commissioners were moving. Her dignity required a more measured progress, and in her own peculiar style she conveyed her displeasure. " Though the (work ?) of your hands be nimble and light, yet I could have wished a clog on your heels when you trotted so far, as our foes will say, after a peace, for that is the common rumour of your flight. If you had, at the first-received letter, made known that Paris, with much ado, was limited your furthest, you should never have made such a Lenten pilgrimage. God be with you," she concludes more gently, " and bestow success upon your beginning."[4]

[1] S. P. For., France, 41/204. [2] *Ibid.*, 42/13.
[3] *Ibid.*, 41/314. [4] *Ibid.*, 41/195.

Cecil wrote his apologies and explanations [1] when the letter came to hand. Meanwhile, he had at last got speech of the King, after spending just a month on the way. He was introduced by the duc de Bouillon and Maisse, and presented his credentials.[2] After a modest reference to himself he defined the purpose of his embassy as the discovery of the real character of the Spanish offers. Elizabeth looked to the King to advise her whether, so far as regarded herself, they were sincere or not. Henry replied in suitable terms, and concluded by inquiring after the Queen's health. " She was when I came out of England," replied Cecil, " according to her custom, comme cette princesse qui n'a jamais senti que c'est de la maladie." Then he presented his suite ; and a less formal interview was arranged for the next day. But the King did not delay so long to be gracious. He took Cecil off there and then to his garden, and talked to him for an hour and a half with that engaging appearance of candour which was no doubt the secret of his charm. He explained that unless the Queen gave him more assistance the long purse of the King of Spain would overcome him in the end ; that his subjects were crying out for peace ; and that, keen soldier as he was, he could not bring himself to buy with blood what might be had for the asking. Then, knowing that no Englishman unreservedly puts his trust in the public honour of a man whose private life will not stand investigation, he added, " I am censured amongst you to be sold over to idleness and delight ; wherein I will confess God has made me a man, and, as I know my frailty is a scar in my forehead, so, the circumstances of my misfortune considered, if I be not guilty of other villainies, I doubt not but I may be

[1] S. P. For., France, 41/317.
[2] I am following the account in the Hatf. Cal., viii. p. 90. The letter is also printed in Birch's *Historical View of the Negot.*, *etc.*, and there are copies of it and of the others here quoted from among the Calthorpe MSS. (vol. clxvi.) at 38 Grosvenor Square.

numbered, if not amongst the better sort yet not amongst the vilest rank of princes."

Cecil was not susceptible to these blandishments. He took leave to doubt—or to seem to doubt—whether the poverty of the country was really so desperate, now that the King had subdued the last remnant of rebellion, and he hinted that certain councillors exaggerated the distress to draw their master along the line of policy which they favoured. Then he dwelt upon the support which Elizabeth had rendered, not only by supplying soldiery for service in France, but by such expeditions as the recent one to Cadiz, which contributed not a little to tie the hands of the King of Spain. As to the Queen's embarrassments they had not been so considerable since 1588. At this the King a little changed his manner, and said abruptly, " Mons. Cecyll, je le confesse tout, vous avez raison, je m'en acquitterai envers ma sœur en façon d'homme de bien." With that they betook themselves to see Madame,[1] the King's sister, one of the promoters of the King's suggested marriage with Gabrielle d'Estrées. " She was well painted," says Cecil in his despatch, " ill-dressed, and strangely jewelled." The next day it was the royal favourite herself. " The King much entreated me to go to see his mistress and his son. She is . . . truly a fair and delicate woman. I stayed little to speak with her, and yet she is very well spoken and very courteous, and spake of Her Majesty with very great respect, and wished she would once command her."

The day after, the envoys had a cabinet-audience. Cecil, saying that he understood that the King called those who made long-winded addresses ' les Haranguers Follastres,' went straight to the point. The Queen was agreeable to peace, and had satisfied all desire of revenge, but she wished before she proceeded further to make sure that the Spaniards were

---

[1] Princess Catherine, afterwards Duchesse de Bar.

in good earnest. Also, and above all, what was to be done if the States would not become parties to the pacification, " seeing they deserved especially to be cared for, both for the honour and obligation of faith given them, as also for the interest which both realms have in their conservation."

Henry renewed his assurances of good faith. He might, as he argued, have already concluded a treaty, but that he wished it should comprise his ally. There is, indeed, no cause to doubt the sincerity of his desire to keep trust with his confederates. His letters to his Commissioners at Vervins[1] tell the same tale as his speeches to Cecil ; and he pressed Archduke Albert to procure from Spain unimpeachable powers to treat with England. But there his fidelity and his effort alike came to a standstill. If war could not be made effective, nor peace be made general, he would not stick at a particular accommodation. He reiterated the alternatives to Cecil. It was in vain that the Ambassador told him that a separate peace was a point that must not be disputed of, for otherwise all leagues were ridiculous. If you will not have me make peace alone, nor you may not make peace without the States, he replied, what is the third way you would wish ?

Cecil could tell him of none. The root of the difficulty, as the King saw, was the United Provinces. Philip would never consent to their independence, and they would never consent to his domination. The arrival of their Commissioners only made this the more clear. These novel diplomatists clothed their attitude in no ambiguous phrases. Their State, they told Cecil, might not hearken to peace or treaty of peace ; their commission was absolutely

---

[1] *Mems. de Bellièvre et de Sillery*, pp. 207, 234, 235: " Je désire aider à les (les Anglais) mettre en repos aussi bien que moi, mais je n'entends pas gâter mes affaires pour leur considération, le salut de mon peuple m'étant bien plus cher que toute autre chose."

to protest against it ; their trust was all in the Queen of England, for those of the King's Council they had spoken with were passionate for a treaty, and the King told them that, " though in his nature he did not desire it, yet by the importunity of his people and the necessity of his affairs, he should be forced to accept it for some time, unless he were better assisted."[1]

That, we may take it, was a very fair summary of the situation till near the end of March, when the Court moved to Nantes—of a situation which, if faith were to be kept, amounted to an impasse. But an obscure incident had already occurred which was to put a different complexion on affairs before the month was out. Some English fishermen, plying their trade, caught a packet of letters, which proved to be despatches from the Archduke to King Philip.[2] From these the English Government learned for certain the real projects and powers of the Commissioners at Vervins. It appeared that the Spaniards were willing to restore all their conquests, even to Calais itself, on condition that all intelligences between France and her allies came to an end. If Henry made a point of bringing England and Holland into the pacification the Commissioners were not to refuse, but they were to treat with these Powers apart from France, and the terms of peace were to include the restoration by England of all conquests or a money compensation, besides free exercise of religion for English Papists, and the submission of the Dutch to King Philip.[3]

These instructions were guileful enough, but the serpent's sting was yet to be found. The papers included, not only the Archduke's advices to his Commissioners, but the advices of the Commissioners to the Archduke. We understand, they told him,

[1] Hatf. Cal., viii. p. 109.
[2] *Mems. de Bellièvre et de Sillery*, p. 208.
[3] S. P. For., France, 41/256.

that the French will treat without their allies. They
only stipulated otherwise before for the sake of King
Henry's reputation. There is no need, therefore,
to get powers from Spain to treat with England
and the States. And four days later they were able
further to inform him that Villeroy had told Richardot
that he would treat without England, though it still
seemed best to get a permission to treat from Philip.
A third letter, dated nearly a week after the second,
declared that the King's intentions are past finding
out, even by his own envoys, but that he insisted
upon the commission to treat with England being
sent.[1]

Elizabeth put the worst construction on these
discoveries and communicated them to Cecil. For a
few days, in order to see whether a power to treat
with England would be sent from Spain, he held his
hand.[2] Then, when the power had arrived, he asked
for an audience, being resolved that plain speaking
was the proper course. He found the King in bed,
recovering from the effect of medicine. " We
warmed him," he tells Elizabeth, " so well that,
whether it were his physic, or our message, Monsieur
Le Grand was fain to fetch drink for him." Henry
muttered broken interjections whilst the lecture was
going on, protesting that the charge was a got-up
thing. Herbert thereupon read him extracts from
the intercepted despatches, suppressing that part of
them which discovered the liberality of the Spanish
instructions in respect to France. The King admitted
that his Ministers might have used large speeches, but
denied the most compromising of the allegations :—
" The Queen shall never find me trompeur ni pipeur,
and when I have a mind to do such an act I will never
deny it, for I had as willingly it were known to-day
as to-morrow." Villeroy backed his master up later

---

[1] S. P. For., France, 41/256.
[2] The following account is taken from the Hatf. Cal., viii. p. 118.

in the day by ' monstrous oaths ' and more particular
denials.   Cecil did not much believe Villeroy, but he
did believe the King.   " If he be not a monster,"
he wrote to Elizabeth, " he hath said true of that
which is past ; yet both of us (and I, the Secretary,
especially, who have had access many times, and
have heard him in many humours, sometime upon
sudden in liberal speech, and sometime serious, discover himself to me with his ends and his natural
disposition) dare not say other to your Majesty than
that I fear France will be France and leave his best
friends, though to his own future ruin, to which I think
God hath ordained it." [1]

    " To tell you the truth," Henry had written to
his Commissioners at Vervins, " I found the English
envoys savage and hostile to the peace from the first." [2]
The Englishmen kept their English manners to the
end.   " Since the closing up of our letter to Her
Majesty," writes Cecil, ". . . the King hath sent to-
night to my lodging to court me and hath intreated
me that I will go to-morrow a-hunting with him to
kill a wolf and play the good fellow and not be
melancholy.   I have absolutely denied him and made
him a sullen answer and have desired that he would
give me to attend him about these affairs for which I
was sent, being at no time fit for hunting and much
less now." [3]   The time had in fact come for winding
up the embassy.   It had never really been more than
a mission of inquiry, and Cecil had no power to proceed
to Vervins, even if he wished.   The limited character
of his instructions, the *intransigeance* of the Dutch,
the inability of the French King to satisfy the English
Commissioners that the Spanish authority to treat
with England was, or would be, drafted in the same
form as the Spanish authority to treat with France—

----

[1] Hatf. Cal., viii. p. 124.
[2] *Mems. de Bell. et Sillery*, p. 207.
[3] S. P. For., France, 42/54.

all made for a speedy conclusion. And Henry was far from averse to seeing the last of a set of visitors who kept his conscience more or less at work and his pleasures more or less at bay.[1]   But Cecil, before he shook the dust of France from off his feet, allowed himself the luxury of a parting thrust at the infidelity of the French. Affecting to return to England for fresh instructions, he accepted the King's proposal of another meeting with the King's advisers [2] which might serve to keep the negotiation alive. The conference between the three allied Powers was arranged for the following Sunday; and the Chancellor and Villeroy were present among other notabilities of the French Court. Cecil opened the proceedings by casting the responsibility for the breakdown of the negotiations upon the States. They must make clear their reasons. Later on he would have something to say about the Queen's part in the matter. Barneveldt, the famous Dutchman, followed with what Cecil calls ' a very wise and plain declaration.' [3] He dwelt upon the terms of the triple alliance of 1596 and the French pledges involved in it. Then with much feeling he indicated the effect of a peace between France and Spain upon the United Provinces, showing incidentally the enormous power of which Spain would be possessed if the revolted territories were restored to her. He concluded with a handsome offer of support if France would but continue the war. Cecil was curious to see what the Council would say in reply. He knew that some of its members were in two minds, and he thought that such plain speaking might have made an impression.

[1] S. P. For., France, 42/1.

[2] The following account is from S. P. For., France, 42/60.

[3] The speech was, I think, an honest one, though on 24th September 1599—over a year later—Neville writes to Cecil and declares that he has learned ' by good means ' that Henry had bribed the Dutch by a promise of 200,000 crowns yearly to oppose the conclusion of a general peace in 1598 (Winwood Memorials, ii. p. 107).

But the Chancellor merely set out the old plea—
the urgent necessity of France—smoothing it over
with compliments. The Ambassador's representations, he said, should be referred to the King. With
that he would have broken up the conference. But
Cecil had not yet done with him. After repudiating
the suggestion that Elizabeth was only trying to
gain time, and associating himself with Barneveldt's
observations, the English Envoy went on to lash Henry
with the utmost rigour. " If an angel of Heaven
had told the Queen that the King would treat without
his allies she would not have believed it." All this
talk of ' necessity ' was hollow pretext. The Queen
and the States would have enlarged the scope of the
alliance if Henry were really unable to defend himself and no peace satisfactory to the allies was to
be obtained. But, he continued bitterly, it is a vain
thing to dispute further against those who hold it a
maxim, " Que l'honneur des Princes gist toujours à
bien faire leur affaires." Then, in conclusion, with
a spice of malice, he brought to mind the undis-
charged English loan of twenty thousand crowns,
of which the Queen would now have the more
need, as she was left to herself. Her dearly bought
experience would teach her, he said, to husband
her resources more carefully for the future, whereby
she might reap more fruit and gather greater thankfulness.

On the 15th April the English Commissioners
took their leave, extremely dissatisfied, reports
Villeroy,[1] as they could not extract any promise
from the King not to conclude peace without them.
All that Henry would do was to engage to keep the
door open for another forty days, after which they
were to signify if they would agree to treat, or else
retire absolutely. But even this pledge he apparently felt under no obligation to observe, as he

[1] *Mems. de Bell. et Sillery*, p. 258.

thought, not altogether inexcusably, that the English were insincere.[1]

Cecil may have felt dissatisfied with the immediate result of his mission. Yet it was probably of some ultimate value to his country, since, in spite of all that had passed, it appears to have left behind some sort of mutual regard between himself and Henry [2]—one of those strange understandings which sometimes arise between a well-principled man of the world and a good-natured rascal. For private reasons, at any rate, he had sufficient cause to be glad to turn his face homewards. For the reports which had reached him of his father's health had been most disquieting, and Burghley's long life was hanging by a thread.

The embassy returned by way of Caen. The wind was good and the crossing should have been quick. But the sailors, for some unexplained reason, missed their way and the passengers were kept two days at sea. Eventually the ships reached the Isle of Wight on the 29th April; and, after dining, the Commissioners proceeded by Ryde to Portsmouth. Staines was reached on the 30th. There Essex met them and accompanied the returning Ambassador back to Whitehall, where the Queen was resident. That night Cecil slept again in his own house in the Strand.[3]

[1] *Mems. de Bell. et Sillery*, p. 270.
[2] See Goodman, *Court of James I.*, i. pp. 38, 39.   [3] Eaton Hall MS.

CHAPTER IX

THE ESSEX TRAGEDY

" Who trusts too much to honour's highest throne,
  And warely watch not sly Dame Fortune's snares,
  Or who in court will bear the sway alone,
  And wisely weigh not how to wield the care,
  Behold he me, and by my death beware,
  Who flattering Fortune falsely so beguil'd
  That lo ! she slew where erst full smooth she smil'd."
          DORSET'S *Complaint of Henry, Duke of Buckingham.*

THE Ambassador, landing, as has been said, at Portsmouth, reached home at the close of April. He was followed a week or two later by the emissaries of the United Provinces — Olden-Barneveldt and Admiral Justinus of Nassau, the natural son of William the Silent. Meanwhile, at Vervins, Villeroy and Richardot had hatched the Peace, which bears its name. France got all she asked for. Her soldiers and her cities were restored to her, and Calais returned from its last captivity. Elizabeth was extremely annoyed, and her indignation fell, hot and strong, upon the heads of the unlucky Dutchmen. The situation in Ireland, the depletion of her own exchequer made peace or payment an imperative necessity. And peace or payment she resolved to have. The Dutch debt was played off against a treaty with Spain, and Olden-Barneveldt was given his choice. He visited Burghley in the hopes of softening the terms, but the Lord Treasurer, racked

¹ S. P. Dom., Eliz., 266/117.

as he was with gout, met him with a fierce countenance
—' een fier gelaat,' as the historian records—and
he retired discomfited. Buckhurst was milder in
appearance but not less firm in purpose. Essex, on
the other hand, was friendly, doubting, so he said,
if the Spaniards could be trusted. To the Lord
Treasurer, who watched him day by day in the Council,
his motives seemed less honourable. Taking a prayer-
book into his hand, Burghley laid his finger upon the
passage in the Psalms where it is said that blood-
thirsty and deceitful men shall not live out half their
days, and showed the verse to his impetuous rival.
The words are strong, and it is not clear that the
application was immediately justified. But Essex
was presently to make them seem prophetic in the
eyes of all men.

The incident furnished, anyway, the exact and
proper conclusion to the labour of one whom the Queen
herself was to designate as ' Pater pacis patriæ.'[1]
The Fates had long been preparing to sever two notable threads upon the loom of life. But neither
Burghley, tormented by attacks of gout so acute
that he signed himself Ἀκέφαλος—without a head—
nor Philip rotting away amid the cold splendours of
the Escorial, had any reason to abhor the shears.
Release came to both of them in the summer of 1598.
The Most Catholic King passed away in such sanctity
as the stately ceremonial of the Roman Church could
afford. Burghley turned his face quietly to the wall
and with a patriarchal dignity said his *Nunc dimittis.*
Each had shown great patience and fortitude in life ;
and their qualities remained with them to the end.
Victor and vanquished, they doubtless realised in
another world the fulness of their rival measures
of success and failure. For to men then living their
contest seemed to be but half fought out.

Cecil, though there appears to be no record of it,

---

[1] Goodman, *Court of James I.*, p. 31.

doubtless followed his father's corpse to Westminster,[1] where the funeral rites were rendered. Thence the poor dust was carried on in solemn procession to be buried in Stamford Church. There was no ostentatious pageantry. " Avoid unnecessary charge "—so ran Burghley's terse direction—" in a long carriage of a dead carcase." Only at every place where the body lay at night forty shillings was to be given to the poor of the parish.

The Lord Treasurer's fortune disappointed expectation. There was some £11,000 in coin, most of it silver. To Thomes Cecil was left the ancestral estate at Burghley, with other Northamptonshire and Rutland properties ; to Robert, Theobalds, with land in Hertfordshire and Middlesex. Burghley House, at Westminster, went with the title ; but the Lord Treasurer gave his younger son one collar of the Garter and its attendant George. Robert Cecil estimated that the income of his lands would amount to £1600 at the outside.[2] To him, however, had fallen, as the wits maintained by borough-English tenure,[3] that which no man can bequeath, his father's best gifts—a great patience and prudence and skilfulness in state-affairs.

There was every call for these then and in the future. Some accommodation had yet to be come to with the Dutch, if there was to be no peace with Spain. By 1st August Barneveldt had been pinched to the point of proposing to redeem £30,000 a year of the debt while the war lasted, as well as to pay another £100,000 for each of the cautionary towns when these were transferred.[4]

---

[1] In S. P. Dom., Eliz., 268/32, Cecil's servants are mentioned, and in Harl., 36/384, in a short diary of his life, Burghley's funeral is noticed. He may have been one of the ' assistants ' who attended his brother, Thomas, the chief mourner.

[2] S. Williams, *Letters of John Chamberlain*, No. vi.

[3] Manningham's *Diary*, p. 82.

[4] Motley, *United Netherlands*, iii. p. 561.

Cecil and his colleagues assented to what seemed a fair offer. But when Elizabeth got wind of it she called her ministers ' great beasts ' and refused to confirm the agreement. A sufficient understanding was at last arrived at. The States were to pay altogether £800,000—one-half in yearly instalments of £30,000, the other vaguely in the future. The restoration of the towns was left in like manner undetermined.

Meanwhile, Essex had entered upon another phase of his career. The failure of the Islands Voyage had accentuated the weak points of his character—his moodiness, his impatience of opposition, his inexhaustible craving for avenues of distinction and positions of power—and there can be little doubt that the curious letter from Cecil,[1] which passes under the title of " Advices to Essex," being in the Queen's disgrace, and purports to belong to the year 1600, was, in fact, an attempt, futile enough as it proved, to instil some ordinary good sense and practical sagacity into his mind in 1597 or 1598.[2] Angry and petulant humours were drawing the man on to his doom. He tended more and more to be, as we should say, ' impossible.' The autumn of 1598 proved the winter of his discontent. It was then, according to Camden's story, that the Queen boxed his ears, and that he replied by laying his hand upon his sword. In his vexation with things in general, he fixed upon Ireland as the principal outlet of his peevishness. He opposed the appointment of Knollys as Lord Deputy ; he was equally hostile to the nomina-

---

[1] Harl. MSS., 35/18.

[2] I have the more confidence in saying this because the date of the letter has long been doubted (see Courtenay on "Sir Robert Cecil," p. 67, in Lardner's *Cabinet Cyclop.*), and the Finch MSS., which are, or were, at Burley-on-the-Hill (H.M. C. Rep., vii. p. 516), contain " An advertisement to Robt. Devereux, Earl of Essex, sent by his Squire the 27th November. *39* Eliz. By the Lord Cecil." The opening words of the Finch MS. show it to be identical with the other (which is printed in Courtenay's *Sir Robert Cecil*, p. 188).

tion of Mountjoy ; from motives of spite he suggested
Sir G. Carew.[1] The Council took the fairest revenge
that lay open to them. He was asked himself to
undertake that for which he thought, or pretended
to think, their nominees were unfit. The attitude
he had taken up precluded a refusal. He accepted
reluctantly,[2] having no love of the job,[3] and made
himself infinitely difficult,[4] hoping perhaps that the
project would fall through. It was of this time that
John Chamberlain wrote to Carleton that Cecil and
Essex played as round a game as if Ireland were to
be recovered at Irish.[5] The Earl had, no doubt, real
ground for complaint, for the Treasury was so bare [6]
that every attempt was made to cut down the cost
of the equipment. But, if much was asked, much
also in the end was given him—plenary powers, large
forces, ample revenues, the flower of the English
nobility and gentry to follow in his train. With so
dashing an armament Elizabeth expected a dashing
success.

And here, indeed, was the mistake, for the conquest of Ireland, as Mountjoy's generalship showed
later on, could be no mere summer campaign. Matters
in the Distressful Isle had long been going from bad
to worse. Bagnal's defeat at the Yellow Ford,
which happened within a few days of Burghley's
death, had discredited the English arms and provoked
a rising of the Septs. It needed time, patience,
opportunity to recover the power and prestige that
had been lost. Essex was statesman enough to see
this. In the remarkable state - paper which he

---

[1] Harington, *Nug. Antiq.*, ii. p. 217.

[2] Hatf. Cal., ix. p. 4: "The hardest job that ever any gentleman
was sent about."

[3] *Ibid.*, p. 10.

[4] S. Williams, *Letters of John Chamberlain*, xviii. (*e.g.*).

[5] *Ibid.*, xiii. Irish=backgammon.

[6] *Ibid.*, vi. The Treasury contained only £20,000 at Burghley's
death.

addressed to the Queen on 25th June 1599,[1] he presents a vivid picture of the advantages and disadvantages which the English army possessed—of the care, the cost, the industry, the time that must be spent upon the Irish enterprise.   And Robert Cecil saw this too. He writes to Neville that Essex " must have wrought miracles to have settled and distributed an army of 16,000 foot and 13,000 horse . . . in a shorter time than he did."[2]   And again : " The Earl is by this time returned to Dublin, and prepareth to go into the North ; he hath done as much as could be done by the sword, on the rebels in Munster and Leinster ; for he hath passed at his pleasure where he listed, notwithstanding all the plots they could use either of force or stratagem.   But the rogues shun fight, and so know how to spend us, and eat us out with time."[3]

Yet Elizabeth was looking for a quick success, and, regardless of the grave warnings of the Irish Council,[4] drove her Deputy forward to the invasion of Ulster, with the stern prohibition not on any account to return home.   From that time all went ill.   Conyers Clifford, sent north to effect a diversion, was defeated and slain, as Essex had gloomily presaged that he would be.[5]   The Lord Deputy himself had no heart for his work, nor any longer adequate troops to compass it   He marched, indeed, against Tyrone, but only as it proved to conclude an empty and humiliating truce with the very man he had come out to conquer. Then he turned his back upon Ireland and his army and hurried home without permission and without renown.   At this point it is necessary to break for a moment the course of the narrative.

In England, Cecil had been discharging those laborious duties to which he was perfectly accustomed.

---

[1] See Devereux, *The Devereux Earls of Essex*, ii. p. 36.
[2] S. P. Dom., Eliz., 273/75.   [3] Winwood Memorials, i. p. 71.
[4] Hatf. Cal., ix. p. 263.   [5] *Ibid.*, p. 289.

The perennial activities of the Jesuits had culminated before Essex set sail for Ireland in Squire's plot—a rather mysterious affair, which was probably designed more to implicate Dr. Bagshaw, the loyal leader of the English secular priests, than to compass Elizabeth's death.[1] The militant party, however, made what capital they could out of this unpromising attempt to poison the Queen by inoculating the pommel of her saddle ; there was some talk of a Spanish invasion ; and Cecil's pacific parleyings with the Archduke suffered accordingly. Whilst Essex was away the Spanish danger assumed more formidable shape. An invasion-panic swept over the country. It was reported in the city that 50,000 men were to be landed ; that the King of Scots had crossed the Border with another 40,000 ; that the King of Denmark was lending aid ; that the Adelantado had sworn on the Sacrament to bring his wife and daughters to London Bridge. One day it went for certain that the enemy had landed at Southampton ; the next day that they had been routed, and so forth.[2] Cecil took the necessary precautions, though he was rather sceptical as to the danger.[3] Fleet and army were mobilised, with Nottingham (the Howard of the Armada) at their head. The Archbishop suggested special forms of prayer on the model of 1588.[4] But the fear subsided after three weeks' duration, leaving little behind except the proof for which the Council were possibly not sorry, that Essex, popular as he might be, was not indispensable to an effective military demonstration. The Queen, indeed, had been afraid that he would break away from his post to take part in repelling the Spaniards ; and it was with this

[1] M. Hume, *Treason and Plot*, p. 385.   [2] Hatf. Cal., ix. p. 282.

[3] Winwood Memorials, i. p. 91 : " I have given way to these preparations that are made, preferring therein the ways of safety, before any matter of charge " (Cecil to Neville).

[4] Hatf. Cal., ix. p. 262.

possibility in view that she had explicitly forbidden him to return without her orders.[1] Essex's biographer thought that he detected Cecil's hand in this special instruction; and that it was the suspicion that his colleagues in the Council were not dealing fairly with him which provoked Essex to rush home.[2] Of the first suggestion there is no kind of proof : the second is possible enough, since the Lord Deputy had freely insinuated that some of the Privy Council—he mentions Ralegh and Cobham by name—were disloyal to him. Rowland Whyte reports in September that " the unkindness between my Lord of Essex and Mr. Secretary is grown to extremity ";[3] and, again, that Cecil has refused mediation because he is convinced that ' there is no constancy ' in the other's love,[3] though Whyte adds that Cecil will not show malice towards his rival. Cecil's own belief, however, was just that Essex wished to secure the Queen's approval of his truce with Tyrone, which he could scarcely hope to do by letter.[4]

Whatever the cause, the event is certain. On the morning of Michaelmas Eve, mud-stained and tired from long riding, Essex entered the Queen's private apartments at Nonesuch. Elizabeth was not yet fully dressed, but, probably supposing some extraordinary reason for such extraordinary conduct, received his homage not ungraciously. She saw him again later, and her mood seemed still propitious. The courtiers began to hang about him ; only Cecil kept aloof. Then the enormity of his disobedience and the real position of matters in Ireland seem to have become apparent to her. It was not, as Cecil says,[4] " the goodness of Tyrone's offers in themselves," but " the necessity of her affairs to which the offers were

---

[1] Winwood Memorials, i. p. 118.
[2] Devereux, *Lives of the Devereux*, ii. p. 49.
[3] Sidney Papers, ii. pp. 122, 135.
[4] Winwood Memorials, i. p. 118.

suitable " that he had really come to acquaint her with. An informal committee of the Council— Cecil among them—was hastily nominated to hear him give an account of himself. Before night he was ordered to keep his chamber.

The Council sat again next day, and had Essex five hours before them. We do not know exactly what passed, but the obvious charges against him— his disobedience, his presumptuous letters, his conduct of the campaign, his reckless abandonment of Ireland, his still more reckless entry into the Queen's chamber, the great multitude of knights whom he had used his viceregal authority to create—were formulated, and he replied to them with gravity and discretion. After a day's reflection the Queen committed him to the custody of the Lord Keeper. The physical and mental agitation through which he had passed had by this time told heavily upon his constitution. He could neither eat nor sleep, and Egerton draws a pitiful picture of his distress.[1] It was not expected, however, that his confinement would last long. Cecil says it was imposed mainly for the sake of example.[2] Nevertheless, it lasted through the winter. In point of fact, Elizabeth was extremely provoked, and not the less because the country in general took Essex's part and pasted the palace walls with libellous attacks upon his supposed enemies in the Council, amongst whom Cecil came in for a full share of abuse.[3] It came to the Queen's knowledge besides that Tyrone had meant all the while to play fast and loose with the treaty.[4] She grew so touchy that anything connected with Essex was liable to rouse the tiger-spirit with which her father had endowed her ; and Sir John Harington, one of the multitudinous knights of the Irish creation, received a rebuke, the sharpness of which his memoirs attest to this

---

[1] Hatf. Cal., ix. p. 36. [2] Winwood Memorials, i. p. 118.
[3] Sidney Papers, ii. p. 153. [4] Winwood Memorials, i. p. 125.

day.   In all this tumult Cecil, on whom the Queen greatly leaned,[1] steered that middle way which was habitual to him.   Though he said no word to lighten Essex's guilt, he did what he might to lighten Essex's confinement.   His speech in the Star-Chamber [2] is a dispassionate condemnation of Essex's conduct.   But it was at his instance that Lady Essex was allowed access to her husband.[3]   It was at his request that Lord Keeper Egerton surrendered his own apartments to his prisoner.[4]   And he too it was who, by timely counsel, saved Essex from being brought before the Star-Chamber, as the Queen proposed, in February 1600.[5]

So generous was his conduct that Ralegh was fearful he would carry it too far, and wrote him the famous letter, which is sometimes, but mistakenly, assigned [6] to 1601.

" I am not wise enough to give you advice, but if you take it for a good counsel to relent towards this tyrant, you will repent it when it shall be too late.   His malice is fixed, and will not evaporate by any of your mild courses, for he will ascribe the alteration to her Majesty's pusillanimity and not to your good nature, knowing that you work but upon her humour and not out of any love towards him.   For after revenges fear them not ; for your own father . . . was esteemed to be the contriver of Norfolk's ruin, yet his son followeth your father's son and loveth him.   Humours of men succeed not [7] but grow by occasions and accidents of time and power. . . . Look to the present and you do wisely.   His (Essex's) son shall be the youngest Earl of England but one, and if his father be now kept down, Will Cecil shall be able to keep as many men

---

[1] Sidney Papers (October 1599), ii. p. 130: " Mr. Secretary is one that Her Majesty exceedingly values, and most trusted by her in all the great affairs and business of her kingdom."

[2] S. P. Dom., Eliz., 273/35, 37.

[3] Hatf. Cal., ix. p. 411.   [4] *Ibid.*, p. 412.

[5] Devereux, *Lives of the Devereux*, ii. p. 93 ; cp. Sidney Papers, ii. p. 143 : " It is said Mr. Secretary hath done all good and honest offices for my Lord of Essex and is sorry it prevails so little."

[6] Stebbing, *Sir Walter Ralegh*, p. 153, states the rival arguments very clearly.

[7] *i.e.* are not inherited.

at his heels and more too. He (*i.e.* Cecil's son) may also match in a better house than his (*i.e.* Essex's son), and so that fear is not worth the fearing. But if the father continue, he will be able to break the branches and pull up the tree, root and all. Lose not your advantage. If you do, I read your destiny.— Yours to the end,　　　　　　　　　　　　W. R." [1]

We do not know what Cecil thought of the warning, but Elizabeth's anger, whether with his approval or not, continued slowly to abate. In March she allowed the fallen favourite to return to his own house, though still under restraint. At length she told Bacon she intended to proceed against him for the sake of chastisement, not for destruction. And so, on June 5th, a special commission assembled at York House to examine him. It included Whitgift, whose Protestant leanings made him especially favourable to Essex, Egerton, Buckhurst, Nottingham, Cecil, Knollys, Fortescue, five judges, and half a dozen peers. The object being to humble the offender as much as possible, the Commissioners gave him no recognition when he entered the room, and left him to kneel until the Queen's Serjeant had concluded the speech. Yelverton, however, only spoke shortly, leaving the burden of the prosecution to Coke, the Attorney-General, who had an unrivalled command of offensive and brutal language. The substance of Coke's accusation fell under five heads : the appointment of Southampton, who had put himself out of favour at Court by a secret marriage with one of the Queen's maids of honour ; the march into Munster instead of against Tyrone, the joint responsibility for which the Irish Council had rather meanly repudiated ; the vast creation of knights ; the equal conference with Tyrone ; and the desertion of command. Fleming, the Solicitor-General, followed with an account of the unsatisfactory state of Ireland subsequent to Essex's departure. To Bacon, Essex's

---

[1] The full text of the letter is printed in Edward's *Life of Ralegh*, ii. p. 222.

former friend and client, was reserved the most odious part in the trial.   He it was who set out deliberately to rub poison into the wounds which had been made. Out of some reckless expressions in Essex's letter to the Lord Keeper, the true value of which he must perfectly have known, the shameless time-server squeezed a comparison of the Queen to Pharaoh and a suggestion that she was the slave of passion.   Essex kept his feelings well under control, repudiated the charge of disloyalty with the utmost fervour, but for the rest threw himself on the Queen's mercy.

The Commissioners then made various observations by way of rebuke.   Cecil's remarks, condemnatory though they were of the expedition to Munster, were nevertheless noticed for their temperate courtesy.[1] Egerton, as Lord Keeper, dealt more fully with the matter than his colleagues, and recommended that Essex should only lose his seat in the Council, and cease to exercise his office as Earl Marshal and Master of the Ordnance ; though, as he argued, had they been sitting as the Court of Star-Chamber, they must have sent him to perpetual confinement in the Tower. The prisoner, however, had to wait upon Elizabeth's pleasure for another six weeks.   He was then allowed to return to his own house under a strict injunction not to approach the Court.

Everyone probably anticipated that his fortunes would now recover.   And so it might have been but for his impatience and the desperate condition of his private affairs.   " After the Queen had read your letter twice or thrice over," Lady Scrope presently wrote him word,[2] " she seemed exceedingly pleased with it, yet her answer was only to will me to give you thanks for your great care to know of her health.   I told her that now the time drew near of your whole year's punishment, and therefore I hoped her Majesty would restore her favour to one that with so much

[1] S. P. Dom., Eliz., 275, 14th June 1600.   [2] Hatf. Cal., x. p. 331.

true sorrow did desire it ; but she would answer me never a word, but sighed and said indeed it was so ; with that rose and went into the Privy Chamber. I do not doubt but shortly to see your Lordship at the Court. . . ."

But Essex could not afford to wait on the time and season of Elizabeth's humour. His creditors were pressing, and, unless he could get a renewal of the profitable monopoly of sweet wines which he had enjoyed, he would find himself a ruined man. He resolved to stake all upon a favourable answer, and when this was withheld [1] he began to run in treasonable courses. He was still quite a young man. If the Queen would not receive him into favour there was everything to be hoped from her successor. And to that successor he might do a considerable service. James wished for nothing more than to be acknowledged Elizabeth's heir. Essex proposed to satisfy the aspiration. He had been succeeded in Ireland by Lord Mountjoy, one of his own friends, who was now reigning there as Lord Deputy in his stead. To this man he turned with some adaptation of an old scheme, concocted in the hour of Mountjoy's appointment and his own disgrace, for diverting part of the Irish army to his defence. But Mountjoy had grown more prudent as the other had grown more rash. Even before he had the Lord Deputy's refusal Essex had resolved to assert the claim of the King of Scots on the strength of his considerable personal popularity with the masses. Essex House, therefore, became a Cave of Adullam, where numbers of discontented persons were gathered together. No one can have been wholly blind to the rise of so formidable an opposition, but few, if any, except his

[1] The lease of sweet wines was, a month after Michaelmas, when Essex's lease expired, given to Sir Henry Billingsley and others ' to husband it for the Queen' (Winwood Memorials, bk. iv., Neville to Winwood, 2nd November 1600).

closest friends can have anticipated to what lengths its leader was prepared to go. Long before Christmas,[1] however, he had taken a resolution to force his way into the Queen's presence. How much Cecil knew of what was going on, or at what moment he acquired his knowledge, we have now no means of learning. The vast and varied mass of documents that have come down to us neither disclose the state of his mind nor the source and character of his information. But, encompassed as he was by a large body of spies, the strong probability must be that he was aware of what was hatching, but thought it wisest to let the chickens live to come home to roost. For, when at last he struck, nothing was overlooked to complete the discomfiture of the conspirators. " The main point," says a contemporary correspondent,[2] " was the providence and celerity of the Secretary who foresaw before he was believed and showed gieat dexterity and courage in ministering sudden remedies."

Christmas passed and January, but still the Court gave no sign. On February 3rd[3] (1601) the confederates met at Southampton's house to mature their plan of action. On Sir Ferdinando Gorges' advice they abandoned the idea of seizing the Tower as being too large an undertaking. There was, besides, a strong and sanguine belief that the City was behind the Earl. To capture the palace at Westminster seemed more practicable, and they determined to secure the various points of vantage within it. When all was ready Essex was to march triumphantly into the Queen's presence and dictate his terms. The realities of the situation would, of course, be veiled by the announcement, customary on such occasions, that the Sovereign had been misled by her Ministers. One thing only was still wanting—the approval of the King of Scots, for whose sake all these things were

---

[1] " Danvers' Evidence," S. P. Dom., Eliz., 278/89.
[2] S. P. Dom., Eliz., 278/49, 50.   [3] Hatf. Cal., xi. p. 69.

supposed to be done. But before his emissaries, charged with a blessing, were on the road, James had seen reason to convert it into a curse. For the man who was ultimately to set him on the English throne had baffled and extinguished Essex's clumsy plot.

On the 7th February, Cecil's understudy, Secretary Herbert, summoned the chief conspirator to appear before the Council. Essex had every reason to suspect the invitation (though, in fact, no more was intended than to order him into the country [1]), and refused to come, making a plea of bad health. It was now plain to him that the execution of his scheme could be no longer delayed. He put everything in train for a rising on the next day, and resolved to time his attempt on the City for the conclusion of the weekly sermon at Paul's Cross. Meanwhile the Council did not sit with idle hands. Early on Sunday morning, Egerton, the Lord Keeper, Popham, the Chief Justice, Worcester, and Knollys were knocking for admittance at Essex House. They were let in readily enough, though their exit was to be less expeditious. To their inquiries as to the meaning of the tumultuous and threatening assembly which was hanging around the courtyard Essex replied that his life was in danger. Then he shut them up and rode off to the City with his adherents, promising shortly to return.

But matters there fell out very differently to what he had imagined. The cry that his life was in peril, which his adherents coupled with that of " God save the Queen!" made no impression on the mob; nor did the vision of the Infanta ascending the throne of England by the machinations of Cecil meet with any better success. Sheriff Smith, on whom, with or without cause, he had relied for effective assistance, gave his troops good cheer, but not the arms of which they stood in need. Whilst the Lord Mayor kept him in play with fair words, Burghley, Cecil's soldier-

[1] *Letters of Cecil to Carew* (Camden Soc., 88), p. 69.

brother, had placarded the City with proclamations
of treason and drawn the nets round the desperate
quarry. There was soon nothing left to him but
retreat. He tried to fight his way home, but Ludgate
was defended, and in the end he had to take boat
at Queen-Hithe. When he reached Essex House
he found that the rats had already begun to fly the
sinking ship. Sir Ferdinando Gorges, who had half
betrayed his leader to Ralegh on the previous day,
had now released the imprisoned councillors and
followed them to Court to get what mercy he might.
There was only one thing left to be done. Essex
set to work to remove the written memorials of the
conspiracy. Among them probably perished that
little black bag for which the Council made afterwards such diligent search,[1] and which is said to
have contained a letter from King James.[2] Had its
presumably compromising contents come to Elizabeth's knowledge it is possible that the Most High
and Mighty Prince would never have sat upon the
throne of England.

Essex House was not defensible.[3] After some wild
talk about dying sword in hand, its owner surrendered
quietly to Nottingham late on Sunday night. Southampton was taken at the same time. It only remained to play out the last act of the drama as
decently as might be. As soon as the principal
conspirators had been examined the two earls were
put on their trial in Westminster Hall. Buckhurst
presided as High Steward, and was attended by the
judges and a jury of twenty-five peers, whom Cecil
had apparently selected after consulting the prece-
dents afforded by the trials of Norfolk and Arundel
in 1571 and 1589.[4] Yelverton and Coke put the case

---

[1] Acts of the Privy Council, 1600–1, p. 166.
[2] Hatf. Cal., xi. p. 69 ; S. P. Dom., Eliz., 279/5 (Exam. of Henry
Cuffe, who affirms this absolutely).
[3] S. P. Dom., Eliz., 278/49, 50.   [4] Hatf. Cal., xi. p. 68.

for the Crown : the examinations of the confederates were read : the narrative of the adventures of Egerton, Worcester, and Popham at Essex House was attested by the Chief Justice.   Essex, having really no available defence, tried to carry the war into the enemy's camp.   He accused Cobham, Cecil, and Ralegh of abusing the Queen's ears with false informations, from which he wished to deliver her, but got no further than a general statement.   Bacon told him, what was palpably the case, that such allegations were but shadows.   He tried to particularise, and asserted that Cecil had told another member of the Council that none but the Spanish Infanta had any claim upon the throne of England.   Cobham was sitting among the jurors : Ralegh was present in command of a detachment of the Queen's Guard : but Cecil had no place in the trial, and Essex may have thought that his unconscionable charge would pass unchallenged.   But if that was so he was quickly undeceived.   Cecil stepped out from behind the arras and, after kneeling to ask the permission of the Court to speak, addressed his accuser face to face.   " The difference between you and me," he said,[1] " is great ; for I speak in the person of an honest man, and you, my Lord, in the person of a traitor : so well I know

---

[1] The account in Camden is slightly but not substantially different from that given in Cobbett's State Trials, from which the above is taken.   Cecil is there made to say : " For wit, wherewith indeed you do abound, I am your inferior ; I am your inferior for nobility ; for I am not in the rank of the prime nobility, yet noble I am.   A sword man I am not, and herein also you go before me.   Yet doth my innocency protect me ; and in this Court I stand an honest man (be)for(e) a delinquent " (Camden *Annals*, iv., 19th February 1601).   In the MS. which Mr. H. L. Stephen has printed in his *State Trials*, vol. iii., Cecil says at one point : " I protest before God I never hated your person, nor envied your greatness, and after you had utterly cast yourself down by your own too much climbing and other follies, so that Her Majesty was highly displeased with you, I continually pitied you, and was a suitor for your restitution, often telling Her Majesty I have verily thought this your cross and affliction might make you fitter to do Her Majesty better service."

you have wit at will. The pre-eminence hath been yours, but I have innocence, truth of conscience, and honesty to defend me against the scandal of slanderous tongues and aspiring hearts ; and I protest before God I have loved your person and justified your virtues : and I appeal to God and the Queen that I told Her Majesty your afflictions would make you a fit servant for her. And had I not seen your ambitious affections inclined to usurpation, I could have gone on my knees to Her Majesty to have done you good ; but you have a sheep's garment in show, and in appearance are humble and religious : but, God be thanked we know you, for indeed your religion appears by Blunt, Davis, and Tresham, your chiefest counsellors for the present, and by promising liberty of conscience hereafter. I stand for loyalty, which I never lost ; you stand for treachery, wherewith your heart is possessed ; and you charge me with high things, wherein I defy you to the uttermost. You, my good lords, counsellors of State, have had many conferences, and I do confess I have said the King of Scots is a competitor, and the King of Spain is a competitor, and you I have said are a competitor ; you would depose the Queen, you would be King of England, and call a Parliament. Ah ! my Lord, were it but your own case, the loss had been the less ; but you have drawn a number of noble persons and gentlemen of birth and quality into your net of rebellion, and their bloods will cry vengeance against you. For my part I vow to God I wish my soul was in heaven and my body at rest, so this had never been."

Bitter at the beginning, the speech by the end had reached a note of lofty pathos ; and there was not a word in the whole that did not possess virtual, though not perhaps literal, truth, for the man who would unmake the Queen's Government was himself a competitor for her throne. Essex was stung to the quick. " I thank God, Mr. Secretary," he retorted,

" for my humbling—that you in the rust of your
bravery came to make your oration against me here
to-day." Cecil repeated the bitter truth. " My
Lord," he said, " I humbly thank God that you did
not take me for a fit companion for you and your
humours ; for if you had you would have drawn me
to betray my Sovereign as you have done." Then,
with rising anger : " But I would have you name the
Counsellor you speak of ; name him, name him,
name him if you dare—I defy you ; name him if
you dare ! " Essex turned towards Southampton
for confirmation of the charge. " Then, my Lord of
Southampton," Cecil continued, " I adjure you by
the duty you owe to God, the loyalty and allegiance
you owe to your Sovereign, by all tokens of true
Christianity, by the ancient friendship and acquaintance once between us, that you name the Counsellor."
Southampton named Essex's uncle, Sir William
Knollys, the Comptroller. He was not present, and
Cecil asked Buckhurst to have him brought. A
gentleman of the bedchamber was thereupon de-
spatched to the Queen. " Let me adjure you,"
Cecil called to him, " that you do not acquaint Mr.
Comptroller with the cause why you come for him."
Knollys presently appeared, and Buckhurst informed
him of the point upon which his evidence was required. " I remember," he replied, " that once in
Mr. Secretary's company there was a book [1] read that
treated of such matters ; but I never did hear Mr.
Secretary use any such words or to that effect."
Cecil expressed his satisfaction at this unqualified
testimony to his innocence. Then, with one of those
sudden uprushes of private feeling which in that age
so often intruded upon public matter, he turned once
more to Essex and said, " I beseech God to forgive
you for this open wrong done unto me as I do
openly pronounce and forgive you from the bottom of

[1] This, it appears, was Doleman's (Father Parsons).

my heart." Essex, who had nothing to forgive, replied with malicious and sarcastic hypocrisy that he also forgave. This was too much for Cecil's patience. "Upon my soul and conscience," he exclaimed, "you are a traitor!" Essex angrily declared that though he might be a traitor in law he was no traitor in conscience. "You do well," commented Cecil sharply, "to deny that last; as you have showed yourself a rebellious traitor, so you should die an impudent traitor." Coke then pressed the prisoner with the weakness of the evidence adduced in support of his charge against the Secretary. Essex bluffed. "Oh, I have other proofs," he said, "if you will needs have me utter them."[1] No one, however, was conscious of the necessity he imputed. The complete collapse of his first allegation had exposed the recklessness of his hatred only too thoroughly.

With the rest of the trial we have no particular concern, and indeed it possesses no particular interest. At the close the jury of peers trooped in to give their decision. One by one, yet with a single voice, they returned the only verdict that was open to them, or to us. Buckhurst bade his old acquaintances submit themselves to the Queen's mercy. Then, with the appalling detail prescribed by custom, he delivered against both the awful sentence of a traitor's death. He supposed, indeed, that mercy might be shown. "No doubt," he told Essex, "you shall find Her Majesty merciful." But the time for mercy had gone by. There is a moment at which everyone must be called upon to bear his own burden. And Elizabeth, though she faltered, did not stay her hand. For Essex had really become, as Ralegh had perceived more than a year before, 'a tyrant.'

A fresh project of conspiracy hastened the execution

[1] These last touches are drawn from the MS. used by Mr. H. L. Stephen in his *State Trials*, iii. pp. 54, 55.

of the sentence. A certain Captain Lee, a military adventurer, who had formerly volunteered services to Cecil and Nottingham for the assassination of Essex, imparted to Sir Robert Cross a scheme for locking the Queen up in her Privy Chamber until she should sign a pardon for Essex. Cross informed against him, and he was hanged in due course. But his action was a new reason for putting the arch-rebel quickly out of the way.

Meanwhile, in prison Essex had entered upon the heavy work of repentance. He had still about some remnants of a noble nature; and one single night in the Tower sufficed to make him regret the asseverations he had so recklessly made at his trial.[1] He besought the Queen to let him see the principal members of the Council,[2] so that he might ease his conscience of its burden of untruth. To Cecil especially he desired to be reconciled. His request was not refused. He received us, Cecil relates, with great penitence for his obstinate denials at the bar. He admitted plotting that with which he had been charged. He altogether withdrew the monstrous fable of Cecil's intrigue on behalf of the Infanta. And of all his enemies he asked forgiveness. A beautiful story,[3] which is not out of keeping with what we know of those times, adds further that he and Cecil took the Sacrament together before they parted.

It was a reconciliation for eternity but not for time. The past could not be undone; and it was in the best interest of the State that treason should meet with its proper reward. Cecil, so far as we know, made no attempt to redeem a second time a man whose restless nature must have been a constant peril to the country. Instead he turned his energies to the

---

[1] S. P. Dom., Eliz., 288/125.
[2] Buckhurst, Egerton, Nottingham, Cecil.
[3] Winwood Memorials, i. p. 299, is the authority.

saving of those numerous noble persons and gentlemen of birth and quality to whose fate he had feel-
ingly alluded at the trial. Southampton's was the
most difficult case of all. " As most of the conspiracies," he writes, " were at Drury House, and he
(Southampton) always chief, it will be hard to save
him, yet I despair not, he being penitent, and the
Queen merciful." [1] Elizabeth seldom if ever shed
a drop of blood that she could afford to spare ; it
was at this point alone that her father's temper was
wanting to her. She sent Essex, whom she had so
deeply loved, to his doom ; Southampton, who had
long been in disgrace, she gave back to a weeping
wife and mother. Sandys too was spared, and wrote
his grateful thanks to Cecil, whom he recognised
as his deliverer.[2] And there were others who to a
greater or less degree owed the mitigation of their
punishment to the Secretary's good offices.[3] His
generosity was, however, no shield against a malignant
tongue. In the fable of Lady Nottingham and the
Ring, which every child effectually learns in the nursery
and every schoolboy ineffectually unlearns at school,
he is allotted the most odious part.[4] It is he who,
after Lady Nottingham has received from Essex in
the Tower the pledge of Elizabeth's undying regard,
prevents her from delivering it to the Queen, and
thus causes his rival's death. Yet no picturesque
justice overtakes him as it overtakes the partner
of his guilt. Whilst Lady Nottingham receives a
good shaking on her death-bed at the hands of the
angry Queen, Cecil is left to flourish like a green bay
tree.

But it is time we were done alike with the miserable story and the old wives' tale which decorates it.

---

[1] S. P. Dom., Eliz., 288/125.   [2] Hatf. Cal., xi. p. 139.
[3] *Ibid.*, p. ix., and see H.M. C. Rep., Rutland MSS., i. p. 376.
[4] *Secret Hist. of the Court of James I.*, vol. i. p. 107. Osborne's
Traditional Mems.

And Cecil's own report will serve as well as any other
to bring it to a conclusion. " The Earl of Essex,"
he told his correspondents,[1] " requested to die
privately in the Tower, and wrote the Queen thanks for
granting his request.   He suffered with great patience
and humility, though the conflict between flesh and
soul appeared in his requiring help in saying ' Our
Father ' and the Creed, which he said was from weakness of the flesh, for no man could pray more Christianly." [1]

[1] S. P. Dom., Eliz., 278/125; cp. Winwood Memorials, i. p. 301.

CHAPTER X

A HOME AND FOREIGN REVIEW

"If we here want the transactions of the Burghleys and the
Walsinghams the loss is in some measure supplied by the
incomparable despatches of the great Earl of Salisbury;
the successor of both in their virtues as well as offices;
to whose memory, if mankind have not paid an equal
regard, it is only because they were unacquainted with
his merits."—SAWYER's Preface to the Winwood Memorials.

THE dramatic unities which at once entangle and
enlighten the paths of history have required that the
tragedy of Essex—or at least Cecil's part in it—should
be played out to its conclusion. But the broad
highway of the nation, crossed and scored though
it was by that ill-omened track, lay, not along any
crooked courses, but between the deep and well-
drawn furrows down which the genius of Elizabeth
and her ministers was patiently guiding it. More
doctrinaire rulers would have allowed the home and
foreign politics of the country to drift into one or
other of the semi-political, semi-religious adventures
of the Reformation. It was the particular merit of
the Cecils that in a time of unexampled change,
when human nature had to a great extent lost its
bearings, they clung tenaciously but not obtrusively
to such solid traditions of the race as they could lay
hold of. For these, having grown up naturally and
in the fulness of time, correspond to the facts of
the situation and will reassert their power as often
as human affairs regain their normal stability. In

nothing was this more apparent than in the sphere of foreign politics. The deep religious antipathy, the prolonged hostilities between England and Spain, had not availed to destroy that fundamental affinity between England and Flanders, which was as much the governing factor in the international situation in the days of Marlborough and of Pitt and of Wellington or the epoch of the Hundred Years War as it has proved in our own.   In all warlike calculations, as a vantage-ground for English armies not less than as a vantage-station for hostile transports and hostile fleets, that which we now call Belgium has always been a subject of anxious and untiring concern to English diplomacy. No great foreign minister, perhaps, has ever been indifferent to its fate.   Burghley, at any rate, kept the Flemish, or, if we prefer to call it so, the Bur-gundian, alliance in view amid conditions of pecu-liar difficulty ; and Cecil did his best to give it back its proper weight in the affairs of Western Europe. It took, indeed, no more than the death of Philip ii. and the assumption, in accordance with the Treaty of Vervins, of an independent sovereignty over the Netherlands by the Archduke Albert and his Spanish bride, for the laws of international gravity to begin to draw the two countries once again together.   Had they been perfectly unshackled, attraction might have operated with rapidity ; as it was, their respective alliances with the United Provinces and with Spain deferred a formal peace until Elizabeth was in her grave.

Two of Burghley's honours had quickly returned to his son—on the 21st May 1599 [1] the Mastership of the Court of Wards, at that time, as Manningham notices,[2] a remarkably potent jurisdiction, and after

[1] Cecil resigned the Chancellorship of the Duchy of Lancaster, which he had held since 8th October 1597 (Sidney Papers, ii. 64), in order to take it.   Apparently the exchange represented a loss of income (Winwood Memorials, i. p. 41).

[2] Manningham's *Diary*, p. 19.

Essex's death, the Chancellorship of Cambridge University in February 1601. But the post of Lord Treasurer had been given to Buckhurst, and Cecil had to wait a decade before he added it to the others. If he lacked the full possession of his father's dignities he obtained all, perhaps more than all, his father's business. Foreign affairs, which Burghley had long directed or controlled, were immediately allotted to his care. And the curious student may pause a moment to reflect that of the three Cecils who have had something to say to the making of their country's history, all have perhaps given their best thought and their best endeavour to diplomatic work. Lacking both the taste and the faculty for popular applause, possessing no extravagant desire to exercise authority or to be called benefactors, they were pre-eminently fitted to ply a trade where reserve and silence are of the essence of the matter, where a man has commonly to be content with his own approval, where the shows and shadows of advantage have often to be sacrificed for the sake of the inchoate or invisible substance. And diplomatic skill must expect no posthumous recognition. A diplomatist's journal may, indeed, live for more than half a century; a diplomatic despatch will scarcely engage attention for so much as half a year. So subtle, so transient, so mobile are the situations with which the art of negotiation has to deal! Satisfying to the brain as is good marksmanship to the eye or dexterous driving to the hand, diplomacy leaves as much or as little trace behind. We see the finished treaty as we see the stricken bird or the goal attained ; but who shall reproduce for us the infinite adroitness, the unfailing nerve, the long apprenticeship to patience, without which these apparently simple results could never have been won ? Even when diversified by anecdote the course of a negotiation like the progress of a parliamentary debate still presents almost insuperable difficulties to the historian. That which was once so full of throbbing excitement and swift anxiety and exasperating disappointment is now a tale where sound and fury are precisely the qualities most evidently desirable.

Among the persons incidentally involved in Essex's rebellion, and mentioned in the last chapter, was a certain Sir Henry Neville, who had held, and indeed still at that time technically enjoyed, the post of the Queen's Ambassador at the Court of France. To him and to his capable Secretary, Ralph Winwood, all students of the period are indebted for certain competent despatches, revealing to those who have the patience to study them the international tangle in the closing years of Elizabeth's reign. Fortunately for the student the Queen instructed Cecil to insist upon each despatch containing at least half a page of Court-gossip,[1] so that the deserts of diplomacy are refreshed from time to time by verdant, if possibly illusory oases, though unfortunately the biographer of Robert Cecil has no concern with these pleasant places, be they substance or only mirage.

It is not too much to say that the first, the second, and the third object of Neville's embassy in 1599 was to extract money out of the King of France. " The best part of your negotiation," writes Cecil simply, "which will best please, is to recover us some money." [2] Unfortunately for Neville nothing in the world was more difficult, for no one knew better than Henry IV. that possession is nine points of the law. Out of the £401,734, 16s. 5½d. which Elizabeth, with exquisite accuracy, computed that he owed her,[3] the King professed that his utmost diligence would only enable him to discharge off-hand the sum of twenty thousand crowns.[4] He was rich, however, in civilities, in pro-

[1] Winwood Memorials, i. p. 167.

[2] Ibid., Cecil to Neville, 14th July 1599.

[3] Ibid., p. 29.   [4] Ibid., pp. 35, 117.

mises, in compliments, in all that smoothed delay
and smothered obligation. Neville was not deceived.
Not good-nature, nor gratitude, but reason of State,
he told his chief, settles the policy that is here
pursued.[1]

The pivot of Western Europe at the time he wrote
was the little marquisate of Saluzzo. Long in dispute
between the King of France and the Duke of Savoy,
it had been seized by the latter during the French
Wars of Religion. Henry iv. was now strong enough
to recover what Henry iii. had been too weak to
retain, provided that Spanish interference—a not improbable contingency, as the Duchess of Savoy was a
Spanish princess—could be averted. It was therefore desirable to keep the Spaniards busy, and no
countries had shown themselves more excellently
qualified for that purpose than England and the
United Provinces. The latter wasted the Spanish
armies ; the former overthrew the Spanish fleets.
There was no surer preparation for the coming glory
of France than the progressive exhaustion of Spain.
Neville saw that if anything was to be got out of
Henry, the question of Saluzzo must be turned to
account while there was time. He wrote, therefore,
to Cecil [2] to know the Queen's real intentions. Did
she, or did she not, wish to come to terms with the
Spaniards ? If she did, English trade, which was in a
precarious condition, could resume its ancient market
in Flanders. If not, every effort must be made to
obtain some measure of free trade with France.
And this he thought could be secured, together with a
discharge of the French debt, by dangling over Henry's
head the prospect of an Anglo-Spanish peace, which
would enable Spanish energies to be diverted towards
Savoy.

Cecil told him [3] that peace would be welcome
enough but that everything really depended upon the

[1] Winwood Memorials, i. p. 34.   [2] *Ibid.*, p. 47.   [3] *Ibid.*, p. 56.

conditions upon which it could be secured. Meanwhile, Neville's policy, on his own showing, was to use the notion as a lever to hasten Henry's halting affections. The Treaty of Blois, which Burghley had negotiated with Charles ix. in 1572, and which had been subsequently renewed by Henry iii., would furnish a good basis for a civil contract with France. For treaties not conceived in the interest of trade, as Cecil told him in a later letter, the Queen had no particular love, ' seeing there was so small assurance by them.'[1]

In accordance with the first part of this scheme Edmondes was sent into the Spanish Netherlands to propagate a gospel of peace, and Henry was invited to show his benevolent approval by affording the English and Spanish Commissioners a place of meeting at Boulogne. The prospects at best were not very hopeful, for the Spaniards had been asking Elizabeth for the surrender of the cautionary towns, besides the abandonment of all commercial intercourse with the Dutch. From this position they had apparently receded before they got to Boulogne;[2] but, as the Archduke and the Queen were more or less anxious to agree, something might still have been effected had not Villeroy taken care to drop a fruitful apple of discord into the midst of the conference. Before he proceeded to Boulogne, Neville had had an interview with the King, in which the latter dwelt upon some of the obvious difficulties of an accommodation. There was sure, he said, amongst other things to be trouble about precedence. Neville asked how this had been arranged at Vervins. The King said the question had hardly come up, as meetings were held under the presidency of the Legate, and went on to recommend that in the present case it should be determined by lot. Then Villeroy, who was standing by, interposed by telling Neville that the English, who had enjoyed precedence until the time of the Emperor Charles v. and had never relinquished it, would by such a course put in doubt that of which they were really in possession.[1] " I am of opinion," wrote Cecil sardonically, in reply to Neville's request for instructions, " that Monsieur Villeroy would have us fall out at the beginning [2] because we should never agree at the end."[3]

In point of fact the Commissioners never got to work at all. From the middle of May to the end of July (1600) they debated etiquette at the delectable seaside town to which they had been sent. The Spaniards supported their claim to priority by alleging that their master derived his title from the blood-royal of the Goths, and by the contention that the shape of their peninsula bore a resemblance to the head of a body. Elizabeth's representatives were instructed to reply that this geographical argument was the fabrication of an idle brain, and, as for the Goths, that the Queen took her descent from the Kings of Britain. Cecil further amused himself by sending some extracts from old authors to bolster up the English contention.[4] But the burden of his letter was to the effect that the Queen, who, as Cecil thought,[5] had already stood ' somewhat too long ' upon her dignity, wished them to cut short all this solemn rubbish and get to work. To that end she proposed that they should ' fall to some indifferent composition, with protestation on either side that no side should be prejudiced.' [6]

She might have spared her pains. The Spaniards still bristled with etiquette. Nothing could be done except these consequential irrelevancies were first resolved. The Commissioners had no course left

---

[1] Winwood Memorials, i. p. 184.

[2] In the original, ' meeting.' I have ventured to recast the epigram so as to give it its proper values.

[3] Winwood Memorials, i. p. 185.   [4] Ibid., p. 205.

[5] Letters of Cecil to Carew (Camden Soc., 88), p. 20.

[6] Winwood Memorials, i. p. 204.

them but to separate ; which they did, not wholly
in ignorance of the fact that they cut a very sorry
figure in the eyes of Europe.[1] Henry meantime was
completing his preparations for the discomfiture of
Savoy, and with the failure of the conference carried
his arms over the border. He might have written
the history of the ensuing campaign in the terse and
memorable language of Cæsar's famous despatch.
By February all was over and Bresse and Bugey had
been ceded to France in exchange for Saluzzo. Cecil's
trump card had slipped out of his hand.

Peace or money—it was still the old dilemma—
and the less Elizabeth could get the one the more
eagerly she clutched at the other. Her hope of
untying the purse-strings of her neighbours depended
in the main on an acceptance of herself as the champion of Europe against Spanish aggression, to whose
equipment everyone ought to contribute. Unfortunately no one saw her quite as she saw herself.
Winwood, who had become chargé d'affaires during
Neville's absence at Boulogne, and who was continued
in that position after Neville became implicated in
Essex's rebellion, tried in vain to get at the ambassadors of the wealthy Italian States who were to be met
with at the Court of France. Neither the Floren-
tines nor the Venetians saw the fun of financing
Elizabeth's armies on the shadowy assumption that
by so doing they were keeping the Spaniards out of
Italy. They gave fair words but doubtless buttoned
up their pockets the tighter. Even a loan was not
to be thought of.[2]

The treaty of commerce with France fared no
better than the financial negotiations. All that
Winwood could extract in addition to another
beggarly fifty thousand crowns in repayment of
debt [3] was a permission for the English merchants

---

[1] Winwood Memorials, i. p. 225.   [2] Ibid., pp. 259, 269.
[3] Ibid., p. 395.

to recover their cloth, which had been seized in accordance with the recent order in Council prohibiting its import.[1] Nor did a conference, which met in London in 1602, under Cecil's own eye, to discuss as well the naval depredations alleged by each party against the other as the Customs duties, bring the dispute much nearer settlement. English merchants were not to be required to pay locally more than the authorised tariff prescribed for the whole kingdom; but any reduction of the imports was deferred to a more convenient season,[2] and in the next reign these were still under a ban.[3] As to the phantom alliance against Spain it was not made plain in what manner Henry's amiable wish that 'something might be done,' that there should be 'a common action' and 'a great design,' was going to be put into execution. "There riseth no fruit of such discourses," Cecil wrote tartly,[4] for of the three kinds of effective assistance which, as the Secretary added, really lay open to the King—the maintenance of an army, the advance of a subsidy, and the accommodation of his diplomatic moves to the advantage of England and the United Provinces and the disadvantage of Spain—Henry showed not the faintest inclination to afford any one.

Commercial negotiations with Denmark went the same way as those with France. There were three well-defined points of discussion — de vectigalibus de piscatione, et de depredationibus—upon which the Danish Commissioners who were sent to Bremen informed Lord Eure, and Herbert, and Dr. Dunn that they were empowered to treat;[5] but, as their notion of diplomacy was always to take and not to give, the colloquy was conducted under difficulties. Apparently the Danes would not reduce by one jot or tittle the heavy duties that were levied in the Sound,

---

[1] Winwood Memorials, i. p. 305.　　[2] Ibid., p. 396.
[3] Ibid., ii. pp. 38, 42.　　[4] Ibid., i. 395.　　[5] Hatf. Cal., xii. p. 472.

though these were to be more clearly specified and defined. As to a licence for Englishmen to fish on the coasts of Norway and in the main ocean, over which the Danes claimed a rather insolent control, it was to be conceded subject to the admission of certain royal privileges. Fishing off Iceland had to be abandoned.[1]

Ireland, then, as so long afterwards, a kind of middle distance between home and foreign affairs, was of necessity constantly in Cecil's mind. He had no time, and perhaps no great ability, to write interesting letters, but his correspondence with his great friend, Sir George Carew, the Governor of Munster, lets us into the secrets of his despondent hours. " God knoweth," he writes, " I labour like a pack-horse, and now that I see how troublesome it is to work things as they should be, I vow to God I wish you out of that country and myself a ploughman rather than to contemplate the vexation which that kingdom will bring upon us." [2] The truth was that the Irish rebels — Tyrone in the north, James FitzThomas, the ' Sugane Earl,' in the south—were costing the English Government £300,000 a year at the least.[3] Elizabeth was both reasonably angry and unreasonably difficult. It was only with great pressure that Cecil could get her to consent to the despatch of James Fitzgerald, the rival claimant to the allegiance of the Geraldines, and then with no more than the promise of a patent of earldom in the future.[4] " The Queen," wrote her Minister,[5] " hath been most hardly drawn unto it—and hath laid it in my dish a dozen times :—' Well I pray God you and Carew be not deceived.' " The ' Sugane Earl,' however, was defeated [6] before his rival was in the field ; but Tyrone

<hr>

[1] Hatf. Cal., xii. p. 500.
[2] *Letters from Cecil to Carew* (Camden Soc., 88), p. 26.
[3] *Ibid.*, p. 148.　　　　　　　[4] *Ibid.*, p. 38.
[5] *Ibid.*, p. 43.　　　　　　　[6] October 1600.

remained, a centre of the liveliest solicitude to the English Government and of the liveliest satisfaction to its foes. Out of the emptiness of his exchequer Philip III. somehow contrived to equip an expedition which landed at Kinsale on 21st September 1601, under the command of Don Juan de Aguilar. The crisis was serious, and, had the Spanish commander met with the response he anticipated, might have been alarming. But, as he afterwards confided to Mountjoy, the Irish were so poor a lot—so inconstant and irresolute—that he believed when the Tempter showed our Lord all the kingdoms of the world he had kept Ireland concealed, ' because it was fit for none but himself.'[1] The jest caused Cecil some amusement,[1] for the problem of ' the distressful country ' was already a millstone slung around the necks of English statesmen. Mountjoy, however, whom Naunton is pleased to regard as Cecil's jackal,[2] had at last got the island under some measure of control ; and the defeat of Don Juan in the end of 1601 brought in its wake the submission of Tyrone, though not until a year and a half later. For Cecil had found the Queen singularly reluctant to grant a pardon which might be construed into a precedent for treachery, or to give to Mountjoy those plenipotentiary powers which Essex had abused ;[3] and the conditions which she insisted upon probably delayed the peace.

The renewal of the Spanish War drove Elizabeth once more to the unwelcome necessity of summoning a Parliament. She desired that its deliberations might be brief and confined to the purpose which she had in view. " The chief intent and scope thereof,"

---

[1] Winwood Memorials, i. p. 378.

[2] Naunton, *Frag. Reg. Mountjoy* : " And so I come to his (M.'s) dear friend in Court, Master Secretary Cecil, whom in his long absence from Court he adored as his saint . . . well-knowing that it lay in his power and by a word of his mouth to make or to mar him."

[3] Add. MSS., 31,022/109.

says D'Ewes of Cecil's official speech, " appeared to
aim at the setting forth of two things especially :
the first the danger the kingdom stood in, in respect
of the power and malice of the Spaniard ; the second
that timely provision of treasure might be made for
the prevention." The Irish crisis was, in fact, at its
height when Parliament met. The ' four thousand
soldiers,' the captain ' valiant, expert and hardy,' to
whom the speaker alluded, were still in occupation
of Kinsale. Ostend, the commercial key of the Low
Countries, was threatened. A Catholic rising was to
be apprehended at home from those who had been
absolved from their allegiance by the papal bulls.
What the representatives of the English people were
asked to do would be done *pro aris et focis*. " Yea,
we do it," he continued, " for a prince that desireth
not to draw anything extraordinary out of the coffers
of her subjects. She selleth her land to defend us,
she supporteth all the neighbouring princes to gain
their amities and establish our long peace ; not
these five, or seven, or ten years, but forty-three
years for all our prosperities. I hope I shall not see
her funeral upon which may be written, Hic solum
restat victrix Orientis. And I pray God I may
not. What we freely give unto her she living be-
stows it to our good, and dying doubtless will leave
it to our profit. Thus have I out of mine own
genius for mine own part delivered unto you what
I know." [1] A few days later Cecil went more into
detail : " The Queen hath occasion to use, as
divers in this House do know, three hundred thousand
pound before Easter. How this shall be raised and
gathered, that is the question. . . . I will by the
leave of a worthy person who sits by me and knows
these things better than I do, yield a particular
account of the state itself. First, the last whole subsidy . . . came not to above four score thousand

[1] D'Ewes, Tuesday, 3rd November 1601.

pounds ; the subsidy of the clergy twenty thousand pound, the double-fifteenth three score thousand pounds ; all which is eight score thousand pounds. Since my Lord of Essex's going into Ireland, she hath spent three hundred thousand pound. So the Queen is behind one hundred and forty thousand pound. Thus we refer the matter to your judicious consideration. We only shew you the present state of the Queen and her affairs, wishing no man to look that we should give advice what is to be done, as though you yourselves, who are the wisdom of the land, could neither direct yourselves nor . . . judge of the necessity of the State." [1]

A grant was clearly inevitable, but the Committee were at issue upon its form. Our modern dilemmas of principle were already familiar. Should men of small means—the ' three-pound men '—be called upon to pay, or should the tax be confined to ' the four-pound men,' and these be made to pay double, with a progressive graduation for those whose incomes were larger ? " The most voices concluded," so Cecil tells the House in his summary of the debates in Committee, " that there should be no exception of the three-pound men, because according to their rate some were sessed under value ; besides, separation might breed emulation, suspicion of partiality and confusion." And this was his own judgment. " It was said by a member of the House," he went on, " that he knew some poor people pawned their pots and pans to pay the subsidy. It may be you dwell where you see and hear ; I dwell where I hear and believe. And this I know that neither pot nor pan, nor dish nor spoon, should be spared when danger is at our elbows. But he that spake this, in my conscience spake it not to hinder the subsidy, or the greatness of the gift, but to show the poverty of some sessed, and by sparing them to yield them relief. But

[1] D'Ewes' *Journals*, 7th November 1601.

by no means I would have the three-pound men exempted, because I do wish the King of Spain might know how willing we are to sell all in defence of God's religion, our Prince and country. I have read," he added, " when Hannibal resolved to sack Rome, he dwelt in the cities adjoining and never feared or doubted of his enterprise, till word was brought him that the maidens, ladies and women of Rome sold their ear-rings, jewels and all their necessaries to maintain war against him."

Upon this four subsidies—eight-fifteenths on the annual value of land and eight-tenths on movables— was voted. Ralegh, however, took some exception to Cecil's argument about the pots and pans. It would, he said, argue poverty in the State if it were known. Cecil hastened to explain. " As for that . . . I said . . . I say it is true and yet I am mistaken : I say it is good the Spaniards should know how willing we are to sell our pots and pans and all we have to keep him out ; yet I do not say it is good he should know we do sell them : that is, I would have him know our willingness to sell (though there be no need) but not of our poverty in selling or of any necessity we have to sell them, which I think none will do, neither shall need to do.' "

Elizabeth had got what she wanted, but she was not to escape without payment. The practice of granting monopolies had been advancing by leaps and bounds, and was no doubt become an intolerable evil. Cecil and Buckhurst had already put their heads together to promote its partial extinction.[1] But the Parliament of 1601 had set its heart upon carrying the affair a good distance farther upon the road to remedy. The difficulty, as Cecil plainly told the House, was that the question trenched upon that of the royal prerogative. " This dispute," he said, " draws two great things in question : first the Prince's power ;

[1] Hatf. Cal., xi. p. 324.

secondly the freedom of Englishmen. I am born an Englishman and am a fellow-member of this House ; I would desire to live no day in which I should detract from either. I am servant unto the Queen, and before I would speak or give consent to a case that should debase her prerogative or abridge it I would wish my tongue cut out of my head." Then, after arguing that the proper procedure was by petition, not by bill, " I had rather," he concluded, " all the patents were destroyed than Her Majesty should lose the hearts of so many subjects as is pretended. I will tell you what I think of these monopolies : I take them to be of three natures. Some of a free nature and good : some void of themselves : some both good and void. For the first, when the Prince dispenses with a penal law that is left to the alteration of sovereignty, I think it powerful and irrevocable. For the second, as to grant that which taketh from the subject his birthright, such men as desire these kind of patents I account them misdoers and wilful and wicked offenders. Of the third sort is the licence for the matter of cards, etc. And therefore I think it were fit to have a new commitment to consider what Her Majesty may grant, what not ; what course we shall take and upon what points." [1]

It was an eminently judicious speech and thoroughly in keeping with the whole spirit of Tudor policy—that policy which, under arbitrary forms and by arbitrary methods, accommodated itself so readily to the temper of English gentlemen. There was, indeed, every call for a calm and steady hand at the helm. The House was profoundly agitated by the fear that in the end the abuse would evade its grasp. In all his time Cecil told the members he had never seen it in such confusion,[2] and he implored them to temper their zeal with discretion. A return of persons

---

[1] D'Ewes' *Journals*, 23rd November 1601.
[2] *Ibid.*, 24th November 1601.

in possession of monopolies had meanwhile been presented to the Committee entrusted with the subject; and on the next day the Speaker and Cecil came down charged with a gracious message from the Queen. Elizabeth had, in fact, had the good sense to see that she must give way, and had acted accordingly. The Speaker began by relating how he had found her in a state of hot indignation at the oppressions of which the monopolists had been guilty. Then Cecil followed with a promise that all monopolies arising from grants in Council should be withdrawn, and the rest be left to establish themselves at the common law. So the controversy terminated with mutual expressions of esteem and courtesy between Elizabeth and her people, and Cecil, who was, in fact, Leader of the House, deserves the credit accorded to a successful political strategist. During the remainder of the session the only other important speech that he made was against the repeal of the Statute of Tillage, which required a certain number of acres to be kept under the plough. " I do not dwell in the country," he told the House; " I am not acquainted with the plough ; but I think that whosoever doth not maintain the plough, destroys the Kingdom." [1]

His financial pre-occupations were by no means confined to public affairs. Three of the most expensive pursuits in the world are building houses, playing at cards, and entertaining the Sovereign. He was doing them all between 1600 and 1603. Besides some landscape gardening at Theobalds,[2] besides the purchase of the Dorsetshire estate of Rushmore,[3] Cecil House was rising in the Strand on the site now occupied by the Hotel Cecil—a quadrangular structure of brick with turrets at the corners,[4] the doors and

---

[1] D'Ewes' *Journals*, 9th December 1601.
[2] Hatf. Cal., xii. pp. 316, 407.   [3] *Ibid.*, x. p. 273.
[4] See the view taken by Hollar in 1630 in Wilkinson's *Londina Illustrata*, i. [98].

windows framed with stone, and the whole, of course, conceived in that style of which its founder left a more fortunate memorial at Hatfield, and its foster-father, Sir Walter Cope, at Holland House. It has long passed away with its compeers—with Durham Place and the rest of the great riverside palaces; with Bedford House and Worcester House, which flanked it; with all the rich vigour of the England that once lay between Westminster and Blackfriars, and which we recover now only here and there in the names of obscure streets. The silver-streaming Thames, running softly between the banks where Spenser walked, no longer carries the pageantry or the life, scarcely even the fortune of the great city. Fashion has shifted once and again—to Soho, to Mayfair, to Belgravia—since Salisbury House was pulled down,[1] not so long after Thomas Hobbes had found a lodging there. We scan the river-bank in vain for the stately courts and sloping lawns and pleasant terraces, of which the back view of the colleges at Cambridge may, perhaps, still convey to us some imperfect suggestion. Only in the dun fog of winter, when London is most truly itself, do the ghosts return; and to the seeing eye the England of Elizabeth rises once more among the mists—a phantasy of dream-palaces and fairy-gardens, a shadow-world that but just escapes our clear vision, whose inhabitants, noble and gentle and simple, glide away in the gloom towards the Tower and the Mermaid and Bartholomew Fair, and whose spectral homes in the returning light of common day turn out to be no more than the Frankenstein's monster of an age of prose and comfort.

Cecil, no doubt, did his building as cheaply as he could. Of one or two bargains the record remains. The Bishop of London let him have, 'without price or measure,' some surplus Caen-stone which had been

[1] In 1695.

bought for the restoration of St. Paul's,[1] and Lady Sidney gave him the run of some wrought stone at Penshurst suitable for his purpose.[2] But Cope insisted on his having gilt hangings for the gallery,[3] which were hard to come by, and must have been expensive in proportion. And not everyone was generous and friendly. The eastern prospect was badly obstructed by a tree growing in the garden of Worcester House. Cecil offered his neighbour's agent a hundred pounds to get it cut down, and the bargain was concluded with Lord Worcester's knowledge. The tree then disappeared, but was shortly after replaced by a substantial brick building which shut out the view more effectually than before.[4]

Nor were the workmen all they might have been. Harassed employers of labour in our own day will find a mild consolation in reading the report which Thomas Wilson, Cecil's agent, sends his master as late as 1605. " I take recreation," writes that genial satirist, " in beholding the going-forwards of your Lordship's building, where I may see labourers work as lazily as myself, whose art in close [5] loitering requireth a surveyor with as many eyes as Argus. They creep about their business so like snails that I am afraid the house will not be ready by the time appointed." [6]

Altogether the house must have been a very expensive affair, and the house-warming only less so. Elizabeth, after postponing her visit twice owing to the bad weather, appeared on the 2nd December 1602 and was entertained, for almost, if not quite, the last time in her life, with the quaint conceits and rich gifts and astonishing compliments in which she took delight.[7] Cope's part in the construction and furnish-

---

[1] Hatf. Cal., xi. p. 362.	[2] *Ibid.*, p. 358.	[3] *Ibid.*, p. 397.
[4] Thornbury, *Old and New London*, iii. p. 101.
[5] *i.e.* secret.	[6] Hatf. MSS., 112/2.
[7] Williams, *Letters of John Chamberlain*, lvii.; Manningham's *Diary*, pp. 99, 100.

ing of the place may be estimated from the fact that he was allowed a share in doing the honours.[1] What the entertainment cost we do not know, but only six weeks later Cecil is plunged in reckless extravagance. " There hath been great golden play," reports John Chamberlain in his registry of Court-gossip : " wherein Mr. Secretary lost better than £800 in one night and as much more at other times."[2] Then, besides, he had lent £4000 to Ralegh in May 1602,[3] which it is improbable he ever set eyes upon again. It is no great wonder—despite the £1600 which his inheritance was estimated to produce, his official income, his farm of silks and velvets,[4] and the considerable though greatly exaggerated income which he derived from his Mastership of the Court of Wards[5]—that he was pressed for money and that we find his agents negotiating loans with opulent aldermen.[6]

Like some other people in straitened circumstances he cherished hopes of a gold-mine ;[7] but there is every reason to suspect that the gold-mine in Scotland turned out a castle in Spain. Spanish ships, however, were not half so likely to prove Spanish castles. In some chance encounter with a Spanish transport, bearing home the spices of the Indies or laden with Peruvian silver, we recognise the South African Rand or the Valley of the Yukon of the sixteenth century. Men took shares and sold interests in these ' mercantile adventures ' just as we shift stocks and lay out capital. So, in March 1602, Cecil is to be found buying a fourth part of the ship *Refusal*, then at sea in cause of reprisal, and of the prizes and gains that have been or shall be taken during the voyage.[8] So, a year later, he takes the

---

[1] *Letters of John Chamberlain*, lviii.   [2] *Ibid.*, p. 172.
[3] Hatf. Cal., xii. p. 163.   [4] *Ibid.*, p. 318.
[5] This was estimated by the Venetian Envoy at £10,000 (Venet. Cal., 22nd May 1603).
[6] Hatf. Cal., xi. pp. 112, 397 ; xii. p. 408.
[7] Hatf. MSS., 118/54.   [8] Hatf. Cal., xii. p. 83.

larger risk in a maritime venture in which Cobham and Ralegh are also interested.[1]

Such practices, even though the Queen herself had participated in them and they had been officially recognised by an order in Council of 1585,[2] were apparently liable to criticism.   Cecil knew that public opinion never dealt too kindly with him.   " I pray you," he writes to Ralegh, " as much as may be conceal our adventure, at the least my name above any other.   For though I thank God I have no other meaning than becometh an honest man in any of my actions, yet that which were another man's pater-noster would be accounted in me a charm."   The last sentiment was natural enough and human enough in the circumstances.   Yet we may happen to reflect that it effectually marks the writer off from that band of high and noble spirits who, neither being subject to public fear nor having hope of attracting public love, become at length, by the very splendour of their indifference to criticism, the object of public pride.

[1] Hatf. Cal., xii. p. 599.

[2] See the chapter (xxi) on Reprisals and Privateering in Cheyney's *History of England from the Defeat of the Armada, etc.*

CHAPTER XI

THE SUCCESSION

"Yet God for us did so provide,
   And held us up when we did slyde ;
And, as Eliza she is gone,
He sent another to ease our mone.
King James is hee, by whose sweete breath
We still possesse Queen Elzabeth."

Shirburn Ballads, lxxvii.

WE are now come to that point in Cecil's life from which his statesmanship and character alike will largely be judged. The great crisis which neither the maledictions of the Pope, nor the armadas of the King of Spain, nor the conspiracies of Mary Stuart and her adherents had been able to bring about, was evidently approaching by the act and in the providence of God. An event long probable was now become certain. And with that certainty measures which must once have been open to reproach and condemnation took on the colour and defence of necessity. Robert Cecil had to consider two things : on the one side, the obligations which loyalty, gratitude, and affection imposed upon him in respect to the Queen ; on the other, the peace and welfare and security of the country whose citizen he was. It would have been happy for him if these two responsibilities had entailed precisely the same course of action. But they did not do so, and a moral and political problem of the first magnitude at once arose.

Elizabeth had long and rightly refused to determine her successor. There was a time in her life when such a course would merely have thickened the plots that hung like threatening swords above her head. And to the end of her days it remained true that the appointment of an heir would have involved the disappointment and consequent disaffection of some part of her subjects. Doubtless private feelings fortified her legitimate objections. Doubtless to acknowledge the claim of one who was no child of hers would have been to set a new sun in the heavens, by whose advance she must have measured the course of her own declining hours. And, in spite of Bacon's opinion to the contrary, there may have been, too, a moral shrinking from the admission that time and the things of time were for her almost gone ; that the reign, whose greatness she must at least in part have perceived, had slipped on to its latter end. She was a brave and a high-hearted woman, but religion formed no great part of her nature, and she can hardly have failed to be sensible that the grave contained little work, or device, or wisdom, or knowledge for which her own life had been in any sort a preparation.

However that was, no thought of laying the matter plainly before his mistress appears to have crossed Cecil's mind. Never easy to deal with, she had not grown less difficult with age. He told Howard of a sharp passage he had with her when, set on by his opponents, she taxed him with the poverty of the country, the expense of the Irish War, and the general discontent.[1] He knew her too well to attempt controversy on more delicate subjects. Yet something had to be done, if only because others would act if he did not, and that, which could be accomplished with prudence, be attempted by a headstrong and disastrous rashness. Precipitancy might ruin James's cause, as it had come near doing in the affair of Essex. He himself and he alone was in a position to effect what was really needful.

[1] Hailes, *Secret Corresp. of Sir R. Cecil*, p. 75.

Among the fourteen candidates to the English throne, of whom genealogy speaks, only four secured any serious attention—the Infanta, Lord Hertford, Lady Arabella Stuart, and King James VI. To the first, who drew a shadowy claim from John of Gaunt, belonged besides whatever title could be derived from Mary Stuart's will ; and her candidature was consequently calculated to satisfy those English Catholics who desired the presence of Spanish armies on English soil. Lord Hertford, on the other hand, had the semblance of being the heir-at-law. He was the son of Catharine Grey and the representative of the right of the house of Suffolk to succeed under the provisions of the remarkable will by which Henry VIII., acting with parliamentary sanction, preferred the descendants of a younger sister before those of an elder. But his mother's marriage lay under a cloud, since Archbishop Parker had declared it void for lack of witnesses ; and public feeling, whilst it did not contest the right of Catharine to gratify her legitimate affections, seized upon the convenient flaw to exclude her son from the succession.

In fact, the instinct of the people was governed, not by legal form, but by moral force. The great-grandchildren of Margaret Tudor, once Queen of Scotland and afterwards Lady Angus, appeared to them to possess a claim which neither laws nor kings could overthrow; and the controversy upon the succession had gradually narrowed to a contest between the two lines of her descendants. Of these James, beyond all doubt, represented the elder branch. But a second legal impediment seemed to block his road. Feudalism was not yet dead ; under feudal law no alien could inherit English land ; and a Scotsman appeared, therefore, to be debarred from occupying a position which theoretically involved a property in the whole land of the realm. Upon this slender quibble Arabella's fragile title was built up.

But worse claims than hers have offered fairer prospects ; and, if she had been an abler and a more enterprising woman than she was, she might have made an effective bid for the crown.   The Venetian Secretary, indeed, credits her with exalted notions, including a firm belief in her own right to the throne.[1] But, in fact, her immediate aims were bounded by a not unnatural desire to escape from the keeping of Bess of Hardwicke ; and the curious attempt, which she made in the last year of Elizabeth to marry Lord Hertford's eldest son, seems to have been prompted by no more ambitious motive.   If, indeed, we do not take our eyes off Arabella herself, it is plausible to argue that the uncontested accession of James was an inconsiderable achievement.   But the real importance of Arabella lay in the fact that she provided a likely focus of disaffection. What Cecil did was to hold together, or at least to hold down, the English magnates, so that the rightful heir enjoyed, beforehand, as good an assurance of his heritage, and, in the event, as fair an entry upon it as a king could look for.

It was, doubtless, a simplifying factor in Cecil's problem that the chiefs of the house of Howard thought as he did about the succession.   With one member of that family he was, indeed, destined in the coming reign to be closely, if not affectionately, associated.   In Camden's courtly metaphor Salisbury and Northampton represented " the two prime wheels " which drove James's " triumphant chariot." And we may, without impropriety, take a passing glance at a figure which must from time to time pass across the background of our stage.   Lord Henry Howard, as he was at this time, has come down to us with the character and reputation of one of the bad men of history. The devil is said, at least by the ingenuous, to be not altogether so black as he is painted ; and Howard

[1] Venet. Cal., ix. p. 541.

may have added to the wit and scholarship he undoubtedly possessed some amiable virtues of which
there is no sufficient remembrance.[1] But to all
appearance it was not so.   To all appearance, at any
rate, he was the possessor of just those kind of defects
which the human race in self-defence has learned to
reckon some of the least pardonable.   To all appearance he was shifty, tortuous, a master of dark counsels
and creeping schemes ;   one of the shrewdest of the
children of this world, yet not unacquainted with the
language of the children of light.   Cecil, if we may
guess his sentiments from a curious letter in which he
has been at pains to delete the epithet ' worthy '
from before Howard's name, held the man at this
time in no great esteem.[2]   But circumstances made
him a valuable, if not an indispensable, auxiliary.
He had been numbered amongst the friends of Essex.
And whilst in one hand he held the broken thread
of Essex's intrigue with Scotland, with the other he
seemed to reassure the Catholic interest in England,
to which he was attached alike by family ties and
religious persuasions.   Above all, he enjoyed the
hearty recommendation of the King of Scots.[3]

The intimacy, then, between James and Cecil
sprang up on the ruins of Essex's failure.   How they
had regarded one another earlier may be judged by a
letter from the Master of Gray, who many years before
had been the Scottish Ambassador in England :—

" Of one thing I am sorry, that your Majesty should speak
so hardly of Mr. Secretary Cecil, for that you allege my Lord
his father cut your Mother's throat.   I am assured your Majesty
knoweth that I know more in that nor any Scottish or English
living, the Queen excepted, and that for I do remember your
Majesty of a note I gave you in that matter ;   that the Earl of
Leicester or Sir Francis Walsingham were only the cutters of
her throat and inducers of Davison to do as he did.   I take on

---

[1] Goodman says a good word for him.
[2] *Corresp. of James VI. with Sir R. Cecil*, p. 8.
[3] *Ibid.*, p. 1.

my conscience it was far from the Queen or his father's mind that she should die when she died as I have yet some witnessing in the world. And, Sir, I assure you this that, if your Majesty shall fall again in good course with the Queen, Mr. Secretary will prove as good a friend as you have in all England. Let them inform you of him as they please, but think never to have him otherways, for he has sworn to me that if he knew to be the greatest subject that ever England bred, he shall never serve any other prince after the Queen. And I think if it were not for love and obligation he would never endure the excess trouble he hath presently, nor almost is it possible for him to serve so ' penibly,' for, albeit he has a very well composed mind, yet the ability of the body is so discrepant that it cannot correspond the capacity of the mind." [1]

The letter is worth citation, not alone because it defines the relative positions in December 1600, but because it is an effective protest against the idea that Cecil, beneath an affectation of patriotism, entertained an immoderate affection for power. No doubt, as we shall see, he resented any attempt to undermine his legitimate influence upon the course and conduct of affairs. But, as Gray intimated, it requires a full-blooded vitality and a sound digestion to keep alive the desire of great place after a man has come to middle life and tasted to the full the so-called sweets of office. Cecil was constantly overworked and constantly ill. The reader will remember his despondent letter to Carew, quoted in the preceding chapter. It is worth while to lift once again the phantom veil of bliss that shrouded the successful Minister. " Mr. Hicks," he was writing to that faithful friend in October 1598, " my head was in such pain when I sent to you that [2] I was fain to will Percival to write." [3] " Mr. Secretary, almost tired with perpetual labour and pains," Rowland Whyte tells Sir Robert Sidney in the following year, " desires leave to go to Theobalds for six or seven days, but I believe it will not be granted, for he cannot be spared." [4]

---

[1] Hatf. Cal., x. p. 414.　　　[2] In the original, ' as.'
[3] Lansdowne MSS., 87/30.　　　[4] Collins, Sidney Papers, ii. p. 119.

" Some ten or twelve days since," writes Chamberlain
to Carleton in November 1602, " we were half afraid
of Mr. Secretary, upon a sudden accident that came
by a cold with a swelling in his throat, or ' squinance,'
which hindered him (so) that he could neither swallow
nor scant breath, but the danger lasted not long, for,
upon letting blood and some other applications, he
presently mended." [1]

So much, then, may be said in defence of the
necessity of action, and of the integrity of Cecil's
purpose. His own further statement of his motives
will be read in due course, as we pass in review the
method and manner of his procedure.

King James's ambassadors, the Earl of Mar and
the titular Abbot of Kinloss, arrived in England by
the end of March 1601.[2] Shrewd observers like Tobie
Matthew and Thomas Phelippes took note of their
quality and drew the conclusion that some greater
matter was in hand than complimentary congratulations to the Queen upon her deliverance from the
late rebellion.[3] James had, in fact, instructed them
to feel the pulse of public feeling. He was not yet
wholly free of the impression, which Essex had
doubtless implanted in his mind, that a serious breach
existed between Elizabeth and her subjects ; and he
wished to discover whether the disaffection was
related rather to the Sovereign or to her Ministers.
The Ambassadors were, besides, to remind the Queen
of her engagement to do nothing to his prejudice in
the matter of the succession and to make a suit for
the lands of his grandmother, Lady Lennox. But

---

[1] S. Williams, *Letters of John Chamberlain*, lvi.

[2] S. P. Dom., Eliz., 279/36 and 53.

[3] A letter from Cecil to Gray (MSS., 213/114), which has been lately
added to the Hatfield Collection, throws a little more light on the
course of the embassy and on Elizabeth's knowledge of what had
been going on. Elizabeth, Cecil says, was ' infinitely distasted '
because the ambassadors were reserved in confessing the traffic
between James and Essex.

the chief of their commission was to Cecil, whom they were to see privately and to coerce by promises of future favour or threats of future disgrace. For, as James told them in words that have often been repeated, " Mr. Secretary is king there in effect." [1]

As the King of Scots still believed Essex's assertion that Cecil leaned towards the Infanta, the ' honourable report ' of his ambassadors must have come as a surprise. They declared, with an honest candour which Cecil gave them credit for [2] though he was aware they were none too well disposed towards him, that they found the Secretary cautious but friendly ; and they presumably instigated the letter from the King, which stands at the head of the secret correspondence and runs as follows :—

" Thus far hath 30 (the cipher by which James indicated himself) thought good to commit to paper to be a witness to 10 (*i.e.* Cecil) of his inward disposition towards him, assuring him that he takes in very good part his wariness in dealing, like as he doth promise, upon his honour, that in all times hereafter the suspicion or disgracing of 10 shall touch 30 as near as 10 and when it shall please God that 30 shall succeed to his right, he shall no surelier succeed to the place than he shall succeed in bestowing as great and greater favour upon 10 as his predecessor doth bestow upon him, and in the meantime ye may rest assured of the constant love and secrecy of your most loving and assured friend, 30." [3]

Apparently Cecil had another interview with the Ambassadors at the offices of the Duchy of Lancaster, of which he was Chancellor, after this letter was received. When all was settled so far as it could be, he drew up the notable document where he laid down with singular frankness the terms upon which he consented to enter into the secret correspondence. One or two passages require quotation.

" I have resolved," he wrote, " in this form to return my

---

[1] Hailes, *Secret Corresp. of Sir R. Cecil,* Letter i.
[2] Hatf. MSS., 213/114.
[3] *Corresp. of James VI. with Sir R. Cecil,* Letter i.

humble thanks.   First, because it hath pleased your Majesty to believe that I have been wronged.   Secondly, because you expect nothing from me to wrong any other.   Thirdly, because you promise hereafter in all accusations to deal with me as God did with Adam, ' Ubi es ? '   Fourthly, because I perceive when that natural day shall come, wherein your feast may be lawfully proclaimed (which I do wish may be long deferred), such shall appear the equity of your mind to all men, that those shall not be rejected (as wanting their wedding garment) who have not falsely or untimely wrought for future fortunes.   For I do herein truly and religiously profess before God, that if I could accuse myself to have once imagined a thought which could amount to a grain of error towards my dear and precious sovereign, or could have discerned (by the overtures of your ministers) that you had entertained an opinion or desire to draw me one point from my individual centre, I should wish with all my heart that all I have done or shall do, might be converted to my own perdition.   For though it is true that natural cares and providence might have importuned me long since to seek some honest mean to dissolve those hard obstructions which other men's practice had bred within your heart, yet had I still determined constantly to have run out the glass of time (though with ideas of future peril) rather than by the least circumstance of my actions (either open or private) to give any ground for insidious spirits to suspect that I would vary from the former compass of a sole dependency, by which I have only steered my courses.   But when I saw that all those whose eyes were blind to all but high imaginations, had left behind them the dregs of foul impressions against some ministers of this estate (especially against myself as one that was sold over to Spanish practice and swollen to the chin with other dangerous plots against your person) . . . when I perceived that the practices which were used to disgrace me must consequently have settled an apprehension in you of an alienation of heart in her Majesty towards you which must have morticed [1] an opinion in your mind, that she must needs be inclined (if not resolved) to cut off the natural branch, and graft upon some wild stock, seeing those that held the nearest place about her were described to be so full of pernicious practices against your Majesty, I did think it my duty to remove that inference, by that occasion which was offered me upon your Ambassadors being here ; though I assure myself (it being known) would prejudice me in her Majesty's judgment, of whom that language which would be tunable in other prince's ears would jar in hers, whose creature I am.   But, Sir, I know

---

[1] Implanted.

it holdeth so just proportion even with strictest loyalty and soundest reason, for faithful ministers to conceal sometimes both thoughts and actions from princes when they are persuaded it is for their own greater service, that [1] albeit I did observe the temperature of your mind (in all your courses) to be such as gave me great hopes that you would do always like yourself, yet I was still jealous, lest some such causeless despair of the Queen's just intentions might be wrought into you as might make you . . . plunge yourself unawares into some such actions as might engage all honest men, out of present duty, to oppose themselves so far against you that [2] they would stand in doubt hereafter what you would do, in the future, towards those which should so lately have offended you.   Wherein I will only for the present lay down this position which I know I can justly maintain, that it is and will be in no man's power on earth, so much as your own to be ' Faber fortunæ suæ.' " [3]

One other passage from a later letter deserves to be added.

"Lastly, renowned prince, when you vouchsafe to show me, that you will use no other steps for your graduation to assure the right you have to your future fortune, but a constant care to conserve the Queen's good will entirely, to retain the affections of her honest subjects, and to invite them to respect you by showing them an example of your kingly government, I have little more to say, besides that comfort I take to see the mind which I do reverence so well tempered, but that when all the roots and fractions of numbers shall be searched by the greatest mathematics you will find that this is only the golden number which will show you veram galaxiam, for all other plots are dreams and all other counsels such as Almighty God will scatter like chaff from off the earth ; to whose blessed protection of you in your religious and just resolutions I do commend you in my devotions and ever remain in humblest affections after one, and her alone, at your Majesty's commandment humbly and honestly,   R. C." [4]

Translated into the simpler language of a more rapid age, Cecil's explanation of his conduct amounts to this—that he moved in the matter of the succession so soon as opportunity offered, for fear that James, ignorant of his real sentiments and distrustful of those of the Queen, might prejudice a winning cause by

---

[1] In the original, ' as.'   [2] In the original, ' as.'
[3] *Corresp. of James VI. with Sir R. Cecil*, Letter ii.   [4] *Ibid.*, Letter iv.

hasty and inexpedient action. To the reservation
of his duty to the Queen, which he explicitly and
uncompromisingly affirmed, he remained unimpeach-
ably faithful. So well defined was his attitude on
this point that, some months after the secret correspondence had begun, an intelligent but unsuspecting
observer reported to the King as follows :—

" If your Majesty shall fall again in sound amity with the
Queen, Mr. Secretary shall prove one of the best friends you
shall have in England, but that ever he will be yours otherwise,
look not for it. I never saw anyone about the Queen that loved
herself better and (was) less mindful of future fortune than he." [1]

It is incontestable that the country was largely
the gainer by the secret understanding. Quite apart
from the question of the succession, the removal of
the wasting feud, which had burnt like the fire of
Vesta from century to century, as well as the supply
of 3000 Scottish footmen whom the King supplied to
fight in the Irish wars,[2] were tangible advantages
even whilst Elizabeth was alive. And yet, because
to serve two masters perfectly is a practical as well
as a psychical impossibility, it is arguable that in
one point Cecil allowed James's opinion to modify
if not to direct his counsel. To the King it seemed
that the conclusion of a peace with Spain during
Elizabeth's lifetime might enable the Spanish party
to secure an advantage and imperil his succession. It
is not clear that the fear was other than an idle one,
or that, even if it was just, the interest of the country
did not demand its neglect. Yet Cecil acknowledges
that his attitude in the Council Chamber became at
this time noticeably more bellicose ;[3] and though he
declares his conscience to have been quite easy in the
matter, that of his biographer is not perfectly at rest.
Here there is, at least, some appearance of a vulner-
able spot in his conduct.

[1] Hatf. Cal., xii. p. 18.   [2] Venet. Cal., ix. pp. 480, 484.
[3] *Corresp. of James VI. and Sir Robert Cecil*, p. 35.

Meanwhile, to the courtiers who hung about the throne as well as to the outer world he presented an inscrutable puzzle.   He was in their eyes as in those of Sully (or rather of Sully's editor [1]) *tout mystère*. They knew not what to make of him, nor whither his steps were tending.   So great was his power that in their perplexity men invented the ridiculous supposition that he meant to marry Arabella Stuart and share the throne.   But from his own clear purpose he swerved neither to the right hand nor the left. There were, of course, hazards to be run.   " Secret de trois, secret de tous ! " says the French proverb, and in this instance there were fully three ' in the know.' Nor did the danger end there.   Many years later Cecil wrote to Sir Henry Wotton to explain the dismissal of Simon Willis, who had been his secretary until within a year of the Queen's death.   It was partly, he told his correspondent, on account of Willis' pride that he had got rid of him, but chiefly because so intimate a retainer must almost inevitably have sooner or later caught sight of some packet or paper, which would have aroused a suspicion of his master's secret practices.   " Wherein," Cecil adds, fearlessly reviewing his own conduct in the light of time, " although I hope you remain secure, if her Majesty had known all I did, how well she should have known the innocency and constancy of my private faith, yet her age and orbity, joined to the jealousy of her sex, might have moved her to think ill of that which helped to preserve her.   For what could more quiet the expectation of a successor, so many ways invited to jealousy, than when he saw her ministers that were most inward with her wholly bent to accommodate the present actions of state for his future safety, when God should see His time." [2]

---

[1] The phrase belongs, I think, to the more lively and less reliable edition of Sully's *Memoirs*.

[2] S. P. For., Venice, 29th March 1608.

Cautious as he was, Cecil could not provide against all contingencies. And Wotton tells a story which, if it be as its narrator claims 'precisely true,' shows that he only escaped detection, and the disgrace which would almost certainly have followed it, by the skin of his teeth. The Queen was one day driving with him as minister-in-attendance on the heath near Greenwich, when a horn was heard and a post-boy came riding along. Elizabeth called the rider and asked him where he came from. He replied that he was from Scotland. Upon which she stopped her coach and told him to deliver the packet to Cecil. The Secretary had reason to suppose that the letters included some items of the secret correspondence, and that in a few moments the Queen would be acquainted with his conduct. A less ready man would have sought some pretext to avoid undoing the bundle. He, however, merely asked for a knife to cut its fastenings ; and, then, while still at a safe distance from the Queen, complained of its evil smell, and advised her to defer its perusal until it had been aired. The Queen, who hated foul odours, fell in with the suggestion ; and Cecil secured the opportunity he sought to remove the compromising papers.[1]

It is improbable, however, that these formed part of the direct correspondence that passed from time to time between James and Cecil. Tradition declares that this went by way of Ireland, and that the conveyance of it was the foundation of Lord Claneboy's and James Fullerton's fortunes.[2] Bishop Goodman, on the other hand, asserts that it was sent by the French post.[3] However that may be, the contents of the tell-tale packet probably belonged to the auxiliary intercourse which was exchanged between

[1] *Reliq. Wotton* (ed. 1672), p. 169.
[2] *Corresp. of James VI. with Sir R. Cecil*, p. xliii.
[3] Goodman, *Court and Times of James I.*, i. p. 32.

Howard on the one hand, Bruce, Mar, and the King of
Scots on the other ; which went by Berwick ; and
which has so long and so falsely passed under the
title that Hailes selected for it—" The Secret Correspondence of Sir Robert Cecil with James VI." In
point of fact, this *dossier* contains no single letter from
Cecil's hand ; but the attribution to him of its contents has brought him all the discredit of what James
brutally described as Howard's ' ample, Asiatic and
endless volumes.' He has been held responsible
as well for the malignant venom which exudes from
beneath those ostentatious pieties, as for the general
purpose of the negotiation which was undoubtedly
his. For the intercourse by which he sought to establish a sound understanding between the King of
Scots and English Government became in Howard's
hands an instrument to poison the mind of James
against Howard's personal foes.

But Lord Henry was not the only member of his
family who had a taste for intrigue. Frances Howard,
the daughter of the Lord Admiral and the widow of
Lord Kildare, was married to Cobham, Cecil's brother-
in-law, in May 1601,[1] just about the time when Mar
and Bruce returned to Scotland. Ambitious beyond
the ordinary, not quite so clever as she supposed
herself to be, she had apparently entered into communication with the King of Scots before her second
marriage, and was extremely chagrined to find the
channel of her confidences [2] suddenly dried up by
virtue of her cousin's more subtle manœuvres.[3]
In her vexation she charged Cecil with doing that
which she herself had already done ; and, instigated by Lord Thomas Howard, was ready to have
accused him to the Queen, if her husband had betrayed her.[3] Why Cobham should have dreamed of
doing any such thing is very far from clear. But

---

[1] S. P. Dom., Eliz., 279/91. [2] Probably Foulis.
[3] *Secret Corresp. of Sir R. Cecil*, pp. 20, 21.

Cobham was a fool and incalculable. Lady Cobham, for her part, though she figures frequently in the *Secret Correspondence*, was at least as petulant as she was effective or dangerous. Cecil treated her as a joke, in spite of the uncomfortable knowledge that she might at any moment, by a lucky stroke, give him cause to pull a very wry face.[1] But in what precise relation she stood to the ' Conferences ' of Durham House, or, which is much the same thing, to her husband's political intrigues, it is not very easy to determine.

Of those secret conferences, Lady Ralegh, according to Howard's account, was the life and soul. In his picture of the proceedings she sits as ' Proserpine '[2] among the ' triplicity of hell,'[3] weaving plans by which the infernal trio — Cobham, Ralegh, and Northumberland — may once more ascend to the mountain-tops of royal favour. The high colouring of the canvas has brought the writer's assertions into legitimate disrepute. And yet we have almost nothing else to go by ; and it is only by washing off his deep splotches of prejudice that we can get some notion of the actual chiaroscuro they pretend to reproduce. Cecil, one is tempted to add, might have done well to take more ample precaution to do the same. For it was from Howard that he derived his information about the course of events at Durham House.[4] And yet we ourselves see here so dimly that we cannot really pass any certain judgment. Howard may have been substantially right, and Cecil have had excellent reason to believe him. At any rate he did so. And our first business is, after all, to try to see all things as he saw them, even if at times we fancy him mistaken.

Amid all the entanglement of ' faction and phan-

---

[1] *Secret Corresp. of Sir R. Cecil*, p. 20.

[2] Edwards, *Life of Ralegh*, ii. p. 439.

[3] *Secret Corresp. of Sir R. Cecil*, p. 39.

[4] *Ibid.*, p. 49 : " I (Howard) were the chief instrument of bringing the chief things to discovery."

tasy '[1] one point at least is plain. Slowly, sensibly,
yet without any passage of words or breach of apparent cordiality, Cecil and Ralegh were drifting
apart. The first faint indication of the coming storm,
the cloud no bigger than a man's hand, had, indeed,
if Harington may be trusted,[2] appeared above the
horizon in the affair of Essex. Cecil—we have
Ralegh's own word for it—showed a disposition towards ' mild courses' which his friend could not
approve, and upon which, as we have seen, that friend
had remonstrated. With the growing importance of
the problem of the succession, the coldness rapidly
advanced. To Ralegh's partisans, it has always
seemed that the other seized upon the opportunity
to discredit an inconvenient rival, whose abilities he
feared, whose merits and greatness he had not the
intelligence to perceive. There is very much to be
said against this view. We must never forget that
the Ralegh whom Cecil knew and with whom he had
to deal was not the Ralegh of 1618—the Ralegh
tempered by adversity and the approach of death—
but rather the Ralegh whom his own associate
Northumberland painted about this very time and
with no unfriendly intention, as " insolent, extremely
heated, a man that desires to seem to be able to sway
all men's fancies, all men's courses."[3] Still, unpopular
as Ralegh unquestionably was, Cecil had given him
the greatest proof of regard that one man can give
another—the care and charge of his own son.[4] It is
surely a cynical and ungenerous view of human character which discovers lurking behind the allusions
to their estrangement contained in his private letters
to Sir George Carew, a secret gladness that he had so
good an excuse for putting down a formidable rival.

---

[1] Howard's phrase, *Secret Corresp.*, p. 124.
[2] *Nug. Antiq.*, ii. p. 151.
[3] *Corresp. of James VI. and Sir R. Cecil*, p. 67.
[4] Hatf. Cal., x. p. 84 ; Collins, Sidney Papers, ii. 214.

And Ralegh himself knew better. After the trial at
Winchester in 1603, when his enemies had shown their
hand, he wrote to Cecil in terms which surely no mere
hope of favours to come could have prompted or
justified :—" For neither Fortune, which sometime
guided me—or rather Vanity, for with the other I
was never in love—shall turn mine eyes from you
towards her while I have being, nor the World with
all the cares or enticements belonging unto it shall ever
weigh down (though it be of the greatest weight to
mortal men) the memory of your Lordship's true
respects had of me ; respects tried by the touch,
tried by the fire ; true witnesses, in true times ; and
then only, when only available." [1]

" Vanity which sometimes guided me ! " Ralegh
had in the end taken to heart the warning of the old
Greek maxim to ' Know thyself.' But in 1602 he was
looking to the coming reign to give him a more ample
success in life, a more definite possession of power
than he had yet secured. Yet there is no certainty
that he had ability in statecraft. Great soldier, great
poet, great explorer, he can hardly have possessed
all the compass of civic talents. Even if it was so,
his repeated efforts to push himself into Cecil's confidence—efforts not probably any the more tolerable
because he had slung the stupid Cobham about his
neck like a millstone—provoked and irritated Cecil
as they would have provoked and irritated the vast
majority of Cecil's critics. Few friendships could
have survived so sharp a test. But Ralegh put his
friend to another. With the advent of the Duke of
Lennox he entered upon a secret negotiation conducted by Sir Arthur Savage,[2] which was of course
designed to bring him into favour with the King of
Scots. This was the last straw. Cecil's position was
not very dissimilar from that of a prime-minister who

[1] Edwards, *Life of Ralegh*, ii. p. 288.
[2] *Corresp. of James VI. with Sir R. Cecil*, p. 43.

should find two of his colleagues—and those two his own familiar friends—attempting now to force his confidences, now to effect his discomfiture behind his back. His letters to Carew show the outraged sentiment that was smouldering behind his great reserve. " Lastly, sir," he wrote, " if I did not know that you do measure me by your own heart towards me, which is likewise the rule of mine towards all others, it might be a doubtfulness in me that the mutinies of those whom I do love and will (however they do me), might create in you some belief that I were ungrateful towards them." [1]   In face of that, even Mr. Stebbing is constrained to admit that Cecil's correspondence countenances the view that his hostility had something in it of hurt affection.[2]

It is not much to the point that he tells Carew in the same letter [3] that he will never make Ralegh a councillor except Ralegh resigns the captaincy of the Guard in his correspondent's favour ; for Ralegh was the last man who could be wisely converted into a powerful pluralist.   Nor is it to the purpose that in a sort of peevish vexation at being persistently pestered about the succession he casually alludes to his brother-in-law and Ralegh as ' gaping crabs,' and tells James that he has tossed a stone into their open mouths.[4]   For the intrinsic evidence of Howard's own letters shows that Cecil had no suspicion of the game his coadjutor was playing behind his back.   " You must not touch one word in your letter (to me)," Howard warns Bruce, " of the consultations and canons of Durham House (Durham House meant Ralegh's lodging), because I had not warrant to advertise them, although I were the instrument of bringing the chief things to discovery." [5]   In that sentence lies Cecil's vindication.

[1] *Letters of Cecil to Carew*, p. 84.
[2] Stebbing, *Sir Walter Ralegh*, p. 179.
[3] *Letters of Cecil to Carew*, p. 86.
[4] *Corresp. of James VI. with Sir R. Cecil*, p. 18.
[5] *Secret Corresp. of Sir R. Cecil*, p. 49.

It is plain that he did not see Howard's letters to Scotland, and knew nothing of their temper. And when Mr. Stebbing argues that Howard would never have propounded a plan [1] for the undoing of Ralegh and Cobham unless he had been certain that Cecil was in sympathy with its object, his contention is exactly on all fours with that of Ralegh's judges—whom he so justly condemns—when they found Ralegh guilty because Cobham had made him treasonable suggestions. The true rule in these matters (to quote a modern Prime Minister) is that "things which cannot be proved ought not to be insinuated."

Meanwhile, events were drifting on to their appointed end. As the year, according to the old Julian calendar, entered upon its last month, the Queen became definitely and undeniably ill. She lost her sleep and with it the healthy action of the skin to which she was accustomed. Cecil says that he found her impatient; [2] and report affirmed that he was the only one of her counsellors who dared approach her during these irritable humours. [3] A discredited story has connected this last phase of her decline with the contemporaneous decease of Lady Nottingham and the dramatic narrative, already repeated, of Essex's ring and the Countess's death-bed remorse. Without any picturesque additions the death of her old friend was enough to hurry Elizabeth towards her grave. She had come to the time of life when every disappearance of a familiar face is a portent full of meaning. Another link had snapped in the long chain of her memories. The future, too, was no longer hers. A generation was pressing on whose thoughts were not her thoughts, nor their ways her ways. She had gradually lost her hold on life, most of all, perhaps, because she had lost her hold over the

[1] See Edwards, *Life of Ralegh*, App. 6, p. 436.
[2] Hatf. Cal., xii. p. 668.
[3] S. P. Dom., Eliz., 287/50.

imagination of her people. Affairs of State wearied
her : she called for the old *Canterbury Tales* which
she must have known and loved in her youth.[1] She
was, in every sense, as Ralegh caustically phrased it,
" a lady whom Time had surprised."

The public eye shifted restlessly from the Queen
to her Minister ; from the known illness of the one
to the unknown purpose of the other. Everyone
said that Cecil's influence upon the crisis must be
paramount, and the old wild stories got about that
he was going to marry Arabella or otherwise make
himself king.[1] No one, in fact, could read the riddle.
" Certain we are," writes an English merchant to his
Venetian correspondent on 9th March, " that his inward mind is averted from the Scot, and it is as certain
that he is altogether opposite to the Spaniards."[1]
Yet, secret as he had been, he had taken all his measures.
Arabella—his imaginary bride—was ungallantly, perhaps collusively, put under surveillance ; Burghley,
not, it may be, fully cognisant of his brother's intentions,[2] was charged with the care of the North,
where the old border-feuds may have detracted
from the popularity of a Scottish succession : the
frontier-fortresses were placed in the hands of persons
well affected towards the Scottish King.[3] James
was apprised of the Queen's condition and the forth-
coming proclamation of his succession submitted for
his approval.[4] As Sanderson tells the story, Cecil
at the eleventh hour sought and obtained Elizabeth's
confirmation of his purpose. Together with Howard
and Egerton he came to her and asked her pleasure.
" My throne," she replied, with her old intense
patriotic pride, " is for a king, none other shall
succeed me." " What king ? " Cecil asked. " What

----

[1] S. P. Dom., Eliz., 287/50.
[2] Hatf. Cal., xii. p. 671.
[3] Venet. Cal., ix. No. 1143.
[4] *Corresp. of James VI. with Sir R. Cecil*, p. 47.

other," she answered, " than my kinsman, the King of Scots ? " [1]

A narrative, which very possibly originated with Cecil himself,[2] relates that the same question was again put to her by the same three councillors on the following day. The Queen was already past speech but not past understanding. Seeing how it was with her, Cecil asked her for a sign whether she would have the King of Scots. Gathering her remaining strength Elizabeth rose in her bed, and lifting her hands brought them together above her head in the manner of a crown. It was an emphatic, if unconscious, approval of the choice which the ablest of her advisers had already taken every measure to secure. Gossip added that she entrusted Cecil with a casket containing some memorials on the art of good government to be delivered to her successor.[3]

She had waned with the waning year, and on the last day of it, before daybreak, the end was reached. The anxious atmosphere of expectation became immediately charged with activity. Robert Cary, Lord Hunsdon's son, got away for Scotland before the official messengers were ready to start. Cecil's private packets may have been despatched sooner. It is not of much consequence ; for everything vital went without a hitch, and the King was proclaimed without opposition at Whitehall and Cheapside. The Secretary took the principal part in the necessary proceedings, reading the proclamation himself at Whitehall, and again, after he had been formally admitted into the City, at Cheapside.[4] The people, torn betwixt sorrow and expectation, listened undemonstratively.[4] Of his own feelings we know

---

[1] Sanderson's *Life and Death of James VI.*, p. 261. There are, of course, other versions (*e.g.* S. P. Dom., Jas. I., 86/50), not substantially different. I merely quote this one because it seems to me the most concisely dramatic.

[2] Disraeli, *Cur. of Literat.*, iii. 331.   [3] Venet. Cal., x. p. 7.

[4] Manningham's *Diary*, p. 147.

nothing. We may picture him the prey of grief, anxiety, elation, or the impassive spectator of his own infallible calculations. For the rest, so smoothly, so silently had he steered the Ship of State into harbour that the crisis scarcely looks an anxious one upon the page of history. Yet Francis Bacon has left it on record that his countrymen awoke to the fair morning of the new reign, ' as from a fearful dream.' [1]

[1] Spedding, *Bacon's Works*, vi. p. 277.

CHAPTER XII

"She told them what a fate
Was gently fallen from Heaven upon this State ;
How dear a father they did now enjoy
That came to save what Discord would destroy ;
And ent'ring with the power of a King
The temp'rance of a private man did bring."
                    BEN JONSON'S *Panegyric on King James.*

THE throne, according to the brutal if beneficent
fiction, is never vacant.   Elizabeth was scarcely dead
before James was invested with all the decorative
and illusory virtues of sovereignty.   The magnetic
needle of public favour, liberated from its long
allegiance to the aged Queen and seeking once again
its lodestone, flew northwards ; and the King advanced
to take possession of a country which was ready to
believe him the most perfect of all the sons of Adam.
He had, in fact, a good deal more than common parts.
Mary Stuart had endowed him with the keen and agile
intelligence which had presumably come to her with
her foreign ancestry ; and Buchanan had worried
and beaten it into a love of learning.   The King had
grown especially curious and intrepid in examining
the doctrines of theology, and his convictions, unlike
those of the majority of his peers, rested upon
strong and rational foundations.   Solomon among
the kings of Israel, Henry VII. among the kings of
England, were the flattering models to which his
subjects compared him, and to which doubtless he

KING JAMES I.

(Painted by P. Van Somer. Hatfield House)

[*To face p:* 192

liked to be compared. But, unhappy in her legacies as in her life, his mother had withheld from him the best part of her qualities. James lacked all the charms and graces which are the most valuable jewels in a monarch's treasury. He was boorish in manner, slobbering in speech, ungainly in gait. And his mind reflected the clumsy disorder of his body. In the immortal portrait in the *Fortunes of Nigel*, Heriot discovers him among the most varied and incongruous assortment of pursuits and papers, where the emblems of the chase mingle oddly with the implements of learning. It is in vain that we turn to study the sage wisdom of the *Basilikon Doron*, or trace the lineaments of his character in Isaac Disraeli's meticulous defence of the philosopher-king. He still looks like a foolish old dominie, shuffling through his days and his difficulties, cumbered with knowledge, cumbered with conceit, cumbered with favourites, cumbered most of all with the stupendous title and empty attributes that our English Bible has given him for a perpetual memorial. In the well-known letter [1] in which Fontenay describes him as a young man to Secretary Nau, the French agent notices particularly three shortcomings in his character— his reckless favouritism, his indolent carelessness, and the magnificence of his ideas in relation to his slender resources. The passage of time had brought no change of disposition. At his accession to the English throne he was still as extravagant, as susceptible, and as lazy as ever. But whilst Cecil was alive, these dangerous faults did not gain ground to an inordinate degree. It was otherwise after Cecil's decease.

When the King crossed the Border he had still to know his minister face to face. But Cecil did not immediately hurry north with the crowd of courtiers who, as Chamberlain sarcastically observed, behaved

[1] Hatf. Cal., iii. p. 60.

as if ' preferment was a goal to be got by footmanship.'
There were urgent matters of public business claiming
attention in London, and the Secretary thought—and
thought rightly—that he could trust James not to
place his confidence elsewhere in the meanwhile.   On
the day after the Queen's death he wrote to apprise
the King of his intentions.   " And I doubt not," he
concluded proudly, " but your Majesty shall in your
service acknowledge me to be a member of that
house which hath never yet been unfaithful to their
masters." [1]

The King meanwhile rode southward, hunting and
feasting as he went.   His jovial familiarity won him
golden opinions,[2] and Cecil did not escape the play of
his good humour.   Burghley, upon whom as President
of the Council of the North and Lord of Burghley
House there fell a fuller share of the entertaining
than his finances welcomed,[2] passed on the royal
witticism to his brother.   " I thought to let you
know," he writes to Robert, " a particular speech
the King [3] used towards you.   He said he heard
you were but a little man, but he would shortly load
your shoulders with business." [4]   By the time James
reached York, Cecil was free to come northward, and
the two met on 18th April.   The Minister has shrouded
his first impression of his new Sovereign with his
accustomed reserve.   He only tells the Council that
an hour's conversation had given him less than time
to deal with the needful business.[5]   He is rather more
expansive a week later in a private letter to the
Master of Gray :—

" For the description you have made of His Majesty this I
must say without flattery, that although you have had the
happiness long to know him and serve him, yet his virtues are
so eminent that [6] by my six days' kneeling at his feet I have made

---

[1] S. P. Dom., Jas. 1., 1/2.   [2] Hatf. MSS., 99/147.
[3] In the original, ' he.'   [4] Hatf. MSS., 99/88.
[5] *Ibid.*, 99/125.   [6] In the original, ' as.'

so sufficient a discovery of his royal perfections that [1] I contemplate greater felicity to this isle than ever it enjoyed. As,
when I was free, my heart never harboured thought against him
either in his person or in his state, which your own soul can best
witness, so that now I am become his humble subject and servant
I am fully resolved (while breath lasteth) to depend upon himself
only, and to associate only [with] those whom I shall find freest
from private ends." [2]

One cannot read the passage without a feeling that
amidst the excitement of change, and in the natural
wish to descry a future as full of promise as the past
had been of glory, the memory of Elizabeth had been
too quickly effaced from the mind of her old servant.
Even the epilogue to the great reign had not yet
been recited. Three days after he wrote,[3] Cecil
was following in the stately procession which accompanied all that remained of his mistress to her
grave at Westminster.[4] Then he turned northwards
once more, for James was due at Theobalds on the
3rd May.

There the King came, riding over from Brox-
bourne on the appointed day, and found a vast con-
course of Londoners, as well as the whole country-
side, in wait to see him. An unknown, or at least
unremembered, chronicler, who has left an account
of the proceedings, tells us how he himself took his
stand with his friends at a window looking on the
street and tried to count the passers-by. To get an
estimate they checked the number with an hour-
glass, but, after half the sand had run through,
abandoned the attempt in despair, since the people
pressed on ' so exceedingly fast.' As far as they
had gone with their computation, they had reckoned
three hundred and nine horsemen and one hundred
and thirty-seven footmen, and the multitude had

[1] In the original, ' as.'   [2] Hatf. MSS., 187/30.
[3] 28th April.
[4] It is interesting to notice that the memorial to Queen Elizabeth
in the Abbey was executed under Cecil's supervision (S. P. Dom.,
Jas. I., 13/8, 9, and Hatf. MSS., 119/8).

been gathering since 4 a.m., 'and the day before also, without intermission.' Whatever their precise number Cecil apparently was ready for them ; and even the poorest found beer and bread, beef and veal and mutton, with which to make holiday. For the maimed and distressed soldiery there was made a special provision of wine and money, 'in very bounteous sort,' as our reporter is at pains to tell us he learned afterwards from their own mouths.[1] He himself and his friends in the meanwhile had had other fish to fry. As soon as the King was announced to be three-quarters of a mile distant, they divided forces, one standing at the upper end of the approach, another at the top of the first court, another at the entrance of the second court, and a 'gentleman of good sort,' whom they chose for the purpose, in the court that leads into the Hall, " to take notice of what was said or done by His Highness to the nobility of our land, or said or done by them to His Majesty." Such a careful and elaborate division of labour deserved a variety of incident. But, in fact, everything passed off so admirably as to make the climax of our reporter's description not a little tame. The King rode past with a troop of English and Scottish magnates, bareheaded, in his train. At the entrance to the outer court these dismounted, James alone remaining in the saddle. At the entrance to the inner court Cecil, with another body of distinguished persons, met him and conducted him into the house, amid general applause, tossing of hats, and invocation of blessings. James, doubtless tired of the tumult, then withdrew to his room, but reappeared again an hour later and showed himself for some time on the balcony. The last glimpse we get of him is among

---

[1] " Whose thankfulness is not altogether unknown to myself, some of whom hearing I was about to publish this small remembrance made means to me to give me true information of such princely exhibition as they daily received during the time of his Majesty's abode at Theobalds."

the shady labyrinths of the garden, walking in the cool of the day.

The visit was concluded in the same magnificent fashion in which it had begun. " To speak of Sir Robert's cost to entertain His Majesty," says the quaint narrator of King James's progress from Edinburgh to London,[1] " were but to imitate geographers that set a little round o for a mighty province." And in the eyes of those who enjoyed his bounteous hospitality Robert Cecil must have appeared an exceptionally fortunate man. But, as his cousin wrote in the essay on *Great Place*, " great persons have need to borrow other men's opinions to think themselves happy." [2] It happens that he has left behind a letter depicting his feelings during that very month of May when the King so greatly honoured him, when he obtained his peerage, and when he seemed to be, and indeed was, mounted more firmly in his saddle than ever before.

"My noble Knight," he replies to Sir John Harington, who had a mind to stand well at Court, . . . " I shall not fail to keep your grace and favour quick and lively in the King's breast. . . . You know all my former steps, good Knight, rest content and give heed to one that hath sorrowed in the bright lustre of a Court and gone heavily even on the best-seeming fair ground. 'Tis a great task to prove one's honesty, and yet not spoil one's fortune. You have tasted a little hereof in our blessed Queen's time, who was more than a man and in troth sometime less than a woman. I wish I waited now in her presence-chamber with ease at my food and rest in my bed. I am pushed from the shore of comfort and know not where the winds and waves of a Court will bear me. I know it bringeth little comfort on earth ; and he is, I reckon, no wise man that looketh this way to Heaven. We have much stir about counsels and more about honours. Many knights were made at Theobalds during the King's stay at mine

---

[1] Millington's narrative in Nichols' *Progresses of James I.*, vol. i. p. 111.

[2] " For if they judge by their own feeling they cannot find it ; but if they think with themselves what other men think of them, and that other men would fain be as they are, then they are happy as it were by report when perhaps they find the contrary within."

house, and more (are) to be made in the City. My father had much wisdom in directing the State ; and I wish I could bear my part so discreetly as he did. Farewell, good Knight, but never come near London till I call you. Too much crowding doth not well for a cripple, and the King doth find scant room to sit himself ; he hath so many friends as they choose to be called, and Heaven prove they lie not in the end. In trouble, hurrying, feigning. suing, and such-like matters, I now rest, your true friend,

"R. Cecil."[1]

The King left Theobalds on the 7th May. A week later Cecil was raised to the peerage under the title of Lord Cecil of Essingdon ;[2] and it was noticed at the investiture that in order to cover the unshapeliness of his figure he and his three companions were robed beforehand according to their new rank, instead of being robed whilst the patent was reading.[3] He had at length attained, with every circumstance of favour and distinction, the dignity which, according to Rowland Whyte, both he and Ralegh had ' infinitely desired' in 1599,[4] when he had taken the significant step of substituting for the sheaves of wheat upon his family crest two sheaves of arrows, crossed and surmounted by a helmet.[5]

It was far different with the other. Ralegh, contrary to Cecil's wishes, had forced his way to Burghley House, only to meet with the coldest of receptions from the King. A few days after he was deprived of the captaincy of the Guard, though some financial compensation was given him by the remission

---

[1] Harington, *Nug. Antiquæ*, ii. p. 263.

[2] The grant book has "Baron de Essingdon in Com. Rutland" (S. P. Dom., Jas. i., 141/3), but Lord Cecil was apparently the form always made use of. Cecil, though he attended the House of Lords previously, did not, it seems, formally take his seat till 8th May 1604 (Lords Journals).

[3] Nichols' *Progresses*, iv. 1056.

[4] Collins, Sidney Papers, ii. p. 126.

[5] S. P. Dom., Eliz., 271/106. The device was apparently drawn from that of some Walpoles, with whom he was connected through his grandmother.

of his debts to the Crown and of a charge upon his
revenue as Governor of Jersey. But for the loss of
influence at Court there neither was nor could be
any amends. The candle of his hopes had suddenly
gone out. All the brilliant visions with which he had
cheated himself had vanished as absolutely as the
visible world from the eyes of a man struck with
blindness. Not unnaturally he attributed his discomfiture to Cecil, though James's known dislike of
him and the substitution of a Scotsman in his place
make it more probable that he needed to look no
farther for his enemy than the King himself. At
all events, the furious, but no longer extant, indictment of his fancied foe, with which he presented the
Sovereign,[1] fell on deaf ears, and he was left to wander
out into the wilderness of disappointment. He did
not find himself alone there. Among the discontented
was one, Watson, a secular priest in Roman orders,
who had been a Catholic agent at the Court of
Scotland and supposed himself to have secured a promise of toleration from the new King. The temper of
James's mind was, in fact, favourable to conversion
by argument rather than conversion by penalty;
but Cecil, though he had no disposition to persecute,
had seen too much of Catholic intrigue to care to
pull down any of his defences against the Pope, and
was, not impossibly, alarmed at the serious financial
embarrassment in which a policy of toleration would
involve the Treasury. At all events, the recusancy
statutes remained in force; and those Catholics who
had taken Watson's word for it that these would
be abolished were no doubt proportionately disappointed. Watson himself appears to have regarded
the failure of his predictions in the light of a personal
insult, and to have resolved that in the long-run his
promise should not miscarry.

Round him gathered a most anomalous band of

---

[1] See on this Gardiner, *Hist. of England*, i. p. 95, footnote.

discontented persons—a Catholic priest,[1] a Puritan peer,[2] a desperado of a knight,[3] an Anglican clergyman disappointed of preferment,[4] and a squire's son [5]—and together they fabricated one of the most absurd conspiracies that insensate vanity has ever devised. A petition against the Recusancy Laws was to be got up, and a number of innocent petitioners assembled to present it. Then at a given moment the harmless sheep were somehow to be transformed into ravenous wolves ; the King was to be seized, the Tower surprised, and the conspirators installed in the chief offices of State—Watson as Lord Chancellor, Lord Grey of Wilton, or Sir Griffin Markham, as Earl Marshal, George Brooke as Lord Treasurer, Copley as Secretary.[6] Once reduced into possession, the government was to be carried on from the Tower in the name of the captive King, and the grievances of the Catholics redressed. Such was the Bye Plot. Alongside of it there grew up, or was thought to have grown up, another and larger scheme—a Main Plot— so that (to use Coke's curious figure) the two were like Samson's foxes, joined in the tail but severed in the head. George Brooke, Cecil's brother-in-law,— a man, according to Weldon,[7] though it is difficult to credit it, ' very learned and wise,'—was the ligament that bound them together. Through him the current of discontent that galvanised the priests and their singular assortment of followers was fortified by the idea that such distinguished persons as Ralegh and Cobham were plotting the downfall of the Government. More than that can hardly be said. For the reader who supposes that these plots can be depicted in sharp and certain outline has misunderstood the character of the men engaged in them.

---

[1] Clarke.   [2] Lord Grey.   [3] Sir Griffin Markham.   [4] Brooke.   [5] Copley.

[6] The assignment of these offices does not appear to have been always the same. Cp. S. P. For., France, 49/221, with Gardiner's list in *Hist. of Engl.*, i. p. 111.

[7] *Secret Hist. of the Court of James I.*, i. p. 342.

Cobham himself afterwards told the Council that his
" fault truly was but a conceit," [1] and it is likely
enough that ' the Main ' was no more than the fragment of a vision.   From all we know of him, it is a
reasonable inference that his ideas seldom leaped the
broad gulf between thought and action.   What he
needed was money ; [2] what he looked to was political
intrigue ; and the *deus ex machina* of his uncertain
plans took shape in the person of the Flemish Ambassador, Count d'Aremberg.

It is as well, perhaps, to unroll the rest of the
story as it disclosed itself by degrees before the mind
of Cecil ; if only because that method is a perpetual
reminder of the dissimilarity between the position of
those like ourselves who can survey historical problems
in the comfortable consciousness that no man's life
and no man's kingdom hang upon our conclusions,
and that of a seventeenth-century statesman whom
one act of ill-judged leniency might set toppling from
his high estate.

The Bye Plot was made known to the Government
by the more intelligent section of the Catholic clergy.
There was still much to hope from James, and neither
the Archpriest Blackwell nor the Jesuits had any
intention of letting him be made away with, at least
before it was seen what stuff he was made of.   The
Bishop of London was therefore informed of what
was going on, and the conspirators were arrested in
the weeks that followed midsummer.   The harmless-
ness of the dove was not without a considerable
tincture of the wisdom of the serpent.   The King
was not allowed to forget the great service that had
been done him ; and in the course of July the recusancy fines were remitted.

So far no suspicion had fallen upon Cobham and

---

[1] Hatf. MSS., 102/56, 57.

[2] Though Ralegh denied this, there is direct evidence of Cobham's
decline of fortune.   See Hatf. MSS., 100/33, 50.

Ralegh. The former, indeed, in his capacity as Warden of the Cinque Ports, had been industrious that same year in apprising Cecil of the arrival at Dover of a Jesuit, "brave in his apparel and wearing a great black feather in his hat," who was subsequently lodged in the Gate-House Prison.[1] He had also been industrious in trying to get permission to go abroad on account of his health. The arrest of George Brooke suggested to Cecil's mind that his elder brother-in-law might not be wholly ignorant of the proceedings of the younger. It was but a very little step from Cobham to Ralegh, and the Secretary resolved, therefore, to know what Ralegh had to say about the business.

History, by the preservation of one or two picturesque trivialities, has lit the scene of Ralegh's downfall with all the significance of allegory.[2] On a July morning, the date of which we cannot precisely fix, but when the pomps of midsummer must just have caught the first faint suggestion of decline, he was walking on the terrace at Windsor in the neighbourhood of the buildings which Elizabeth had set up twenty years before. Half a century of life, or thereabouts, full of the variegated and incalculable movement that made him in a subtler sense than the poet intended a Shepherd of the Ocean, lay behind him : and before, all undetected, stretched the cage against whose bars he was to beat so piteously for the fifteen years that were yet to come. It is irresistible to fancy that, with his fortunes trembling in the balance, he meditated, superb poet as he was, upon the intractable hours of chance and change in which human life consists ; upon the pageantry of the seasons—the cozening illusions of spring, the gorgeous mortalities of summer, the swift and fading glories of the fall,

---

[1] Hatf. MSS., 100/52, 57, 73.

[2] I am, of course, especially indebted to Edwards' *Life of Ralegh* in the passage that follows.

the dark sepulchral prisons of a northern winter.
Tragic irony seems to demand so much. Yet very
possibly he thought of nothing of the kind. The King
was going out hunting : he was himself in attendance, and the King, it seems, was late. Suddenly
Cecil passed and stopped him. His presence was
desired in the Council Chamber.

We possess no record of the exact interrogations
that were put to him, but they were doubtless of the
kind which lawyers aptly style ' fishing.' Cecil
apparently had not communicated his thoughts
about Cobham to his fellow-councillors. Ralegh
was examined about the Bye Plot, or, as it was
called alternatively, the Surprising Treason, in regard to which he can have had little or nothing to
say. Then (though Cecil appears afterwards to have
forgotten it [1]) the examination shifted towards Cobham. Ralegh was asked whether he knew of any
practices between his friend and the Netherlands
Envoy. He denied all knowledge of them, if they existed. But after he had left the Council it occurred to
him that on one occasion Cobham had left his lodgings
at Durham Place to go on and visit La Rensy, one
of d'Aremberg's creatures. The natural inference
was that there existed some intelligence between the
two, and it seemed more prudent to acquaint Cecil
with the incident. He wrote accordingly, without—
so his biographers [2] charitably suggest—any real
idea of what he was doing. Cobham—within the
knowledge both of Burghley and Cecil—had held
communication with d'Aremberg in the past, and the
same practice might mean no harm in the present.
Unfortunately for Cobham, still more unfortunately
for Ralegh, the letter fell upon the top of the revelations of George Brooke.

None of the principal conspirators had made much
difficulty about betraying his confederates : Watson

[1] See his speech at Ralegh's trial.   [2] Edwards and Stebbing.

had even made plans to do so before he was arrested, and probably before he had any suspicion that he was to be. There was no need of threats or torture to set the tongues of the poor creatures wagging.[1] They spoke willingly—more willingly a good deal than was consistent either with truth or honour. They accused each other ; and they went on presently to accuse Cobham and Ralegh. Brooke affirmed that his brother had been negotiating with d'Aremberg " touching the procuring certain crowns, to the value of 500,000 or 600,000 ; the intent of which was to assist and furnish a secret action for the surprise of His Majesty." And he indicated La Rensy as the channel of communication.

Cobham was, of course, arrested. Meanwhile, Ralegh (" out of what strange humour," as one contemporary narrator observes, " the God of Heaven knows "[2]) was advising the apprehension of La Rensy. His letter was shown to Cobham, who behaved exactly like a man betrayed by his confederate, exclaiming again and again, " O traitor Ralegh ! O wretch ! I will utter all ; it is you that have procured me to all this villainy." His performance did not lag behind his promise. He affirmed that the plot had been instigated by Ralegh ; that he himself had intended to go abroad to obtain money from the Archduke and the King of Spain ; and that on the way home he was to meet Ralegh in Jersey to consult about its application.[3]

Meanwhile, Brooke and Watson had been embellishing their stories. Cobham, they asserted, had confided to the former the existence of a Main Plot to take away the King and his issue, or, in Watson's more vivid, perhaps more accurate, narra-

---

[1] Hatf. MSS., 101/44.
[2] See Jardine, *Criminal Trials*, i. p. 462.
[3] Cecil's account of the Main Plot is to be found in S. P. For., France, 49/221.

tive ' the King and his cubs . . . not leaving one
alive.'

Ralegh, of course, at the first breath of accusation,
had been confined. He denied, however, from the
beginning, as he denied to the end, any kind of
complicity in the plot. But one circumstance told
heavily against him. It came out that, after Cobham's
arrest, he had sent his retainer, Keymis, to advise
his friend not to be dismayed, for that the evidence of one witness could not condemn him, and that
he himself had cleared him of all. The message
was exactly such as one conspirator might well
send to another. It was not rendered the less
suspicious later on by Ralegh's disavowal of it in
face of the separate affirmations of Keymis and
Cobham.

Nor was Cecil's perplexity diminished by an
incident which followed Ralegh's committal to the
Tower. The Secretary relates how one afternoon,
whilst he was examining prisoners there, he was
informed that Ralegh had attempted suicide. " We
came to him," he writes to Parry,[1] " and found him
in some agony, seeming to be unable to endure his
misfortune, and protesting innocency with carelessness of life ; and in that humour he had wounded
himself under his right pap, but in no way mortally,
being in truth rather a cut than a stab, and now very
well cured, both in body and mind." " What to
judge of this case yet," he goes on, " we know not,
for how authentically soever the Lord Cobham did
before us all accuse him in all our hearing, and most
constantly, yet being newly examined seemeth now
to clear Sir Walter Ralegh in most things, and to
take all the burden to himself, so, as the matter
(. . . how apparent soever) . . . is *in foro con-
scientiæ*, yet you may be assured that no severity

---

[1] The letter is printed in Birch's *Court and Times of James I.*,
i. p. 13.

shall be used towards him, for which there shall not be sufficient proof." It is the fashion not to give Cecil credit for his perplexity. No one who reads the passage just cited has any right to doubt it. Later on, as the formal trial approached, he reached, it is true, a more definitely adverse conclusion. " Sir Walter Ralegh," he wrote to Winwood on 3rd October,[1] " yet persists in denial of the main treasons ; which though he doth by having gotten some intelligence of Lord Cobham's retraction, yet the first accusation is so well fortified, with other demonstrative circumstances, and the retraction so blemished by the discovery of that intelligence which they had, as few men can conceive it comes from a clear heart. Always he shall be left to the law, which is the right all men are born into."

Doubtless the law was a birthright for which men had cause to be thankful. Yet, in fact, as we know, a seventeenth-century trial fell not a little short of the justice of to-day. So unstable was the State that the famous maxim was virtually reversed. Once a man was charged with high treason he was, to all intents and purposes, held to be guilty until he was shown to be innocent.[2] No one now supposes that Ralegh met with the incidents of justice : very few people, probably, suppose that he met with justice itself. He received what the law gave him, full measure and running over.

But this is not the place to try him again for the hundredth time. All that Cecil's biographer requires to show is that Cecil threw all the weight of his influence upon the side of such an equitable trial as legal practice allowed. Sitting as he did as one amongst the Commissioners, and not being himself a lawyer, he had neither the power nor the knowledge to do more than press the claims of common sense and fairness : but so much he

---

[1] Winwood Memorials, ii. p. 8.
[2] I am, of course, only repeating Gardiner.

unquestionably did. Ralegh's plea that the evidence of one witness was insufficient to convict in case of treason was overruled by the Chief Justice. From that time it became the prisoner's endeavour to have Cobham brought into court. Cecil intervened to support him. " Sir Walter Ralegh presseth often," he said, " that my Lord Cobham should be brought face to face ; if he ask a thing of grace and favour, they must come from him only who can give them ; but if he ask a matter of law, then, in order that we, who sit here as Commissioners, may be satisfied, I desire to hear the opinions of my Lords, the Judges, whether it may be done by law." The Judges replied that the law did not suffer it ; that it would shelter treason and be prejudicial to the King. Later, in the trial, of his own accord Cecil took up the point again on the score of equity. " I am afraid," he said, " my often speaking may give opinion to the hearers that I have delight to hear myself talk. Sir Walter Ralegh hath often urged, and still doth urge, the producing of my Lord Cobham. I would know of my Lords, the Judges, if it might not stand with the order of our proceedings to take a further time and know His Majesty's pleasure in that which is desired." The Judges were obdurate : the proceedings, they said, must ' go on and receive an end.' Cecil was not satisfied, and turned to the prisoner. " Sir Walter Ralegh," he said, " if my Lord Cobham will now affirm that you were acquainted with his dealings with Count Aremberg, that you knew of the letter he received, that you were the chief instigator of him, will you then be concluded by it ? "

" Let my Lord Cobham speak before God and the King, and deny God and the King if he speak not truly," replied Ralegh, " and [if he] will then say that ever I knew of Arabella's matter or the money out of Spain, or the Surprising Treason, I will put myself upon it. God's will and the King's be done with me ! "

" Then, Sir Walter," said Cecil, " call upon God to help you, for I do verily believe my Lords will prove this."

My Lords had, in fact, what seemed a conclusive document up their sleeve. It was no less than a solemn confession [1] from Cobham that his former retractation in Ralegh's favour had been wrung from him in pity for Ralegh's wife and children. He went on to say that he was resolved to set down the truth, and then affirmed that Ralegh had dealt with him to obtain a pension of £1500 from Spain, in return for which Ralegh was to give d'Aremberg intelligence affecting Spain, the Low Countries, and the Indies.

The impression which Cobham's letter produced was the crisis of the trial. Up to this time Ralegh's bearing had been so manly, and Coke's language so outrageous, that there must have been room to doubt which way the event would go. Now for a moment Ralegh was dumbfounded. Presently he gathered himself together to make one last fight for life. " What say you," Popham asked him, " to the pension of £1500 a year ? " " I say," he answered evasively, " that Cobham is a poor, silly, base, dishonourable soul." True as the words were, Popham scented the evasion. " I perceive," he said, " you are not so clear a man as you have protested all this while, for you should have discovered this matter to the King." Ralegh made no direct reply, but begged leave to read the letter exculpating himself which Cobham had now retracted. Coke broke in, declaring that the letter had been unfairly obtained. Cecil advised in the contrary sense. " My Lord Cecil," shouted Coke angrily, " mar not a good cause." Cecil had already had occasion to rebuke Coke's insolent treatment of the prisoner. This time he did not

[1] " I protest upon my soul to write nothing but what is true."

veil his meaning in civil phrases. " Mr. Attorney,"
he said, " you are more peremptory than honest ;
you must not come here to show me what to do."

Ralegh asked Cecil to look at Cobham's letter, as
Cecil could best swear to his brother-in-law's writing. It
contained as solemn an assertion of Ralegh's innocence
as its successor had contained of Ralegh's guilt.   The
prisoner sought to give it a higher value. But evidently
it proved nothing. As Gardiner says : " The only point
which Cobham succeeded in establishing was the un-
doubted fact that he was himself a most impudent liar."
Making, however, what he could of it, Ralegh went
on to deal with the Chief Justice's question.   And
now he acknowledged that there had been speech of
a £1500 a year pension from Spain between him and
Cobham, though he had never had any idea of accepting it. He admitted the fault of concealment, but he
denied any implication of treason.

The confession came too late.   His defence had
now that fatal appearance of shiftiness from which
no case ever perfectly recovers.   The jury found him
guilty, and Popham pronounced judgment in the usual
form. Then, or perhaps at some earlier point in
the proceedings, Cecil was seen to weep.[1]

It would not, of course, follow that he thought
the sentence unmerited. Nor is there the least
reason to think he did so. Even the judicious
historian of the seventeenth century does not avoid
the conclusion that " Ralegh was evidently not
anxious to tell the whole truth " [2]; and Cecil's
official despatch to Winwood [3] suggests that his own
cautious judgment had reached a similar opinion.
He notices especially the two points that have never
been satisfactorily explained—the message by Keymis,
and the offer of the pension—and he points out that a

---

[1] Lodge, *Illustr.*, iii. p. 74.
[2] Gardiner, *Hist. of Engl.*, i. p. 136.
[3] Printed in Jardine's *Crim. Trials*, i. p. 458.

certain additional value seemed to attach to Cobham's evidence, because no man would recklessly incriminate himself. It is probable enough that Ralegh (as indeed he himself admitted after his conviction [1]) had given ear to some things which he had best not have heard.

To the 'irresolute and revengeful' Cobham Cecil meets out the same dispassionate treatment. And in Cobham's case the enumeration of facts—"all which, with many other circumstances being inferred against him, made it clear that he was worthily found guilty of treason"[2]—promoted a far more definite condemnation.

Still, the Main Plot was a shadowy affair beside the Bye. All the confederates in that conspiracy were condemned by their own confessions, and the treason was of such a kind that there was no great place for mercy. Cecil saved where he could. Parham, to whom Watson had only opened part of the matter, owed his life directly to the Secretary. "He had gone the same way as the rest (as it is thought), save for a word the Lord Cecil cast in the way as his cause was in handling, 'That the King's glory consisted as much in freeing the innocent as condemning the guilty.'"[3] But in the case of Cecil's own brother-in-law there was no room for repentance. In vain George Brooke wrote those piteous appeals which one can hardly read even now without a pang :—

"Sir, I perceive that I am fallen quick into hell, neither can I find any other comfort in it but this, that I hope I shall be excused from it in the world to come. . . . I hold myself bound to solicit . . . that you will not be weary to move the King for grace." And again : "She that loved me and whose memory you yet love, beholds from heaven the extreme calamity

---

[1] Edwards, *Ralegh*, ii. p. 277.
[2] The letter is printed in Jardine, *Crim. Trials*, i. p. 459.
[3] Carleton to Chamberlain (Jardine, i. p. 465).

of her father's house. Shall I need say any more after this ? . . .
If I promise you anything of myself you may truly say you need
it not, nor care not for it.   Therefore I must stand only upon
your free disposition and shall be as much the more bound because nothing binds you.   Leave now, I beseech your Lordship,
to be nice and stick not to discover yourself in my relief." [1]

It was all in vain. Not even the memory of his
wife availed to induce Cecil to save the arch-con-
spirator ; nor ought we to doubt the propriety of his
conduct. What he might fairly ask the King to
grant—some alleviation of his brother-in-law's confinement in view of Brooke's particular infirmity [2]—
he asked. But to solicit Brooke's life was to solicit
that which the King had no more than a bare right
to give. Justice therefore took its course. The
priests, in Carleton's grim phrase, ' led the dance.'
Brooke followed, looking his last from the scaffold
at Winchester upon Saint Cross, ' which drove him
first to discontent.' Markham, Grey, and Cobham
were brought out to die, and then reprieved by an
act of grace, of which his ministers had no previous
knowledge, on the part of the King.[3] Ralegh was
saved from the preliminaries as well as the reality of
death to beat his wings against the Tower walls until
his brilliant plumage grew rusty with age and his
heart sick with yearning.[4] It is suggested that Cecil
deliberately kept him there. More probably, powerful
as he was, Cecil had no power to open the cage. If
we are to read between his words, the Minister,
waited upon the times and seasons of James's pleasure
to effect Ralegh's liberation.[5] In the event it is true
the faint shadow of hope which he had thrown
upon Lady Ralegh's supplications faded into nothing.
But to Ralegh's eyes, and in spite of one unfriendly

[1] Hatf. MSS., 101/85, and 187/106 ; S. P. Dom., Jas. 1., 4/84.
[2] *Ibid.*, 101/107.   [3] Winwood Memorials, ii. p. 11.
[4] See Ralegh's letter in Edwards' *Life of Ralegh*, ii. p. 329.
[5] Stebbing, *Sir Walter Ralegh*, p. 245.

passage in 1609, he continued to the end to seem a friend at Court.[1]   And the fact that Cecil died in 1612, and that Ralegh, in spite of the favour shown him by the Queen and the Prince of Wales, remained a prisoner until 1616, seems to show conclusively that it was the King and not the Minister who was the real opponent of a release. Cecil, besides, has all the appearance of having done what he could. He had, as Ralegh's biographer observes, saved Lady Ralegh and the child from destitution after the catastrophe of 1603.   Of that the acknowledgments of the stricken wife and husband leave no room to doubt.[2] One not over-friendly act may, however, perhaps be laid at his door. From a sentence of the King's it is to be inferred that he had brought forward Carr's name as the donee of the manor of Sherborne, of which the Crown, by virtue of a legal flaw, was in a position to deprive the hapless Ralegh.   The injury did not amount to much, for compensation was intended (though in the event this fell short of the just value of the estate), and James would probably in any case have given the property to another if he had not disposed of it to Carr. But a fastidious conscience will be left wishing that Cecil had had no kind of share—outside his official duty—in the undoing of one to whom he was tied by memory, affection, and esteem.

[1] See Ralegh's letter in Edwards' *Life of Ralegh*, ii. p. 329.
[2] Edwards, *Life and Letters of Ralegh*, i. p. 461.

CHAPTER XIII

CHURCH AND STATE

" Bodies politic being subject as much as natural to dissolution
by divers means, there are undoubtedly more estates over-
thrown through diseases bred within themselves than
through violence from abroad; because our manner is
always to cast a doubtful and a more suspicious eye towards
that over which we know we have least power; and therefore the fear of external dangers causeth forces at home to
be the more united; it is to all sorts a kind of bridle, it
maketh virtuous minds watchful, it holdeth contrary dispositions in suspense, and it setteth those wits on work
in better things which would be else employed in worse:
whereas on the other side domestical evils, for that we
think we can master them at all times, are often permitted
to run on forward till it be too late to recall them. In the
meanwhile the commonwealth is not only through unsound-
ness so far impaired as those evils chance to prevail, but
farther also through opposition arising between the unsound
parts and the sound, where each endeavoureth to draw
evermore contrary ways, till distraction in the end bring
the whole to ruin."

HOOKER, *Eccles. Pol.*, bk. v., Ep. Ded. to Abp. Whitgift.

THE year 1604 opened with the assembly of the
Hampton Court Conference. Cecil, together with the
other Lords of the Council, was impressed to attend
that momentous ecclesiastical tournament, where, according to the pardonable exaggeration of the most
cautious of historians, the King ' in two minutes '
contrived to ' seal his own fate and the fate of
England for ever.'[1] It does not appear that the
Secretary contributed anything of consequence to the

[1] Gardiner, *Hist. of England*, i. p. 157.

debate. He had not got James's love of theological
disputation. In early life, when Puritanism was a
less aggressive force than it had since become, he
had criticised the action of the Bishops in driving
the Puritan ministers from their cures ;[1] and at
the assembling of the Conference he had been long
enough in power to have a statesman's dread of
stirring the muddy waters of ecclesiasticism. Barlow's offer to dedicate an account of the proceedings
to him does not appear to have been welcome.[2]
Probably his interest in such questions as the use of
the cross in baptism and the ring in marriage was of
the smallest. So far as we know he only intervened
on two occasions—once to attack the licence that
obtained in respect to the sale of ' seditious and
popish pamphlets ' at the Universities and in St.
Paul's Churchyard, once to put the King in mind
of the indecency of what passed by the name of
' ambling communions.' But, as might be expected,
he agreed with the general tenor of the King's discourses, and, just after James had made his famous
speech upon the theme of ' no bishop, no king,' he
told his colleagues—in language which reads pleasantly beside the egregious flattery of the Bishops—
that great thanks were due to God who had given
them ' a king of an understanding heart.'[3] A letter
to the Archbishop of York shows that in ecclesiology
as in other things he was a disciple of the middle
way. But, more logical and more clear-sighted than
many later adherents of his Church, he affirms that
" there are schisms in habit as well as opinions " ;
that " Non servatur unitas in credendo nisi adsit in
colendo."[4] Uniformity is not indeed the kernel of
unity, but, as he saw, it is the shell which guards that

[1] Ickwellbury MSS., " A Speech made to Queen Elizabeth touching
Jesuits, etc. etc. By the Earl of Salisbury."
[2] Hatf. MSS., 188/109 and 108/44.
[3] Barlow's account of the Hampton Court Conference.
[4] Hatf. MSS., 108/76.

kernel from destruction.   Bacon, it is true, thought
otherwise and recommended a policy of compre-
hension which would have retained the Puritans.
But Bacon fell into the mistake, common to persons
of a philosophic turn of mind, of supposing that things
theoretically indifferent are practically unimportant.
James, philosopher though he was, had seen enough of
the Scottish Presbyterians to know better.   Toleration
within the Church would have merely made confusion
worse confounded.   What was needed was a generous
toleration outside the borders of the Establishment.
But no one had as yet conceived such a thing to be
possible.

The course which had been resolved upon was
carried out with a decent lenity.   The dissentient
ministers were given time to conform to the in-
junctions of their ecclesiastical superiors.   It was not
until 1605 that ejectments began.   In April of that
year the gentlemen of Leicestershire wrote up to
Cecil to try to move him to sustain the interest of
some favourite clergymen who had fallen under the
ban.   He replied with characteristic courtesy and
firmness.

" For the request you make that I shall interpose my mediation in favour of divers ministers that show themselves uncon-
formable to the ordinances of the Church, in respect of that
comfort which you have received by their ministry, this is that
I must say, that for the religion which they profess I reverence
them and their calling, but for their unconformity I acknowledge
myself no way warranted to deal for them because the course
they take is no way safe in such a monarchy as this, where His
Majesty aimeth at no other end than, where there is but one
true faith and doctrine preached, there to establish one form
(so as) a perpetual peace may be settled in the Church of God ;
where contrarywise these men, by this singularity of theirs in
things approved to be indifferent by so many reverend fathers of
the Church, by so great multitudes of their own brethren (yea
many that have been formerly touched with the like weaknesses)
do daily minister cause of scandal in the Church of England and
give impediment to that great and godly work, towards which

all honest men are bound to yield their best means according
to their several callings, namely, to suppress idolatry and Romish
superstition in all His Majesty's dominions. . . . Let me entreat
you now to give me leave to change the case and make myself
the petitioner to you in this kind, that you (foreseeing the dis-
honour and danger like to ensue by these separations of ourselves one from another, in matters of this nature, concurring
otherwise in all main points of faith and doctrine) would so
interpose your private authorities over these poor men (who are
easily carried by your breath in things indifferent) that [1] they
may not be found ready to strain a gnat and swallow the camel,
nor wilfully to stop their own mouths from instructing those of
whom they profess to take so great care, but rather to conform
themselves to the ordinances of the Church, to which they owe
obedience, seeing we so fully agree in one true substance of faith
and religion and ought all to strive in a brotherly course to
maintain the bonds of unity and conformity for the advancement
of God's glory and furtherance of our own salvation." [2]

In the same spirit Cecil conceived his instructions
as Chancellor to the University of Cambridge. Everyone preaching at St. Mary's ought in his judgment
to subscribe to the Prayer Book, the Articles, and the
Royal Supremacy.[3]

If there was trouble in the Church there was
trouble also in the State. Goodwin's Case and
Sherley's Case, interesting as they are to students of
constitutional history, are too uninteresting to the
rest of the world to claim recapitulation here. But
they exercised the mind of the House of Commons
and were doubtless reflected in the great budget of
business with which the indefatigable minister had to
cope. It was not the least of his difficulties that by
his accession to the peerage he had lost personal
touch with the Lower House. There was no one in
the administration to replace him there. Large questions were coming up. The abuses of purveyance and
the incommodities of wardship stood in the forefront
of the programme of reform. The latter grievance
touched Cecil very nearly. Though he had apparently

[1] In the original, ' as.'   [2] Hatf. MSS., 110/117.   [3] Ibid., 136/199.

been deprived of the Mastership of the Court of
Wards soon after the King's accession, he had been
quickly reinstated in that lucrative office.[1]   But
the country had outgrown alike a theory of marriage
which took from the ward all freedom of affection
and a theory of taxation which attached the family
income to the capricious chances of age and sex.   No
one pretended that the recommendations of the
Commons were otherwise than reasonable.   The
most that could be said about them was that they
were untimely, because a greater project than the
abolition of *corvées* or of *mariages de convenance*
was in the air.   The King wanted the field clear in
order that he might draw England and Scotland
into a union.

In respect to this greater issue there can be no
doubt of the abstract excellence of James's reasoning.
When at last, a hundred years later, Scotland
reluctantly submitted to the unwelcome bondage,
she entered upon a period of prosperity such
as she had never dreamed of before.   The un-
soundness of the King's design lay in the total
absence of friendly sentiment between his Scottish
and English subjects.   The enemies of five hundred
years' standing were in the twinkling of an eye, with a
stroke of the pen, to be united in all their members
as they were now united in their head.   Cecil, if, as
Gardiner maintains, he never harboured one original
thought, escaped at least the dangers of the visionary
which Gardiner equally laments in Cecil's master.
He wished the nations to get to know one another,
to be allied in marriage before they were allied in
constitution.[2]   He wished, in fact, as every statesman who knows his work does wish, that the pain of
a new idea might be first allayed by the gentle hands

[1] Venetian Cal., x. 55 and 66.
[2] See Baschet Transcripts, Beaumont au Roi, 19/29th February
1604.

of Time.   The King, however, was urgent, and conveyed his displeasure at the dilatoriness of the Lower
House.   They accordingly dropped their attack on
purveyance and wardship for the moment and proceeded to pass a Bill appointing commissioners to
treat of the Union.   It is unnecessary to say that
Cecil was one of them.

The weight of public business had now grown
enormous. The simmering resentment of the Commons, which showed itself in the famous Apology
of 1604, where the religious and political principles
of 1688 were clearly foreshadowed ; the vague but
deep-seated hostility to the Union, which in itself
required time and attention ; the overtures of peace
from Spain, now coming to a point—all these needed
careful and deliberate handling.   But Cecil did not
save himself for great issues.   His name appears
at committees, where he might well have deputed the
work to less busy men.   He is appointed by the House
of Lords to consider Bills directed against the im-
portation of popish and seditious books, against the
unlawful hunting and stealing of deer and conies,
against the residence of married men with their
wives and families at the universities, colleges, and
halls, as well as one for the confirmation of letters
patent : [1] and he sits as a member of the conference
of the two Houses to determine what shall be done
in the matter of the Bishop of Bristol's book, which
violated the then privileges of the Commons by
its antagonistic criticisms.[2]   It is no wonder that
he begged the Venetian envoy to have a little
patience with him, since he had hardly time to
breathe.[3]

By the time Parliament was up, the negotiations
for the Spanish peace were nearing a conclusion.
Few men who were then alive can have remembered

---

[1] Lords Journals, 3rd and 5th May, 23rd June, 28th June, 1604.
[2] *Ibid.*, 30th May.   [3] Venetian Cal., x. 227.

Spain as other than the inveterate enemy of their country. Robert Cecil had grown to manhood in an England where the thought of a Spanish invasion held the place which the thought of a French invasion had for a later age, which the thought of a German one has come to have for our own. But if on all hands he heard the call to battle, from his father he learned the tradition of peace. In an interesting state-paper,[1] which sets out in the quaint orthography of some Scotsman about the Court ' the reasons which the Lord Cecil did use to induce His Majesty of England to consent to the peace with Spain,' the restitution of good relations between the two countries is treated as Burghley's dying charge to his successor. . . .

"Pardon me, dread sovereign," Cecil is alleged to have said, " if I reveal that which I had . . . left (me) as the greatest part of my patrimony . . . by my father who foresaw this happy arrival of your Majesty to England. Having then his body wearied with sickness, his mind mightily perplexed with the State besides his old age which of itself is a most great cross (he) called me to him almost weeping—' Son,' said he, ' I found a sick and diseased commonwealth. How much I have laboured in her God knoweth, and these to whom my pains are best known can partly record, but the most that ever the industry of this weak body could perform was only to minister physick to the sick and wounded commonwealth, to keep her in the same state I found her and to preserve her from falling into further frenzies. But how oft I have pressed to make this commonwealth go of her self and stand alone . . . (finding her so straightly linked to others which were so heavy a burden to her and did rather weigh her down than support her),[2] being but one unless I would have opposed me to all the rest of the state (which is a dangerous matter), I could not develop her from this remorse. But, son,' said he, ' thou art young and perhaps thy father's care . . . and thy own good behaviour may move thy prince to impose a part of that heavy weight which I have all my time carried . . . upon thy weak shoulders; which, if (it) happen, upon my blessing I charge thee that these three things thou have before thy eyes . . . the first, tend in all thy actions in the state to shun foreign wars and . . . seditions;

---

[1] S. P. Dom., Jas. I., 9/18 (i).   [2] The brackets are mine.

labour (with thy prince's honour) to reconcile her to all her enemies so far as may stand with honour and safety ; thirdly, have regard to the tottering commonwealth after thy mistress' death to invest the true and lawful successor.' "

The wisdom of these instructions Cecil, if the document be authentic, impressed upon the King. He told James how, within his own experience, Elizabeth had increasingly realised that the welfare of English commerce was of far more consequence to the community than the contentment of the hot young bloods of the nobility who were clamouring for new avenues of distinction. He compared the policy of privateering to the vehement mineral medicines of a chemist, which perhaps dispelled the disease in cases of extremity but left the stomach ' mightily weakened.' He quoted an old saying of his father's that the Low Countries were but ' a wooden leg ' to England and ' no natural one.' And he insinuated the two considerations to which James was likely to pay very particular attention—that the Hollanders were, in fact, rebels against their proper Sovereign, and that the maintenance of their cause was an extremely expensive affair. It must not, however, be supposed that he contemplated the restoration of the United Provinces to Spain. Even had he desired it, the revolt in the Netherlands was long past the stage at which a return to the *status quo* was conceivable. He fully recognised that we lay under certain obligations towards our old ally, and the recognition of these obligations fell into line well enough with the international economy which he had in his mind. There were, he told the Venetian envoy, three Christian Powers in Europe—England, France, and Spain—nicely poised in equilibrium, as things were, but liable to be thrown out of balance if the weight of the United Provinces were cast into any one of the three scales.[1] The key of his diplo-

[1] Venetian Cal., x. p. 107.

macy—it is the skeleton key which unlocks the
secrets of every pacific diplomatist in every age and
country—was therefore to maintain the balance of
power. This would have been best attained by
welding together the Netherlands—both Catholic and
Protestant—under an independent Sovereign, after the
fashion of medieval Burgundy. But the childlessness
of the Archduke and the consequent prospect of the
reversion of his territories to Spain rendered such a
solution impracticable for the moment. Cecil therefore
professed himself ready to recognise ' a species of independence ' in the United Provinces, ' if they showed
they were capable of using it.' [1]

A policy, so evidently sagacious as far as England was concerned, was not likely to commend itself
abroad. The Provinces had no wish to be left to
fight their battles for themselves, however well able
they were to do it, and the French, for all their smooth
speaking, were reluctant to see their allies delivered
from the incubus of the Spanish War. Rosny,
charged with present guile but excogitating for the
future the beneficent purposes of the Great Design,
came over to felicitate James on his happy accession
to the English throne and to propose an offensive
alliance against the Spaniard. The King, moved
the more by the discovery of a supposedly Spanish
plot, fell an easy victim to the Frenchman's grandiose
flatteries. In Cecil the Ambassador found less susceptible emotions. He was blandly informed that
war cost money, that France was already largely
indebted to England, and that unless the French
undertook to discharge their obligations within two
years it would be impossible for James to put an army
into the field or a fleet upon the sea. The challenge
was very much more direct than Rosny cared about.
He took refuge in the infinite periods of the old
diplomacy and reported that his opponent was a

[1] Venetian Cal., x. p. 107.

master of mystification. " Cecil," he wrote home, " subtle as is his custom, and intent on snatching an advantage at every turn, was always trying to make the States' Envoys and myself admit that we had said things which we had never thought of, and manifested great satisfaction when he had brought matters to such a point that no one could make anything of them." [1] The truth was, as Rosny knew well enough, that Cecil was not to be decoyed from the straight paths of peace :—" Lord Cecil and others like him are of the old English temper, that is to say, enemies of France, not too friendly towards Spain and resolutely bent upon reviving the House of Burgundy and reducing the States to this necessity." [2] Nothing, therefore, came of all the fine speeches but a permission to recruit soldiers in England for the defence of Ostend, and some indefinite understanding that the royal children of France and England should presently intermarry. But Rosny boasted of a great diplomatic success ; and there were doubtless those who believed him.

As soon as the Frenchman was gone, d'Aremberg began to get to work by requesting the mediation of the English King between the Archduke and the States. In September, Villa Mediana arrived in England as Spanish Ambassador. The situation was peculiar. The two Countries were not at peace, but neither were the two Sovereigns at war. For as King of Scotland James had no quarrel with the King of Spain. Villa Mediana, however, had no authority to treat. The Ambassador extraordinary and plenipotentiary—the Constable of Castille—was sent to dally at Brussels whilst Spain endeavoured to enforce her old contention that England was an inferior power by luring the English diplomatists across the water. The Mountain, however, resolutely refused to come to Mohammed, and Mohammed, therefore, in the person of the Constable,

[1] Econ. Roy., t. ii. c. 19.   [2] Ibid., c. 20.

came in due course to the Mountain. All—or·almost
all—the essentials of the business, however, were
settled by special commissioners before his landing.
The conference took place at Somerset House,
where the Spanish Ambassador was lodged. In
spite of Cecil's fear that James's indiscretions would
weaken his position [1] the English contrived to drive
a solid bargain. After the usual bickerings about
credentials had been dismissed,[2] the Spaniards proposed an offensive and defensive alliance. Cecil
rejected it more peremptorily than that offered by
Rosny. It was inconsistent, he said, alike with the
Protestant religion and the existing treaty with
France. He went on to speak of amity. Rovida,
the Senator of Milan, with whom rested the burden
of the Spanish case, asked him to be more definite,
and of three alternatives—an offensive and defensive
alliance, a defensive alliance, and ' a peace of firm
amity and friendship with a condition not to attempt
anything to each other's prejudice '—to choose one.
Cecil asked leave to refer them to the King. James
declared the third to be the only alternative worth
discussion. Let them, he said, treat the conference
like a treaty of marriage, " wherein the articles of
covenant are handled between the parents by way
of admission upon presumption of a future liking
to follow between the parties."

Rovida then proceeded to cast the chief apple of
discord into the arena. The English, he said, had
spoken of their existing treaties as impediments to
the peace, but the King of Spain was not, in fact,
at war with any state in Christendom. Richardot,
Cecil's old acquaintance of 1588, pointed the observation. Was James, he asked, prepared to abandon

[1] See Baschet Transcripts, Beaumont to Villeroy, 29th February
1604.

[2] The following account is based upon Add. MSS., 14,033. Cp.
the account in H.M. C. Report, viii., App. 1, p. 95 (Jersey MSS.),
where the deliberations are summarised at length.

relations with the King's rebellious subjects in
Holland ?

Cecil replied that he did not wish to discuss whether
they were rebellious or not.   His late mistress, upon
' very just and good cause,' had allied herself to
them, and by her action the English nation was bound.
Was the cessation of the English trade with Holland
essential to the conclusion of peace with Spain ?

But Rovida pressed the question.   Cecil replied
that it had little significance, for James, even as King
of Scots, had traded with the United Provinces, and
he could not now be reasonably asked to accept worse
conditions of commerce than he had had before his
accession.   Rovida was cornered.   He could not deny
that good relations between Scotland and the States
had subsisted side by side with friendship towards
Spain.   He was obliged to urge, therefore, that the
magnitude of the trade involved affected the principle
for which he was contending.   We ought, besides, to
be governed by laws and not by examples.   Examples,
retorted Northampton, are the means of interpreting
laws.   Cecil offered to make munitions of war contra-
band.   Still the Spaniards were not satisfied.   Then
he quietly reminded them that, if England was more
prejudiced in her trade by peace, it would be to her
interest to continue hostilities.

Other points came up for discussion.   Cecil made
a bid for the trade of the Indies, but that prize was too
rich to be voluntarily divided, and by tacit consent
there continued to be ' no peace beyond the line.'
His revenge was not slow in coming.   When Rovida
asked for the surrender of the cautionary towns—
Brill, Flushing, and Rammekens—he was told that
the King's honour was bound up with their restoration
to the States if the Dutch debt was discharged within
a reasonable time.

In spite of these differences it was plain that there
was a sufficient basis of agreement.   One or two

points only were left over to the Constable's coming—
in particular the secret articles securing immunity
from the Spanish Inquisition for English merchants
and sailors so long as they offered no insult to the
outward practices of the Roman Catholic faith.
On the whole the negotiation was as successful as
a minister could reasonably look for. The trade of
Spain, so long closed by war to English traders, was
thrown open on the ancient terms. Merchandise
drawn from or destined for any of the three kingdoms
or the Spanish Netherlands was freed from the new
thirty per cent. duty on imports and exports ; the
incessant drain of men and money for foreign service
was stayed; and, if the Indies were still forbidden fruit,
there remained the more adventure for those who
plucked it.

In spite of the hatred of a Spanish connection
which lay deep in English breasts, the Constable met
with a very tolerable reception at his coming. Enough
expressions of goodwill, at any rate, were heard—so
Northampton told the King—to provoke the Ambassador to remark that it was the work of God under
princes of sweet and gracious disposition to reconcile
the hearts and affections of Christians.[1] Doubtless
there were others to whom that which had been
done was far from grateful, and on the continent of
Europe the exhaustion of Spain was believed to be so
great that it was thought she had scored a treaty on
remarkably easy terms.[2] It was obvious to argue
that Cecil had been bribed, and we shall have in due
course to examine the ground of that and similar
suspicions. But for the present, at least, we may accept
the explanation which Cecil gave to the Venetian
Ambassador that the English Crown was itself too
much embarrassed to find money for any continuance
of the war to be practicable ; that, in fact, as he put
it, ' necessity knew no law,' or else the treaty would

[1] S. P. Dom., Jas. I., 9/7.   [2] Winwood Memorials, ii. p. 75.

not have been signed.[1] Such an admission precludes
the possibility as well as the need of any other defence.
If it were not so, one might have urged that Cecil
had at any rate given to his country the best gifts of
all diplomatic activity—commerce and peace.

Canvas has a better life than parchment. The
treaty which the Constable came with so much pomp
to conclude has passed into a long oblivion from which
only from time to time the student of history is at
pains to rescue it. But many a casual wanderer in
the National Portrait Gallery must have cast a glance
at its negotiators. There they still sit as Marc
Gheeraedts saw them, ranged around the conference-
table, over three hundred years ago : the Constable
with that ' long, black Spanish face ' of his which
Northampton thought a replica of his own ;[2] Rovida,
in all the strength of his grim, set brows ; Richardot,
grown grey in astuteness ; Villa Mediana and d'Aremberg, unmistakable past-masters in all the arts of
plausibility ; Verreiken, the only one of the party,
perhaps, whom the eye is inclined to pronounce at
a glance to be perfectly honest : and, over against
them, Buckhurst and Nottingham, weary with age
and services ; Devonshire, all aglow with honours and
success ; Northampton, steeped in secret cunning ;
Cecil, with his pallid skin already betraying the sickness of the body, and his long, white, nervous fingers
hardly concealing the tension of the mind. Altogether
an interesting and distinguished company, of whose
co-operation some pictorial reminiscence is not ungrateful !

On August 20th, in reward for his services, Cecil
received a viscountcy. Why he chose to take his
title from the remote Dorsetshire manor, which, in
fact, he was not fully possessed of until 1611, instead
of from his extensive estates in Hertfordshire, is not
apparent. Perhaps the mere charm of a name caught

<hr>

[1] Venet. Cal., x. p. 176. [2] S. P. Dom., Jas. I., 9/7.

THE CONFERENCE OF THE ENGLISH AND SPANISH PLENIPOTENTIARIES, 1604

(Painted by Marc Gheeraedts the Younger. National Portrait Gallery)

[*To face p.* 226

his fancy ; perhaps the King was already to his knowledge casting envious eyes upon Theobalds, which James had visited again in the beginning of the year (1604). Anyhow, it was with the great freshness and freedom of the down-country of the west, where he was soon after to be found adding field to field, that he chose to associate the fortunes of his family. At Salisbury they show a house in the Vicars' Close which he is alleged to have inhabited and which certainly bears a crest of the Cecils, although the one which he abandoned. And it was from that delectable cathedral town that when he obtained his earldom in 1605 he chose to take his style. A year later the grant of Old Sarum from the Crown gave the best of titles to his choice.

He had a less pleasant reason than estates or dignities for frequenting the west of England. In the summer of 1604, as soon as the Spanish negotiation was disposed of at the end of August, he set out for the waters of Bath. Fear of the plague or pressure of business brought him back again almost directly.[1] He was in London once more early in September, and the rest of the year was devoted in the main to the work of the Union. The joint commission which sat to consider it was, so Bacon tells us, ' a grave and orderly assembly,' a model of counsel. Matters were propounded one day and not discussed till the next, according to the maxim, *in nocte consilium*. This sage procedure had all the appearance of success. Conclusions were reached with such singular unanimity that the King fancied he had run down his quarry and despatched hasty congratulations to his ' little beagle '[2] upon the success of the conference. But, though Cranborne's nose may have been keen enough, the prev was by no means within the huntsman's grasp.

Proposals for a commercial union proved as un-

[1] Hatf. MSS., 278/3.   [2] S. P. Dom., Jas. I., 10/41.

popular with the English merchants as proposals for the naturalisation of Scotsmen were unpopular with the country gentlemen who controlled the Commons. In the end the King tried to force the pace. Colvin's case settled that subjects born under one King belonged, for all the purposes of inheritance, to one country. But the decision of the judges in the one matter only hardened the obstinacy of the Commons in the other; and free trade in commerce between the two peoples was left to wait a century. Cranborne probably suffered no great disappointment at the failure of his efforts. He had never been, if the conjectures of the French Ambassador are to be credited, a friend to the enterprise,[1] knowing as he did much better than his master the part that time and occasion require to play in the affairs of men and nations.

---

[1] Baschet Transcripts, 19th/29th February 1604, Beaumont au Roi: " I know that the Sieur Cecil is uneasy about it (the Union) and that besides as an Englishman he rejects and distrusts it more than he desires it."

CHAPTER XIV

GUNPOWDER TREASON AND PLOT

" Thus you see now what those men be, that under the mantle of
holiness and piety do countenance the foulest and most
abominable treason that ever was conceived against their
Prince and country."
Salisbury to Wotton, 19th March 1606 (S. P. For., Venice, 3).

THE student of latter-day France has suggested the
doubt whether in any modern community the deliverance from destruction of its legislative bodies
would appear a benefit sufficiently precious to be
inscribed in a ferial calendar.[1] If that unkind, but
not improbable, suspicion be just, Guy Fawkes, we
may assume, will continue without a rival to illuminate
the blackness of a November night, until at least
kings have utterly lost their crowns and parliaments
have been replaced by some more rational form of
government and small boys have lost their natural
habits. But good pantomime as it makes, Gunpowder Plot deserves to be remembered as something
more than a winter's tale. More, probably, than anything else it has served to implant in the English
mind that deep, often prejudiced, hatred of Catholicism in all its forms, which the lapse of centuries and
some progress in equity have not entirely sufficed to
dispel. The mere horror of the design was quickened
by the horror that English gentlemen, men of substance and reputation, should have conceived it ;
and the statesmen of the time are little enough to

[1] Bodley, *France*, i. p. 211.

blame if they regarded the ministers of a religion which appeared thus to warp and poison the conscience as no better than agents of darkness. For Catesby and his fellow-conspirators, with the one exception of Tresham, showed themselves to have all the panoply of men of honour. Neither in their adventurous lives nor in their grim and hideous deaths did they behave in a manner which we might not, every one of us, be proud to emulate. Throughout their enterprise they enjoyed all the comfortable assurance of deep conviction; and, when failure had brought home to them some dim perception of the enormity of their offence, they fell back without effort upon the consolations of religion. So high a courage, so strong a resolve, so good a conscience, so foul a purpose seemed a combination almost diabolical.

If Gunpowder Plot determined the judgment of Englishmen upon the Catholic system, as set forth by the Roman missionaries, so conclusively that Titus Oates could make capital out of it seventy or more years afterwards, it determined also in its own time any lurking hesitancy in the mind of the King. Persecution, which he had once declared to be one of the infallible marks of a false church, became in the end the note of his own government. Hence it has been inferred that Cecil got up or at least fostered the conspiracy in order to frighten a timid Sovereign into a policy more agreeable to his own opinions; and Cecil's biographer has as usual to work in face of the knowledge that there is no degree of infamous cunning of which some of his critics have not supposed him capable—not even the decoying of misguided wretches to a violent and hideous death.

Whatever castles we like to build out of them the stones of the story are no longer likely to be much augmented. The excavations seem to have been thorough, and the experts to have left no sod unturned. A singularly able lawyer, a singularly painstaking historian, and, one may add, a singularly sceptical priest, will not, we may be confident, have let much escape their independent investigations. And it only remains to decide whether with Father Gerard we should leave the broken fragments lying in disorder on the ground; or should build with Gardiner after the traditional plans; or whether we should merely seek to fit the pieces together like a child's puzzle without a key. Whatever course we take, the edifice or the ruin will clearly present similar angles of vision, and it is plainly Cecil's that we have, so far as possible, to consider here.

The best way of combating error, it has been well said, is by setting forth truth. But in a perverse world error, or what we take to be so, does not immediately surrender to such gentle methods, and, where the question is urgent, statesmen have sometimes to look to other means for its overthrow. Neither James nor Cecil was by nature a persecutor.

"I did ever hate alike both extremities in any case," the King had told Cecil in their secret correspondence, "only allowing the midst[1] for virtue, as by my book now lately published doth plainly appear. . . . I will never allow in my conscience that the blood of any man shall be shed for diversity of opinions in religion, but I should be sorry the Catholics should so multiply that they might be able to practise their old principles upon us. . . . I am so far from any intention of persecution that[2] I protest to God I reverence their church as our mother church although clogged with many infirmities and corruptions; besides that I did ever hold persecution as one of the infallible notes of a false church."[3]

Cecil, though he did not occupy James's ecclesiastical position, entertained very similar views in regard to the matter in hand. Early in life he had considered very carefully and dispassionately the political aspect of the papal claims and the papal propaganda—far more carefully and dispassionately

[1] 'Middes.'   [2] In the original, 'as.'
[3] *Corresp. of James VI. with Sir R. Cecil*, xiv.

than we should be likely to suspect.   In a state-
paper which he drew up for Queen Elizabeth before
1590 [1] he sets out in the most enlightened fashion
the argument against seeking to reduce the number
of the Papists by persecution.

"No way," he affirms, " do I account Death to lessen or
diminish them since we find by experience that Death works
no such effect, but that, like hydras' heads, upon one cut off seven
grow. Persecution being ever accounted as the badge of the Church,
. . . they should never have the honour to take any pretence of
martyrdom especially in England where the fulness of blood and
greatness of heart is such that they will ever for shameful things
go bravely to death, much more when they think they climb
heaven. And that vice of obstinacy proximitate boni seems
to the common people a divine constancy."

He goes on therefore to affirm that ' he wishes no
lessening of their number but by preaching.'   The
safety of the State, however, required that they should
not be allowed to promote their opinions by occupying
official positions, and that their dependents should be
protected from pressure by the appointment of a commission of Anglican gentlemen in each locality, which
measure, he declares, ' would greatly bind the hearts
of the Commons, in whom the power and strength
of . . . England consisteth,' to the Sovereign.   And
the oath which he recommends to be required of
Catholics is one of a purely political character, viz.
" That whosoever would not bear arms against all
foreign princes, and namely the Pope, that should
anyway invade your Majesty's dominions, he should
be a traitor."   The existing oath he thought excessive ; being such that a Catholic ' must either think,
as without the especial grace of God he cannot think ;
or else become a traitor.'   And though, as things
were, Catholics must inevitably be discontented, in

---

[1] This MS. is among the Ickwellbury (Harvey) MSS. under the
title of " A Speech made to Queen Elizabeth touching the Jesuits,
etc. etc.   By the Earl of Salisbury."   I infer the date from a mention
of the King of Navarre.

order to keep the rest of the nation in contentment, yet they ought not to be made desperate.

Such were Cecil's early cogitations over the most difficult problem of his time, and nowhere else is the character, the prudence, and the clear-sightedness of his political judgment more plainly to be read. Time and experience did not alter his opinions ; and the language he used to King James in the secret correspondence was dictated by the same temper of mind :—

"For the matter of the priests I will also clearly deliver your Majesty my mind. I condemn their doctrine ; I detest their conversation ; and I foresee the peril which the exercise of their function may bring to this island ; only I confess that I shrink to see them die by dozens, when (at the last gasp) they come so near loyalty, only because I remember that mine own voice, amongst others, to the law (for their death) in Parliament was led by no other principle than that they were absolute seducers of the people from temporal obedience and confident persuaders to rebellion, and which is more, because that law had a retrospective to all priests made twenty years before. But contrariwise for that generation of vipers (the Jesuits) who make no more ordinary merchandise of any thing than of the blood and crowns of princes, I am so far from any compassion, that [1] I rather look to receive commandment from you to abstain than (to) prosecute." [2]

But whatever sentiments of pity and moderation germinated in their minds, neither King nor Minister could change the soil and climate in which they had to work. The fears that haunted them were, indeed, no idle ones. The propaganda of the Roman Church had been exceptionally successful. The Venetian Ambassador estimates, doubtless with some exaggeration, that one-half of the nation at least were adherents of the Pope.[3] Every advantage, in fact, was taken of any leniency in the enforcement of the statutes against recusancy, and there seemed to be a fair prospect that

[1] In the original, ' as.'
[2] *Corresp. of James VI. with Sir R. Cecil*, No. xiii.
[3] Venet. Cal., x. p. 302.

a generation desiring to go back upon the work of the Reformation would presently arise. The conduct of the King led the hopes of the Catholics in the same direction. Amid the visionary projects that haunted his mind was one for the reunion of Christendom, and through Sir James Lindsay he began to exchange communications with the Court of Rome. His refusal to remit the recusancy statutes, which had prompted Watson's plot, was reversed after the conspiracy had been brought to light by the aid of the Jesuits ; and for a short twelvemonth the Catholics enjoyed an unwonted security of possession, which they mistook for the earnest of a perfect toleration. Then in the summer of 1604—contemporaneously with the negotiation of the treaty with Spain—a Bill re-enacting all the recusancy statutes of Elizabeth was carried through Parliament. It was not, indeed, designed to be more than monitory, and those who came under its penalties were intended to be excused from its operation. The judges, however, particularly in the north, took the law at its face value ; and the death-sentences which they passed must have seemed to many to cry out for retribution. To Robert Catesby and his associates their conduct brought to maturity a long-fermenting desire to avenge the Catholic cause; and as soon as Cranborne and the Commissioners for the Union vacated their place of meeting with the approach of Christmas, the conspirators entered in and began to undermine the wall which divided it from the Houses of Parliament.

The negotiations with the Holy See did not prove less disappointing to the persons interested than is usually the case. To the King's overtures for a General Council the Pope had responded by inviting him to let his son be brought up as a Catholic, and by appointing a commission of twelve cardinals to inquire into the condition of England. The last suggestion

was more than James could stomach; and, since the
Pope himself was out of reach, he proceeded to take
vengeance upon the Pope's adherents. A word
from him was enough to open the flood-gates of
Protestant antipathy, and over five thousand recusants
were presently brought to book. It happens that
Cranborne's views are very exactly known to us, for
Nicholas Molin, the Venetian Ambassador, taxed him
directly with this renewal of severity, the reason of
which was so little apparent. The King's excessive
clemency, he replied, had brought them to this—
that priests went openly about both in town and
country to say Mass, and gave a great deal of offence
by doing so. The news from Rome had made an
uproar amongst the English bishops, and people
fancied that the King was going to grant freedom
of conscience, though he had in reality no such intention. All the trouble came from Lindsay, a ' feather-
brained fellow ' who had overstepped his instructions
by inducing the Pope to appoint a congregation of
cardinals, whilst all he was enjoined to do was to
make civil speeches, assuring the Pope of the King's
goodwill towards him as a temporal sovereign, and
undertaking not to persecute the English Catholics,
either in goods or person, so long as they remained
loyal. Some increase of severity was therefore required in order to repress the licence of the priests
and convince the world that no change of religion was
in contemplation.[1]

The miscarriage of the negotiation with Rome
coincided with an increasing distaste on the part of
the King for the discharge of public business. He
told the Council in the February of 1605 that he
intended thenceforward to live much more in the
country, where alone he could get adequate physical
exercise, and that he should leave the administration
of public affairs more generally in their hands.[2] On

[1] Venet. Cal., x. p. 227.   [2] *Ibid.*, p. 216.

4th May he created Cranborne Earl of Salisbury, and it is probable—contrary to the opinion of certain of his critics—that the Minister was never more powerful than in the months which preceded the discovery of the plot. Burghley, his brother, and Philip Herbert, who had married his niece, Lady Susan Vere, received simultaneously the honour of an earldom ; and George Carew, his great friend, was given a barony.

The summer did not pass without vague presages of a Catholic plot ; but Salisbury had lived too long in an atmosphere of treason to make much account of the warnings. He was more troubled by the applications which he received to farm out the lands of recusants during their sequestration [1] and by the lavish expenditure of the Court, which continued to deplete the Treasury. The question of the Union and the question of a subsidy alike involved the meeting of Parliament ; but he seems to have shrunk from the encounter, and the date of assembly was postponed once and again. The 5th of November seemed both to him and to Ellesmere soon enough to face the tale of ' empty coffers.' [2]

Ten days before Parliament met, on the 28th October,[3] Salisbury was preparing to sit down to supper with some of his colleagues at Whitehall, when Lord Mounteagle unexpectedly joined the company. The newcomer, who was only thirty-one years of age, if he had not quite boxed the compass of opinion, had made a fair attempt to do it. As a young scapegrace he had had a hand in Essex's rebellion ; as a Catholic zealot he had promoted an intrigue for a Spanish invasion ; and now, having sown his wild oats and exhausted his enthusiasms, he was apparently following

---

[1] Hatf. MSS., 190/148.		[2] *Ibid.*, 111/142.

[3] Salisbury (Winwood Memorials, ii. p. 170) and Levinus Munck (G. P. B., 129) say 26th October. Gardiner (*What Gunpowder Plot was*, p. 128) says, by way of correction, 28th October.

in the track of that judicious form of Catholicism which
Northampton had contrived to reconcile with the
favour of the King. Mounteagle drew the Secretary
aside and they passed into another room. Salisbury
must have known the man and cannot have been
tempted to set any undue value upon his communication. This was, in fact, one of those affairs which were
in the Minister's ordinary way of business—an anonymous letter couched in vague terms and convey-
ing the existence of indefinite danger. All that was
plain was that the recipient was advised to keep clear
of the House of Lords at the meeting of Parliament.
The missive had been handed to one of Mounteagle's
footmen in the evening by a bearer whose face could
not be clearly seen in the darkness. Salisbury, as he
told Cornwallis afterwards, thought that either ' sport
or frenzy ' had begotten the letter,[1] but he made the
discreet comments of one who has been long in office.
He began by applauding Mounteagle's conduct in
making him a party to the affair. Such advertisements as this, he said, in spite of their loose style
and appearance, did not deserve to be neglected,
for the writer might have been distracted by apprehension and terror. Also, since he knew Mounteagle
to be attached to the King, he might tell him that for
months past the Papists, both at home and abroad,
had been in agitation to procure the free exercise of
their religion, and were proposing the delivery of a
petition, at the ensuing session of Parliament, in such
force as should make the Government fearful to refuse
it. Mounteagle was still uneasy lest the whole thing
should turn out to be nothing worse than a bad
joke, and asked for an explicit assurance that he
should be exonerated if it ended in vapour. Salisbury
reassured him and then called into council Suffolk,
who, as Lord Chamberlain, had care of the Houses
of Parliament and the adjacent buildings. Suffolk

[1] Winwood Memorials, ii. p. 171.

undertook to look to his charge. Mounteagle then departed, and his communication was disclosed to the other Lords of the Council who were present. They reached no fresh conclusions except that it was best to let the matter develop. Other peers might receive other anonymous letters bearing on the same issue ; and, besides, premature action would scare the malefactors, if they existed, and, as likely as not, bring the searchers into ridicule.

So things remained until James returned from Royston, three days later, on the 31st. Salisbury then put the letter into his hands, tactfully withholding his surmises, so that the King might have the credit of its interpretation. James read it and remarked that the project of overthrowing a legislature seemed as improbable as the origin of the warning was vague, but that though it might possess no serious significance, the document smacked of fire and powder, and that all places from which an attempt of that character might be made had best be looked to. He went on to commend Mounteagle, and told the Secretary to keep his eye about for peers who showed an inclination to be absent from their places in Parliament. The general sense of the Council continued to be in favour of letting the plot develop.

Salisbury, indeed, was not yet inclined to abate his scepticism. Though he had been frequently warned that a plot was brewing amongst some of the very men afterwards found to be guilty, his mind rejected the probability of so amazing and prodigious a treason.[1] Suffolk, perhaps actuated by a sense of more immediate responsibility, took a more serious view of the affair, and on the following day determined to visit the threatened locality, taking Mounteagle with him. Under the pretext of seeing after some

[1] Hatf. MSS., 227/109. An interesting and candid letter from Cecil to Edmondes, showing the extent of his previous knowledge.

stuff belonging to the King they sought admission to the cellar which lay under the House. There they saw some coal and faggots piled up which they were told belonged to Thomas Percy, a gentleman-pensioner attached to the Court. The name gave both men food for reflection. Suffolk recollected that Percy was a Catholic. Mounteagle, who knew him well, was astonished at never having heard him mention the place, though he was said to have rented it for over a year. They said no more, however, and presently left. Guy Fawkes, for Fawkes it was who had admitted them, may have reasonably thought that the terror was now overpast. He was mistaken. They returned to the palace, carrying their suspicions with them, and the King reaffirmed his belief in the Gunpowder theory. But to avoid ridicule, if the plot proved a mare's nest, he ordered a rumour of stolen stuff to be put about, and then sent Sir Thomas Knyvet down, apparently on that errand, at dead of night. Fawkes was still lurking about the concealed explosives as a miser lurks about his hidden gold. Knyvet's posse detained him whilst the faggots were removed. Thereupon the wretched man, with the same resolute composure that had characterised his actions throughout, confessed his purpose, making no pretence of shame or sorrow. It was now 1 a.m., and Knyvet hurried back to Salisbury with the news of the discovery.

The Council, or such members of it as were available, hastily assembled; and the prisoner was interrogated by the King himself. " Why would you have killed me ? " James asked him. " Because," he replied (if Coke is to be believed), " you are excommunicated by the Pope." " How so ? " said James, doubtless surprised to find that anathemas flourished beside the Pope's fair speeches. " Every Maundy Thursday," replied Fawkes, " the Pope doth excommunicate all heretics who are not of the Church

of Rome ; and you are within the same excommunication." [1]

The prisoner passed to the Tower, and for three
days Popham and Waad cross-questioned him in vain.
He told his story to the Commissioners, but neither
threats nor promises availed to drag from him the
names of his accomplices. On the 9th November
Waad had better news to communicate. Fawkes
agreed to speak, but to Salisbury alone and without
committing his words to paper. Waad, who knew
the psychology of criminals as well as any man living,
made light of the conditions. " When he hath confessed himself to your Lordship I will undertake he
shall acknowledge it before such as you shall call,
and then he will not make dainty to set his hand to
it. . . . He will conceal no name nor matter from
your Lordship . . . and I know your Lordship will
think it the best journey that ever you made." [2]
Salisbury doubtless went down to the Tower to
receive the confession, but he has left no record of the
pungent interview. Already he had his hands upon
the conspirators, and Fawkes' informations can only
have been valuable as confirmatory evidence against
them. How he learnt their names, if we reject, as we
well may do, Father Gerard's conjecture that Thomas
Percy was a spy, is no doubt an obscure point in
the story. But the assurance given to Fawkes that
his associates were known by their flight was not at
all necessarily fictitious in a society still sufficiently
small for men of substance to be men of mark.

In the last scene at Holbeche, where Catesby and
Percy were shot fighting, Salisbury had, of course,
no share. His work lay in London, where, in cold
blood, he had to send the surviving traitors to their
hideous death. The verdict in such a case as theirs
was, of course, a foregone conclusion. Yet Coke

[1] Jardine, *Narrative of the Gunpowder Plot*, p. 103.
[2] Gunpowder Plot Book, 53.

conducted the prosecution in his usual vehement style
—a style which for once, at any rate, matched the
matter of the offence. Salisbury had warned him
beforehand of what ought to be brought out and of
what ought to be left obscure.[1] He does not appear
to have fulfilled his instructions with much fidelity.
It is true that he made it plain that the design of a
conspiracy had begun whilst James was still showing
leniency to the Catholics and even before he had
ascended the throne ; and that he emphasised as far
as he was able the complicity of Hugh Owen, a centre
of Catholic conspiracy in the Netherlands, a man
" whose finger hath been in every treason which hath
been of late years detected," and one whose acquaintance was presumably as damning a distinction as
persons on trial for their lives could possibly possess.
But in spite of the Secretary's instructions he was
too honest or too inconsiderate to conceal the fact
that the anonymous letter to Mounteagle emanated
from one of the confederate traitors. And he said
nothing particular to vindicate Mounteagle's character, though Salisbury was eager to clear him of
the current suspicion of participating in the plot
and afterwards betraying it.[2] Great part of his
speech was devoted to showing the incompatibility
between certain Catholic instruction with regard to
the Pope's power of dethroning sovereigns and a loyal
allegiance to the King. And we can better understand Salisbury's uncompromising hostility to the
Jesuits and all their kind if we bear in mind the
assertion of Cresswell, cited by the Attorney-General,
that "Regnandi jus amittit qui religionem Romanam
deserit." No Protestant Government of those days
could afford to tolerate teaching which affirmed
unblushingly that only a king of the true faith was
a king at all.

Sir Everard Digby was tried separately from his

[1] S. P. Dom., Jas. I., 19/94.   [2] *Ibid,*

associates, and Salisbury took occasion at his trial to
say a few words about the treatment which had been
meted out to the Catholics. He distinguished between toleration and exemption from penalty, and
affirmed that the first had never been promised and
the second only conceded by the King in July 1603,
in respect to the fines which had accrued up to that
time and in consideration of the loyalty which had
been shown by the Catholic gentry on his accession.
According, however, to the version of the King's
speech, which is commonly received, more than this
had been assured ; there was to have been a lasting
immunity from the recusancy fines so long as the
Catholics were faithful to their allegiance. If that
was so, doubtless Salisbury's words fell short of the
fact. But the evidence is not sufficient to justify
Gardiner's sweeping verdict that " he said what he
must have known to be untrue." It may, indeed,
have been so ; but it would have been more in
keeping with the practice of that generally most
patient and equitable historian if he had indicated
that a lie does not exhaust the possibilities of
accounting for the discrepancy. No verbatim
reporters existed in Salisbury's day to whom one
may turn with the same confidence as to a recording
angel. Nor did persons in great place read their
speeches on occasions of importance. Impromptu
and perhaps hesitating words, such as the King made
in replying to the Catholic deputation at Hampton
Court, may have had a different significance for, and
have left a different impression upon, those who heard
them, according as their sympathies inclined towards
Catholicism or its opposite. To Degli Effetti, the
accomplished young man of fashion who filled the post
of papal emissary, they may have seemed to possess a
fairer promise than they had in the eyes of experienced
statesmen like Salisbury. Or, again, Salisbury may
never have heard them himself and have felt bound

in honour and fealty to accept James's own version of
their meaning. At any rate, his statements at Digby's
trial passed unchallenged, and it is dealing out hard
measure to affirm that they were deliberately false.

The work of exposure was but half accomplished
with the condemnation of the active agents of the
plot. Behind Fawkes and Catesby, Salisbury was
looking for the agitators, whose doctrine and countenance,
as he believed, had been the secret root of all
the mischief. To label as a ' visible anatomy of
Popish doctrine and practice ' [1] that long series of
conspiracies which extended as far as his earliest
recollections, became the object of his earnest endeavour;
and, though such a diagnosis inevitably
confounded the natural form and substance of the
Church of Rome with the curvatures and excrescences
of its disease, still the harshness proved salutary,
and Catholic propaganda in England were thenceforward
more commonly conducted by Christian
methods. Four men in particular fell under suspicion.
Garnet, the superior of the English Jesuits, Greenway,
and Gerard had all been intimate with the traitors.
Oldcorne, who with too great a modesty refused to
judge the associates in the hour of their distress,
leaving it, as he said, to God and their consciences to
condemn or justify them, was, by a generous attempt
to give shelter to Garnet, drawn into the fatal circle
of the conspiracy after its failure, and paid for his
humanity by death and torture.

Gerard and Greenway succeeded in escaping—
Gerard, as far as we can judge, deservedly, for,
though he gave the conspirators communion, he is
thought to have known nothing of their design ; but
Greenway perhaps undeservedly, since, if Bates' statement
is to be admitted, he not only received knowledge
of the plot in confession but gave the penitent
absolution. Upon Garnet, at all events, fell the

[1] The phrase was used by him at Garnet's trial.

defence of his order. He was taken in hiding with Oldcorne on 30th January 1606, and was sent up to London with every consideration for his comfort and welfare. The principal conspirators had already been executed by the time he arrived, and his own trial furnished a kind of aftermath to the great conspiracy. There were, of course, endless examinations to be got through before he could be satisfactorily set upon the public stage; and the desire to draw admissions without any appearance of roughness made the extraction of evidence unusually lengthy. Torture, indeed, was once applied, but not probably with any great severity;[1] and in his examinations he met with gentle usage. Salisbury, it is true, could not resist the temptation of chaffing him about the innocent attentions of one of those excellent but embarrassing ladies who in all ages are to be found dogging the steps of eminent ecclesiastics. "I never"—so Garnet relates the incident to the Jesuit Fathers—"had discourteous word of the Commissioners, but only once. Having taken a letter of Mrs. Vaux to me subscribed 'Your loving sister, A. G.,' my Lord of Salisbury said, 'What! you are married to Mrs. Vaux? She calleth herself Garnet! What! Senex fornicans!' But the next time he asked me forgiveness, and said he spoke in jest and held his arm long on my shoulders, and all the rest said I was an exemplar in these matters."[2]

---

[1] It is commonly stated that Garnet was not tortured at all. But his letter to the Jesuit Fathers (Hatf. MSS., 115/13) proves, I think, that he was tortured once. The passage runs: "After I had acknowledged all that was true, my Lord Chief Justice said that they must have more of me. For I must, forsooth, confess I was the very original of all and the plot, and, besides, I must confess such noblemen as Catesby and the rest did build on both in this action and in this intended invasion from Spain; and for these two points I was to go to torture the *second* time upon Friday, which was Good Friday beyond sea." The threat was not apparently executed.

[2] Hatf. MSS., 115/13.

It would have been well if Garnet's standard of truth had stood as high as his standard of honest living. His copy of the *Treatise of Equivocation*— a manual perhaps composed by Father Southwell —shows that in this essential matter he did not belie the reputation of his Order ; and the Council, confident of his guilt, but yet unable to extort proof of it, eventually determined to meet guile with guile. He was placed in a cell which communicated with Oldcorne's, and was made acquainted, by an apparently friendly jailer, with the opportunity for intercourse. He fell unsuspiciously into the trap ; and, whilst he exchanged confidences with his colleague, one of Salisbury's secretaries, together with a magistrate of repute, were so placed as to overhear his speeches. The listeners caught enough to prove his complicity ; and, when he found the game was up, he substituted a new story for his old denials. It came to this : that Greenway had spoken to him in general terms of a Catholic design ; that Catesby had put him hypothetical questions in casuistry of a suspicious character ; and that ultimately Greenway under the seal of confession had made him acquainted with the whole affair ; though he affirmed that he had never given them anything but discouragement or contemplated their purpose otherwise than with horror. Under the cloud of such admissions he was brought to his trial at the Guildhall on March 28th.

No one can read the report of the proceedings in Court without becoming sensible of the particular pains Salisbury was at to make them fair and conclusive so far as the manner and fashion of legal practice in that ungentle age permitted. Even Coke kept his bitter tongue under restraint, and the compliments which Salisbury paid him on the rare clarity and compactness of his argument were probably no idle ones. The Minister did not intervene until after Garnet had replied to the four heads of Coke's

indictment — to the Attorney's strictures upon
Romish doctrine and recusancy, upon Jesuits in
general and Garnet in particular. Then he virtually
took over the prosecution and pricked the prisoner
in the vital points. One of the Jesuit's pleas had
been his attempt to get the plot, and all like plots,
forbidden at Rome ; Sir Edmund Baynham was to
have seen the Pope and brought back the prohibition.
" Baynham," said his pitiless interlocutor, " was only
at Florence in October ; do you not think he had need
to be well horsed to go from thence to Rome, get a
prohibition, and return to England before the fifth of
November ? " To which Garnet made no great answer.
Later on Salisbury broke down his guard again :—

" I would further ask you, why you would not
write to your superior Aquaviva, as well of this
particular Powder-Treason as to procure prohibition
for other smaller matters ? "

Garnet faintly answered " he might not disclose
it to any, because it was matter of secret confession
. . . but that fault might justly be laid upon him in
that he had disclosed none of those things whereof
he had general knowledge."

" Did not Catesby tell you of the Powder-Treason ? "
pursued Salisbury. " I may not answer," replied
Garnet. " Then," said his examiner, " I will say no
more, but leave it to the judgment of the hearers."
. . . ' But why, if you were desirous to prevent it, did
you not seek particulars from Catesby, when he would
have told you for the asking.' [1] " Because," replied
the prisoner, " after Greenway had told me (in
confession) what Catesby intended, my soul was so
troubled that I was loth to hear more of the matter."

Salisbury then turned to the jury and spoke of
the wider issues which the trial involved—the vindication of English justice and the exposure of the

[1] This is a paraphrase, but conveys, I think, the meaning of the
sentence.

effects of Popish doctrine. He required Garnet to
answer whether he had not been ' as Christianly, as
courteously, and as carefully used as ever man could
be of any quality or any profession.' The prisoner
acknowledged it ; and, the suspicion of ill-usage being
thus removed, Salisbury drove home the damning
inconsistencies of Garnet's confessions :—

" All your defence, Mr. Garnet, is but simple
negation ; your negatives compared with your
affirmatives are merely contradictory ; and your
privity and activity laid together approve you manifestly guilty." He went on to remind the accused
how, when Catesby had asked him whether it was
lawful to kill a person if by so doing he would
endanger the lives of ' innocents,' he had replied that
the battering of walls and houses was justifiable
though ' innocents ' were within, if the guilty were
more numerous. " What warranted Fawkes but
Catesby's application of your arguments ? " Garnet
protested, and then Salisbury struck his hardest
blow—" I must needs be bold with you to drive you
from the trust you have to satisfy the world by these
denials by putting you in mind that you have said
that you think it not unlawful to deny the truth—
a doctrine which it grieveth me to hear from the
mouth of a man of religion. And here I must mention how, after the interlocution between you and
Hall,[1] you were called before the Lords and were
asked, not what you said, but whether Hall and you
had conference together, desiring you not to equivo-
cate ; yet you stiffly denied it upon your soul, re-
iterating it with so many detestable execrations that [2]
our hair stood upright and it wounded our hearts to
hear you. Afterwards, Hall being called, he at first
denied that you had any conference together ; but,
being examined apart, confessed it ; and, after he had
confessed it, you also confessed what you had so vehe-

[1] That is, Oldcorne.   [2] In the original, ' as.'

mently denied an hour before, and cried us mercy, and said you had grievously offended if equivocation did not help you."

The case was going unmistakably against the prisoner ; and Garnet tried to shake himself free of the thick cloud of infamy that was settling upon his conduct by some cheap invocation of blessings upon the King.   It was a futile move, and Salisbury turned it at once to his discomfiture by asking him whether, if the King were excommunicated, the King's subjects were any longer bound by their allegiance.   Garnet could only desire ' not to be pressed at that time with such questions.'   He made one more protest—probably a just one—when his examiner affirmed that he was a special director of the Powder-Treason, though he sat at his ease in a gentlewoman's house.   But when Salisbury went on to ask him for ' but one argument that he was not consenting to it that could hold in any indifferent man's ear or sense, besides his bare negative,' he remained helplessly silent.

The trial drifted on its way.   Coke spoke again, and afterwards Northampton.   Then Garnet urged that, though he had done more than he could excuse, yet he was bound to preserve the secrets of the confessional.   Nottingham, no Catholic himself if we are to allow old tradition to be reversed by modern authority,[1] brought the general proposition at once, with a sailor's bluntness, to the test of the concrete : " If one confessed this day to you that to-morrow morning he meant to kill the King with a dagger, must you conceal it ? "   Garnet answered in the affirmative.   Salisbury's keen intelligence was not asleep.   " I would fain, Mr. Garnet," he said, " ask you some questions of the nature of confession."   The prisoner replied that he would do his best to

[1] Cheyney, *A History of England from the Defeat of the Armada*, p. 43.

answer them. " Must there not," asked his interlocutor, " be confession and contrition before absolution ? "   Garnet readily admitted it.   " Did
you absolve Greenway," continued the other.   Again
Garnet made an affirmative answer.   " What had he
done," Salisbury inquired, " to show his penitence ?
Had he promised to desist ? "   " He said he would
do his best," was the reply.   Salisbury now had the
prisoner in a vice.   That could not be so, he said, for
afterwards, when Catesby and Percy were in arms,
Greenway tried to induce Abington and Hall [1] to
assist them.   " Hereby it appears that either
Greenway told you out of confession, and then
there needs no secrecy ; or, if it were in confession,
he professed no penitency and therefore you could
not absolve him."   " Besides," he added, " this
one circumstance must still be remembered and
cannot be cleared.   When Greenway told you what
Catesby meant in particular, you must then have
called to mind what Catesby had spoken to you
in the general before ;   and after that, if you had
not been so desirous to have the plot take effect,
you might have disclosed it out of your general
knowledge from Catesby ; but, when Catesby offered
to deliver you the particulars himself, as he had
done to Greenway, you refused to hear him, lest
your tongue should have betrayed your heart."
Garnet protested that he had gone into Warwickshire in the hope of dissuading Catesby as soon as
he came down there, and that Greenway had done
very ill in trying to persuade Hall to join.   " Your
first answer," observed Salisbury, " is most absurd,
seeing you knew Catesby would not come down
till the 6th November, which was the day after
the blow should have been given, and you went
into the country ten days before.   And for the
second, I am only glad that the world may now

[1] *i.e.* Oldcorne.

see that Jesuits are condemned by Jesuits, and
treason and traitors laid naked by traitors themselves."

There we may leave the cross-examination and the
trial. There is room for doubt as to the extent of
Garnet's guilt ; there can be no doubt about the guilt
itself. He was hanged ; but the customary concomi-
tant barbarities were not inflicted until life had left
the poor body, and, if we take the trouble to transport ourselves out of our own age by reading the
account of Ravaillac's contemporary execution in
France, we shall reach the conclusion that in the
vengeance they took for the Gunpowder Plot James
and Salisbury showed themselves to be men of considerable clemency.

" When these things shall be related to posterity,"
Coke had said in opening the prosecution of Fawkes
and his confederates, " they will be reputed matters
feigned, not done."   So they have seemed in our time
to the late Father Gerard.   With a critical scepticism,
which, had he applied it to the canon of Scripture,
would have been fatal to his belief in the Biblical
narratives, he massed together every improbability
and inconsistency in the story of Gunpowder Plot
until he had convinced himself that the whole was
little better than an old wife's fable, a knavish trick
directed against the Roman Church.   Point by point
the great historian of the period refuted his unbelief
and his conclusions ; and it would be tedious now to
repeat that which has been once for all thoroughly
and decisively accomplished.   The substructure of
Gerard's argument crumbled away with the rest.
" The attempt to make Salisbury the originator of the
Plot for his own purposes breaks down entirely, if
only because, at the time when the plot was started,
he had already pushed James to take the first step in
the direction [1] in which he wished him to go, and that

---

[1] *i.e.* the anti-Catholic direction.

every succeeding step carried him further in the same direction."[1]

Gunpowder Plot, however, caused an undeniable acceleration of speed. Salisbury's usual good sense forsook him, and he hurried into panic-legislation. The Holy Communion was for the first time degraded into a civic test. The penalties of recusancy were stiffened both for rich and poor. Catholic gentlemen, who neglected to attend the Established Church, found that two-thirds of their estates lay at the King's mercy. Catholic servants who fell into a like offence laid their masters open to a fine of £10 a month for retaining them. Catholic priests were reminded by proclamation that their proper place was on foreign soil. " If they shall not obey," wrote Salisbury, " then the laws shall go upon them without any more forbearance."[2] And Catholics generally found the gates of the liberal professions closed against their reasonable aspirations. Travel, except within a circumscribed area of five miles from their homes, was forbidden them without permission. Their children might not be baptized according to the Latin rite; and even their religious books were subject to destruction.

It is true, no doubt, that the bulk of the anti-Catholic legislation was only intended to be a sword of Damocles—to frighten rather than to fall. But the King had enough favourites to find a use for confiscation; and no laws are more deplorable than those which are administered with caprice. There was, besides, a new statute which brought ecclesiastical theory and constitutional law into sharp collision. An oath of allegiance, formally repudiating the deposing power of the Pope, could be tendered to all except the nobility; and the Pope proved as rigorous in requiring its rejection as the King was tenacious of its

---

[1] Gardiner, *What Gunpowder Plot was*, p. 200.
[2] Winwood Memorials, ii. p. 219.

acceptance. The unhappy subjects of a double
allegiance, driven this way by their spiritual pastor,
that way by their sovereign lord, behaved according
as spiritual or temporal terrors seemed to them the
more real.   Yet we cannot reasonably blame James
for insisting upon loyalty ; and it is perhaps equally
unreasonable to blame Paul v. for demanding a strict
adherence to the Canon Law.

Gunpowder Plot—at least so far as we have any
certain knowledge of it—was a conspiracy of country
gentlemen, countenanced though perhaps not encouraged by one or more Jesuits of the baser sort.
The Council looked in vain for the magnates, without
whose co-operation the treason seemed inconceivably
audacious.   One man alone attracted suspicion.
Northumberland was not only the head of the distinguished family to which Thomas Percy belonged,
but he had, as it presently appeared, omitted to
exact from his relative the oath of supremacy required of every gentleman-pensioner not only by
custom but by an express minute of the King.   After
some confinement in the Tower and a trial in the Star
Chamber, the Earl was fined £30,000, though that sum
was subsequently reduced by a little less than two-
thirds.   It is supposed that Salisbury thus gratified
his personal animosities.   To this charitable opinion
one can only oppose the apparently honest ring of his
own language and the apparently sincere protestation
of his victim's testimony.   " For the other great
man . . ." wrote the Minister, " considering the
greatness of his house and the improbability that
he should be acquainted with such a barbarous plot,
His Majesty is rather induced to believe that whatsoever any of the traitors have spoken of him hath
been rather their vaunts than upon any other good
ground ; so I think his liberty will, the next term, be
granted upon honourable and gracious terms, which,
for my own part, though there hath never been any

extraordinary dearness between us, I wish ; because this State is very barren of great blood and great sufficiency together." [1] " I protest," wrote Northumberland to the Secretary, " I believe you would do me any good were in your power." [2]

[1] S. P., Ireland, 3rd March 1606. Salisbury to Brouncker (cited by Gardiner).

[2] Hatf. MSS., 192/112. When Northumberland was re-examined in 1611, after Elks had made his charges, Salisbury concluded that though the fresh admissions then elicited did not prove his guilt, they did justify a suspicion of it (Winwood Memorials, iii. pp. 287, 288).

CHAPTER XV

PROTESTANT TENDENCIES

" For four things our Noble sheweth to me—
King, Ship and Sword, and Power of the Sea."
HAKLUYT'S *Voyages* (ed. 1809), i. p. 207.

PROTESTANTISM, as it informs the story of Garnet's trial, so also gives some point and purpose to the rather shapeless years that followed the failure of Gunpowder Plot—years not really unimportant or uninteresting, but yet wanting in the high colour and definite outline of those which went before or came after them. England was resting between the two greater phases of her religious difficulties, between the Reformation and the Great Rebellion ; and the forces were not yet grouped afresh for the renewal of the struggle.

But for Salisbury there was no rest. Those who surrounded him had supposed that with the advent of his new dignities he would resign the influential, but not highly esteemed, office of Secretary for one of greater outward appearance.[1] They were mistaken. Though all the trappings of great place had now been laid upon him, though the Garter had been bestowed with a pomp and circumstance which caused the Venetian Secretary to write home to his Government that all confessed they had not seen the like even at the King's Coronation,[2] yet it is no rash assertion to declare that what he looked for was the reality, not the semblance of power. And this

[1] Winwood Memorials, ii. p. 59.   [2] Venet. Cal., x. p. 354.

ROBERT, FIRST EARL OF SALISBURY, K.G.

(Painted by Marc Gheeraedts in 1608. Hatfield House)

[*To face p.* 254

also he obtained in abundance.   The same authority
affirms that his position had become so secure that
" all envy of him had died away." [1]   Such omni-
potence could only be had at a tremendous price.
It meant work, tedious, unremitting, immensely
laborious as well as immensely responsible, in an age
of ill-distributed endeavour.   He learned to absorb
business with that fatal facility which grows upon men
with widening experience and perfected talent, but
which, often enough, in the end rises in judgment
against them and presents its long-neglected account
at the least convenient moment and with the most
merciless insistence.   As one turns over the files of
his endless correspondence the dim forgotten pleas
of endless suitors come to seem like the wishes recorded on the *peau de chagrin* in Balzac's famous
story, each of which is paid for with some particle
of the man's ever-shrinking vitality.   We cannot
wonder, in face of his incessant toil, that some have
found Salisbury lacking in initiative, lacking in
freshness and vigour of understanding, lacking in the
fulness of insight without which no man can perfectly
fulfil the demands of great place.   There is such a
thing as the dissipation of energy in mere industry,
as blurring the high vision of great affairs with
petty business.   And if Salisbury fell short of the
highest quality of statesmanship, it is but fair to
remember that what blame there is may have sprung
as much from excess of labour as from any natural
deficiency.   Light and leading, as well as some other
good things, need the nourishment of leisure.

One of the greater crises in the history of Ireland
occurred while Salisbury was steering the Ship of
State, and furnishes a test by which we may take
his measure at this stage of his life.   He had shown
singular discrimination in his selection, first of Mountjoy and then of Chichester, to govern that distracted

---

[1] Venet. Cal., x. p. 354.

island. No two Viceroys, perhaps, have been more generally recognised as representative of that dispassionate justice upon which Englishmen particularly pride themselves. Mountjoy, indeed, had not scrupled to harry the country with relentless severity wherever rebellion raised its head; but, given his resources and his aims, his method was probably better calculated to bring hostilities to a close than any other. He left Ireland effectively garrisoned and, which was the same thing, England effectively vindicated. To his successor fell the problems of the civil administration.

In Chichester's conduct of affairs there are two capital features—the attempt to force the English Church upon the Irish Catholics and the plantation of Ulster. Each raised a great issue and each was decided in accordance with principles very widely held then and very widely rejected now. Protestantism at the present day is commonly supposed to be radically inconsistent with the temperament of the Irish Celt. To Salisbury and King James in the seventeenth century it represented the true faith of Christian men, the path of loyalty, and the way of salvation. Confident of its universal efficacy, they were anxious to secure it a fair hearing, and were the more stimulated to do so, because the Catholic propaganda in Ireland, as elsewhere, had been latterly both active and forcible. Their own measures were comprehensive ; they sought both to fold the sheep and to rehabilitate the shepherds. The Catholic laity, separated from the pastors of their own choice, were to be compelled to get sound knowledge and instruction ; the Protestant clergy to give it. Both tasks proved to be beyond the very limited powers of Dublin Castle. The Irish, gentle and simple alike, offered a stubborn resistance to the royal proclamation enjoining their attendance at Church. In vain the shilling fines for recusancy, which were legal enough, were fortified by hundred pound fines, which were not legal at all. Chichester, finding himself at war with the convictions of a whole people, learned to urge the merit of a policy of pacific penetration —the advantages of ' time ' and ' conference ' and ' the education of youth.'[1] And to these recommendations the English Government was wise enough to agree.[2]

The Viceroy fared little better in his efforts to infuse some sort of spiritual vitality into the Anglican clergy. From the Archbishop of Cashel downwards they were, many of them, pluralists of the worst description, deficient in knowledge, deficient in sympathy, deficient, so far as we can judge, in the bare desire to do their duty according to their lights. None of the Reformed Churches stood in more need of Reformation than the Established Church of Ireland in the seventeenth century. Grooms and horseboys murdered the sacred offices, whilst their principals fattened on the incomes which were paid to have those offices properly performed. Chichester did what he could. A new type of bishop was introduced into vacant sees, and the Book of Common Prayer was done into Irish. But the evil lay deeper. Character and conviction were divorced from obedience and order. Enforced uniformity drove the more energetic ministers into Ulster ; and the blind were left to lead the blind. Fifty years later Ormonde was still talking of a reform of the Protestant clergy.

In the midst of these embarrassments there occurred the momentous flight of Tyrone and Tyrconnell, which, according to English notions, at least, placed their property, comprising great part of Ulster, at the disposal of the King. Alarmed at the steady advance of English law and justice, implicated, or

<hr />

[1] Irish Cal., ii. p. 43, 1st December 1606.
[2] Hatf. MSS., 195/17 (17th June 1608). Advices from Ireland: " All persecution is left off."

thought to be so, in a treasonable conspiracy with Spain, the two Earls fled the country, never, as it proved, to return. Salisbury and Chichester had no difference of opinion as to the course to be pursued in so providential an emergency, though which of them first gave expression to it is still debatable.[1] The most turbulent province of Ireland must clearly be ' planted,' as the phrase went, with a race of settlers. " It is of great necessity that those countries be made the King's by this accident," the Secretary wrote to Chichester in September 1607.[2] The conditions seemed to him favourable beyond all expectation. Not a man had ' moaned ' at the flight of the Earls, he wrote to Edmondes, " neither was there this thirty years more universal obedience nor more appearance at seats of justice than now there is." [3] The great thing to avoid, as he thought, was any repetition of the mistake, made in Munster twenty years before, when a body of bankrupt adventurers and English country gentlemen had been pitched into a locality whose conditions and people were alike unknown to them, with disastrous results. But Salisbury was wise enough to avoid anything like dogmatism. " Errare possum, hereticus esse nolo," [4] he wrote ; and in the details of the settlement there is nothing to show that he ever attempted to overrule the advice he received from Chichester and Chichester's representatives.

The Lord Deputy's recommendations provided alternative courses. Either their lordships might graft a body of colonists upon the existing Irish occupants of the land who, whenever they were men of worth and substance, were to be put in possession of such an acreage of ground as with the aid of their dependents they could properly stock and manure ;

---

[1] Irish Cal., iii. p. lv.   [2] *Ibid.*, ii. p. 284.
[3] S. P. For., Flanders, 8, 30th September 1607.
[4] Irish Cal., ii. p. 284.

or else the Irish must be expropriated, with adequate
compensation, in the waste lands beyond the Ban and
the Blackwater. The former was, as he thought,
the juster and the wiser method, and the more likely
to make for peace and happiness ; but if the Council
preferred the latter, he held it to be ' void of iniquity
or cruelty,' ' an honest and laudable act.' [1]

The Council, acting on the advice of Davis and Ley,
whom Chichester sent over to London to represent
him, did in fact adopt this less excellent way. We
can hardly doubt that they were actuated by a lively
recollection of what had happened in King's County
and Queen's County, where the cohabitation of a
mixed population, consequent on a plantation of
English settlers, had resulted in incessant conflict.
There were, indeed, difficulties every way. Labour
was insufficient without the Irish ; friction was
inevitable if they remained. A compulsory emigra-
tion involved an outrage upon sentiment which no
compensation could cure. Permissive re-settlement
at home under their own chiefs left the English Government face to face with the prospect of a continuance
of the tribal faction, which had made Ulster the most
turbulent province in Ireland. The English side of
the affair was hardly less difficult than the Irish.
Colonists of the sort that was required were not to
be had for the asking. Only under pressure was the
City of London induced to undertake the plantation
of Coleraine. Chichester himself was not too consistent amid the difficulties that surrounded him.
He became the severest critic of his own recommendations. He disapproved the limitation of estates, which
he had advised, and their apportionment by lot, which
he had desiderated.[2]

Still, on the whole, the plantation of Ulster
stands out as the most successful of the English
attempts to put fresh blood into Ireland. For the

[1] Irish Cal., ii. p. 277.   [2] See *Ibid.*, iv. pp. xiii, xiv.

time being it did give to the country an air of prosperity and peace which had long been wanting; and those who had promoted it congratulated themselves upon its results. That was not, of course, the whole tale. The Parliament of 1613, which met after Salisbury had been laid in his grave, showed the existence of a dangerous temper among the better sort of Catholics. How deeply the iron had entered into the soul of the expropriated peasantry was not apparent, however, until the massacre of 1641. But, if it would be unjust to exonerate Salisbury wholly from blame, it would be inequitable to lay it heavily on his shoulders. His knowledge of Ireland was, as he well knew,[1] imperfect enough; he had to act upon advice—the advice of Chichester's agents; and, most fatal of all, the instruments he had to employ were not the instruments he required. What was needed in Ulster was love and labour; what was sent was hatred and financial speculation. The work was work for a mission; yet it was a garrison that undertook it. A chain of monasteries, bringing the simpler arts of peace, bringing sympathy, bringing faith in its more tangible, more imaginative forms, might have solved the problem which a chain of forts could at best only suppress from view. But Salisbury had no monks to send; and he would, besides, have been the last man to send them. His was a shorter way with Catholics, which proved, however, in the end to be the longest road home. Yet to think of the Irish question of to-day as altogether a legacy which he has left us is a serious historical mistake. Antrim and Down had already been planted by the private enterprise of energetic Scotsmen, and would have had to be reckoned with, whether Tyrone and Tyrconnell had ever fled the country or not. All Salisbury did was to extend a settlement, already admirably conceived from a commercial standpoint.

[1] Irish Cal., ii. p. 284.

He became himself personally interested in the results. He consented to be responsible for the plantation of a district ; and there fell to him by lot the barony of Clogher in Tyrone, a fertile region of 12,500 acres, which, according to the regulation, he transferred in lots of 2000 to 1000 acres to lesser undertakers.[1] Among these is mentioned a certain William Parsons, whom we may probably identify with the notorious Lord Justice Parsons of 1640. But Salisbury cannot have entirely disposed of his interest, for there is an allusion to a silver mine, of which he possibly entertained great hopes, and from which he probably obtained small profits.[2]

The flight of Tyrone and Tyrconnell affords us a passing glimpse into the great system of espionage which Salisbury had by this time brought to a science. A detective, whom we only know now by the name of Henry Richardson, is sent to the Continent to shadow Tyrone. He is paid by the English Ambassador, who is instructed to furnish him also with journey-money if his business should entail extended travel. Arrangements are made, by means of which his reports to Salisbury may enjoy the maximum of security. He is to address them to Mr. James Brookesby to the care of one Thomas Yong, the commercial correspondent at Florence of an honest London merchant. But more than this, the information is to be transmitted in the language which one Catholic would use to another.[3] A specimen of this elaborate fiction, endorsed in Salisbury's hand " Advertisements from Rome written with some clauses to disguise the affection of the intelligence," remains to us among the Foreign State Papers. " Italians," says that curious document, " speak much good and very honourable of these Earls ; and the Earls themselves keep their state gallantly. It seemeth some good

---

[1] Irish Cal., iii. p. 434; and iv. p. 201.   [2] *Ibid.*, iv. p. 251.
[3] S. P. For., Flanders, 40, 21st January 1608.

vein of gold as yet flows with full tide, which I pray
God may not soon fall to a low ebb. I send a picture
of the canonized . . . and by Father Midford 40
Agnus Deis. I would have sent more if I had them,
for I know here are more store than with you. I
send Father Parsons' commendations."[1]

Henry Richardson moved among the purlieus of
his craft. In the higher walks of diplomacy Salisbury had more eminent correspondents; though if
Wotton's epigram,[2] which cost its author so dear, is
to be accepted, the moral situation of these highly
placed personages was hardly more fortunate. The
Secretary was well served—so well served, indeed,
that the English envoys appeared abroad to be
rather his creatures than the King of England's
ambassadors.[3] Cornwallis from Madrid, Winwood
from The Hague, Edmondes from Brussels, Carew
from Paris, Wotton himself from Venice, kept the
kaleidoscope of European affairs revolving briskly
before his eyes ; and there are worse ways of catching
the drift of foreign politics between 1604 and 1612
than by picking a casual acquaintance with some
of the more than half-forgotten diplomatists who at
that time represented England abroad.

At Wotton, whom alone of all the group we may
really know, whose memory is raised by exquisite
song above all delusive dependence upon pomp and
place, we can, alas ! only allow ourselves a passing
glance. His post lay outside the real sphere of
English policy, and his finished talent [4] spent itself
beneath a brilliant but declining sun. Nevertheless,

---

[1] The above is a little paraphrased. I have read and noted the
original, but cannot again disinter it. I registered it as among the
S. P. For., Venice, 5—a loose and disorderly collection.

[2] " Legatus est vir bonus peregre missus ad mentiendum rei
publicæ causa."

[3] Winwood Memorials, ii. p. 231.

[4] Salisbury thought highly of him as a diplomatist. Venet. Cal.,
xi. p. 351.

the mention of his work is no unfitting introduction
to some account of those Protestant influences which
dominated Salisbury's later administration of foreign
affairs. For Wotton went to Venice at that curious
and interesting moment when it looked as if a state of
Italy might withdraw itself from the allegiance of the
Pope. Under the influence of Fra Paolo the Venetian
Republic was fighting out with partial success those
ancient quarrels with the Papacy about ecclesiastical
jurisdiction and ecclesiastical property which had
been faced in England at a much earlier date. An
interdict still furnished an available weapon in the
papal armoury ; and Venice had to brave its terrors.
In face of so tremendous a conflict the Venetians
wished to stand well with Protestant Europe, and
applied to James to draw his friends in Denmark and
Germany into ' an association of war with them
against the Pope.' [1] The King, however, was the
reverse of warlike. He gave expression to the excellence of his disposition towards the Doge and Senate ;
but he thought their suggestion premature, and he
thought, too, that they might very well carry on their
own negotiations without his mediation.[1] In fact,
he did not anticipate that the quarrel would run to
extremities. " His Majesty," Salisbury told Wotton,
" expecteth to be advertised from you how things
proceed, in which he shall take pleasure as he
hath done, though he will not flatter himself with great
hope because his opinion is adverse to his desire." [2]

James's judgment for once did not prove to be at
fault ; and, in the May of 1607, Wotton communicated
the terms of reconciliation between the Republic
and the Holy See. The incident had, however,
served to direct attention towards the famous friar
who had been the backbone of resistance to the papal
aggression.

[1] S. P. For., Venice, 3, 2nd October 1606.   Salisbury to Wotton.
[2] Ibid., 16th June 1606.   Salisbury to Wotton.

"I send your Lordship," Wotton wrote to Salisbury, "a very true picture in portable form of Maestro Paulo the Servite, taken from him at my request, presuming that since it pleased His Majesty to bestow upon him some gracious and honourable words . . . it may be likewise some pleasure unto His Majesty to behold a sound Protestant as yet in the habit of a Friar. Which I affirm unto your Lordship, not out of that vanity (which maketh Jesuits register every great wit in their catalogue), but upon assurance thereof given me by my chaplain who hath sounded him in the principal points of our religion. By him I deal with him, for less observation, in diverse things of importance; and they spend upon agreement together every week almost one half-day. . . . In their very last conference he acquainted him from me with the taking of Blackwell, and with some things in the late published book touching the said person. . . . Wherein is mention of a *breve* of the Pope's . . . a copy of the which *breve* he hath desired me by all means to procure that he may out of it inform the Senate palpably and authentically that the Pope's ends are to resist all natural obedience, and finally to dissolve the jurisdiction of princes and states. And in this he is the more eager because he holdeth this position, that it is the point of sovereignty under which other parts of God's truth must be replanted here. Now, to say yet a little more of this man upon whom and his seed there lieth so great a work. He seemeth, as in countenance, so in spirit, liker to Philip Melancthon than to Luther, and peradventure a fitter instrument to overthrow the falsehood by degrees than on a sudden which accordeth with a frequent saying of his own that in these operations non bisogna far salti. He is by birth a Venetian, and well-skilled in the humours of his own country. For learning I think I may justly call him the most deep and general scholar of the world, and above other parts of knowledge he seemeth to have looked very far into the subtleties of the Canonists, which part of skill gave him introduction into the Senate. His power of speech consisteth rather in the soundness of reason than in any other natural ability. He is much frequented, and much intelligenced of all things that pass, and lastly, his life is the most irreprehensible and exemplary that hath ever been known. These are his parts set down (I protest unto your Lordship) rather with modesty than excess."[1]

It is an interesting letter, at least, for English Churchmen, and was doubtless acceptable to Salisbury, who entertained a great admiration for Father

[1] S. P. For., Venice, 13th September 1607. Wotton to Salisbury.

Paul [1] and was himself credibly believed to be the
author of a book upon the differences between Venice
and the Pope.[2]   But, for the most part, his diplomatic
correspondence ran in duller courses, and the reader
needs to equip himself with a very panoply of patience
before he sets out to pursue its mazes.

Cornwallis, though he occupied the most distinguished post, is the dimmest figure of all the
prominent diplomatists of the day. We meet him
afterwards as the treasurer of Prince Henry's household and the author of a feeble presentation of Prince
Henry's life. His despatches give the impression
of a humorous, large-minded, plain-spoken Englishman, operating creditably on a field of no little difficulty. Since the distant days when Elizabeth and
Philip had expelled each other's envoys there had
been no resident English ambassador at the Court of
Madrid,—or rather, as it was in 1605, of Valladolid,
—and Cornwallis received at the outset elaborate
instructions. He was assiduously to cultivate amity
with the Spanish king, and as studiously to avoid
any recognition of the papal nuncio as more than the
legate of a secular prince ; and he was to keep a sharp
eye on the interests of English merchants, and a
sharper on the persons of any English fugitives he
might get wind of. For the rest, he was to be a
prophet of peace, promising his master's best assistance to compose the war in the Netherlands, whenever a convenient season should present itself.[3]

The Ambassador was not slow to discover beneath
the shows and splendours of the Spanish Court the
rottenness and exhaustion of a defeated country.
It is ' a proud misery,' he told Salisbury, choosing
the same phrase which came to the mind of Dudley
Carleton after a tour through Spain in the same year.[4]

---

[1] Venet. Cal., x. p. 404.   [2] *Ibid.*, p. 391.
[3] Winwood Mem., ii. pp. 65-7.   Instructions to Sir C. Cornwallis.
[4] Winwood, ii. p. 85.   Cp. Birch, *View of the Negot.*, p. 227.

The administration was on a par with the rest.
" Daily doth the weakness of the Government of this
State discover itself more and more to me."[1]   So
badly did he think of it that he assured Salisbury with
blunt candour that " England never lost such an
opportunity of winning honour and wealth . . . as
by relinquishing the war with Spain."[2]   The fires in
his English blood kindled at the helpless ineptitude
of the old enemy of his country.   " To be short;
their estate (were they now well set upon) is irrevocable : this peace being an impediment to the
greatest advantage and means to enrich our king
and realm that in any age hath ever been offered."[3]
Fortunately for England, Salisbury had slower pulses
than the Envoy, and a better knowledge, besides, of
the state of the English Exchequer.

The condition of Spain was hardly to be wondered
at when the Prime Minister was given over to sport.
" If there be a bird to be shot at in the wood, a
hare in the field, a rabbit in the burrow," reports
Cornwallis of the Duke of Lerma, " the papers
lie dead, though they concern the life or soul of
the poor, or the greatest good whatsoever of the
commonwealth."[4]   Foreign suitors fared no better
than domestic ones.   " There are papers deeply concerning some of His Majesty's subjects which have
lain in that sort almost two months, being promised
to be despatched in two days.   Very grievous it
hath been and is to me, in lieu of being His
Majesty's Ambassador to become here the Merchant's
solicitor."[4]

The commercial treaty, of which so great things
had been hoped, had in fact proved a vast disappointment.   The old hatred between the Englishman and
the Spaniard flared up afresh at every occasion.
Justice was denied and delayed ; and the new export

[1] Winwood, ii. p. 96.   [2] Ibid., p. 75.
[3] Ibid., p. 235.   [4] Ibid., p. 150.

duty in Portugal[1] on wines and oils threatened to defeat the intention of the Commissioners.[2] Cornwallis prided himself on the good quality of his plain speaking,[3] but apparently it failed to produce any marked effect. Still, he did not think there was any desire on the part of the Government to be on other than friendly terms with their late opponents. " An old saying and wish of the Duke of Alva (that Spain might have peace with England and then would not care though they had wars with all the world) hath now gotten the force and reputation of a general rule and maxim amongst them, and is so settled that I think it will not leave them ; which moves my Lord[4] to believe that. plainly and faithfully they intend to use all means to conserve and increase their amity with England."[5] So the Ambassador's secretary reported to Salisbury ; and the opinion was very possibly true. Salisbury, however, had his own opinion about the reason of the manifold delays in redressing legitimate and crying grievances. They are dissatisfied, he told Cornwallis, with the provisions of the late treaty ; they do not like to see Englishmen serving in the Dutch armies, though this was not prohibited ; and they are disappointed, because the fear of Dutch interference has repressed the Anglo-Flemish trade. And then, bidding Cornwallis build upon them, he adds a few words which may be taken as the motto of his foreign policy, and might well be the model of any man's : " Whatever you hear or collect, thus standeth His Majesty's inward affections . . . to conserve peace as long as he may with honour and safety, or to make a war upon good foundatio ."[6] He gave the same answer in more ample terms to the deputation from the Commons which waited upon him to press the griev-

---

[1] Portugal was, of course, at this time united to Spain.
[2] Winwood, ii. p. 147.   [3] *Ibid.*, p. 152.
[4] Namely, Cornwallis.   [5] Winwood, ii. p. 169.   [6] *Ibid.*, p. 252.

ances of the English merchants in June 1607, and
whose interference on this occasion in a matter of
foreign policy was, according to a learned student,[1]
'symptomatic of a change in the constitution.'
Salisbury's speech, preserved in Bacon's report of
it, is perhaps the best and longest example of his
eloquence that has survived. It is courteous, prudent,
and well ordered, and appears to justify, even in the
oblique rendering that is all we have to judge it from,
the praise which Bacon accorded to its author—" this
worthy Lord, whose speeches, as I have often said,
in regard of his place and judgment, are extraordinary
lights to this House ; and have both the properties
of light, that is conducting and comforting." [2]   It
would, however, be tedious to reproduce it here, and
is the less necessary as the speech is already in print.[3]
What the speaker said amounted to this. After alluding
with great sympathy to the distresses of the merchants,
he pointed out that their unprotected position was
largely the effect of the abolition of monopolies.
They had, with the abolition of privileges, lost union,
which is strength, and were paying the price of their
desires.   Shopkeepers and handicraftsmen had begun
to compete in the trade and were promoting their
personal interests by bribing the Spanish officials to
the great disadvantage of honest merchants.   The
English Government did what it could, but was not
prepared to regard the dilatory character of Spanish
justice as furnishing a *casus belli*.   Spaniards, he told
his audience, were proud ; and proud men were
full of delays, which must be put up with by those
who dealt with them.   The grievances, too, were
rather vexatious than intolerable.   And he went on
to remind his hearers that the matter, raising as it
did questions of peace and war, lay properly within
the sphere of the King's prerogative, and not in that of

[1] Spedding, *Letters and Life of Bacon*, iii. p. 346.
[2] *Ibid.*, p. 359.   [3] *Ibid.*, pp. 347–59.

parliamentary control. As for the remedy suggested by the Commons, it was unhappily chosen. Letters of marque—letters, that is, authorising reprisals—were not likely to prove an efficacious retort so long as the volume of our merchandise lying in Spanish ports far exceeded that belonging to the Spaniards in English ones.

So Salisbury argued, with a good sense and breadth of wisdom that checked any further criticism. Still, there was no denying that the Anglo-Spanish treaty had proved a disappointment. The Spaniards themselves were as dissatisfied as the English. They had hoped that it would tend to the subjugation or restoration of their revolted provinces, but all it had done was to expose their own weakness. Alone, or at least not openly assisted, the Dutch ' Beggars ' were withstanding the greatest of the kings of the earth. Even the genius of Spinola, though it redressed the balance, could not turn the scales. On land, indeed, the United Provinces were ' driven by the power of the enemy from an offensive war to a defensive.' [1] But at sea the Dutch navy was threatening the coasts of Spain and the treasure-ships from the Indies ; [2] and in their extremity the Spaniards tried to tempt Cornwallis with some vague talk about a marriage between the Prince of Wales and the Spanish Infanta and an ultimate transfer of the United Provinces to the married pair. Cornwallis duly reported these overtures to his chief. " Loose discourses ! " was the old diplomatist's comment, which the Ambassador would doubtless have too good judgment to be " catched by . . . except the generals were reduced to particulars." [3]

Salisbury had, indeed, already put the value of

[1] Winwood Memorials, ii. p. 218. Salisbury to Winwood.
[2] Cf. Ibid., ii. p. 223 : " Until a new reveil of fears I look no more to hear of the motion of alliance."
[3] Ibid., ii. p. 293.

Spanish amity to the test.[1] Among the persons implicated in the Gunpowder Treason were two, by name Owen and Father Baldwin, whom the Narrow Seas shielded from the hand of English justice. Application was made to the Archduke, in whose territories they resided, for their apprehension and delivery; but the reply was that Baldwin, by virtue of his orders, lay under the jurisdiction of the Pope, and that Owen was a servant to the King of Spain. Representations at Madrid proved equally fruitless. Justice was as usual delayed, if not actually denied. A ' great coldness '[2] presently set in. Spain began to look for a French marriage; and the affair, insignificant in itself, probably gave to Salisbury's later foreign-policy the decisive bias against Spanish overtures which distinguishes it from that of his Sovereign.

The trouble about Owen and Baldwin draws the eye by a natural transition from Madrid to Brussels— from Spain itself to Spain's shrunken and already half-dissevered limb. Here Sir Thomas Edmondes, a man ' very trusty and sufficient,' was in charge of British interests. His work, as had been pointed out to him in his instructions, was of an exceptionally difficult character. Goodwill with Flanders could hardly be shown without manifesting ill-will towards the United Provinces.[3] Trade interests represented the crux of the situation. The commercial effects of the treaty of peace had not satisfied the expectations of the Flemings. So long as English merchant-men were liable to be captured by Dutch men-of-war there could be no great revival of Anglo-Flemish trade. The Archduke considered that he had been cheated. He expected England to extract from her old ally immunity from seizure for her commerce,

---

[1] Birch, *View of the Negot.*, p. 236.
[2] Winwood Memorials, ii. p. 249 ; cp. p. 319.
[3] S. P. For., Flanders, 7/119. Instructions to Sir T. Edmondes.

and threatened, if this were not granted, that he would revenge himself on English vessels bound for Holland. Edmondes would not tolerate the threat. The King of England, he told the Archduke, had done what he could to influence the United Provinces in the direction desired ; but if it came to choosing between the trade of Holland and the trade of the Spanish dominions, the former was the more valuable to his country, and that consequently which his countrymen would be the less inclined to forgo. To President Richardot, still the most prominent of the Flemish statesmen, he pointed out how seriously the good understanding between England and the Catholic Netherlands was impaired by their dependence on Spain.[1]

The conditions, indeed, were for the moment very adverse to an effective revival of the old alliance. The Low Countries were no longer a compact and vigorous entity, nor even, as they had still been to Charles v., the choicest jewel in the imperial crown. Philip ii. had made them definitely subservient to what he conceived to be the interest of Spain ; and the policy of the Archdukes [2] rested in uncertain and uneasy dependence upon the will of Philip iii., or rather of the Duke of Lerma. Salisbury felt his way as best he might in the changing circumstances. An alliance such as the Archdukes could give him was hardly worth the having ; so heavily were they shackled by the bonds of Spain. Still, he had no wish to make himself otherwise than agreeable to them, and the despatches record his use of one of those singular blandishments which sometimes enliven the tedious annals of diplomacy. Through Edmondes and d'Aremberg he contrived that the Archdukes should be initiated into the mysteries of a cock-fight. He despatched the birds with attendants to keep them in

[1] S. P. For., Flanders, 8, 11th March 1607.
[2] The common phrase used to describe Albert and Isabella.

good feather ; and on the appointed day the match was held.   But an unexpected obstacle frustrated the fair promise of his intentions.   Use and wont are dominant in these affairs ; and the eye that must have been accustomed to see bulls and their tormentors in gory conflict shrank from the blood of cocks. " The Archdukes," so Edmondes reported, " could not at the first comprehend the delight thereof, as well for want of understanding the sleights and practice of the said game as also for that the Infanta is so compassionate that she will not permit the battles to be thoroughly fought out to a destruction of either side : according as the laws of the Council of Trent, which are here in force, do forbid duels upon pain of excommunication.   But," he adds, gilding his report as well as he might, " your Lordship's favour in having been a means to make them partake of this sport is very thankfully acknowledged." [1] Aremberg wrote with a more finished politeness and a greater economy of truth : " Je ne puis donc laisser de vous baiser les mains bien humblement de la faveur qu'il vous a plu me faire par l'envoi de ces coqs, que je vous assure ont donné de grand plaisir à leurs Altesses et ont démontré leur vaillantise, y étant demeurés des morts et blessés à la bataille ; et, outre le plaisir qu'ils en ont eu, ils ont confirmé ce que je leur en avais dit que plusieurs ne voulaient croire."   Then, he adds, recalling their old acquaintance in England, " Je suis ici en ce lieu que j'ai acheté pour l'envie que je pris de votre beau parc à Tibols,[2] mais pour beaucoup que je travaille je n'arriverai de la ressembler." [3]

Even while d'Aremberg wrote, however, more serious matters than the cock-fight were beginning to swell the volume of diplomatic correspondence. Early in 1607 John Neyen, a Franciscan friar, had,

[1] S. P. For., Flanders, 8, 23rd April 1607.
[2] Theobalds.   [3] S. P. For., Flanders, 8, 2nd May 1607.

on behalf of the Archdukes, opened negotiations for a truce with the United Provinces ; and on 9th May an armistice was signed. The world had seldom been more profoundly moved with astonishment. The saying is, wrote Edmondes to Salisbury,[1] that there is no novelty but spends itself in nine days, but the wonder at this truce has disproved it. It is said to be the work of Richardot, who hates the Spaniards, and of Spinola, who wants to rest upon his laurels. The soldiers and the Jesuits exclaim bitterly against it ; and the Flemings resent remaining under the yoke of Spain, now that the Hollanders are free.

Financial exhaustion, weariness of the war, despair of success, had carried the first ditch, but there still remained a great gulf fixed between proposals of peace and their consummation—a gulf dug by Spanish pride and widened by Dutch distrust. Philip III. could not bring himself to recognise the independence of the United Provinces ; the United Provinces could not bring themselves to believe in the good faith of the King of Spain. Meantime, Friar Neyen came and went, and in the end with deceptive assurances cajoled the Duke of Lerma into consenting to treat the Dutch as a free and independent nation. The Dutch, on their part, determined to insure against deceit. They refused to enter into any treaty with their opponents except it were guaranteed by France and England. France raised no obstacles : England had her own reasons for proceeding with less alacrity. The war, as Salisbury pointed out to Cornwallis,[2] suited her well enough. Whilst two powers were busy in tearing each other to pieces, the strength of a third was augmented beyond the ordinary. And a quittance from the struggle in the Netherlands would set Spain free to

[1] S. P. For., Flanders, 8, 29th April 1607. Paraphrased.
[2] Winwood Memorials, ii. p. 401.

meddle in Ireland.   But James I. was honest enough
not to allow ' reason of State ' to stand before the
welfare of Christendom,[1] and, if the Dutch made good
their debts, he was willing to make sure their liberties.

It is at this point that Winwood may be called
upon to take up the tale.   He was, perhaps, Salisbury's favourite in the diplomatic service,[2] and, to
judge from the importance of his missions, one at
least in whom his chief placed very great reliance.
He had been a soldier and was credited with a soldier's
quick temper, though James, who must have come
to know him intimately when later on he became
Secretary of State, declared that he never spoke ill of
any man.   However that may be, he was the envoy
selected in conjunction with Sir Richard Spencer to
represent England at the European conference, where
such veteran diplomatists as the President Jeannin
and Richardot were the principal figures.

Thanks to Friar Neyen's exertions, the combatants
had been brought to treat on equal terms.   The
obstacles to peace were still, however, formidable
enough ;   and, if hard fact had not imperatively
demanded peace, doctrine and theory would have
made short work of the peacemakers.   Antagonism
rose high over the question of the Dutch trade with the
Indies, and of Catholic toleration in the United Provinces.   The one was vital to the physical existence
of the merchant-republic : the other to the spiritual
pride of Spain.   For Philip to assent to the first was
to tear up the world-famous Bull of Alexander VI.;
for the Dutch to agree to the second was to open a
door to the inexhaustible activities of the Jesuits.
Through a long twelvemonth determination battled
with necessity.   But Salisbury was not deceived by

[1] Winwood Memorials, ii. p. 401.

[2] See H.M. C. Rep., Buccleuch Papers, i. p. 38.   De la Fontaine
to Winwood : " Sortant d'avec sa Majesté, j'ai dîné, avec M. Cecylle,
lequel par occasion m'a montré avoir une grande opinion et contente-
ment de vous."

protestations of impossibility. " I am still persuaded," he wrote to Winwood in the end of July 1608,
when the conference showed signs of breaking down,
" (that) peace or truce will be the issue, and is so
resolved inwardly on every side, howsoever you see
they stipulate."[1] He had, in fact, from the first
motions for peace, believed in its advent.[2] But he
did not desire to see the Dutch sell it for anything
less than its proper value, and he impressed upon
Winwood and Spencer the importance of keeping the
Provinces firm in their resolution not to come to terms
unless the King of Spain fully renounced any claim
of sovereignty over them.[3] The establishment of the
Dutch Netherlands was only to be secured ' by the
maintenance of an active war or the assurance of a
firm peace.'[4] And in spite of the desperate condition of English finance he undertook to see them
through their difficulties. " We," he makes his master
say, " will never suffer them to run any dangerous
hazard to the overthrow of their estate."[5]

Disinterested, however, Salisbury neither was nor
pretended to be. England was desperately in want,[6]
and, if the peace was to bring her a renewal of Spanish
aggression, she might fairly insist that it should bring
her a discharge of the Dutch debt. Therefore, though
he had no intention of letting Dutch liability stand in
the way of pacification, he told the English envoys
not to let it be forgotten.[7] Whilst the French were
abounding in good offices, the English made it
plain that they would only guarantee Dutch independence at a price. That price was the solution
by instalments of the £818,408 which it was computed had been lent by England to the United
Provinces.

The diplomatic situation, so far as England was

---

[1] Winwood Memorials, ii. p. 422.   [2] Ibid., p. 332.
[3] Ibid., pp. 331, 332.   [4] Ibid., p. 331.   [5] Ibid., p. 332.
[6] Ibid., p. 376 : " Our necessities here."   [7] Ibid., p. 376.

concerned, was not a little delicate. So heavy a
grant of credit hung like a millstone about her neck
and prevented anything like buoyancy or initiative
in her diplomacy. Of this Jeannin, the French
envoy, took full advantage. He is the Bismarck
of The Hague Congress of 1608. Fertile in expedient,
cynical in purpose, solemn in speech, he made himself
agreeable to both parties and controlled all. England,
on the other hand, from the very equity of her conduct, lost colour both with Spain and the Provinces.
Philip and the Archdukes accused her of violating
the lasting amity she had sworn to bear them, by
undertaking to guarantee the position of their opponents ; and it was in vain that Salisbury pointed out
that she was only proposing to guarantee a peace to
which they would have first assented. On the other
hand, Count Maurice, representing the warlike faction in
the United Provinces, treated Winwood to an insolent
complaint of King James's Spanish sympathies and
indifferent friendship toward the young Republic.

It would be beside the point, or at least confusing
to the purpose, of this book to follow the negotiations
at The Hague in closer detail. England, as has been
said already, played no brilliant part : those doubtful
honours fell to France and Jeannin. But at the close
of the long business " she was," as Gardiner well
points out, " found in her right place." [1] Though
to save Spanish susceptibilities it was called a truce,
the United Provinces had secured the essentials of
a firm and lasting peace. Their independence was
recognised ; their trade with those parts of the Indies
which were not actually in occupation by the
Spaniards was connived at ; they retained intact
their right to refuse any exercise of the Catholic
religion within their dominion. Of these terms
both France and England became the guarantors,
though the Winwood Papers preserve the record of

[1] Gardiner, *Hist. of England*, c. xi.

one poignant hour at the very end, when the
English Envoys thought they would, in their own
phrase, ' having ridden out so many storms in much
foul weather in this wearisome negotiation . . .
naufragium in portu facere '—make shipwreck in
harbour.[1] After they had consented to warrant the
trade with the Indies, instructions arrived from
England that no warranty was to be given except
the archducal Commissioners first gave an assurance
that such a liberty of commerce was within their
own intentions. But the Commissioners had, or
said they had, no power to do so ; and Winwood complained piteously by letter to Salisbury that " either
the Treaty must fall to the ground . . . or else our
private reputation must hazard the shame of a disavowal, having promised that which His Majesty
will not be pleased to perform." [1] Salisbury got the
anxious letter four days later, and his reassuring
reply contains one of those rare glimpses of zealous
service to the State and delicate consideration for
his subordinates, which give the true measure of
what a man is like to work with. " I received (your
last despatch)," he writes, " at eight of the clock, and
find so necessary for me to answer with expedition,
that [2] I should accuse myself of breach of private
friendship, as well as neglect of public duty, if I
should not use my best endeavours for removing
those doubts and fears which now possess you, that
are so good servants and so much my friends. In
which consideration I have resolved before I close my
eyes to return this answer that followeth . . ." [3] He
was a considerate ' chief ', yet he was not content
with any easy-going service. He expected his agents
to use their full energy and to keep him well supplied
with information. Both Cornwallis and Edmondes
knew what it was to meet with his rebukes, yet even

[1] Winwood Memorials, ii. p. 490.   [2] In the original, ' as.'
[3] Winwood Memorials, ii. p. 491.

then there was enough evidence in his language of a kindly regard.[1] " Sir," he writes, for example, to Edmondes,[2] with a delicate irony that for many of us at least would have salved the sting, " the letters you write are so good arguments of your public care, as His Majesty approveth them, and taketh good contentment to read them, bringing with them variety of matter. Only, howsoever it hath happened, the last cessation [3] was far gone and known unto us here before (it seems) you have been suffered to take notice thereof in your quarters."

These, however, are but observations in passing, for we have still to wind up the long negotiation at The Hague. The English guarantee assured to the States, in the event of any violation of the twelve years' truce, a force of six thousand English foot and six hundred English horse, beside twenty ships. The Dutch on their side gave a similar, though not so considerable, promise of assistance if England were to be attacked, and, which was more to the point, agreed to repay their debt by regular instalments. The terms were not ungenerous, and of the Peace as a whole we may perhaps say that it was not unworthy of a pacific minister and a philosophic king.

The Truce between the Archdukes and the Provinces was signed on the 29th March 1609. A few days earlier the Duke of Juliers and Cleves had been gathered to his fathers. As Winwood indicated,[4] it was a very fortunate circumstance that this event had not occurred before, since it would have gravely interfered with the prospects of peace. The Duke left no certain heir ; his Duchy was so situated as to make its fortunes of considerable consequence as well to France and Spain and the Emperor as to the Dutch

---

[1] Winwood Mem., ii. p. 340. [2] S. P. For., Flanders, 8, 8th May 1607.
[3] *i.e.* of arms. [4] Winwood Memorials, iii. p. 2.

Republic and the Union of the Protestant Princes of Germany ; and the eyes of Europe, forced at last from the Netherlands, fixed with eager interest upon the double Duchy commanding the banks of the Rhine.

Henry iv.'s shrewd intellect was then dominant in the affairs of Europe. With English aid he had forced the Hapsburgs to their knees at The Hague ; and, stimulated by a private passion for the Princesse de Condé, who had fled from his solicitations to the Court of the Archdukes, he immediately challenged another encounter. King James was actuated by better motives. He coveted the reputation of a peacemaker, and, if he had not an entirely single-hearted desire to see justice done, he had in all probability the power of persuading himself of his own integrity. The instructions issued to Winwood contain very explicit directions about the satisfaction of the King's conscience. " First you must take it for granted," the Ambassador is warned, " that, if His Majesty could have heard or could conceive that any other had right, . . . his respect to no man (never so near) could have drawn him against his honour and conscience." [1]

Fortunately in this case might and right ran pretty closely together. The nearest heirs in the disputed succession were the Elector of Brandenburg and the Count Palatine of Neuburg, who had the rare wisdom to patch up their private difference and hold the territory in partnership pending the arbitration of their respective claims. They were not so quick, however, but that the Archduke Leopold, enforcing the Emperor's pretension to the disputed fee, had thrown himself into the town of Juliers, which he proceeded to hold on behalf of his cousin. From this position the rulers of north-western Europe were resolved to dislodge him ; and Henry iv., the United

[1] Winwood Memorials, iii. p. 76.

Provinces, and King James drifted into a grudging and suspicious understanding.

"Now that the French King will make himself a formal party of the religion and join with Princes Protestants (and that in solemn and public treaty) against the Pope, is a deeper mystery than every man's capacity can conceive and a project more strange than any man (I think) will easily believe."[1] Yet Winwood, who thus set out the problem, had himself already more than half guessed the solution. "The issue of this whole business," he had written a month before, "if slightly considered, may seem but trivial and ordinary, but duly examined with all the consequences necessarily ensuing . . . doth, as it shall be carried, uphold or cast down the greatness of the House of Austria and of the Church of Rome in these quarters."[2] The shadow of the Thirty Years War was, indeed, already beginning to darken the chessboard of international policy; and Henry was evolving that grotesque but fruitful alliance with the Protestant Powers which the genius of Cardinal Richelieu was ultimately to perfect. He was set upon large and far-reaching combinations against the Hapsburgs. He constructed schemes, in conjunction with the Duke of Savoy, against the Milanese. His armies were simultaneously to pass the Pyrenees, the Alps, and the neutral but helpless territories of the Archdukes. Old man as he was, he was young enough still to wish to cross swords with Spinola and to abduct the Princesse de Condé from her refuge.

In the midst of all his preparations Ravaillac struck home. The substantial visions of the King's living imagination faded immediately into thinnest fancies; the fortresses he had looked to capture from the Spaniards became at once the most impregnable

---

[1] Winwood Memorials, iii. p. 83. Winwood to Salisbury, 2nd November 1609.
[2] Ibid., p. 78.

of all castles in Spain. The French Court was split
with faction, and Marie de' Medici wavered between
the rival policies which were pressed upon her.
Her natural inclinations led one way ; her husband's
purposes pointed another. But if French assistance,
or at least French countenance, were withdrawn, the
success of the expedition to Juliers would be gravely
imperilled.

Salisbury had shown himself far from eager to
use English resources in a quarrel which was not
primarily England's own. He realised, however,
the urgency of the crisis, and Sir Thomas Edmondes
was at once despatched to Paris, with instructions
to invite the good offices of the House of Guise, King
James's relatives.[1] Whilst watching the situation
he was, according to directions, characteristic of their
author, to exercise great prudence, neither allowing
the French to suppose that the English troops,
already ' appointed to repair ' with those of the
Dutch to the frontiers of Cleve, would engage precipi-
tately without French assistance, nor on the other
hand that they would refrain from action if French
aid were withheld.[2] French statesmen were not to be
allowed to think that they could lightly shirk their
promises ; nor were the well-wishers to the expedition to be disheartened. Edmondes found Villeroy
very chilling at the first encounter.[3] A few days
later he sent a better report. It had been resolved
in full council to carry out the undertaking given
by the late King. Eight thousand foot and one
thousand horse were therefore to be sent to support
the allied forces in Juliers. Edmondes felt justly
proud of his diplomacy. " The Ambassadors of
Germany," he wrote, " do plainly confess that the
interposing of His Majesty's authority by the sending
of me so seasonably hither was of the greatest consideration with them here for consenting to the

[1] S. P. For., France, 56/102.   [2] Ibid.   [3] Ibid., 56/146.

succour of Cleves, and that otherwise there was great
danger that they would have retracted all their
former promises, and the Councillors themselves here
do not make difficulty to confess almost as much." [1]
Guise and Bouillon, we may gather, had not served
King James so ill. [2]

As has been already suggested, the moral support
of France was of more value than the military, and
the event establishes the opinion.   Count Maurice of
Nassau and the Dutch, supported by a contingent
drawn from the English garrison in Holland and led
by Sir Edward Cecil, had pretty nearly captured
Juliers before Marshal de la Châtre, in command of
the French, had arrived.   The city fell in the end of
August.   " The honour of the conduct of that siege,"
Winwood reported, " no man will detract from the
Count Maurice, who is the *maître-ouvrier* in that
métier : but that the siege hath had so speedy an
end, he himself will and doth attribute it to the
diligence and industry of Sir Edward Cecil." [3]

With the fall of the town the succession to the
Duchies ceased to be of international consequence,
though the competitors were far from having brought
their claims to any final settlement.   But the ultimate issue lies altogether outside the province
of Salisbury's biographer.   For the end of our road
is already full in sight, and we have to take short
views of worldly matters.

We may equally neglect the lesser matters incidental to Winwood's Embassy at The Hague—the
rebellion at Emden, the revolt at Utrecht, the theological protestations of King James against the
appointment of the unorthodox Vorstius to the Chair
of Divinity at Leyden.   Salisbury's correspondence
is reminiscent of them all, but they were not of a

---

[1] S. P. For., France, 56/170, 12th June 1610.
[2] *Ibid.*, 56/183 and 204-7.
[3] S. P. For., German States, 26th August 1610.

character to cause his diplomacy to swerve either to the right hand or the left. Of that diplomacy the principal features should now be plain enough. Working on the traditional hypothesis of friendship with Flanders, he had made peace with Spain in 1604, only to discover that Spain had no effective friendship towards England, and the Archdukes no real vitality apart from Spain.[1] When, by the Peace of 1609, the Dutch Republic took an acknowledged place among the Powers of Europe, he gave a firmer recognition to an alliance of which, so long as it was an alliance with rebels, England had always been a little ashamed. This was to achieve a kind of reconciliation between the old policy and the new ; to walk, one might fairly say, in the ancient paths with the assistance of a modern compass. Protestantism and Peace had at last met together ; and the balance of power had been redressed afresh within the confines of ' waterish Burgundy.' What the Catholic Netherlands for the time being seemed too inert to give, the Protestant Netherlands were at last in a position to supply.

Not indeed for ever and everywhere ! The New World was presently to try to the uttermost the balance of the old ; and the equipoise which Western Europe had half regained was to be shaken once more in the struggle for colonies and oceanic trade. But these things lay plainly beyond the utmost range of Salisbury's vision. And yet not much beyond. In 1606 a royal charter had been granted authorising and regulating the colonisation of Virginia, and in 1609 a second charter revised and amplified the government of the new colony. Such acts can have seemed to their authors no more than uncompromisingly Protestant denials of the famous Bull of Pope Alex-

---

[1] Salisbury told Boderie (Le Fèvre de la Boderie, *Ambassade en Angleterre*, i. p. 114) that " séparer l'Archiduc d'avec lui (Spain) était une vanité."

ander VI., restricting the profits of adventure and discovery to Spain and Portugal. But in fact they are the proof of a spirit which was to play havoc with the Protestant alliance. It was not for nothing that in the summer of 1597 Salisbury had taken Hakluyt into counsel about the colonisation of Guiana and had impressed that first apostle of empire with his knowledge of the navigation of the Indian Seas.[1] England, as well as Holland, was beginning to dream imperially; and in those imperial dreams there lay dormant the stern realities of a future antagonism.

For the moment, however, Protestant influences were everywhere victorious in British foreign policy. They are not least apparent in the projects of marriage which once again began to occupy the serious attention of diplomatists as a new generation of royal personages grew to maturity. We have seen how little value Salisbury attached to Spanish offers; a wise negligence fully justified by the dying declaration of Philip III. to the effect that he had never seriously meant to let a daughter of his marry the Prince of Wales.[2] But this game of cheats and shuffles deserves to be recalled, if only because it drew from Salisbury one of the very rare touches of high colour in his commonly restrained correspondence. " What is like to be the issue," he writes to Edmondes, " I must leave yourself to judge ; all that I will say is this, that the conclusion with France [3] is only of consequence, for our brave Prince [4] may find roses

---

[1] Hakluyt's *Voyages*, vol. ii., Ep. Dedicatory (to Salisbury).

[2] Cited in Motley, *Life and Death of John of Barneveld*, i. p. 267. The insincerity of the proposal was made patent to all who had eyes to see when, after the betrothal of the elder Infanta to the King of France, an attempt was made by the Spaniards to substitute her younger sister in the marriage-project.

[3] That is, of the project for the marriage of Louis XIII. and Anne of Austria.

[4] Henry, Prince of Wales.

elsewhere instead of this olive there."[1] The letter
shows that, like all his countrymen, he had set high
hopes on the engaging figure, who, if an early death
did not provoke too hasty a canonisation, united to
the charm of the Stuarts a wisdom and a sincerity
altogether foreign to his race. To sacrifice the
happiness of such a man on the altar of diplomatic
expediency was an act for which Salisbury had no
wish to be responsible.

Against mixed marriages, indeed, he set his face.
When the Duke of Savoy, eager to snatch some solid
advantage out of the tantalising visions of dynastic
and territorial aggrandisement, which Fortune
dangled before his eyes, sent a special embassy to
England to invite a double alliance between his
children and those of King James, the difference of
religion came under discussion. "We . . . shortened
that disputation," Salisbury wrote to Edmondes,[2]
"with this peremptory conclusion, that to make her
(the Princess Elizabeth) Queen of the world the King
would not so abandon her." Upon this the Ambassador declared he had commission to grant her as
much religious freedom as the King would give to a
Savoyard Princess. Salisbury's wits were not asleep.
"To this," he goes on, "it falling to my lot to reply,
I then said he had sufficiently cleared the argument
of his master sinning against his conscience, seeing,
by way of permutation, liberty should be granted.
For either it was good or evil. If evil in them, our
doing the like excused not theirs ; to which there
was no other reply but . . . an acknowledgment of
lack of power to conclude." But, in fact, an alliance
with Savoy was not one in which he discerned any
advantage. "For my part, I conclude that, as Savoy
will never break with Spain, so but in contemplation
of all circumstances of his high thought, unquiet

[1] S. P. For., France, 58/143, 5th September 1611.
[2] *Ibid.*, 57/113, 30th March 1611.

nature, and poor purse, his fortune single would be but of small use to England, if Spain and he were asunder." Still, with true diplomatic caution, he made no absolute or direct refusal of the offer. Savoy was invited to reconsider the religious objections—the incompatibility of creed and the hostility of the Pope. Only in the end of 1611 and in strict confidence did he reveal to the duc de Bouillon that the proposal was finally rejected.[1]

To Bouillon as much as to anyone the English Court had looked for assistance in the crisis which followed the death of Henry IV. Between him, the leading magnate among the French Calvinists, and Salisbury, still no less than in his youth an ' English settled Huguenot,' there was a sympathy of conviction and purpose which did as much to promote the Palatine marriage as any other cause. In October 1611 Edmondes conveys the intelligence, which Bouillon has communicated, that a resolution has been taken in Heidelberg to solicit the hand of the Princess Elizabeth for the young Elector Palatine.[2] The resolution, however, had something of a tentative character. The counsellors of the Regent required to be assured, before they made any definite proposal, that the Princess would not be too smart or expensive for the country.[2] To such cautious wooing Salisbury took exception; and he told Edmondes to make play with the offer from Savoy[3] in order to stimulate the rival competitor. This simple expedient proved effective; and before the year was out—the last year of which Salisbury saw the end— the Palatinate was prepared to invite the marriage and the King to entertain it.

We may fairly regard that eventful alliance as the

---

[1] S. P. For., France, 58/277. Salisbury to Edmondes, 26th December 1611.

[2] *Ibid.*, 58/197, 5th October 1611.

[3] *Ibid.*, 58/234, 20th November 1611.

culminating feature of Salisbury's administration of
foreign affairs. Little by little he had set English
foreign policy in a way where the dynastic alliances
of the Stuarts might blend with the predilections
of the people and the interests of the country. The
leadership of the Protestant forces of Europe, which
the assassination of Henry IV. had made vacant, and
which Cardinal Richelieu afterwards assumed, lay
within the grasp of England at the time of his decease.
The rôle would have been congenial to the growing
Protestantism of the nation, and would have accorded
with the known inclinations of the Prince of Wales
and the coming marriage of Princess Elizabeth.
More than this, the event proved that the European
ascendancy of the country lay in the same direction.
At the moments of our greatest effectiveness—in
Cromwell's time, and again in the time of William
of Orange—English continental policy turned upon
the Protestant interest. It was then no fault of
Salisbury's if after his death England lost her position
in the counsels of Europe. No man can ensure the Ship
of State against the seamanship of his successors ; and
from his day to Cromwell's no great statesman
touched the helm of foreign affairs. Public policy
under the Stuarts lay at the mercy of fancy marriages and vainglorious expeditions, of financial bargains and of civil war. Yet, beside all these, we
are conscious of a sinister personal influence.
In the year after Salisbury died, one of the
greatest of diplomatists left the shores of Spain.
Don Diego Sarmiento de Acuña, afterwards Count
of Gondomar, arrived in England in 1613. Though
Salisbury never crossed swords with him, he is nevertheless Salisbury's great opponent. It was his plausible address and seductive tongue which tempted
the King away from the course which Salisbury
had marked out, on to the treacherous shallows of the
Spanish marriage. And even yet his dark and hand-

some presence seems to haunt the place where, if
anywhere, Salisbury's wan and wasted phantom is
to be encountered.   By a curious irony there is no
finer or more striking portrait in Hatfield House than
Van Ceulen's likeness of Gondomar.   But of Hatfield
we have yet to speak.

COUNT GONDOMAR

(Painted by Cornelius Jonson Van Ceulen. Hatfield House)

[*To face p.* 288

CHAPTER XVI

FINANCE: PUBLIC AND PRIVATE

" Neither will it be that a people overlaid with taxes should
ever become valiant and martial. It is true that taxes levied
by consent of the estate do abate men's courage less; as it hath
been seen notably in the excises of the Low Countries; and,
in some degree, in the subsidies of England. For you must
note, that we speak now of the heart, and not of the purse. So
that although the same tribute and tax, laid by consent, or
by imposing, be all one to the purse, yet it works diversely
upon the courage. So that you may conclude that no
people overcharged with tribute is fit for Empire."

BACON'S *Essays. Of Kingdoms.*

THE great cataclysms of society, into whatever
surface-elements we may resolve them, will always
in the last resort be found to bear a witness to the
double nature of man. It is when spiritual enthusiasm becomes allied with material need or
material cupidity that the statesman needs to mount
his guard and the seer his watch-tower. For the
waters are then massing for a deluge. The one source,
almost as in Chatham's famous parable of the Rivers
of the South, is sweet and pure; the other fierce and
muddy; but, allied together, they are potent to carry
us far out into the unfathomable ocean. The Reformation, which, whatever we make of it, was at least
an effort after purer morals and deeper spirituality,
had its grosser side in the Peasants' War and the
spoliation of the Church : the French Revolution,
beneath its shocking animalism, concealed a just
protest against spiritual wickedness in high places.

And in the more sober and deliberate action of the Great Rebellion one of the chief points of interest is the interplay of Puritan idealism with the common sense of national economy.

If 1604 is to be taken as the year in which the lines of the religious struggle were first defined, 1610 is as certainly that in which the financial issue was first set forth. And the historians have devoted to it proportionate attention—Spedding an all too lavish wealth of detail ; Gardiner a special care and a special research. In its chronicles Salisbury is as much the protagonist as James in the annals of the Hampton Court Conference ; and posterity regards his work with no very different eye. If success be the measure of all things certainly there is not much to choose between the King and his Minister. Each tried his hand at one of the two great problems of their age ; each failed in his endeavour ; each left to his successor the legacy of an unsettled dispute. Yet no two men worked in a more opposite temper or saw their plans miscarry from a more dissimilar fault. The King was hasty, prodigal, impatient of opposition, incautious in speech. Salisbury abounded in the contrary virtues ; and it is no slight tribute to his diplomatic talent that he contrived so long to satisfy a master so different. If we treat as something of a fable that curious story [1] of his causing a roomful of silver to be heaped up so that the King as he passed might realise the significance of the bounties so lightly bestowed upon a royal favourite, it is at least a fable which aptly illustrates the conflicting natures of the Sovereign and the Minister. James was a reckless spendthrift, with all the spendthrift's genius for fair promises of reform ; and, long before Salisbury came to the Exchequer, the exchange of strong remonstrance and plausible contrition—the one as idle as the other—had begun to pass.

[1] See Lloyd, *Worthies, Observ. on the Life of Sir R. Cecil.*

" I cannot but be sensible of that needless and unseasonable profusion of expenses," so the King assured him in October 1605,[1] " whereof ye wrote in your last to Lake. Ye best know both my part and my mind in all the unnecessary waste that comes that way. . . . When I consider the extremity of my state at this time, my only hap and hope that upholds me is in my good servants that will grieve and labour for my relief upon such ground as I said at my parting : otherwise I could rather have wished with Job never to have been than that the glorious sun-shine of my entreaties should be so soon over-cast with the dark clouds of irreparable misery. I have promised, and I will perform it, that there shall be no default in me."

So he wrote once and again,[2] but he was not the less touchy and difficult, and Salisbury had to make haste to excuse himself for an impatient word.

" I have . . . understood . . . that your Majesty hath been troubled with a word that fell from my lips, wherein I only glanced that I saw a fatality in the State that it would never be rich. . . . If your Majesty observe the time wherein it was written and the person that wrote it : the time being, when I was newly come from attending four or five of your faithful labourers, who had been looking upon the glass of your state for point of treasure and revenue, which hath been and must be for seven or eight days yet the best part of our meditation; the person being myself that love rather to speak too little (like myself) than too much : in such cases I will (let the law be as sharp as it will against words) conclude that a sticking beagle may some-times have a sticking master who, having such a piercing and a multiplying brain that [3] he can make what he list of everything, hath stuck so long upon such a word." [4]

Thus with sagacious humour Salisbury retrieved the chance expression. But to retrieve the fortunes of the State there was needed the power to convert a fool, immoderately vain of his own wit and knowledge, into a wise man. Here lay the psychological factor in the economic situation, without some appreciation

[1] Hatf. MSS., 134/72.
[2] Cf. Hatf. MSS., 134/113: " I shall facilitate your cure by all the means possible for a poor patient." And see also Hatf. MSS., 126/75, Lake to Salisbury.
[3] In the original, ' as.'   [4] Hatf. MSS., 134/95.

ot which the student will never judge the statesman fairly.

National finance is never an engaging subject to depict in words, and seldom an agreeable one to handle in practice.   In Salisbury's time it was more than usually unpleasant.   Though the nation was growing yearly richer and the national expenditure inevitably expanding, the proceeds of national taxation, as measured in the returns from subsidies, showed a distinct decline.[1]   Elizabeth, with all her economy, was beginning to outrun the constable before her death ; and it is doubtful whether her successor, whoever he might have been, could with the best will in the world have made both ends meet without some loss of prestige.   Parsimony in a new sovereign is a fault pardonable, indeed, but seldom pardoned ; and cheese-paring might, as Spedding has suggested, have done James a greater injury in popular esteem than all his thriftlessness.   When we look with reproach at the swelling expenses of the Cofferer of the Household, representing no doubt a formidable array of masques and banquets, we may in fairness remember that there lay upon the King the burden of national joy at the conclusion of a great war and the achievement of an unchallenged succession.

The financial situation, when in 1608 Dorset closed his long and honourable career by a death at the Council-table itself, stood approximately thus. The annual sum which the Sovereign derived from his estates and his other settled revenue amounted to £320,000 ; and in addition there was the parliamentary grant of three subsidies and six-fifteenths, voted in the exultation attending the discovery of the Gunpowder Plot, which secured to him, up to 1610, a further income averaging £100,000 a year. His resources thus reached something in the neigh-

---

[1] See the Memorandum by Salisbury in Spedding's *Letters and Life of Bacon*, iv. p. 149.

bourhood of £425,000. But on the other side of the balance-sheet there lay an annual expenditure of £500,000, leaving him at an annual disadvantage of £75,000. And there was, besides, at this time, or just afterwards, a debt of £1,400,000,[1] partly inherited, partly of his own making.

Between two items of the King's revenue there lay a debatable country. ' Impositions ' were customs duties lying outside both the immemorial custom on wool and hides and the custom on wine and merchandise, which, under the title of tonnage and poundage, had, since the advent of the Tudors, been granted by Parliament to every Sovereign at his or her accession for the term of life. The King claimed an administrative supervision over the trade of the country, and by virtue of this claim a duty on currants, which the resistance of John Bate made famous, was imposed in 1606. The action of the Government was admittedly reasonable and the decision of the judges against Bate admittedly free from unlawful pressure and generally approved at the time by the common sense of the community, however wrong-headed we may think it. But in the *obiter dicta* of the Bench there lay cause for uneasiness ; and the case, as we shall see, was not forgotten when the conflict between Parliament and the Crown began to grow. For the moment it supplied a new source of revenue of which Dorset took advantage. Salisbury would have been less than human if, in his urgent need, he had not pursued the example of his predecessor ; the more as he was a convinced believer in indirect taxation.[2]

His presence at the Treasury was followed by a burst of activity, to which his two principal subordinates—Sir Julius Cæsar, the Chancellor, and Sir Walter Cope, the Chamberlain of the Exchequer—

---

[1] Gardiner, *Parl. Deb. in 1610*, p. 5. This was, I think, however, in 1608, not in 1603, as there printed. See Harl. MSS., 737/4.

[2] Winwood Memorials, ii. p. 415.

have left a testimony.[1]   He " found the Exchequer
a chaos of confusion "; Cope tells us " he found the
debts thereof £300,000 or £400,000 ; but which
were good, which were bad, which separate, which
desperate, no man knew." To bring order and
solvency into this chronic muddle might have given
pause to a man with large leisure and a full complement of health. Salisbury, who had neither, did
not quail.   He set to work on the instant to see what
was owed as well as what was owing. Letters,
received with very ill-favour, inconveniently reminded noble lords of debts to the Crown, which
they had conveniently forgotten. With lesser men
he took the sharper method of a process. Some old
dues from the sheriffs, which had grown rusty with
disuse, awoke suddenly to life ; and copyholders on
the Crown-lands were made aware of certain fines
they had supposed would never be remembered again.
Into the returns from another kind of fine—the
penalties of a court of law—an inquisition was pro-
jected. Further, commissioners were set to review
the royal properties, and revise the royal rents, and
survey the royal woods, and dispose of the royal
timber. Everywhere there was unwonted activity.
A scheme for bringing water to the drier parts of
London, from which in time the Sovereign might
derive a comfortable revenue, entered the untiring
brain of Salisbury's tired body ; and his plans for
increasing the national wealth included the en-
couragement of various industries by which the native
subject might be set to work—the manufacture of
alum, of copper, of steel, and, as Cope quaintly puts
it, ' of salt by the sun.'   He had some idea of mining
silver in Scotland ; [2] but experiments showed him that
the nature of that admirable country, like the nature

---

[1] S. P. Dom., Jas. I., 35/43, and Cope's *Apology* (in Gutch, *Collect.
Curiosa*, i. p. 119).

[2] See S. P. Dom. Jas. I., 38/23.

of those, at least, of its children with whom he had formed acquaintance, was rather adapted to absorb money than to provide it.

In the matter of the Customs his activity brought up the revenue by leaps and bounds—from £86,000 to £120,000, and again to £125,000.[1] This was accomplished by an extension of the principle which, as we have seen, the judges had sanctioned in Bate's case. But though Salisbury did not invite the co-operation of Parliament, he knew better than to be arbitrary in his methods. Representative merchants of the City were taken into council, and the new Book of Rates was issued with their assent if not with their approval. The fresh impositions even made some bid for popularity. On currants and tobacco the duty was reduced ; and the underlying principle of the revised tariff was the taxation of luxuries and the exemption of necessaries. Munitions of war and re-exports were privileged to escape paying toll altogether.[2]

There was another expedient to which the Treasurer had recourse. Among the obligations of a feudal tenant was that of making ' an aid,' or contribution in money, at the knighting of his lord's eldest son. So far, indeed, as subjects were concerned, this exaction had long been obsolete. But Henry vii. had made use of it ; and Salisbury, perhaps with a purpose which will presently appear, took advantage of its legal existence. The figure of Prince Henry, on whose account the levy was nominally made, was no doubt popular enough to take the edge off the requisition ; but there must have been many excellent and loyal gentlemen who felt that the time had gone by for such unwonted charges. And Salisbury himself was at heart of the same opinion.

By dint of this strenuous finance he had, at the beginning of 1610, raised the King's income by some-

---

[1] Cope's *Apology*.   [2] *Parl. Deb. in 1610*, p. 157.   S.'s speech.

thing near £150,000,[1] and had paid off debt and checked deficit to the amount of at least £1,100,000.[2] It was an achievement which, in other circumstances, would have brought him the name of a great financier. But the circumstances in his case were paralysing to the most brilliant effort. For James was now in peace-time living at the rate of over £500,000 a year,[3] a sum which rivalled Elizabeth's expenditure in the hour of her direst crisis ; [4] and the utmost that Salisbury could raise fell short of this figure by £46,000. Where the leakage lay is made only too apparent even by a cursory inspection of contemporary documents. In the beginning of 1610—the very year of the financial crisis—John Chamberlain, the Horace Walpole of the day, sends Winwood an account of the Christmas festivities at the Court. " If the charge do not hinder it," he tells his correspondent, " the Prince would fain undertake another triumph or show against the King's day in March, and the Queen would likewise have a masque against Candlemas or Shrovetide. She hath been somewhat melancholy of late about her jointure, that was not fully to her liking : whereupon to give her contentment there is £3000 a year added to it out of the customs with a donative of £20,000 to pay her debts." [5]   And two months later no less a sum than £700 is expended on ' fine gold and silver spangles ' for the ' coats of the Guard, the footmen, and the messengers of the royal household.' [6] In face of this, Salisbury's attempt to deprive the

---

[1] Gardiner, *Hist. of England*, ii. p. 13. In 1606 it was £315,000, in 1610 it was £460,000.

[2] Gardiner, *Hist. of England*, ii. p. 13 and footnote (³), and see *Parl. Deb. in 1610*, p. 5, and Harl. MSS., 737/14. The amounts do not precisely tally, and I have stated the lower figure—£1,100,000—instead of the higher, £1,200,000.

[3] *Parl. Deb. in 1610*, p. 6.

[4] Gardiner, *Hist. of Engl.*, ii. p. 12.

[5] Winwood Memorials, iii. 117 [10th February 1609 (10)].

[6] S. P. Dom., Jas. I., 53/106.

Prince's second kitchen-clerk of the enjoyment of
five dishes at his dinner appears a work of supereroga-
tion—the more idle, indeed, as the hungry fellow had
taken the precaution to secure a special warrant
from the King authorising the full satisfaction of his
appetite.[1]

The King, according to our fanciful Constitution,
can do no wrong ; and accordingly Salisbury, when at
last in 1610 he was forced to the expedient of applying
to Parliament for assistance, cast a decent veil over
the open secrets of the Court. The new session, so he
told the conference of the two Houses, had two objects—to witness the creation of the Prince of Wales
and to obtain supply. The first gave him occasion
to pay a tribute which, amid the dry and meagre
reports of his speeches, pleasantly arrests the eye of a
biographer. Prince Henry had evidently fascinated
him as he fascinated all men.

" What do I speak of time, place, and suchlike
circumstance," he said, " which are but the shells
and shadows of this action. Let us leave this and
behold the Prince himself with comfort and admiration—a prince in whom there are more strange
images of external formosity, vigour, and activity,
and, for the internal faculties of the mind, greater
capacity, promptness to learn, and judgment in point
of election than ever appeared in prince of England.
It is true I might have forborne this commendation
amongst you, whose eyes I need not open to behold
his virtues, yet such is my joy when I see him, and so
do my affections kindle when I must speak of him,
that,[2] though I never had *promtum ad adulationem
ingenium*, yet when I am speaking I cannot choose but
speak what I think." [3]

He went on to set forth the King's necessity.
Spedding has criticised his action, arguing that he,

---

[1] Hatfield MSS., 128/150.
[2] In the original, ' as.'   [3] Harl. MSS., 737/4.

who is generally accused of over-subtlety, was in this case unduly frank.   His plain admission of the state of the Exchequer gave Parliament, we are told, the advantage in the coming struggle with the Crown, since the Commons learnt that they had only to wait their time to secure their ends.[1]   It is a strange piece of criticism.   If there is one thing which moves the generosity of Englishmen it is a straightforward appeal—the candid confession of error or difficulty. And conversely there is nothing more damaging to solicitation than a detected deception.   In this case, moreover, there can be little doubt that the deception would have been rapidly brought to view.   Salisbury's policy was at once the most honest, the most safe, and the most politic.

There is no need to follow him through a waste of figures.   Those that are most material have been already cited; and mention of the rest is more likely to confuse than to enlighten counsel.   After the worst was said, he conjured his hearers to come to the rescue of the sinking fortunes of the country, using that time-honoured simile of the Ship of State which never grows old.   He went on to anticipate obvious objections.   If it was alleged that the precedent was rare, he replied that on the contrary the Kings of England had but thrice in six hundred years asked help of their parliaments and been denied it.   Again, if it were urged that the King was not at war, the answer was that the pacification of Ireland entailed exceptional expense.   Nor was the King's well-known generosity without purpose or precedent. Bounty is essential to a sovereign.   Queen Mary, ' a queen full of moral virtues and of great devotion according in her kind,' had made large gifts and restitutions out of the revenues of the Crown.   Further, the outlook in foreign politics was not reassuring.   Some breach of treaties was to be

[1] Spedding, *Letters and Life of Francis Bacon*, iv. p. 175.

feared, and the enterprise in Cleves ought not to be abandoned. " For my particular," he continued, " I must say thus much, that, if sitting so near the storm and seeing it come in the air, I should have suffered it to break and bemoaned myself in a private corner without resorting to the natural place for remedy, I were not worthy to carry this staff in my hand." [1] Then followed one of those passages, customary, no doubt, as the preface of the Authorised Version of the Bible is there to remind us, but from which, nevertheless, a biographer would gladly avert his eyes. " Remember what a king you have," Salisbury told his hearers, " not only the wisest of kings (well I may say of men) but the very image of an angel, that doth both bring good tidings and puts us in the fruition of all good things." [1] These amazing if conventional compliments opened the way for rational truth. In the matter of supply the speaker said Sovereign and People had complementary duties : " Kings though they were so great ought not to demand contributions and subsidies at their pleasures ; neither ought subjects to deny them out of humour, when there is just cause *pro bono publico*." In conclusion he alluded to the King's prerogative, which he affirmed absolute and unassailable in respect of impositions and feudal tenures, ' the times and places of the Courts of Justice, and the execution of the penal laws,' yet subject to some permissive modification in view of popular grievances. Here was the first tentative cast in the matter of the Great Contract.

The speech was, we learn,[2] very persuasive ; and the Commons eyed the bait, but not greedily. It was argued that the Catholics, whose existence the growing Puritanism of Parliament bitterly resented, had not been as sharply mulcted as the law allowed ;

---

[1] Harl. MSS., 737/4.
[2] Winwood Memorials, iii. p. 123. Beaulieu to Trumbull.

and there was some allusion made to the extravagance of the pensions granted to courtiers as well as to the leakage entailed by farming the customs. The financial situation would be ameliorated if more thought were taken about such inlets and outlets of revenue. But these were the by-products of debate. The conclusion of the whole matter was that the Commons would be glad to hear more of the fore-shadowed concessions and particularly of the question of tenures.

A conference was therefore arranged, so that the Lord Treasurer might be heard again. Salisbury rather wittily told the assembled legislators that the Commons had converted the King's demand for assistance into a " *Quid mihi dabis ?* " on the part of the King's subjects. He tried to bring them back to what was after all the main purport of their session—supply to discharge the King's obligations and support to carry on the King's Government. For the one he said he needed £600,000 ; one-half of which was to clear the debt, the other half to furnish the navy and to be stored as treasure against an hour of need. For support he needed £200,000 a year. He was pressed by the representatives of the Commons to speak about tenures, but, though he adumbrated various other alleviations of law and practice, he pro-fessed himself unable to deal with that matter, and advised the appointment of a committee to learn the King's pleasure about it. In due course, however, he became the spokesman of the King's intention or rather absence of intention. James declared that he must have time to make up his mind ; that he was as yet uncertain whether it consorted with his honour or his conscience to release young nobles and gentlemen from the royal tutelage. The Commons respectfully urged that wardship was not a regal but a feudal prerogative, and that a relative was the natural, the Sovereign only the artificial, guardian

of a minor. To this representation James assented ;
and, the pricks of honour and conscience being thus
easily allayed, the question of the tenures was approached from the standpoint of utility.

It is important that at this point we should call
to mind the then theory of the Constitution. To us
it seems all important that Parliament should be
annually in a position to strike the sceptre out of the
hands of any administration by the simple expedient
of withholding supplies. The men of the early
seventeenth century had not so far elaborated the
mechanism of government. They found, indeed,
in the refusal of supply a convenient method of
obtaining the redress of grievances. But supply
and support represented to them extraordinary and
not ordinary incidents in the working of the Constitution. Their ideal was to be free of requests for
money ; and there was nothing they more devoutly
desired than, as the phrase went, to see ' the King
live of his own.' The difficulty which Salisbury
had to face was merely that ' the King's own '—the
revenue derived from crown-lands, feudal incidents,
tonnage and poundage, and impositions—was no
longer sufficient ; and we are reading into his time
the ideas of a later age if we see in his attempt to
secure for the Sovereign a sufficient annual revenue
a subtle design to make the Sovereign independent of
Parliament. With this caution in our minds we are
likely to view the Great Contract more justly than
would otherwise be the case. It was, in truth, a
remedial measure, consisting, as all the best remedial
legislation does consist, in a development rather
than in a reform of prevailing practice. Feudal
incidents had fallen out of date with feudal lords and
feudal castles ; and their charges had become burdensome with the decay of the society to which they
corresponded. But their financial equivalent might
be properly demanded as a contribution to national

defence ; and what Salisbury sought to do was to set this contribution upon a convenient and stable basis.

If public finance ever lent itself to dramatic effect, a tragic drama could be built up out of the course of the negotiations relating to the Great Contract. There is in them an ebb and flow of action—one party making a move forward, and the other retorting with a counter-move—such as Mr. Bradley has taught us to look for in the constructive mechanism of Shakespeare's plays. And there is in them, besides, a crisis, when the hero's fortunes (if we give Salisbury that rôle) seem on the very point of triumphing, followed by a collapse complete and irretrievable, of all his schemes, in which he himself is closely involved, and for which, it is no great exaggeration to say, he pays forfeit with his life. But it would be tedious to any ordinarily constituted reader to be taken in detail through the scenes in which this tragedy is worked out ; and most men will be content, and more than content, to know the outline of the story.

Salisbury occupied the interlude, whilst the question of the feudal tenures was under the royal consideration, by an adroit repudiation on the King's behalf of the doctrines of Cowell's *Interpreter*. That famous book had exalted the pretensions of the Crown beyond the point to which even a Stuart laid claim. James, the Lord Treasurer told the conference of the two Houses, " did acknowledge that he had no power to make laws of himself or to exact any subsidies *de jure* without the consent of his three Estates ; and therefore he was so far from approving the opinion that [1] he did hate those that believed it." [2] It was a politic declaration, but it did not serve. There was as yet too great a gulf fixed between the desires of the Minister and the disposition of the

---

[1] In the original,' as.'   [2] Gardiner, *Parl. Deb. in 1610*, p. 24.

Parliament. Salisbury estimated the value of the
prerogatives to be surrendered at £200,000 ; the
Commons rated them at just half so much. On the
very day on which the negotiations collapsed Henry
IV. was murdered in Paris. Salisbury broke the
news to the Lower House, turning the sinister event
very dexterously into a plea for supply. " This
King," he told them, reviewing the loss which England had sustained from the dagger of Ravaillac,
" stood in the breach betwixt foreign enmity and
our King. A king rich and powerful in arms and
ours in want and indigence . . .! We must now
give occasion for foreign despatches to advertise
how careful we are of our King and how we provide
for him. And money is the only antidote for future
mischief." [1]

He charmed wisely, but as yet in vain. The
House, ' packed ' though it had been at least to some
extent,[2] began at this juncture to agitate the question of
the general legality of impositions ; and neither King
nor Council could stop its murmurs. In the end James
bowed to the storm, and, in the fairer weather which
followed, the negotiation for the Great Contract was
again revived. The creation of the Prince of Wales
brought the sun back into the sky. In that function
Salisbury bore the chief part after the protagonists.
" At their coming to the chair of estate the Prince
kneeled down before the King ; and then the herald
delivered the patent to the Lord Treasurer, who read
it openly, and, as he came to the clauses mentioning
the parts of the investiture, the King received them
and put them upon the Prince. . . ." [3]

A few days later Salisbury addressed a conference
of the two Houses again. The rough notes of his
speech have come down to us among the manu-

---

[1] S. P. Dom., Jas. I., 54/29.
[2] See Gardiner, *Hist. of Engl.*, ii. p. 63.
[3] Gardiner, *Parl. Deb. in 1610*, p. 49.

scripts at Hatfield [1]—a few incoherent words on a
sheet of paper, which yet, by their vivid carelessness,
throw a surer bridge across the chasm of three
centuries than the most elaborate and painstaking artifice. " Marigold " he sets down, for example,
upon that strange relic of eloquence, now so dull
and faded ; and we learn from the fuller edition
of the speech which he caused to be prepared that
he exhorted subjects to ' open their joy ' in their
Sovereign ' like the marigold opens to the sun.' The
creation of the Prince of Wales and the assassination
of the King of France gave him two more texts for
loyalty which he was not slow to use. Let the
Commons, he urged, bring to a close those "months
—almost five—spent in matters impertinent, and
extravagant discourses, whereof some (are) square,
some long, some short, but all circular, for we are there
almost where we first begun " ; and let them vote
the King ' supply,' enough to free him from debt and
to give him some small deposit of treasure against
immediate necessity. ' Support '—the reconstitu-
tion of the revenue—could wait, whilst the members
made themselves better acquainted with the state
of the country.[2]

The appeal was successful, but not instantly.
The Commons were resolved to lay to rest the question
of the impositions, and only after Salisbury had
defended both in general and in particular the impositions he had exacted,[3] only when the King had
undertaken to levy no new rates on merchandise without parliamentary consent, were they agreeable to
a meagre grant of one subsidy and one-fifteenth.
But in the matter of the Contract better progress
was made. The King had asked for an annual income of £220,000 in exchange for the rights to be
surrendered : the Commons offered £180,000. Salis-

---

[1] Hatfield MSS., 140/217.   [2] Gardiner, *Parl. Deb. in 1610*, pp. 52–4.
[3] This speech is given in *Parl. Deb. in 1610*, p. 154.

bury brought them to a bargain at £200,000 ; the
King's assent being characteristically given in what
his courtiers doubtless regarded as a ' merry ' conceit,
but what a less courteous age can only commend as
a pedantic witticism. To have closed at £200,000
was, so His Majesty averred, a course he liked better
than if they had fixed upon £190,000 or £210,000 ;
for nine was the number of the Muses or Poetæ,
who were ever beggars, whilst eleven was the number
of the Apostles when Judas was away.[1] To one
observer, whose opinion has been preserved to us,
Salisbury's achievement appeared very considerable.
" The matters now concluded," wrote Sir Roger
Aston to an unknown peer, " have had long debate,
and yet in the end, God be praised, (are) come to a
good and sound resolution : and that chiefly by the
wise, grave, and careful carriage of this worthy counsellor, your dearest friend, who by his wisdom hath
so governed all things that [2] they are come to a final
end. The little Beagle hath run a true and perfect
scent, which brought the rest of the hounds to a
perfect tune, which was before by their voice much
divided." [3] And the historian of the time has not
stinted his praise : — " Regarded from a merely
financial point of view, the arrangement was excellent. It is difficult to say which of the two parties
to the bargain would have gained most if it had been
finally carried out." [4] For the King, as he goes on
to point out, would have secured an increase of
income : and the subject would have been secured
against much troublesome litigation.

The Lord Treasurer wound up the proceedings of
the session in a ' long and pithy speech ' which gave
good satisfaction.[5] The Contract itself, he impressed
upon the Commons, was no longer in doubt ; all that

---

[1] S. P. Dom., Jas. I., 56/42.　　[2] In the original, ' as.'
[3] S. P. Dom., Jas. I., 56/42.　　[4] Gardiner, *Hist. of Engl.*, ii. p. 84.
[5] S. P. Dom., Jas. I., 56/42.

remained to do was to fix the incidence of the new taxation. He was reasonably but prematurely, sanguine. He should have recalled the familiar dictum, which is to be found more than once in his letters :—" Multa cadunt inter calicem supremaque labra." [1] The King's speech proroguing the assembly betrayed a little rift in the lute. In response to the petition that the Puritan clergy should be restored James undertook to look himself into the working of the Ecclesiastical Commission. It was not such an answer as had been hoped for, though it was the answer which the King, with his conception of a Church-establishment, was bound to give. Uniformity of doctrine and discipline are, as he affirmed, essential to the well-being of every visible Church. In regard to other grievances — the issue of proclamations, and the administration by the Council of Wales of the four English counties adjoining— his reply was still more evasive.

When the Legislature re-assembled in October it was manifest that the situation had changed for the worse. The Commons felt that they had not secured the things they had been fighting for ; and they came to their work, resolved at all costs to set the matter of the impositions at rest, and generally to obtain redress of grievances. James on his side had looked into the bargain and found it not quite so good as he supposed. There were those about him —and Sir Julius Cæsar, we have every reason to think, was one of them [2]—who advised him, doubtless with a plausible apparatus of figures, that he could by an ingenious manipulation of existing sources of revenue, secure a large increase of income without any surrender of his prerogatives. He raised his demands accordingly. He must have a supply of £500,000 before the Contract was even considered ;

[1] *e.g.* Hatfield MSS., 213/117.
[2] See Gardiner, *Parl. Deb. in 1610*, pp. 163/79.

and his share of the bargain was, besides, to be raised by one-half—£300,000 instead of the £200,000 agreed upon—as well as by the amount of a compensation to the officers of the Court of Wards, whose places were to be swept away.

The new propositions severed the fabric of the Contract as sharply as the scissors of Fate. To Salisbury, indeed, the rending of his hopes seemed so sudden, so incalculable, that he could only attribute it to the finger of Providence. He had seen, we are told, that the Commons " had a great desire to have effected that great contract," and that the King " had willingly given his assent to the same, and that yet, nevertheless, it proceeded not, wherein he could not find the impediment, but that God did not bless it." [1] He groped wearily amongst the shreds of his diplomacy, striving at least to secure the means of carrying on the King's Government. Even that was denied him. The blood of the Commons was up : they would have nothing but complete concession ; all their grievances must be allayed ; it was not enough that the King agreed to forgo new impositions and proclamations and arbitrary government in the Welsh border counties, besides several lesser prerogatives or practices. And, if the Commons' blood was up, James's blood was on fire. Salisbury, urging conciliation and patience, met with the hot breath of his anger. " He (the King) followed your Lordship's advices," Lake wrote to the unhappy Minister, " in having patience, hoping for better issue. He cannot have asinine patience. He is not made of that metal that is ever to be held in suspense and to receive nothing but stripes." [2] No counsel could now deter the angry man from dismissing the assembly which had so coolly defied him ; it was all his Ministers could do to restrain him from sending his enemies to the Tower.

[1] Somers, *Tracts*, ii. p. 151.   [2] S. P. Dom., Jas. I., 58/35.

So ended the project of the Great Contract. It was a statesmanlike attempt to settle on conservative lines one of the pressing problems of the age. Far-reaching principles underlay it, which, if they had been accepted, might have preserved to the Sovereign more power than remained to him at the end of the century, and secured to the nation more peace than in the event it was to enjoy. We cannot say that civil war would have been avoided, for the Great Rebellion was primarily a war of religion, but it might not have been reached so soon, and it might have terminated sooner. One issue is clearly more easily determined than two. Enlightened conservatism, however, fell a victim, as it constantly does, to the conservatism which knows no change. Sir Julius Cæsar, in that critical dialogue to which we have already alluded, warns his readers that the Great Contract will work " an innovation of the fundamental laws of the kingdom and give a ready passage to a democracy, which is the deadliest enemy to a monarchy " ; [1] and there were doubtless many such Cæsars among the idle band of courtiers which thronged the King. They got their way, though by a seeming defect in the justice of the gods they never lived to see the end of their road. Human justice has been equally kind to them ; and the Minister whom they thwarted has been made to bear the burden of their reproach. " Salisbury's mistake," Gardiner tells us, " was that he had attempted to drive a financial bargain without taking care that it should be preceded by a political reconciliation." [2] Doubtless it was a mistake, but the common phrase teaches us that some mistakes are ' unavoidable.' It is no great blame that Salisbury's plans, intrinsically excellent, were wrecked upon the incalculable elements of human pride and passion ; for even the purposes

---

[1] *Parl. Deb. in 1610*, pp. 177, 178.
[2] Gardiner, *Hist. of Engl.*, ii. p. 111.

of God can, as we read, be made of none effect by the foolishness of men. To the more specific indictment of Spedding[1] that "the total result of Salisbury's financial administration appears to have been the halving of the debt at the cost of almost doubling the deficiency," Gardiner has himself furnished the crushing rejoinder that "the former was the result of Salisbury's own labour; over the latter he had but little control."[2]

The papers that have come down to us afford one or two glimpses of the stricken Minister in the hour of his defeat. His overstrained nerves almost gave way. When Levinus Munck, his secretary, imprudently laid Winwood's bill of extraordinary expenses before him, he put it off, saying, "Sir Ralph Winwood is no poor man; he can stay well enough:" and "so from this matter his Lordship presently fell into a great passion about the penury of the Exchequer and the exceeding difficulty that would be found in the replenishing of the same."[3] To Lake he wrote that he knew not to what to compare the vexations of the late Parliament so much as to the plagues of Job.[4] Meanwhile, the King remained helpful as ever. The extinction of the last hope of parliamentary supply was succeeded by a petulant gift of £34,000 to six royal favourites. With such a master to serve a younger man might have despaired of bringing round the national affairs. Salisbury was frail in health as well (if feeling be the right measure of age) as old in years. He must have known his life had not long to run. As things were, it only remained to him to live from hand to mouth, and to leave to new men and more propitious seasons the restoration of the common weal.

He resorted, therefore, to temporary expedients.

---

[1] Spedding, *Letters and Life of Francis Bacon*, iv. p. 276.

[2] Gardiner, *Hist. of Engl.*, ii. p. 144.

[3] Winwood Memorials, iii. p. 235.   [4] Hatf. MSS., 128/172.

One of these — the creation of baronetcies — will
always be remembered against him, though, in fact,
the idea sprung ' from the earnest suit of two hundred
prime gentlemen of birth and estates.' [1]   On the
pretext of providing funds to meet the heavy burden
of the Irish administration any knight or esquire,
worth a thousand a year in land and agreeable to the
sacrifice of approximately a year's income, was enabled to gratify himself with a petty dignity and a
social precedence.   The sale of titles is a practice on
behalf of which no moralist would care to be briefed ;
and certainly none the more where the recipients had
been previously reputed honest gentlemen of good
report.   Honours, if they are to be worth anything
to the nation or the individual, must carry upon them
the stamp of public service and public esteem.   Yet,
if cynicism be ever healthy, it is healthy here.   There
will always be, so long as the world lasts, a certain
number of people who believe that honour can be
extracted from the purchase of the emblems and
trappings of merit. Salisbury gave these people
exactly what they asked for and exactly what they
deserved.   They wore badges and were pointed at
with the finger.   But no one was under the smallest
illusion as to how they came by their dignities ; for
they carried their own colours and flaunted their
own plumes.   They were an aristocracy of purchase ;
no one could mistake them for an aristocracy of
honour.   The modern world is more hypocritical.
Titles, in general belief, are commonly sold ; but
the common people who buy them pass among the
vulgar for the possessors of uncommon distinction.
Salisbury's plan had notable merits, which only the
lapse of time has made fully apparent.   Not only
would the principle, if systematically applied, have

---

[1] The author of *Aulic. Coquin.* (p. 149, ed. 1811) says that he copied
the list of signatures to this petition before it came into Salisbury's
hands.

preserved the peerage from an egregious and damaging contamination, but it would have diverted the purchase-money in these ignoble bargains from the party chest into the national exchequer. The scheme only suffered from one defect. When it came to the point there proved not to be enough snobs in the kingdom. Salisbury had calculated for two hundred, and less than one hundred put in their claim. Thus the creation fell short of the estimate by just one-half. Time, there is reason to think, would have corrected the deficiency with a good deal to spare.

Other expedients for raising money did not fail to occur to his ever-active mind. Privy seals, inviting a loan from men of substance, were issued with the King's approval,[1] though they met with no success.[2] There was some talk of calling in the full fine of £30,000 to which Northumberland had been condemned.[3] A project was set on foot to release the Dutch from the bulk of their debt in return for a good round sum of ready money.[4] Local compositions in lieu of purveyance were arranged in the various countries.[5] Finally, Salisbury abandoned all his profits as Master of the Court of Wards to the use of the State.[5]

Those who are disposed to think hardly of him will be likely to moderate their judgment if they consider how little, as he himself was well aware,[6] he had to gain, by the conclusion of the Great Contract. The abolition of his office would have left him undoubtedly the poorer, and, though in the King's ultimatum to Parliament compensation had been demanded for the dispossessed officials, this formed no part of the original plan.

---

[1] S. P. Dom., Jas. I., 66/69.
[2] Prothero, *Statutes and Const. Doc.*, lxxx.
[3] S. P. Dom., Jas. I., 67/67.   [4] Winwood Memorials, iii. p. 275.
[5] Gardiner, *Hist. of Engl.*, ii. p. 113.
[6] Winwood Memorials, iii. pp. 193, 194.

One measure of widespread importance, connected with his administration of the public finances, deserves a passing mention. The monetary problems of the age arose out of the depreciation of silver, consequent upon the discoveries of that metal in America ; and Salisbury, like his predecessors, had to deal with the continuous efflux of the gold coinage to the Continent, where it obtained a higher value. He gave the subject careful attention and was eventually convinced of the correct remedy. By a proclamation of November 1611 the value of all gold coins was raised 10 per cent., or (which was the same thing) the artificial relation between gold and silver was readjusted to the natural. With a bi-metallic coinage and foreign exchanges shifting from day to day the proclamation could only have a passing effect. But so far as principle was concerned it was right enough.[1]

What Salisbury's personal income amounted to is an interesting question, at which we may not inappropriately glance at the close of a chapter dedicated to finance. It happens that among the papers at Hatfield there are extant the balance-sheets of his revenue and expenditure in some of the last years of his life.[2] The figures indeed elude anything in the nature of a nice precision, for capital and income are recklessly intermixed, and the separation of these two accounts is often a speculative and consequently rather arbitrary matter. It is, however, a safe approximation to the truth to say that he had about £10,000 a year ; and this is, in fact, the figure at which his agent puts his income in 1608.[3] If we make our calculation of the difference in the value of money

---

[1] See on this W. Shaw, *History of Currency*, p. 136.
[2] Hatf. MSS., 160/1. Mr. Gunton makes his income £13,423 in 1609, £10,033 in 1610, £8473 in 1611.
[3] Estate Papers, Accounts, 8/8.

between his day and ours on the basis of a comparison of the wages of unskilled labour,[1] this might represent £30,000 a year in our own time.

The sources from which this revenue was derived were in the main three—official salaries, rents, and what we should call investments. The first of these yielded to a modern eye a strangely inadequate remuneration. As Secretary of State, Salisbury was entitled to £100 a year ; as Lord Treasurer to £365 ; as Master of the Court of Wards to something under £250 ; as High Steward of the Queen's lands to £20.[2] According to Chamberlain, the bailiwick of Westminster, which he held at the time of his death, was worth £500 a year.[3] Smaller sums were owing to him in various capacities, among which a title was apparently one. " For your Lordship's creation-money," we read, " for being Earl of Salisbury, for half a year £10 ; " " for your Honour's creation Viscount Cranborne, for half a year £5." But there were, of course, other and more lucrative means by which a Minister obtained remuneration for his services. Though the profit of the Court of Wards and Liveries fell far below the figure conceived by the mercantile imagination of the Venetian Secretary or his informant,[4] they represented in the half-year between Michaelmas 1608 and Lady Day 1609 the substantial sum of £650. The profits of the farm of

---

[1] Salisbury paid his labourers about 10d. a day : we pay them now something in the neighbourhood of 30d.

[2] The authorities for these figures are the Hatf. Estate Papers, Box Q, 2, and the Hatf. MSS. Accts., 160/1. A complete list of the salaries of the great officers of State will be found in H.M. C. Report, Montagu of Beaulieu, p. 55.

[3] Cham. to Carl., 27th May 1612.

[4] Venet. Cal., x. p. 3. The Venetian Secretary of Legation in England estimates his profits ' at a moderate computation ' at 40,000 crowns (£10,000). ·That this figure is a huge mistake seems to be attested not only by Salisbury's balance-sheets at Hatfield, but also by the fact that he regarded the resignation of the Chancellorship of the Duchy of Lancaster and acceptance of the Mastership of the Court of Wards as a financial loss (Sidney Papers, ii. p. 64).

silks appear to have been more regular and averaged, perhaps, about £1000 a year.[1]

Still, when all these sources of income have been named, it is in the great grants of land from the Crown that we have to seek a minister's real reward. Salisbury, at the time of his death, had land in twenty counties and a rent-roll of £6000 a year or more.[2] His scattered property, part of it, of course, inherited, included places of historic interest like St. Michael's Mount and Old Sarum, and also the house of Alterinnes in Herefordshire, which had at least the reputation of being the first home of the Cecils. Extensive, however, as it was, the total acreage had been diminished by various sales, to which (taken, at any rate, in conjunction with his resignation of the profits of the Court of Wards [3]) the decline in his income in the last years of his life must be mainly attributed.

There is, as has been said, a third source of income, which appears on the credit side of his balance-sheets. Those were the days before stock-markets existed, but his accounts show that he lent, as he also borrowed, money extensively. There is nothing to say at what rate the lending and borrowing took place, nor can we very well calculate whether he was the richer or the poorer by these involved transactions. As he was constantly in need of money to finance his building operations it might have been a good deal simpler to have let his revenue accumulate to meet his bills, instead of investing the revenue in loans and borrowing to replace it. But a man is supposed to know his own business best ; and we must hope that

---

[1] Chamberlain (S. P. Dom., Jas. I., 69/57) gives them as £2100 for three years.

[2] *Ibid.*; and the valuation of lands in possession of the first Earl of Salisbury, drawn up at the time of his death.

[3] I take the profits he is said to have resigned to refer to the fines. The Hatf. MSS. Accts., 160/1, shows that he was receiving certain fees from the Court of Wards during 1611.

he did so. According to a statement,[1] drawn up just before his death, of debts owing to and owed by him, the first balanced the second with something to spare. This is more likely to be correct than the gossip of Chamberlain,[2] which in truth pretends to be nothing more, to the effect that he left £50,000 of debts, to be found out of his estate.

It is now generally supposed that he supplemented his revenues by the acceptance of a pension from Spain. Upon this point, turning as it does largely upon our conception of his character, something will be said when this biography enters upon its last austere office of psychological diagnosis ; and to that occasion we may defer any consideration of it. In his own time people, having regard to the Batavian bias of his policy, were inclined to believe that he had large interests in Holland ; and the Venetian Ambassador reports that he was said to have invested 500,000 crowns in that country.[3] It may have been so, but the silence of the Hatfield Papers does not countenance the opinion ; and to this, as to some other loose suggestions about the way in which he enriched himself at the public expense, we may be wise to turn a deaf ear.[4]

[1] Hatf. MSS., 143/146—£37,867, 6s. 8d. owed by, as against £38,150, 13s. 3d. owing to him.

[2] S. P. Dom., Jas. I., 69/57.

[3] Barozzi e Berchet, *Relazioni, Inghilterra,* i. p. 61.

[4] Weldon has a rambling accusation, which I do not sufficiently comprehend to be able to explain (*Secret Hist. of the Court of James I.,* i. p. 372). There is also an allegation that he received a pension from the French Government (see Gardiner, *Hist. of Engl.,* i. p. 216).

CHAPTER XVII

MORTALITY AND IMMORTALITY

"Even such is Time, that takes in trust,
  Our youth, our joys, our all we have,
And pays us but with earth and dust;
  Who in the dark and silent grave,
When we have wandered all our ways,
  Shuts up the story of our days;
But from this earth, this grave, this dust,
  My God shall raise me up, I trust.
                    RALEGH, *The Conclusion.*

" IT was perceived at the first, when men sought to cure mortality by fame, that buildings was the only way." [1] So meditated Bacon, thinking, one must suppose, of the sepulchral splendours of Egypt, and, perhaps, of those half-buried cities of the East, whose life and thoughts and activities are even now returning to us through the muffled voices of their stones. To the age he was addressing his words may have had some appearance of a truism. Facing death, as they did almost daily, in many forms of which we no longer need to take account, measuring their length of days by a standard which we half flatter ourselves we have thrown out of date, the men of the seventeenth century possessed, we can hardly doubt, a juster and more settled perception of human conditions, of the insecurity and instability and brevity of human life and human labour. Their poems, their dramas, their prayers, their stately and rhythmical prose, are the

[1] Spedding, *Letters and Life of Francis Bacon,* i. p. 148. *Gesta Grayorum.*

work of men who had pondered much upon time. Ralegh and Andrewes and Vaughan and Taylor and Browne, to make no mention of Shakespeare and Bacon, have spoken of mortality and mortal things with a depth and feeling which has no equal in the English language, and to which we still gratefully turn amid the dæmonic haste of our own ever-quickening courses as to the shade of cypresses upon a dusty road. Knowing how to take so just a measure of man's destiny, the children of that generation were in no great difficulty to find the best way with man's remembrance. That way—the only way, as Bacon thought—was ' buildings.' And these eternal memorials remain deeply reminiscent of the hidden secret of their being. The shadows of mortality lurk everywhere about that which we boldly call immortal. The clocks shouting from the housetops the passage of the hours ; the dials set in the garden or upon the panes of a window and surrounded by the warning legend of the fleeting day ; in the church the grinning skeleton beneath the slab mocking the recumbent figure above, still clothed in all its panoply of worldly splendour ;—these were the grave companions of the Elizabethans and their successors amidst all that building of palaces and planting of vineyards and getting together of men-servants and maid-servants, which has suggested the most poignant of all texts to the greatest of all human preachers.

Yet vanity in the last resort as such various monitors proclaimed the work to be, its authors have not failed of their desire. Even as we secure an increasing ease and comfort from the zealous pursuit of luxurious accommodation, even as the men of the Middle Age learned the knowledge of mysteries from the space and darkness of their dim cathedrals, so also these others have obtained what they sought— the long remembrance of a glory that is gone. Fame,

which Dante had thought to be but an idle breath of
wind, was, as it were, trapped like some Puck or Ariel
in its flight, and made to render up its magic.   The
gorgeous fabrics that delight our eyes have given
to their founders' names a perennial praise which
more strenuous, if not more skilful, work would have
failed to bring them.   For statecraft perishes in the
using ; and great speeches lose their subtle virtue ;
and good legislation falls out of date ; and brilliant
diplomacy is absorbed into the tangled network of
contending issues.   Even pregnant thought dissolves
at last into platitude.   Only art really survives from
age to age.   And many, to whom Salisbury's long
years of public service are no better than a blank,
remember him by virtue of that enthralling passion
for bricks and mortar, which, as Bacon tells us, is the
only safe insurance against the eclipse of death.

Architecture in his day still preserved its anon-
ymity.   The self-effacement of the medieval artists,
who built without care for the praise of men, had not
yet been displaced by schools and master-builders.
Inigo Jones, indeed, was born, and his name is even to
be found in incidental connection with the building of
Hatfield.   But the glory of a great house still fell in
undisputed lustre upon him for whom it was built,
and who, according to the old phrase still in common
use, was held to have built it.   In architecture alone
of all the arts there was no republic.   And doubtless
there was more justice in this arrangement than at
first appears.   Building was the hobby as well as
the work of the age ; and noble lords had in all probability a very good amateur knowledge of the art.
Those, too, who worked for them were rather skilful
craftsmen than men of original or inventive genius.
Salisbury, at any rate, must have known pretty well
as much about domestic architecture as either Thomas
Wilson, his agent, or Robert Leminge, the clerk of
the works.   Before Hatfield was dreamed of, in the

last years of the sixteenth century, he had received
through Lady Dacre [1] what Anthony Bacon rather
vindictively styled 'that unnatural legacy of the
goodly house in Chelsea.' [2] It was a house already
of historic interest, for it had been the home of
More and the scene of that exquisite idyll of family
love which William Roper has left on record.
Salisbury, during the fleeting idyll of his own happiness, had doubtless intended to inhabit it ; and if
a modern student of Elizabethan architecture is
to be believed,[3] he was chiefly responsible for its
ultimate appearance. Beaufort House, as it afterwards became,[4] presented all the characteristic
features of the Elizabethan age—the bay windows,
the gables, the lantern, the angular lodges in the
long approach running up from the river, the spacious
garden and bowling-green behind, with an expanse of
meadow again beyond stretching up to a site where,
presently, Sir Baptist Hicks was to place Campden
House. It does not appear that Salisbury spent
much time there.[5] There were doubtless memories
to deter him. In 1597 his appointment to be
Chancellor of the Duchy of Lancaster gave him an
official residence.[6] And in the following year his
father's death threw Theobalds upon his hands.

Attractive as that house must have been to him it
can have given him little opportunity for gratifying
the only passion he possessed. Burghley had done so
much to it that there was little left for his son to do ;

[1] Lady Dacre left it to Burghley in 1595, with remainder to Cecil.
Burghley seems very soon to have handed it over to Cecil. See R.
Davies, *The Greatest House in Chelsey*, pp. 43, 44.

[2] Birch, Bacon Papers, ii. p. 169.

[3] Gotch, *Growth of the English House*, p. 147. If the letter (Hatf.
Cal., v. p. 360) alludes, as I think it does, to this house, Salisbury's share
in it is proved.

[4] See Kip, *Nouveau Théâtre de la Grande Bretagne*, i. plate xiii.

[5] He seems to have been living there in July 1596 (see Hatf. Cal.,
vi. 292).

[6] Hatf. Cal., vii. p. 428.

and this lover of bricks and mortar had to seek satisfaction elsewhere. He built, as we know, Salisbury House in the Strand, of which such account as we have has already been given. Beside it he placed a building which promised to give him a wider and more generous fame. " Britain's Burse " was an attempt to give to Westminster such conveniences as had been secured to London by Gresham's Exchange in 1571, and which are provided for us by Harrod's or Selfridge's or the Army and Navy Stores. One building was to cover the sale of all kind of wares and to afford the purchasers certain amenities which they would not find elsewhere. The project at once aroused the jealousy of the inhabitants of the City. The merchants of the Royal Exchange in particular began to murmur and to petition the Lord Mayor.[1] Salisbury was a good deal nettled. He told the Lord Mayor that he had as great regard for the welfare of the City as anyone could be expected to have. No man, he said, could be a good servant to King or country who should ' go about to wrong or weaken that place.' [2] But he protested that it was unreasonable that he should not be allowed to benefit a locality which gave to London itself all the advantages of the proximity of the Court, which had been his father's residence, and where he himself was born.[3] All he had done was to assemble together shops, which anyone might have built in batches of six or less between Long Ditch and Temple Bar, and to do away with ' an old wall, noisome stables, and base sheds,' which made no very pleasant impression on the eyes of the foreign ambassadors when they went to Court.[4]

The New Exchange was opened on 11th April 1609 by the King in person. There had been some notion of calling it " Armabell," in allusion, pre-

[1] S. P. Dom., Jas. I., 35/13.   [2] Hatf. MSS., 195/30.
[3] S. P. Dom., Jas. I., 35/13.   [4] Hatf. MSS., 195/30.

sumably, to Lady Arabella Stuart, if she was ' the graceful lady ' referred to by Thomas Wilson as its godmother;[1] but in the end James conferred upon it the more prosaic name of Britain's Burse. It consisted of two great galleries, lavishly adorned with carving and sculpture and containing all kind of stores. On the day of the royal visit, one shop, more splendid than the rest, bore the inscription : " All other places give for money, here all is given for love " ; and at this Utopian place of commerce Salisbury, with a nice discrimination, presented the King with a handsome cabinet, the Queen with a silver plaque of the Annunciation, reputed to be worth four thousand crowns, and the Prince with splendid trappings for his horse ; nor was the royal suite forgotten.[2] Formed out of the purlieus of Durham House the Burse must have suggested an agreeable contrast to eyes familiar with the site. Whatever regulations could do was done to make it clean and pleasant.[3] Only tradespeople of reputable vocation were to have stalls there, except by special licence. Jewellers were not to ply their noisy hammers. There was to be no solicitation of customers by calling them. Beggars were to be altogether excluded. Masters were to be fined if they railed or scolded ; and ' a private room ' was to be set apart where noisy and quarrelsome servants and apprentices were to be whipped into good behaviour. For pickers and stealers there were to be stocks ready at hand. The amenities of the place were to be cared for by keepers who, as well as the owners themselves, would sweep the shops and see that the grass plot and gravel walks adjoining the arcade were kept smooth and tidy. Doors and windows were to be open from 6 a.m. to 8 p.m. from Lady Day to Michaelmas, and from 7 to 7

[1] S. P. Dom., Jas. I., 44/46.   [2] Venet. Cal., xi. p. 269.
[3] The summary of regulations which follows is taken from S. P. Dom., Jas. I., 44/46.

the rest of the year, but on high days and holidays they were to be closed.

How far this mass of good intentions prospered we have now no means of knowing. The Burse itself was at first no great success. But in the larger London of the Restoration, under the title of the New Exchange, its long galleries were filled with the wealthiest merchandise; and in its walks were to be seen the fashionable young men of the day, flaunting their best finery and flirting with the young shopwomen at the stalls. And consequently Grand Duke Cosmo, taking his view of the sights of the town in 1669, does not fail to mention this New Exchange with its ' façade of stone, built after the Gothic style, which has lost its colour from age and become blackish.' [1]

Far away from this busy scene, in a remote corner of Dorsetshire, where the down-country of the west begins to reach out toward the valley of the Stour and the still-distant sea, Salisbury was again to be found heaping up his endless tale of stones. How much he really achieved at Cranborne will probably be always something of a matter for speculation; but the facts that in the early years of the new century his neighbours were offering to sell him the adjoining acres [2] and that he chose to take his title from the place are some evidence that he was even then beginning to contemplate the conversion of the house into something more than the hunting-box and court-house it had been ever since the days of King John. In 1608 Sir Thomas Gorges writes to compliment him on the contrivance of the house and the convenience of the offices.[3] And the report that he received from his agent in 1610 shows that all the coming splendours of Hatfield had not destroyed his desire to beautify the homely English manor, which the King formally bestowed upon him in 1611. Between 1608 and 1612

[1] Magalotti, *Travels of the Grand Duke Cosmo*, iii. 296.
[2] Hatf. MSS., 106/108, 106/136.   [3] *Ibid.*, 213/104.

he spent upon it and upon the repairs at the castle of
Old Sarum (which was then or shortly after used as
a farm) the sum of over £3000.[1]   He was building, it
is plain, both at the east and west ends of the house ;
and at the latter was placing those new amenities of
the Tudor house—a dining-chamber and a drawing-
room.[2]   The Civil Wars played havoc with this part
of his work, but it is hard to believe (though the evidence is wanting) that we do not owe the great distinction of the place—its northern façade and portico
—to him rather than to his son, the artless William.[3]
Nor would it be any disproof of this if, as is quite
possible, some of the work was actually executed after
his death.   We know, at least, that the alterations
were sufficiently advanced for the King to be accommodated there in August 1611, when there appears
to have been something like a house-warming.

   " Wisdom," says the Son of Sirach, " cometh by
opportunity of leisure, and he that hath little business
shall become wise."   The fascination of Cranborne
is the fascination of those sources of good sense and
good feeling and good courage which, rising noiseless
and unobserved in the background of English life,
amidst the call of the wild game and the cawing of
the rooks and the long shadows of the trees, feed the
full stream of English character with the things that
are true and honest and of good report.   Those who
have touched that life at any point are dull of eye
or steeped in prejudice if they have missed its worth
and meaning.   There is another fascination, more
brilliant but less serene—the fascination of a great
house, where the politics of centuries have been focused
and the shadows of statesmen haunt every room, and
causes that have seemed long dead wake again with

[1] See *Blackwood's Magazine*, April 1908, p. 507.
[2] Hatf. MSS., 128/153.
[3] Hutchins (*Hist. and Antiq. of Dorset*, iii. p. 380) affirms that the
arms over the north porch are Robert's.

cogent and mysterious life. Such a temple of
memories and traditions Salisbury was now to build.

Hatfield was, however, rather the outcome of
accident than of design. It was probably on the
occasion of that not too creditable visit which he
paid there, in the company of his brother-in-law,
the King of Denmark, in July 1606, that James took
away a fancy to Theobalds. He had been all too
royally entertained.[1] Harington, who was present,
thought he had never seen such licence before, and
declares he almost fancied himself in Mohammed's
paradise. Wine and women were in the ascendant ;
and it seemed to him that the English nobility had
forgotten their traditional sobriety and been con-
quered afresh by the brutal Danes.[2] Poets, however,
had recklessly blessed the nascent orgies. Jonson,
under Salisbury's correction,[3] had composed lines
which were put into the mouths of some airy mortals,
impersonating the Three Hours and sitting upon
clouds over the porch :—

> "Enter, O long'd-for Princes, bless these bowers
>   And us, the three (by you made happy) Hours ;
>   We that include all time, yet never knew
>   Minute like this or object like to you :
>   Two Kings, the world's prime Honours, whose access
>   Shows either's greatness, yet makes neither less.
>   Vouchsafe your thousand welcomes in this shower [4]
>   The Master vows, not Sibyll's leaves were truer."

And the Dean of Salisbury, one Gordon, was
moved by the event to write an imaginary conversation between the House itself and a passing
traveller, which has come down to us in the French
translation, made by his faithful wife. The following
lines may represent the rest :—

---

[1] The five days' visit cost £1180 (Hatf. MSS., 119/162–3).
[2] Harington, *Nug. Antiq.*, ii. p. 130.   [3] Hatf. MSS., 144/272.
[4] The original has ' shewer,' but ' shower ' must, I think, have been
intended.

"Le Voyageur

Ces lieux dignes de rois, pour Dieu, dis-moi pourquoi
De si rares beautés enrichies je les vois
Pourquoi ces tables encore sont [1] passant magnifique
Les banquets orgueilleux des friands sybariques.

La Maison

Afin d'un jour servir de gloire à mon pays
Mon géniteur m'orna de ses meubles exquis
Et de même voulut que ces tables friandes
Pûssent à deux grands rois fournir toutes viandes." [2]

Harington gives us a glimpse of Salisbury toiling as usual in the midst of this ill-judged and ill-requited hospitality: "The Lord of the mansion is overwhelmed in preparations at Theobalds, and doth marvellously please both Kings with good meat, good drink, and speeches." [3] The chase played a large and discreditable part in the proceedings. "I have spent much time," continues the scandalised Harington, "in seeing the royal sports of hunting and hawking, where the manners were such as made me devise the beasts were pursuing the sober creation, and not men in quest of exercise or food." [4] But the King saw with other eyes than Harington's; and it is plain that the prospect of the excellence of the sport which the locality afforded was the principal reason he was anxious to possess himself of the house.[3] No wise minister opposes the private wishes of his sovereign if he can avoid it. On 15th April 1607 Salisbury wrote to Lake recounting how he had borrowed "one day's retreat" to visit his old home, "now," as he said, "drawing near the delivery into a hand which, I pray God, may keep it in his posterity until there be neither tree nor stone standing." From there he had gone on to Hatfield, where Suffolk, Worcester,

---

[1] Emendation for 'vont' in the original.
[2] Hatf. MSS., 119/162.
[3] Harington, *Nug. Antiq.*, ii. p. 130.
[4] Clutterbuck, *History of the County of Hertford*, ii. p. 93.

and Southampton had helped him to determine the site of his new house.[1]   Then, on May 22nd, to the accompaniment of feasting and a Jonsonian masque, he made Theobalds over to the King.   The dramatist had devised a sufficiently pretty piece of symbolism to celebrate the occasion.   The Genius Loci was discovered on a darkened stage, mourning over the rumour that his loved lord must

> " Now in the twilight of sere age,
>   Begin to seek an habitation new,
> And all his fortune and himself engage
>   Unto a seat his fathers never knew."

The rumour is confirmed by Mercury and Clotho ; and the Genius then asks whether it be gain or necessity or the ambition to build a house of greater fame which prompts his master to forsake a ' father's monument.'   Mercury replies with perhaps some little economy of truth :—

> " Nor gain, nor need : much less a vain desire
> To frame new roofs, or build his dwelling higher.
> He hath with mortar busied been too much
> That his affections should continue such."

The Genius is puzzled, arguing that men do not take joy in labour, unless they intend to eat the fruit of it, but is warned by Mercury not to expostulate but to obey.   And then, to the accompaniment of sweet music, a voice is heard singing :—

> " O blessed change !
>   And no less glad than strange,
> Where we that lose have won,
>   And, for a beam, enjoy a sun." [2]

According   to   Weldon — the   untrustworthy Weldon — Salisbury received fifty years' purchase

---

[1] S. P. Dom., Jas. I., 27/7.

[2] Ben Jonson, " Masque on the occasion of the delivery of Theobalds to King James."

for the surrender of Theobalds.[1]   However that may
have been, Hatfield was granted to him on May 27th,
1607.   The new possession included the old palace of
the bishops of Ely which Henry VIII. had purchased
by the surrender of Icklington and where both Mary
and Elizabeth were subsequently confined.   It was a
quadrangular building, of which one side containing
the hall still remains and was until recently used as
the stables of the present house.   But it found no
place in Salisbury's imaginative palace of art, and
would perhaps have been actually too small to accommodate his retinue.   Like all deep dreamers, perhaps,
in brick and stone, he regarded the coming triumphs
of creative power as of far greater moment than its
past successes ; and he placed his house on a spot
which made the partial destruction of the old Palace
an artistic necessity.   There can be little doubt that his
confidence was justified.   Beautiful as Hatfield Palace
must have been, Hatfield House has far outstripped it.

It would be tedious, even if it were feasible, to
describe that which was now brought into being.
A thousand prints, a thousand photographs, have
brought the famous pile within the imagination of all.
And many of us can say that our eyes have seen it.
It was the work of an age that was drawing on towards
its close.   Inigo Jones and Palladian architecture
and sash-windows were close at hand.   But the
change had not yet come.   And, as we turn from
the stern perpendicular lines of the north side of
the House and face the light horizontal aspect of the
southern front, the eye may at will traverse all the
rich experience of half-a-century in a moment of time
and find there before it a consummating reminiscence
of that incomparable world of Elizabeth, with its
stern commencement and its sumptuous close, whose
romantic features, just when the House was rising,
were themselves fading away from the country and

[1] *Secret Hist. of the Court of James I.*, i. p. 361.

passing into a dream before the chilling influences of
a more critical and less spacious age, even as daily
at the appointed hour the Italian arcade before us
and its flanking wings of ruddy brick lose the rich
radiance of the westering sun and turn again to
shadow. England possesses larger houses than Hatfield ; and there are, doubtless, some among them
which compel the eye with a more imposing splendour.
But there is probably none where the stately presence
of a bygone world wears a more friendly face, none
where the warm hues of mellowed brick blend more
kindly with wood and glade and garden, none where
the heart may warm itself more readily at ancestral
fires, or the spirit find a better contentment in the
subtle influences of history and tradition.

Salisbury spent to our knowledge about £40,000 [1]
on the House with its amenities of garden and vineyard ; and there may have been more disbursed of
which we have no record. At the very lowest estimate this would represent £120,000 of our money.
Still the work was very far from being done regardless
of expense. The papers show that Salisbury looked
carefully into the liabilities he was incurring ; and
as time went on the building was shorn of some elements of its intended splendour. There had been, for
example, an idea of covering the roof with copper,
which would have cost 19d. a square foot ; and lead,
which cost only 12d. the square foot, was ultimately
chosen.[2] But to say that some expense was spared is
not to say that no trouble was taken. Advice and
materials were sought where they were best to be
had. Caen-stone was brought over to relieve the brick.
Inigo Jones was employed to carry through a negotiation for some work executed in Antwerp.[3] A French

[1] This figure is given me by Mr. R. T. Gunton, who has made a
most thorough investigation of the bills, etc., relating to the house.
[2] Hatf. Estate Papers, Genl., 3/11.
[3] Hatf. MSS., Agents' Accts., 8th November 1610.

HATFIELD HOUSE, THE SOUTH FRONT

[*To face p.* 328

painter—Lewis Dolphin (Louis Dauphin)—was employed to design some, though not all, of the chapel
windows.[1] And as much thought was taken for the
grounds as for the house itself. Salomon de Caux, a
Frenchman in the service of the Prince of Wales,
constructed the fountain [2] in the gardens which one,
Mountain Jennings, was laying out.[3] Tradescant
scoured France and the Low Countries to procure
for his master what was choicest in fruit and flowers.[4]
Four hundred sycamore trees were sent by Sir Edward
Cecil from the Netherlands.[5] Five hundred mulberry
trees, in the introduction of which James had greatly
interested himself, were bought by Salisbury, presumably to plant at Hatfield.[6] And from M. de la
Boderie there came thirty thousand vines,[7] a number
more than sufficient to furnish " that most pleasant
and delicious vineyard," watered by the Lea, " which "
(as Chauncy [8] puts it), " having performed her devoir
there, hastens away to Essendon."

Was it a time to plant vineyards, and to build
houses, and to add acre to acre and field to field ?
Among the endless bills there is one which turns one
suddenly cold :—" Mr. Steward,[9] this bearer, Mr. Colt,
having this morning brought my Lord a model of his
tomb and demanded fifty pounds in imprest towards
his workmanship of the three chimney-pieces at
Hatfield, his Lordship commanded that you should
deliver him so much money. Withall first November 1609." Did Salisbury guess thus soon that
it was not towards the spacious rooms and sunlit

---

[1] Hatf. MSS., Agents' Accts., 8th and 22nd November 1609.

[2] *Ibid.*, 31st January 1612.

[3] *Ibid.*, 14th December 1609 and 26th February 1611.

[4] See Hon. Mrs. E. Cecil's *History of Gardening in England*, p. 152.
Cp. Hatf. MSS., Agents' Accts., 3rd November 1609.

[5] Hatf. MSS., Box V, 71, 25th February 1610.

[6] *Hist. of Gardening in England*, p. 139.

[7] S. P. Dom., Jas. I., 61/50.

[8] Chauncy, *Antiq. of Hertfordshire*, p. 3.

[9] Presumably Roger Houghton. In the original, ' Stuard.'

gallery of the great house but to the narrow chamber of the tomb that his steps were even then most swiftly tending ? We cannot tell. We do not even know whether he ever slept beneath the roof he had been at so great pains to raise. The presumption perhaps lies that way, for in May 1611 the report runs : " If this chapel were despatched, your Lordship might have use of your house to lie in," [1] and on 1st July the works are said to be nearly completed, and the house shortly to be ready for his reception.[2] But nothing can be argued from the fact that the King saw the place in that same month,[3] for it is likely enough that he came over from Theobalds for the day only. So we have no assurance, and, it may be, the tragic issue was unrelieved. All we know for certain is that the workmen were not out of the house before its master had gone to his long home.

It only remains to mark the milestones on that last journey. The failure of the Great Contract was the point at which, so far as can be seen, Salisbury definitely entered upon his last decline. The disappointment had been doubtless aggravated by a suspicion that he had lost the King's favour and by the knowledge, which Lake communicated in confidence, that Carr was intriguing against him.[4] James, indeed, to give him his due, wrote not unkindly to his old servant, affirming, what was no more than the truth, that he was never accustomed to withdraw his affection from any man, except " the cause were," as he put it, " printed on the other's forehead."[5] If their personal relations were unaltered, there was, however, no concealing the fact that, in regard at

---

[1] S. P. Dom., Jas. I., 63/88.　　　　[2] *Ibid.*, 65/3.

[3] This is shown by the bills at Hatfield for July 1611. But they are only labourers' and gardeners' bills.

[4] Hatf. MSS., 128/171.

[5] *Ibid.*, 134/144: "All that know me do know that I never use to change my affection from any man except the cause be printed on his forehead " (James to Salisbury).

least to what had just occurred, the King and his Minister no longer saw eye to eye. The very letter which establishes the one point is proof also of the other ; and it is significant that Carr had grown almost frankly insolent.[1]

So much, or so little, foundation, then, exists for the posthumous gossip [2] that Salisbury's death alone averted Salisbury's disgrace. But before the end the historian will find the evidence of returning ascendancy ; and nothing is more striking in the contemporary reports of the Venetian Ambassador in 1612 than the references to James's frequent visits to the dying Minister, to their long consultations together, and to the earnest solicitude of the one at the prospect of losing the other.[3] " The King," we are told in March 1612, " is fully aware of the value to himself of this great Minister." [4]

The conduct of the Prince of Wales was an indirect but hardly less striking testimony to Salisbury's continuing influence in public affairs. Anxious, as he grew to manhood, to associate himself with the work of government, and especially to obtain the post of Lord High Admiral, the Prince paid most assiduous court to the Minister, and is reported to have been ' almost always with him ' [5] in the autumn of 1611 ; [6] nor did he relax his attentions as Salisbury's illness gained ground in the early part of 1612.[7] Never perhaps did the dying statesman seem more omnipotent or more powerful than in the months that preceded his death. Even after he had left for Bath

[1] Hatf. MSS., 128/174, Carr to Salisbury: " . . . the manifold occasions I shall have ere long to trouble you shall give you assurance that I am content to owe much of my fortune to your care and favour." That the strained relations between the two men were very apparent and turned on the jobs which Carr wanted Salisbury to perpetrate is shown by the " Dialogue between two friends, servants to His Majesty," in the Ickwellbury MSS. belonging to Mr. J. A. Harvey.

[2] Weldon and Goodman.

[3] Venet. Cal., xii. pp. 298, 303, 312, 314.   [4] *Ibid.*, p. 305.
[5] *Ibid.*, p. 227.   [6] *Ibid.*, p. 305.   [7] *Ibid.*, p. 314.

never to return, when the end was as sure as it could be and his offices had been put into a kind of commission, the Venetian still assures his Government that " Salisbury in spite of ill-health and absence governs everything."[1]   But this is to anticipate by a little the proper course of the narrative.

The spring and summer of 1611 brought on the concluding episodes in Arabella Stuart's famous and miserable love-story ; and Salisbury's ministerial burdens included the correspondence entailed by the affair.   He had been on the best of terms both with Arabella herself and the Seymour family, into which she had married ; and in the first passages of the romance he had thrown his weight on the side of leniency.[2]   But the escape of the lovers had, from a ministerial standpoint at least, put both of them hopelessly in the wrong ; and he frankly said that he would not attempt anything on Seymour's behalf.[3] To have tried to mitigate the pains and penalties of Arabella was almost certainly out of the question, for James's rage was fanned by his fears.   And, so far as we know, Salisbury made no response to the piteous account which Arabella sent him of her condition of mind and body.[4]   Meantime his own illness was gaining ground.

It happened that the King had in this very year secured the services of a new and very remarkable physician.   Experts regard Sir Theodore Turquet de Mayerne as the father of English clinical studies ;[5] and to this day his name is honourably remembered in his profession.   To him Salisbury turned.   On

---

[1] Venet. Cal., xii. p. 356.

[2] See the letter to Trumbull printed in Cooper's *Letters and Life of Arabella Stuart*, ii. p. 202.

[3] Cooper, *Letters and Life of Arabella Stuart*, ii. p. 202.

[4] The letter in Cooper's *Letters and Life of A. Stuart*, ii. p. 235, is, I think, clearly addressed to Salisbury (" My Lord Treasurer "), though the biographer suggests Northampton as the recipient.

[5] See Norman Moore, *Medicine in the British Isles*, p. 93.

August 1st, in the town of Salisbury and presumably
at that house in the Close which the Lord Treasurer
is supposed to have inhabited, Mayerne made an
examination of the patient. It was the first important
case he had had to deal with since his new appointment; and his elaborate notes upon it may still be
read by the curious amongst his Opera Medica.[1]
The diagnosis revealed " a large abdominal tumour
occupying nearly the whole hypogastrium on the
right side and associated with prolonged diarrhœa." [2]
Serious as it was, Mayerne thought that with care and
a rigid dietary the disease might yield to treatment.[3]
Salisbury, however, continued to sicken, though not
without one or more fallacious appearances of returning strength.[4] Painful symptoms of disease
and debility became more and more manifest—
rheumatism in the right arm,[5] ague, depression,
and shortness of breath;[6] and towards the close
scurvy and dropsy.[7] By February of 1612 it was
generally assumed that the end, at least of his official
life, was not far off.[8] He himself grew melancholy
and heavy-spirited; and the business of the State,
now that his once ubiquitous presence was withdrawn, came pretty nearly to a standstill.[8] In March
he rallied again, to the vexation doubtless of those
who, as Chamberlain says, were ' forward to part
the bear's skin.' [9] But the amendment did not last,
and five weeks later the same retailer of current news
affirms that he was sustained only by the vigour
of his mind.[10] Mayerne, indeed, who saw him constantly, would not despair of a case where the patient

---

[1] Ed. Browne, pp. 78–90.

[2] Moore, *Medicine in the British Isles*, p. 96. I am also much
indebted to Dr. Moore for a private letter upon this subject.

[3] " Nullum numen abest si sit Prudentia," etc. etc.

[4] See S. P. Dom., Jas. I., 67/114.   [5] *Ibid.*, 67/82.

[6] Winwood Memorials, iii. pp. 332 and 338.

[7] S. P. Dom., Jas. I., 68/102.   [8] Winwood, iii. p. 338.

[9] S. P. Dom., Jas. I., 68/78.   [10] *Ibid.*, 68/104.

exhibited such singular force of will ; [1] and it was probably on Mayerne's advice that he decided to try what waters would do for him. From the time of his leaving London at the end of April the story has come down to us in pathetic and painful detail.

Before departure Salisbury had, perhaps, spent the night with his friend and colleague at the historic mansion which the world has long learned to call Holland House, but which in those days was known as Cope Castle. At all events it was from Kensington and in Cope's company that he set out for Bath on April 28th. The old comrade of earlier and happier days—Sir Michael Hicks—was also of his party, as well as Salisbury's chaplain, Mr. Bowles, from whose memorials [2] the ensuing narrative is derived.

The first day's travelling took them as far as Ditton, where they lodged with Lord Chandos. Short as the distance seems to us, Salisbury, afflicted with his painful malady and after some hours of rolling in a heavy coach along indifferent roads, had reason enough for the remark, which he made to Bowles in the evening, that it was a long and troublesome journey on which they had set out. Then he ' fell into a double discourse ' of the two things that were nearest his heart—of his son, whom he loved so greatly that he would gladly die for him, and of the tranquil resolution which he had come to in respect of his own present condition, to be prepared for either event, whether life or death, whatever God should please to send. The odds, as he felt, lay heavily against his ever returning to London ; and he said

---

[1] Winwood, iii. p. 363 : " . . . C'est une disposition à l'hydropisie compliquée avec le scorbut ; les quels sont deux mauvais hôtes en un corps faible et délicat : mais par la force de son courage invincible nous ne laissons pas d'avoir espérance de la guérison bien qu'elle soit longue et difficile " (Mayerne to Sir T. Edmondes).

[2] "An Account of the Lord Treasurer's Last Sickness," addressed to James Mountague, Bishop of Bath and Wells. Printed in Peck, *Desid. Cur.*, bk. vi. No. 4.

that he would as gladly be buried in Bath Church as elsewhere, knowing, as he did, 'that from any place there was a means of resurrection and a way to heaven.' Then falling into prayer he confessed to God his particular sins. He was conscious of having fulfilled the great condition of forgiveness. "There was never a man in the world," so he protested to his hearer, "but he could take him by the hand, if he now were a-dying."

Hicks and Cope were aware that too close a pre-occupation with the proximity of death does not tend to fortify an already failing hold on life ; and they resolved to take what steps they might to draw their old friend's attention back to earth and to the transient drolleries, without which earthly living might prove for most of us too austere a pilgrimage.   In the early morning, before they left Ditton Park, Hicks indited a chaffing letter[1] to a certain Sir Hugh Beeston, who was evidently a funny fellow and well calculated to dispel depression of spirits :—

"And because I think my Lord would be merrier if he had such a merry man as your Worship is in his company, I have thought good to advise you, setting his Majesty's service apart, to make your present repair to the Bath without delay.   In this advice of mine Sir Walter Cope doth join with me.   Now to persuade you (besides your love and duty to my Lord) the best argument I can use to you is *ab utili*, for assure yourself, if my Lord be in any case fit to play at tables, we shall be sure to get £4 or £5 a piece from him and Sir Walter Cope ; for you know, God wot, they cannot play anything well, and you can, without cause chafe, swear and brabble, and for a need enter and bear a man falsely too.   Therefore we have good advantage of them. But, if this should fail, yet it is hard luck if you wring not one fiddling suit or other from him, or at the least some velvet cloak or saddle not much the worse for the wearing, for Sergeant Goddins hath gotten a velvet pair of breeches already.   My Lord is ready to take his coach for this day's journey . . . and I am ready for my breakfast."

Such humours are apt to seem profane in close

[1] Lansdowne MSS., 92/114.

juxtaposition with human suffering. But constant reaction is the stay of life, and human kindness, we do not need to be told, is most refreshing in the very quarter where human fancy is swiftest and most alive.

They made that day for Lord Knowles' house of Cowson.[1] The painful jolting of the coach caused the patient to ask for the carrying-chair, which offered an alternative method of advance. The servants in charge of it had, however, lagged behind ; and their master was provoked to a show of irritation. By the time they reached Cowson his anger had melted. " You will say, I am impatient. Alas ! what would you have me to do when my servants do forget themselves so much, that, if I had not remembered myself, I had not come hither this night ? " He was told that his servants had failed from error, not from want of love, for that they would gladly do any servile work to promote his health or ease. " I know it," he answered. And then later : " God knows it is my pain and weakness ; but I will forbear all passions."

He struggled on wearily and painfully, sleeping at Newbury, at Marlborough, and at Lacock, and making ' many stops and shifts ' from his coach to his litter or to his chair, though, as his secretary saw only too clearly, the ' ease lasted no longer than his imagination.' [2] Bath was reached on May 3rd. At first the waters gave surprisingly good results, and by the 8th he was visibly better. On that day, after returning thanks to God, he wrote an affectionate letter intimating his improvement to the son who was ever in his thoughts.[3] But the revival was only temporary, and four days of renewed health were paid for by two days of intense weakness and a new and ugly development in the disease. It was about this time that his

---

[1] Courtenay (*Robert Cecil, Earl of Salisbury*, p. 177) identifies this with Caversham, near Reading.

[2] Winwood Memorials, iii. p. 367.   [3] Hatf. Papers, 129/106.

old friend Lord Shrewsbury, who was in close correspondence with Hicks, caused some ' scorbut ' grass
to be gathered at Castleton in the Peak district and
despatched to him fresh every fourth day.[1] Whether
he made trial of it and, if so, what effect it had, we
are ignorant; but it was at least as likely to have
been efficacious as the singular remedy of quintessence
of honey which Lady Shrewsbury recommended as
the finest cordial of her acquaintance and one peculiarly adapted to Salisbury's disease.[2]

On the 15th he spoke again with his chaplain
about the issues of life and death, and was especially
comforted by a quotation which Bowles made from
St. Augustine : " Is it not better that He chastise
thee and spare thee, than that He spare thee and
damn thee ? " He reiterated his confession of faith
in Christ, saying he was of the same mind as when
he had formerly made his peace with God and received
the Sacrament in the presence of the Dean of Westminster and his present adviser. He said he found
the great goodness of God in the very slowness of his
disease, which had drawn his soul more and more away
from earthly things and taught him the vanity of
worldly happiness. " But yet," he added, " one
thing troubleth me, that I could not have come to
this resolution if God had not thus afflicted me."
The chaplain spoke of the two great parables of God's
mercy—of the Prodigal Son and the Lost Sheep—
indicating a difference between them, inasmuch as
the prodigal had returned of himself whilst the
sheep had needed to be sought by the Shepherd. The
sufferer caught eagerly at the story which seemed
the more nearly of the two to mirror his own case.
" That sheep am I ! " he repeated again and again.

He was now come to that state of mind in
which life itself appeared burdensome; and it may
well have been at this juncture that in conversa-

---

[1] Lansdowne MSS., 92/101.   [2] Ibid., 92/102, 103.

tion with Cope he framed a sentence, the simple
pathos of which has caused it to be long remembered :—" Ease and pleasure quake to hear of
death ; but my life, full of cares and miseries, desireth
to be dissolved." [1] His attendants feared that this
great desire to depart and be with Christ would lead
him to neglect the means to a still conceivable though
unlikely recovery. He was reminded of the examples
of St. Martin and St. Paul and of their willingness
to forgo their own wishes and abide in the flesh for
the sake of others. Some clumsy spectator, using
" St. Paul," as was afterwards explained or asserted,
to mean the existing hierarchy, affirmed that the sick
man was even more needful to them than that Apostle.
Salisbury kicked at the parallel but was presently
pacified by the explanation. Hicks, by way of
comfort, here interposed with a reflection, which
seems in point, just so long as religion is bounded by
' la morale des honnêtes gens,' and becomes pointless
as soon as the soul feels itself alone with God. " His
Lordship," he said, " was not in that degree a sinner,
but that he might sooner find mercy at God's hands
than many other, if we consider their sins." Salisbury replied quite simply that his only trust was in
the saving mercies of Christ. The doctor, one Atkins,
begged him not to neglect remedies ; to which he answered that he would do whatever was prescribed him.

In the night his attendants heard him praying.
" Do you hear me ? " he said ; " then know that if
God now take my soul out of my body I am prepared for Heaven." On the next day it seemed to
him that the end was drawing on. In the afternoon,
after prayer, he commended his servants, some to
the King, some to his son. " And this being done,
he leaned on his crutches and lifted up his eyes to
Heaven. And,[2] his gesture in the likeness of a rapt

---

[1] Cope's *Apology*, in Gutch, *Collect. Cur.*
[2] I have very slightly altered this sentence to make it grammatical.

passion, his mouth smiling, his hands stretching out, he uttered this saying, ' O Lord Jesus, now, sweet Jesus, O Jesus, now, O Jesus, let me come unto Thee ! My audit is made. Let me come, now, O Jesus, in the strength of my understanding, in the act of my memory ! For, if otherwise, what will the people say ? But, O Jesus, I care not ; Thy will be done. I am safe : I am safe.' And here the tears ran down his eyes and stopped his speech, which was seconded by the tears of the standers-by, (so) that for a great while, there was nothing but a mournful silence."

But the long agony had still some days to run. At one interview he spoke to Bowles about the religion of his three children, inquiring the chaplain's opinion of their principles. Then, on the 18th, Sir John Harington, now a helpless paralytic, was brought to see him. He greeted him with a half-humorous allusion to their common infirmity :— " Sir John, now doth one cripple come to see and visit another." Then in a more solemn vein he went on to speak of their condition :—" Death is the centre to whom we all do move—some diameterwise, some circularly, but all men must fall down to the centre. I know not, Sir John, which of us two is nearest, but I think myself. And it is true, *moriendum est quia nati sumus*, we must therefore die because we were born, yet God, by His visitation, hath sweetened death unto me, because He hath given me the light of His grace. . . . I do not despair ot life, and I do not fear death : God's will be done, I am prepared for it. And now, Sir John, let me ask you, what good have you found by the Bath ? " He himself was no longer finding any. On the next day he fell into a fit, and was so nearly gone that he bade the chaplain close his eyes. That afternoon his son came to him, contrary to his express instructions. He had at an earlier date enjoined upon William to keep away, fearing, perhaps, that the agitation entailed

by talking with one from whom he could scarcely bear
to think of parting would prejudice the treatment.
But he recognised that the time for such precautions
was gone by, and when he was asked if it would not
be a comfort to him to see Lord Cranborne, he answered
that it would be the greatest comfort in the world.

Comfort though it doubtless was, he broke down
before the grief of parting. " Oh, my son," he cried,
" God bless thee ! The blessing of Abraham, Isaac,
and Jacob light upon thee ! My good son, embrace
true religion, live honestly and virtuously, loyally to
thy prince, and faithfully to thy wife. Take heed,
by all means, of blood, whether in public or in private
quarrel : and God will prosper thee in all thy ways."
" So they fell again to weeping," adds the spectator,
" and my Lord commanded me to administer the
Sacrament to him : which incontinently was performed." After this he was better. The following
Wednesday the Bishop's chaplain, by name Russell,
who was apparently giving some addresses at the
church, concluded a previous sermon upon the text,
" My power is made perfect in weakness." Though
the coincidence was thus apparently accidental, all the
congregation must have turned their thoughts towards that bed of mortal sickness, where the truth
of the words was being exemplified. Bowles, who
thought the sermon particularly good, retailed the
main points to his master, upon which Salisbury
asked that the preacher might be brought to see him.
Russell was fetched, and the dying man praised him
for his discourse that morning. " You see how God
hath humbled me," Salisbury added, " and laid His
rod upon me. But I trust in His mercy because
that I know I am one of those for whom the blood
of Christ was shed upon the Cross. I know likewise
that God's power is made perfect in weakness, and
that His infinite power is able to restore me from
corruption to health. But I do not expect it, but

desire rather to be unburdened of all mundane cares and to enjoy rest in the bosom of Abraham." He went on to speak of Bath Church, in which he had an especial interest, since his father's steward had been one of its benefactors ; and he expressed his willingness to be buried there.

The same day there came a last token from the world, which had lavished upon him so many fading honours. Lord Hay arrived from the Court, bringing ' a fair diamond set, or rather hung square in a gold ring without a foil.' With the gift, the King had sent a message ' to the effect that the favour and affection he bore him was, and should ever be, as the form and matter of the ring, endless, pure, and most perfect.'[1] Sir John Hollis brought a like acknowledgment from the Queen.[2]

The last remedy had been tried and had failed, for the doctors were come to the opinion that the waters were doing more harm than good.[3] It only remained for the dying man to determine where he would lay his bones. In the night, by a reaction perhaps after his talk with Russell, he was seized with a longing to be back in London.[3] At all events, the next day he resolved to return there, and set out forthwith, Hay and Hollis accompanying him. They lay the first night at Lacock, as they had done the last night of the journey out. Here he was seized with fits, and his mind wandered. At one point Bowles, seeing him distressed with the thought of his sins, told him that God did certify him by his chaplain that he was in the estate of salvation. The theology of the English Church was then, as it still is, full of obscurities ; and Salisbury seems to have been puzzled by the assurance. " Then," he said, " you have a power ? " Bowles assented. " From

---

[1] Winwood Memorials, iii. p. 368.

[2] The Queen was very fond of Salisbury. See S. P. Dom., Jas. i., 65/80.

[3] Winwood Memorials, iii. p. 368.

whence ? " he asked. " From the Church, by im-
position of hands," replied the chaplain. Salisbury
pressed to know whence the Church had it. Bowles
told him, " From Christ." " Oh," he said, " that is
my comfort ; then I am happy." The next day,
though they did not know it, was to be the last of the
journey. They got as far as Marlborough and there
the sufferer became desperately ill. On the outward
journey he had put up at, or rather on the site of, a
now deserted and dilapidated house lying on the out-
skirts of the town which had formed part of the
former Priory of St. Margaret's, and in his day was in
the possession of a Mr. Daniel.[1] There, in all probability, they carried him in again, though the authorities
are at variance and we cannot be certain.[2] His
weakness had by this time grown to be extreme, but
his mind still struggled, as of old, against the frailty
of the body. Then the next day, just after the
chaplain had returned from the midday meal, the
end came. He asked to be raised up once more, and
as he took hold of the doctor's hand for support,
suddenly, with one last ejaculation to God, but ' without groan or sigh or struggling,' he passed away. It
was the 24th of May and ' the Sabbath.' " And
I doubt not," concludes the witness, who had

[1] The house now stands in the grounds of Mr. R. L. Merriman's
place called Sempringham. I am much indebted to Mr. Merriman
for allowing me to see it, and also for the information he supplied
me with respecting it. It has upon it the date 1680, but it very
possibly incorporates part of the house, where, as I think, Salisbury
died.

[2] Naunton (*Fragmenta Regalia, Sir Robert Cecil*) seems to me the
most reliable contemporary authority. He says : " For he (Salisbury) departed at St. Margaret's near Marlborough in his return from
the Bath, as my Lord Viscount Cranborne, my Lord Clifford, his son
and son-in-law, myself and many more, can witness." So also *Aul.
Coq.*, ii. p. 157. Mr. Wordsworth (*Wilts. Arch. and Nat. Hist. Mag.*,
xxxiv. p. 246), following Chamberlain, takes the view that Salisbury
died at St. Peter's Vicarage. But Chamberlain had probably only
gossip to go by, and quite possibly confused St. Margaret's Priory
with the Parsonage.

followed the long agony to its peaceful close, " but it was the passage of one Sabbath to another."

The world received the news that the long struggle was at an end without regret, or even the appearance of it. The King, whatever his inmost feelings,[1] put off his intended departure for Eltham only until he had had his dinner ;[2] and the most part of his subjects set to work to invent and propagate and believe all manner of discreditable rumours about the character of a statesman[3] who had only served the State too long for their taste. Some, who had had occasion to know better, asserted that the dead man had ' juggled with religion, with King, Queen, and their children, with the nobility, Parliament, with friends, foes, and generally with all.'[4] His chaplains could hardly make their voices heard amid the general clamour, and their protests met with small attention.[5] The old precept had been utterly reversed, and about the dead man there was nothing spoken but what was bad. " More ill-spoken of and in more several kinds, than I think ever anyone was," is Dorset's report to Edmondes.[6] Meanwhile the poor body had been embalmed[7] and faithful servants had carried it to the burial. But even at Hatfield the general hostility was apparent ; and the day of the funeral came near being desecrated by unseemly resentment. The enclosure of Hatfield Wood had provoked a certain amount of feeling ; and a plan which proved abortive was made to break down the enclosure paling.[8] The funeral itself was far from being splendid

---

[1] The Venetian Ambassador declares he was " greatly disturbed."

[2] Cham. to Carl., 27th May 1612 (S. P. Dom., Jas. I., 69/57).

[3] *Ibid.*, 25th June 1612 (S. P. Dom., Jas. I., 69/75).

[4] *Ibid.*, 2nd July 1612 (S. P. Dom., Jas. I., 70/1).

[5] S. P. Dom., Jas. I., 70/1.

[6] Stowe MSS., 172/319, 22nd June 1612. [I have altered the order of the words.]

[7] *Secret Hist. of the Court of James I.*, ii., p. 157.

[8] S. P. Dom., Jas. I., 70/1.

according to the standard of those times. To Chamberlain's surprise Salisbury had only allocated £200 to the cost of the ceremony, directing at the same time that a like sum be given to the poor.[1] Imbued with the graceless curiosity of the born carrier of news, that amiable gossip sent a servant to observe what sort of company composed the procession. The result, from his standpoint, was disappointing. He had run up against that dislike of publicity which Salisbury has imparted to most of his descendants. The county was scarcely represented at all, not having been invited.[2] Of the colleagues and relatives of the dead man there were present [3] Cranborne ; Suffolk, Pembroke, Worcester, Coke, and Bacon ; Montgomery, Clifford, Burghley, St. John, Hay, Denny, Sir Edward Hobby and Sir Edward Cecil ; besides one or two more, like Sir Michael Hicks, who came to fulfil the last offices of friendship ; and, of course, the more prominent members of the household—secretaries, ushers, physicians, and chaplains ; altogether, in the quaint words of an anonymous eye-witness, ' a train of noble personages, in sable habits trailing on the ground, witnesses and presenters of England's heaviness.' [4] For some heaviness there was even amidst the general jubilation ; and the Venetian Ambassador, who had liked Salisbury well, even declares that he found at Court ' striking signs of grief.' [5] We may suppose then, in charity, that those intimates at least who followed the hearse mourned with no idle or perfunctory lamentation.

Whether the 9th June 1612 was a day of sunshine

---

[1] S. P. Dom., Jas. I., 69 /57.

[2] *Ibid.*, 69/67.   [3] Hatf. MSS., 206/61.

[4] *A Remembrance of the Honours due to the Life and Death of Robert, Earl of Salisbury*, p. 23.

[5] Venet. Cal., xii. p. 372. I have felt great difficulty in reconciling this passage with the contrary evidence of Dorset and Chamberlain. But no doubt the Venetian generalised from a very narrow observation.

Monument to Robert, First Earl of Salisbury, in the Salisbury Chapel, Hatfield Church

[To face p. 344

or of shower there is nothing now to tell us. But at least we know that summer must have been wearing her softest and most shining garments at a date which, according to our reckoning, would have fallen in the month of May. And as the dark procession passed on into the church there must have been some who, according to varying disposition and sensibility, meditated upon the grim ironies of human existence ; casting their thoughts now back toward the glowing pile of buildings, just risen to its full height of pride and splendour and designed to be immortal as men count such things, and then forward to poor mortality borne thankfully to its last home after not so much as fifty years of toil and conflict.

A monument in the fashion of the time marks the place in the church where the frail and tired body was laid to rest. The Cardinal Virtues keep watch around the tomb. Upon their shoulders is raised a slab of black marble supporting the effigy of the Lord Treasurer, robed and still holding in his hand the very staff [1] of his high office ; his eyes gazing upward towards the house he built, and beyond the house towards the dawning lights upon the eastern sky. Beneath him grins the emblem of death, muttering its solemn reminder of the transitoriness of human life and human glory. Canon Liddon used to say that the whole formed a very edifying subject of contemplation.

[1] It is said to be the one he actually used.

CHAPTER XVIII

A CHARACTER AND AN ESTIMATE

"Nay, to let all other things pass, how holily and Christianly
in his last will and testament doth he commend his soul
unto God! I must profess, when I saw it first, it did very
much affect me."—ABP. ABBOT'S Funeral Sermon upon
Thomas, Earl of Dorset.

"IL di loda la sera"—with that picturesque reflection Cope introduced the apology for his chief
which in the flood-tide of slander and abuse he
presented to the King. "The night praiseth the
day; the death the life; the end the action."[1]
It was, beyond all doubt, the evening of Salisbury's
days which illumined and ennobled and explained
all that had preceded it. Before that bed of mortal
sickness, of whose pains and sorrows we have received
so full a narrative, we may learn, as at no earlier date,
to know the character we have followed through all
the changes and chances of a swift and crowded life.
It would be a shallow as well as a heartless gibe
to maintain that what we catch sight of amid those
restless tossings is but the wreck or shadow of the
man, and not the very man himself. Men are plainly
most disclosed when all the veils and garments of
convention are rending of themselves, when the soul,
gazing out over the waters of eternity, perceives at
its feet its very image in clear vision unswept by
pride or passion or any other thing. Nor is it other
than a poor diagnosis which would find in the travail-

---

[1] Cope's *Apology* for Salisbury, in Gutch, *Collect. Cur.*

ings of the spirit of which we have been witness just the uneasy forebodings of an evil-liver brought at last to judgment. Salisbury's anxieties were those of a good man, not of a wicked one. Death, as such, had no terrors for him. " Ease and pleasure," so he told Cope plainly, " quake to hear of Death ; but my life, full of cares and miseries, desireth to be dissolved." [1] What weighed upon him was the thought of sins, presently to be set against the light of Perfect Holiness ; not the recollection of crimes for which he himself would shortly have to pay the price.

And, doubtless, there was much to repent of. No one could occupy great place in that century without having to face moral situations of great danger and great difficulty. Even Laud and Andrewes, living the comparatively sheltered lives of clergymen, became involved in affairs of no pleasant character and where their own conduct is not susceptible of easy explanation—the one in the business of Devonshire's marriage, the other in that of Essex's divorce. Men, like Salisbury, who trod the highways of public life, were necessarily confronted at almost every turn of the road with cases of conscience by which the most skilful of casuists in that age of casuistry might have been perplexed. And doubtless they were blind, by force of custom, to much that seems to us intolerable in the practice and incident of the time ; just as many a modern democrat, capable of high hopes and fine ideals, has a conscience thrice-armoured against the pains of log-rolling, or platform oratory, or posters, or the thousand illicit artifices of canvassing. It probably never crossed Salisbury's mind to inquire into the morality of torture ; or to wonder what kind of soul a paid spy would carry with him into another world ; or to ask himself whether the profuse compliments which, in common with others, he paid to Elizabeth and

[1] Cope's *Apology*.

James, had the slightest relation to actual fact. He was educated for a man of the world, not for a cloister, nor for the mystic scenery of Camelot and the flowery meadows of Mont Salvat. The morality by which he was surrounded was that which has been called ' la morale des honnêtes gens,' and to which Burghley's famous precepts of worldly wisdom form an incomparable guide. What is interesting in him are the glimpses of a higher character struggling against the trammels of circumstance and training, and raising him at last—unless, indeed, his words bore no relation to thoughts and feelings—to a plane where he had long desired to be and where his tired spirit at length found peace.

At bottom he was something of an idealist, and at moments, like all idealists, felt out of touch with the world that now is, and in the government of which he was called upon to take so great a part. The traces of that inner conflict are most apparent in the letter to Harington, where the expression of them is so poignant that probably none of Bacon's well-turned sentences in the essay on Great Place leaves on the mind so vivid an image of the cheats and penalties of public office. " 'Tis a great task to prove one's honesty and yet not spoil one's fortunes. . . . I am pushed from the shore of comfort, and know not where the winds and waves of a Court will bear me. I know it bringeth little comfort on earth ; and he is, I reckon, no wise man that looketh this way to heaven." Less emphatic but not less touching is the passage in a letter addressed to some anonymous correspondent, perhaps Prince Henry's tutor, in which he says that the Prince's rectitude ' in a court, where private ends never lack mediation,' puts all their grey hairs to shame.[1] It is, indeed, impossible for anyone who has made himself familiar with the various memorials of him to doubt that he thought

[1] Lansdowne MSS., 91/20, 31st August 1609.

and thought earnestly about the things that are most worth thinking about. If there had been nothing else to show it, the long exordium to his will, in which, whilst still (as he assures us) feeling himself to be ' in perfect health and memory,' he sets forth, after the fashion of the day, his confession of faith, would be evidence of a mind strong in its possession of some ultimate realities. " Because I would be glad," so, after a commendation of his soul to the mercies of Christ, the passage opens, " to leave behind me some such testimony of my particular opinion in point of faith and doctrine, as might confute all those who, judging others by themselves, are apt to censure all men to be of little or no religion which by their calling are employed in matters of state and government under great kings and princes, as if there were no Christian policy free from irreligion or impiety, I have resolved to express myself and my opinion in manner following." [1]

He goes on to affirm his conviction of the truth of that which is contained in the Apostles' Creed, " the best rule of necessary faith and points of salvation." Then he speaks of the two Sacraments admitted by the Church of England. In regard to Baptism he declares that it is " the ordinary way and means appointed in the Word for our admittance into the Church, without which Church whosoever is, is also without salvation." With the more vital question of the Eucharist he deals more fully. " As I could never render to myself any reasonable account of carnal presence in the Sacrament of the Supper, either without or within the Elements of Bread and Wine, because God Himself hath taught me that flesh and blood availeth nothing with him but the Spirit and life, so on the other side I always dissented (yet without scandal) from them that make it but a bare sign or signification of Christ's death and

[1] The will is to be seen at Somerset House.

was ever resolved upon the oracle of my Saviour, that it is really and truly His body and blood to all purposes of spiritual nourishment and life and graces whatsoever to him that receives it if he be a penitent and true believer." This was the doctrine of Calvin ; and it was among the disciples of that rigid thinker that Salisbury placed himself.[1] But he had nothing about him of Calvin's iron intolerance, and all his letters suggest that he was essentially a moderate man, impatient of extremes and probably impatient of the fine theological reasoning by which extreme positions are attained. He fully recognised the loyalty of the Puritans,[2] but he also recognised what we probably recognise too little, how impracticable they often were.[3] Barrow he puts down for a dissembling, lying fool ; but it is in the same letter [4] that there occurs the statesman's exceeding bitter cry : " By God, the priests swarm ! "

Principles are the foundation of morality, but not, of course, the structure ; and there was enough gossip started about Salisbury to suggest that his conduct was out of keeping with his convictions. Much of this dates, indeed, from a time when he was no longer able to reply to it, and issues from the muddy and discredited sources of Osborne and Weldon.[5] One gives him a mistress named Walsingham ; both credit him with dying of the Herodian disease. The second statement is as much disproved, the first as little proved as such allegations can be. But they remain, of course, on the printed

---

[1] Hatf. MSS., 192/16, Pickering to S.: " I am glad to hear you declare yourself a Calvinist."

[2] Hatf. Cal., xi. p. 148.

[3] See H.M. C. Rep., Cowper MSS., i. p. 56, S. P. Dom., Jas. i., 10/66, and Hatf. MSS., 109/48.

[4] Cal. MSS., Inner Temple, 538/54, f. 200.

[5] *Secret Hist. of the Court of James I.*, i. pp. 234, 236, and 326. His name had also apparently been coupled with a certain Lady Sherley's (Hatf. MSS., 107/75).

page for cynics to shake their heads over, and still, in spite of all possible repudiation, cause Salisbury's reputation, in the eyes of the casual reader, to lie under something of a cloud. Even had they been formulated in his lifetime, it is doubtful whether he would have thought them worth notice. It was one of his maxims that " he that will not be patient of slander must provide himself a chair out of the world's circle." [1] And his general principle " never to spend breath in excusing particular imputations . . . because innocency scorns apologies " [2] was doubtless the wisest way to take with that ' busiosity ' [3] of the times, of which he elsewhere complains.

And the vindication of his character might, perhaps, have been safely left in the hands of such intimates as Dorset and Cope if it had not been for the existence of Francis Bacon and the long line of Bacon's admirers. Bacon suspected, and his biographers commonly insinuate, that Salisbury was the snake in the grass who thwarted and belittled talents, the reach and splendour of which he had only the instinct to envy and to fear, and not the wit to realise and appreciate. It will come, then, as a surprise to many to learn that Salisbury said of his cousin that " he had the clearest prospect of things of any man in his age." [4] That is very judicious, very accurate praise. And it perfectly harmonises with a more familiar remark from the same lips, that Bacon was ' a speculative man.' [5]

If these two criticisms are authentic—and there is no reason to doubt them—it seems probable that

[1] S. P. Dom., Eliz. and Jas. I., Add., 35/59.
[2] Hatf. Cal., xi. p. 21. [3] S. P. Dom., Eliz., 243/83.
[4] Lloyd, *State Worthies*, " Observ. on the Life of Francis Bacon," p. 833. Salisbury's corresp. with Cæsar (Add. MSS., 36, 767/196, 202) shows that he asked and valued Bacon's council on financial questions.
[5] Montagu, *Works of Bacon*, xvi. (i) p. 26.

Salisbury had taken just that measure of Bacon which commends itself to minds not bewitched by Bacon's genius. More than most men he had reason to know at once his cousin's strength of vision and weakness of purpose. That which afterwards became so manifest to all—the littleness and meanness of Bacon's immediate ends—must have been apparent to him and to his father from the first. They had been the first objects of the inexhaustible flattery and the inexhaustible solicitation with which their poor relation pressed his claims to present or prospective advancement. Salisbury, we may be sure, was not blind to the calculated servilities of which we catch a most damning glimpse in Bacon's private note-book :—" At Council-table," so we read in that intimate record, " chiefly to make good my Lord of Salisbury's motions and speeches." [1] And again :—" To correspond with Salisbury in a habit of natural but noways perilous boldness and in vivacity, invention, care to cast and enterprise (but with due caution, for this manner I judge both in his nature freeth the standes and in his ends pleaseth him best and promiseth most use to me." [2] And once more :—" (to) insinuate myself to become privy to my L. of Salisbury's estate." Bacon was in a fuller degree, perhaps, than Salisbury realised ' a speculative man.' He was one, that is, whose wide views and profound thoughts never became fruitful and active principles of conduct ; one who, despite all that nature had given him of wisdom and understanding, never shook off the motives and desires of common clay. His cousin promoted him according to his ability,[3] and repressed him according to his character. For character is the first and not the second qualification for great place.

Bacon, though not a revengeful man, was probably

---

[1] Spedding, *Letters and Life of Francis Bacon*, iv. p. 93.
[2] *Ibid.*, p. 52.   [3] Bacon was made Solicitor-General in 1607.

not altogether without the spirit of malice ; and
posterity has scented in his essays on Cunning and
Deformity the satisfaction for his disappointments.
If the observations in the latter were really pointed
at Salisbury—and people would have been likely to
give them that application—the thing was ignobly
done. " Whosoever," so Bacon has warned succeeding generations, " hath anything fixed in his person
that doth induce contempt, hath also a perpetual
spur in himself to rescue and deliver himself from
scorn, therefore all deformed persons are extreme
bold—first, as in their own defence, as being exposed
to scorn, but in process of time by a general habit.
Also, it stirreth in them industry, and especially of
this kind, to watch and observe the weakness of
others that they may have somewhat to repay. Again
in their superiors it quencheth jealousy towards
them as persons that they think they may at pleasure
despise ; and it layeth their competitors and emu-
lators asleep, as never believing they should be in
possibility of advancement, till they see them in
possession ; so that upon the matter, in a great wit,
deformity is an advantage to rising."

If a finer taste would have shunned that passage,
no exception, on the score, at least, of fairness, can
be taken to the unmistakable allusions to Salisbury's
cunning. Nor can there be much doubt that this was
the weak joint in the harness. There is an early
letter, written when he was twenty-five, in which
Salisbury asks Hicks to put off a troublesome suitor
by pretending to have seen a letter from himself to his
father, asking the desired favour.[1] And always he
lacked that utter frankness of disposition which,
even if attended by a rough and hasty manner, leaves
men comfortable in the conviction that they know
exactly how they stand in the other's opinion. He
was smooth, courteous, friendly, but with a reserve

[1] Lansdowne MSS., 65/71.

which aroused suspicion. Bacon, baffled by the manner, thought that it was nothing but a disguise to conceal hostile practices.[1] And in the essay he paints Cecil's craftiness of a Machiavellian hue :—
" It is a point of cunning to let fall those words in a man's own name which he would have another man learn and use, and thereupon take advantage. I knew two [2] that were competitors for the Secretary's place, in Queen Elizabeth's time, and yet kept good quarter between themselves, and would confer one with another upon the business ; and the one of them said that to be a secretary in the declination of a monarchy was a ticklish thing, and that he did not affect it ; the other straight caught up those words, and discoursed with divers of his friends, that he had no reason to desire to be secretary in the declination of a monarchy. The first man took hold of it, and found means it was told the Queen ; who, hearing of a declination of monarchy, took it so ill, that [3] she would never after hear of the other's suit."

This, no doubt, was the view of Cecil that passed current in Essex's circle, though there is room enough in the story, as Bacon tells it, for a good deal of false accusation. " Robertus Diabolus " he was to Antonio Perez ; and Robert the Devil he seemed, no doubt, to many of that great Elizabethan public whose heroes mostly carried fine figures and open purses. But it is rather of *diablerie* than of devilry that the memorials we have of him are suggestive. The story of his guile in suggesting to the Queen that the compromising packet from Scotland required to be aired from evil smells before she perused it, has already been told. Bacon adds the record of another piece of mischief :—" I knew a counsellor and secretary that never came to Queen Elizabeth of England with bills to sign, but he would always first put her into some

---

[1] Cp. Spedding, *Letters and Life of Francis Bacon*, iv. p. 11.
[2] Cecil and Bodley, presumably.　　　[3] In the original, ' as.'

discourse of state that she might the less mind the bills." [1] And throughout Salisbury's correspondence there is to be felt a certain Puckish playfulness of which the reader has been shown one or two specimens, and which, once one has become familiar with it, takes all the harsh lines and dramatic horrors out of the portrait of him as ' *tout mystère* ' or as ' the proud and terrible hunchback.' [2]

And of Machiavellism in its most sinister sense he was guiltless. He did not certainly discourage those who threatened the lives of rebels,[3] actively in arms and proscribed as outlaws under the royal proclamation ; but in this he merely followed the common practice of English statesmen, which Ralegh approves in the most definite and unmistakable terms.[4] Once Tyrone had fled the country and the rebellion was over, however, he repudiated with horror the constant offers which were made him for the assassination of both Owen and the Irish Earl :—
" I had rather serve my country in any other kind than, together with the blemish of mine honour, to stain my conscience with the blood, which, shed by a lawful course, were acceptable service to God, but, spilt by indirect means, would cry for vengeance from above." [5] The truth is that the constant juxtaposition of his career and the careers of men whose claims upon our sympathy are stronger, has led people [6] to fancy that there hung about him, in the same manner, though not, of course, in the same degree, as Shakespeare's Richard III., a sort of clandestine

---

[1] *On Cunning.*

[2] Quoted by Motley, *United Netherlands* (iv. p. 160), from Molin's *Relazione.*

[3] Edwards, *Life of Ralegh,* i. p. 321. Hatf. MSS., 213/116.

[4] Edwards, *Life of Ralegh,* ii. p. 198. Ralegh says: " We have always in Ireland given head-money for the killing of rebels who are evermore proclaimed at a price."

[5] Birch, *View of the Negotiations,* p. 291.

[6] Martin Hume, for example, always views him in this light.

malevolence which enabled him to outstrip better men than himself. They contrast his rapid and lasting eminence with the slow success of Bacon, the swift failure of Essex, the living death of Ralegh ; and they are half disposed to suspect him of some compact with the devil which they cannot discover. Macaulay, who is responsible for so many popular opinions, must bear, too, some share of the blame. Though he has done something to dispel the popular illusion he has rather confirmed the popular dislike. He has told us, indeed, that the secret of Burghley's success was the possession of those kind of abilities ' which keep men long in power,' and that of these abilities his son was the inheritor.[1] But to him Salisbury's reputation owes one of those casual, but not the less piercing stiletto thrusts, which were inspired rather by a regard for picturesque suggestion than by any strong obligation towards ascertained truth. The little clause in the essay on Bacon, in which he tells us how " Robert Cecil sickened with fear and envy as he contemplated the rising fame and influence of Essex," is nicely calculated to leave upon the reader the most odious and damaging impression. Cecil, no doubt, at that early stage of his career, was as anxious as most young men of ability to attract notice ; and there is reason enough to think that he preferred his own promotion before that of other people. But ambition is at a good remove from fear and envy ; and to assert that he sickened with these unamiable qualities by reason of his rival's success is as gratuitous as it would be to affirm of a disappointed candidate for political office in our own time that he grew sour with indignation at a rival's preferment. The truth is that, at first starting, Cecil was not any better and not any worse than the average young courtier of his own day or the average young parliamentarian of ours. Later, when time and experience had

[1] In the essay on *Burghley and his Times*.

mellowed his judgment, and when the things which had
looked sweet to the eye had turned sour in the tasting,
he rose, as we have seen, to a nobility of feeling to
which time and experience and the vanity of human
wishes do not always suffice to raise the human race.
And it is from those, like Cope and Dorset, who
enjoyed his rare intimacy in later life, rather than
from the pale and uncertain shadows which he casts
across the path of men like Bacon and Essex and
Ralegh, that—if we are just—we shall seek to know
him as he really was.   A sociable man may be known
from his friends, but a reserved man must be made
known by his friends.

There is another and a different reason why the
memory of Salisbury has been blighted. He is said
to have been in receipt of a pension from the Court
of Spain ; and the statement is—very properly—
seldom, if ever, omitted from any modern account
of him or his career. The charge is authenticated
by Gardiner, and as that good historian was always
generous, always unprejudiced, always careful, no one
probably has felt the inclination or the curiosity to
carry the point further than he has done.   And yet,
as he himself fully realises, the matter is not without
its difficulties.

The facts, as he has them, are that, after the
conclusion of the peace between England and Spain,
and continuously until the end of his life, Salisbury
received, through the Spanish Embassy, a pension of
£1000, and subsequently of £1500 a year, in return
for which he supplied the Spanish Ambassador with
information respecting English affairs.

It does not escape Gardiner's observation that
there are two circumstances which may make us
pause before we accept the story in its naked form.
One is the high character for incorruptibility which
Salisbury bore. Subject, as was every man in high
office at that time, to the proffer of gifts, he laid

down for himself a standard of conduct which almost certainly rose above the standard of the times.[1] His letter on this subject to Northumberland, in the year 1600, is in certain respects so significant that it deserves to be quoted as well for the illustration that it offers of the difficulties entailed by opposition to the common practice, as for the impression which it leaves of his own integrity of intention :—

"My Lord, I love not to use many words by a letter, in a matter of this nature, wherein the greatness of your own mind may lead you to mistake mine, especially when I must maintain my arguments with replies, which a letter cannot do. But, Sir, in short, I have received a coach and four horses from you, a gift greater than ever I was beholding for to any subject, and that, which I protest before God, I would have refused, whatsoever had come of it, if I could have been present to have argued with you. For first, Sir, even as far as I respect myself only, I must needs say, that gifts of value, ought not to pass between those, whose minds contemn all the knots that utility can fasten. Toys, which argue only memory in absence, may be interchanged, as long as they are no other, either in substance or circumstance. Secondly, there is at this time, some thing in question, which doth concern you in profit, wherein the care I have showed to further your desires, will now be imputed to this expectation, and so give a taint to that profession, which I have made, only to delight in your favour, in respect of the honour I carry to your person, and the knowledge I have of your sincerity, and ability to do her Majesty service. Thirdly, I confess it grieveth me to think, that divers of my adversaries, who are apt to decry all values that are set upon my coin, may think that you, who should know me better than they do, find me either facile, or not clear from servile ends: the conceit whereof, I do confess, doth so much trouble me, as it had almost made me adventure a desperate refusal, but that I feared to have made you doubtful that I had judged you by others scantling. And so much for the relations of mine own particular. Next my Lord, I pray you think, whether the eyes of the world can wink at these shows, and whether if the Queen shall hear it, she will not be apt to

---

[1] " . . . la grazia e la protezione di alcuno dei consiglieri, il che non si può fare in quel paese con altri mezzi nè con altre vie che con presenti e donativi," gives the general impression of a foreign diplomatist in 1607 respecting the English Council (Nicolo Molin's *Relazione* in Barozzi and Berchet, *Inghilterra*, i. p. 58).

suspect me, that I am the earnester in your cause for it. But what should I now call back yesterday ? for I have accepted your fair present, rather than to discomfort you, and for my own satisfaction, have only reserved an assurance to my heart that this was given me, out of the vastness of your kindness, and not out of any other mistaking my disposition ; for requital whereof, I can only return this present, that though I have neither gold nor silver, yet I have love and honesty." [1]

Salisbury's conduct, so far as the evidence enables us to judge, agrees with the spirit of this letter. He made a conscience, but not a close or unmannerly conscience, of receiving presents. Bishop Goodman assures us that he refused New Year's gifts to the amount of over £1800.[2] And Chamberlain tells the same story to Carleton :—" The great lord refused a world of New Year Gifts and accepted very few and those but from near friends." [3] It was no doubt sufficiently difficult to pick a clear road between the claims of common civility and the claims of the public service. Gifts of every kind were tendered—venison pies [4] as well as live deer,[5] cherries and apricots,[6] a page-boy,[7] a chest,[8] the guardianship of a lunatic.[9] Against the seductions of the venison pasty, at all events, we have every reason to think that he was not proof ; and of the other items it is probable that more than one found acceptance. Money, however, we know that, on one occasion at least, he firmly declined.[10] And we know, too, that he combated the distribution of illicit fees in the Court of Wards at the risk, as he says, of raising a suspicion that he had received some secret consideration for doing so.[11] There is nothing, in fact, so far as domestic affairs are concerned, to disprove that more than

---

[1] Hatf. MSS., 250/31.   [2] Goodman, *The Court of James I.*, i. p. 36.
[3] S. P. Dom., Jas. I., 43/14 (January 1609).
[4] H.M. C. Rep., Rutland Papers, iv. p. 457.
[5] S. P. Dom., Jas. I., 57/17 ; Hatf. Cal., vii. p. 182.
[6] Hatf. MSS., 101/56.   [7] *Ibid.*, 118/162.
[8] S. P. Dom., Jas. I., 32/16.   [9] Hatf. Cal., vii. p. 4.
[10] *Ibid.*, ix. p. 8.   [11] Lodge, *Illustrations*, iii. p. 45.

ample indication of his honesty which, after his death, in the dark night of his good name, Cope, his subordinate at the Exchequer and a man of admitted integrity, put forward :—" The heart of man was never more free from baseness or bribes ; he hated the bribe and the taker. He was one of those of whom king David speaketh, ' Qui munera super innocentem non accepit.' So clear his hands were from those base corruptions, that I supposed rumour and report would have been afraid once to have raised such slanders on him." [1]

Such, then, was Salisbury's common reputation in the light of the documents that have descended to us and according to the witness of one who was well qualified to judge. Whatever precisely we may think of it, it is clearly not a reputation which will lightly suffer to be called corrupt in the larger sphere of foreign affairs. And, in fact, the very course and conduct of those affairs is in itself a second and a formidable objection to the story of the pension in its naked form. For, as the reader has already seen, " we know," to borrow Gardiner's language, " that up to the day of his death, Salisbury's policy, whenever he had free play, was decidedly and increasingly anti-Spanish." [2] To that careful judgment Spanish testimony might be added. Salisbury was to the end of his life regarded as the great enemy of Spain. " The news of the Lord Treasurer's death," writes the English Ambassador at Madrid,[3] " is very welcome to the Spaniards." And, if this be criticised as the opinion of those who were ignorant of his real relations with their Government, another unimpeachable witness may be called into court. Don Alonso di Velasco, the Spanish Ambassador in London, through

[1] Cope's *Apology*, in Gutch, *Collect. Cur.*
[2] *Hist. of Engl.*, i. p. 215.
[3] H.M. C. Report, Eglinton, Maxwell, etc., p. 584. Sir J. Digby to Sir T. Edmondes, 2nd July 1612.

whose hands all the pensions passed (if they passed at
all), reports to the Council of State in December 1611
" that of all the confidants only El Cid, who is the
Earl of Northampton, is trustworthy and reliable ;
and that Cecil is as bad as he can be." [1]

It is clear, then, that Salisbury did not sell his
country. The information he gave (or was thought
to have given) was a grave caricature of the
information that the Spanish Ambassador desired.
And the natural explanation of the evidence, so far
as we have at present carried it—and probably the
explanation of the evidence so far as it can be carried—
is that Salisbury encouraged a piece of fictitious
treachery, in which he himself pretended to take
the principal part, and thus, to use a now classical
phrase, stewed the Spanish Ambassador very prettily
in his own juice. It is quite a credible supposition,
that, knowing with whom he had to deal, he conceived
it to be advantageous to his diplomacy to accept
rather than to refuse the illicit Spanish overtures ;
and that he turned the deception to good account,
perhaps with, perhaps without, the knowledge of the
King. This theory, and this theory alone, reconciles
the evidence with his policy and with that view of
him which was expressed by a contemporary and disinterested observer that he had never been willing
to accept pensions.[2] And it might be added that
this theory more easily perhaps, than any other, ab-
sorbs two curious facts—the apparent indifference of
Salisbury when Cornwallis, the English Ambassador
at Madrid, informs him that he is using every effort
to discover the names of persons near the King
who were receiving pensions from the King of

[1] Simancas Archives, Bundle 2513. Consultation of the Council
of State, 3rd January 1612 : " Que de los confidentes solo El Cid,
que es El Conde de Nortampton es seguro y puntual, y Sicil es el peor
que puede ser."

[2] " . . . Nè ha mai voluto accetar pensioni . . . " (M. Correr's
Relazione in Barozzi and Berchet. *Inghilterra*, i. p. 123).

Spain,[1] and the patent inaction of James himself, when Digby, Cornwallis' successor, detected and named the English pensioners after Salisbury's death.[2] One might have expected the one to fly into a panic, and the other to fly into a rage. But, in fact, Salisbury displayed no fear, and James disgraced no courtiers.[3]

If Salisbury were on his trial in a court of law a great deal more would, of course, have to be said, and a great many more interrogatories would have to be put. The whole question of the taking of pensions and gifts from foreign powers would have first to be argued. Though there can be no question that to a mind like Digby's the acceptance of pensions from a foreign power appeared a grave affair, still it would be in point to recall that so actually good a patriot as Olden Barneveldt in that age,[4] and so reputedly good a patriot as Algernon Sidney in the next,[5] were, as we should say, in the pay of foreign powers ; that Villeroy was a pensioner of Spain ; [6] that James himself made presents of a most costly character to the Spanish Commissioners at the conference of 1604 ; [7] that the English Privy Councillors on that same occasion had no hesitation in taking

[1] Winwood Memorials, ii. p. 153. Salisbury, that is so far as I am aware, made no attempt to check Cornwallis' investigations.

[2] S. P. For., Spain, 8th Aug., 9th Sept., 24th Dec. (1613), 16th Dec. (1615), 3rd April (1616). It is true that the Spanish spy—Joseph de St. Andex—procured the information for Digby on the understanding that Digby would use every effort to prevent James from taking action, lest suspicion should fall on St. Andex. But after St. Andex had been taken in flagrant delict (S. P. For., Spain, 3rd January 1614) there was little reason why James should have spared the English pensioners.

[3] Four of the pensioners were still alive in the spring of 1614, when Digby made his revelations to the King—Northampton, Lady Suffolk, Sir William Monson, and Mrs. Drummond (Gardiner, Hist. of Engl., ii. p. 224)—but though Lady Suffolk and Monson got into trouble on other accounts later on, no steps were taken against them at this time.

[4] Motley, United Netherlands, iv. p. 534.

[5] Macaulay, Hist. of Engl., i. p. 230.

[6] Motley, Life and Death of Barneveldt, i. p. 234.

[7] Venet. Cal., x. p. 179, 8th September 1604.

the gifts of the Spanish Commissioners, and scoffed at those who made a scruple of it,[1] and finally that the Venetian Ambassador reports in the following year that the matter of the Spanish pensions was expected to be put to the King in such a manner as to lead him to sanction them.[2] Such a loose catena of considerations makes it clear that, even if the pension had been accepted in its naked form, Salisbury's conduct—to borrow the phraseology of one of his namesakes and descendants in relation to another matter [3]—might have probably to be treated as ' an indelicacy ' rather than as ' corruption.'

But again, any legal investigation of Salisbury's conduct would require a much closer proof of his complicity. His case is very far from being on a par with that of Bacon, where we have both the verdict of the House of Lords and the admission of the accused to go upon. Salisbury was never tried ; he never had an opportunity of making any explanation ; and he has left behind him no jot or tittle of written matter or of oral tradition to show his guilt. The evidence against him is all of it ultimately derived from Spanish sources : the memorandum of Villa Mediana instigating and outlining the pensions ; [4] the despatches [5] of the Spanish Ambassadors in London reporting their disappointment at the insufficiency and untrustworthiness of the information supplied ; and the despatches of the English Ambassador at Madrid, himself much puzzled to read the riddle of the revelations [6] and whose considered reflections on

[1] Venet. Cal., x. p. 179. [2] Ibid., p. 262.

[3] Exam. of Sir R. Isaacs by Lord Robert Cecil. Marconi Commission. Reported in The Times of Friday, 28th March 1913.

[4] Simancas Archives, Bundle No. 2512, 18th July 1605.

[5] Ibid., Bundle No. 2513. Consultation on Don Pedro de Zuñiga's letter of 22nd December 1607 and Don Pedro de Zuñiga's letter of 4th May 1611.

[6] S. P. For., Spain, 24th December 1613. Digby to the King: " This business is full of intricacies." Digby points out the importance of not confusing the allocation of pensions with their acceptance.

the subject are buried for us beneath the symbols of a cipher despatch.[1] What certain proof is there that the money sent over from Spain ever passed out of the hands of the Spanish Ambassador, and that the alleged complaints of Cecil at the amount of the payments made him were not a fraudulent shift to cover the Ambassador's peculation and to increase the Ambassador's opportunities of lining his own pockets ?

Again, there is more than one passage in the papers which strongly suggests that Lady Suffolk played the part of intermediary between the Spanish Ambassador and Salisbury.[2] After the latter's death that lady came into unenviable prominence, not only through the reflected notoriety of Lady Essex, whose mother she was, but also on her own account and that of her husband for malversation of public moneys. One section of public opinion made her the centre of a conspiracy of ' Spaniolised Romanists ' for tolerating Roman Catholicism in England ; [3] Weldon, who also has the pension story, made her Salisbury's mistress.[4] She was, in fact, the mother-in-law of Salisbury's son. What is there to show that she did not trick the Spanish Embassy into paying to her and to that inner circle of her friends, who in the Spanish correspondence appear as ' the confidants,' and of whom her relative Northampton was plainly one, ever-increasing sums of money on the assumption

---

[1] S. P. For., Spain, 16th December, 1615. Digby to the King. I am not aware of the existence of the key to this cipher.

[2] Simancas Archives, Bundle 2512. Council of State, 18th March 1606 : " Que el Conde de Villa Mediana dejó prometidas quatro mil libras y le han dicho los que las han de aver que tardan para la presente necesidad que tienen de casar sus hijos. Que la Condesa de Sufolt dice que la mitad desto es para Cicil y que ella no se atreve a hablarle en nada sino es cumpliendo con el y assi suplica Don Pedro se provean luégo." Also see Bundle 2586, f. 84.

[3] S. P. Dom., Jas. I., 67/149 : " An advice from an anonymous hand " (1611–12).

[4] *Secret Hist. of the Court of James I.*, i. p. 338.

that she had access to Salisbury's secrets and was the paymaster of his confidences ?

This, like the last, is, of course, only a hypothesis, and not, as the present writer thinks, the most likely hypothesis. But it would equally have to be exhausted before we can confidently affirm that Salisbury received continuously large sums of money from Spain. It is not enough to show that money was allocated to bribe him ; the accuser has to show that the money reached his pocket. With that caution we may quit a question which will never probably be absolutely resolved on this side of the grave, and pass by a not unnatural, if seemingly abrupt transition, to a pleasanter topic—Salisbury's relations with the Howards, with his son, and with his kinship and acquaintance.

Thomas Howard, Earl of Suffolk, was, as Salisbury tells us in his will, " the person in whom he had found so much sincerity and constancy and so much honour and virtue in all . . . actions and conversation," that he had held it, next the favour of the King, to be " the felicity of his life to exchange his dearest thoughts with him whenever he had cause to use and trust a friend." And to this tribute of affection the testator adds the touching assurance that towards Suffolk " this heart of mine did never offend in thought since my first contract of friendship with him." History has on the whole endorsed Salisbury's opinion of his beloved intimate. Though, years after Salisbury was in his grave, Suffolk fell, it is generally agreed that he fell as Adam did. Lady Suffolk was incurably designing and avaricious, and the bribery and corruption which flourished at the Exchequer during Suffolk's tenure of office as Lord Treasurer is for the most part laid at her door. In Salisbury's lifetime Suffolk's character stood exceptionally high ; and it is significant that (if Digby's information was correct) the man with whom Salisbury loved to exchange ' his dearest thoughts ' declined a Spanish pension.[1]

The Howards, during the greater part of James's reign, enjoyed a power which they have never enjoyed since. Nottingham, Northampton, and Suffolk were all in the Council, and there is no reason to suppose that Salisbury's relations with any of them were other than good. But the idea that he rested his power on their support is rather a perverted expression of the fact that he maintained good relations with them. He was himself infinitely the most powerful man in the realm; and after the death of Essex and the fall of Ralegh the Council seems to have been free of faction. To Ellesmere he bequeathed some gold plate as a token of friendship, and correspondence ' both as private friends and public ministers '; and Ellesmere was the opponent of the Howards' policy of Spanish alliance. Nottingham and Northampton, on the other hand, are not even named in his will; and the kindly letter which he wrote to the latter on his death-bed implies an estrangement of policy and opinion,[2] which in the last hours of his life he desired to obliterate. The truth is that his friendship with Suffolk was as much a personal as a political one, and that it had been consolidated by a family connection which was of the closest interest to him. On 1st December 1608, Cranborne had been married—' very privately,' for some reason which does not appear, ' at the Lady Walsingham's lodging by the tilt-yard '[3]—to Suffolk's daughter, Lady Katherine Howard. The alliance had, as the Venetian Ambassador perceived,[4] more than surface advantages. Lady Cranborne's sister was Lady Essex, lately married and of course still guiltless of the blood of Sir Thomas Overbury. Salisbury no doubt hoped

---

[1] Gardiner, *History of England*, i. 215.
[2] Cotton MSS., Vesp. F. XIII. Art. 237.
[3] S. P. Dom., Jas. i., 38/17.   [4] Venet. Cal., x. p. 308.

that in the new generation the memory of his own just dealing with Essex's father would be wiped away by a brotherly affection. Even towards himself the young man had already shown himself friendly.[1]

It is high time that something should be said of the boy upon whom Salisbury lavished all the ineffective desires of a devoted parent.[2] Cranborne was possessed of a disposition which proved in the event as good a road to King James's favour as a better. He was a first-rate horseman,[3] and had a perfect aptitude for all the lore of the racecourse and the hunting-field. His father, on the other hand, though he did not perhaps hope to see him carry the political honours of the family into a third generation, was reasonably anxious that he should bear the common marks of a liberal education. Every effort, therefore, was made to get the young man ' to take delight in his book.' He was sent to Cambridge, and there appeared no native vice in him to prevent his acquiring the features of a complete gentleman. A scholarly eye, indeed, detected in his pupil ' all complements of nature, all good parts of wit, capacity, and memory,' though, alas ! ' not that delight in his book that he had [4] in other things.' [5] " As Themistocles," continues the worthy pedagogue, " could not sleep in the night for dreaming of Miltiades' triumphs, so neither can he go to his study all the day for revolving and recounting in his mind the sports and pastimes abroad in the world." The truth, as indeed the observer perceived, was that the delights of the

---

[1] See the letter from Essex to Salisbury in Hatf. MSS., 193/118, 9th June 1607.

[2] Mr. Dennis, in his *House of Cecil*, suggests that Salisbury may have had another son, perhaps illegitimate, on the authority of a letter in Lodge's *Illustrations of British History*, iii. p. 171. This letter is erroneously attributed to the first earl. It was written by the second, and the date (1605) given it by Stewart (when calendaring the Hatfield Papers) was given by mistake.

[3] Hatf. MSS., 193/15.   [4] In the original, ' doth.'

[5] Hatf. MSS., 104/60.

Court had estranged the young man's fancy from the delights of the classics. Salisbury administered appropriate rebukes. Cranborne promised amendment, and, to give him his due, diligently sought the uncongenial company of Tully. Latin was even adopted as a channel of communication ' both travelling and hunting,' though, as his tutor lamented, " the sound of it was so harsh amid the cry of dogs that it came not off with a wonted facility." [1] Reassuring reports attended these stupendous endeavours :—" I find that as his Lordship grows in years, so his love of learning and liking of his book doth daily increase." [2] Salisbury's anxieties, however, were not long laid to rest. Cranborne's letters home told their own tale. " Ill orthography," the watchful parent observes, " agreeth not well with an University. . . . Your letters are without date, from any place or time ; which makes me doubt whether you be at Royston at some horse-race, or at Cambridge. Your name is not well written, and therefore I have written it underneath as I would have it. I have also sent you a piece of paper folded as gentlemen use to write their letters, where(as) yours are like those that come out of a grammar-school." These things were, however, as he said, but toys. The root of evil lay deeper :—" Keeping running horses I will no more allow." Hounds fell for the time under the same condemnation. Of all the delectable four-footed beasts in whom Cranborne delighted he was to have but one horse, upon which ' to take the air.' [3]

Stimulated by these privations, the uneasy student made some little progress in handwriting, though only so far as to make it resemble that ' of a scrivener,' and even this not without the aid of ruled lines. To the end of his time at Cambridge it remained an eye-

[1] Hatf. MSS., 117/85. ' Of ' in the original I read as ' off.'
[2] Hatf. MSS., 118/49.   [3] *Ibid.*, 228/19.

sore to his father :—" Though it be Roman, yet it doth lean in your letters as gentlemen's hands do not, but rather like a woman or a scholar." [1]   But there was worse than this to lament.   The boy came down from Cambridge profoundly ignorant, as his father presently discovered and conveyed to his tutor :—

" He cannot speak six words in Latin, out of which language I did expect you and he would seldom have discoursed.   In any part of story without book he is not able to show memory of four lines, neither is his manner of repeating anything like to those whom tutors teach to speak distinct and ornate.   For his logic, a month would beget more knowledge than he hath, in one of no greater capacity.   If you say that his mind hath affected other pleasant studies, either the mathematics, language, or that he hath given himself to music, or any other gentleman-like quality, then must I answer you that I find no such thing.   So as I conclude that either the fault is in my suffering him to be out of the University, or in your neglecting him in the University." [2]

Marriage did not bring Cranborne's education to an end.   Very soon after he went over to Paris and received all the attentions which his father's son could command.   Henry iv. took daily notice of him ; [3] he attended the Queen's ' ballett ' ; [4] and in the general alarm which followed the King's assassination the Queen went so far as to offer him guards for his special protection. [5]   The catastrophe brought him home for a time, but later in the year (1610) he travelled in Italy, visiting Turin, where he was handsomely entertained by the Duke of Savoy, [6] Milan, and Venice.   Such experiences cannot have been wholly wasted upon him ; and, indeed, the dreary and painstaking chronicle [7] of his movements, which he compiled in French under the impression

---

[1] Hatf. MSS., 228/23.   [2] *Ibid.*, 228/14.
[3] *Ibid.*, 228/25.   [4] *Ibid.*, 228/24.
[5] S. P. For., France, 56/112.   [6] Sidney MSS., Collins, ii. p. 327.
[7] The 2nd Earl of Salisbury's Journal of his travels in France, Italy, Germany, and the Low Countries, 1609.   At Hatfield.

that he was keeping a journal, is proof how hard he tried to profit by his opportunities. But Salisbury knew better than to pay much attention to the pretty compliments [1] upon his son's attainments that reached him from abroad ; and there is too much reason to think that Pepys selected the exact, right epithet, when, recording a visit to Hatfield Church one Sunday evening in October 1664, he described how he saw sitting in the gallery " my simple Lord Salisbury." Cranborne was one of those unfortunate men who, gifted with a good deal less than average ability, are called upon to bear the honours of a great name through the storms and trials of a revolution. Between the day when, being just of age, he took a last leave of his father at Bath, and the day when Pepys viewed him at evensong in Hatfield Church, he had been a noted master of irresolute counsels, had been washed hither and thither by the terrors of the time—first into the King's incipient camp at York and finally into Cromwell's House of Commons— and had earned the contempt which Clarendon has so bitingly conveyed by affirming that he at any rate would not lightly enter into the rest which Seneca has provided for the children of illustrious parents :— " Hic egregiis majoribus ortus est, qualiscunque est, sub umbra suorum lateat ; ut loca sordida repercussa sole illustrantur, ita inertes majorum suorum luce resplendeant." [2]

But the real interest of the correspondence between father and son lies in the discovery of the qualities of the one, not in the exposure of the defects of the other. No one, probably, will rise from reading the letters which Salisbury wrote to Cranborne without receiving a confirmation of every good impression he held

[1] Hatf. MSS., 228/32 : " I know this world too well to believe reports, where flattery so much aboundeth and especially of you, in whose youth false reports so much betrayed me."

[2] Clarendon, *Hist. of the Great Rebellion*, vi. 403.

about the elder of the two. No callous man would have been at the pains to write his son letters of such untiring and tender solicitude. No pompous man would have contrived such unaffected good sense, strangely different both in matter and method to the famous precepts which Salisbury had himself received from his own father. And no hypocritical man would have constructed the simple sentences in which he applauds his son's attendance at the Holy Table :—
" I thank you and love you for having given so good a testimony to the world (as well as to your own conscience) that you are perfectly established in religion by coming to the Lord's Supper. Do it, I pray you, when you may conveniently, though I require it not frequently, for it will strengthen your faith and confirm God's grace and mercy. Your wife and sister have done the like at Hatfield this Easter." [1]
And elsewhere [2] there may be read the scorching sentence in which the father tells his son that honour exacts that one should not suppress one's religion in face of the world.

Whatever Salisbury may have been he was certainly not the forbidding parent of tradition. A rebuke with him ushers in a new outbreak of affection. " However," he writes, " you may find in this letter plainness, and fatherly admonition, you may promise yourself that all proceeds from care and love, and that I free you from any fault for lack of duty towards me. And therefore, let nothing trouble your mind that I write, though you make use of my counsel and direction, for if I may know anything you desire or want for your ease and comfort while you are abroad, be not afraid to ask it of your loving father, that prays to God to bless you." [3] Nor were these mere idle assurances. Cranborne was travelling for seven months and a half in the autumn and winter of

[1] Hatf. MSS., 228/32. [2] Add. MSS., Egerton, 1525/33 (Br. Mus.).
[3] Hatf. MSS., 228/32.

1610–11, and during that time his expenses, of which we have a most explicit account, amounted to £2565, 17s.[1] Salisbury would have held his own with the most indulgent parent of modern times ; and no doubt there will be those to say now, as there were those (so he tells us [2] himself) who said then, that he was ' fond and foolish.' But it would be a mistake to suppose that Cranborne turned out badly. He was never vicious ;[3] only deficient in that which perhaps no human being can really implant, the love of wisdom.

In the interval between Cranborne's two journeys abroad, his sister, Frances, was married on 25th July 1610, and with considerable pomp,[4] to Henry, Lord Clifford, the eldest son of Lord Cumberland. Lady Dorset, the first cousin of the bridegroom, has left it on record [5] that she regarded the marriage as a malicious attempt on Salisbury's part to cut her out of the succession to the Cumberland estates. The idea is, of course, preposterous. Any marriage that Clifford contracted would have had a similar effect ; and he could hardly be expected to remain a bachelor in order to let her succeed to his inheritance.

Of Frances we know little, though a little more than we know of her sister Catherine. One of the two, almost certainly the latter,[6] was deformed ; and there is a pathetic letter, written after his wife's death, in which Salisbury, himself familiar with the treatment accorded to deformity in the society of the Court, invites his sister-in-law, Lady Sturton, to be-

---

[1] Hatf. Estate Papers, Accts., 9/13. [2] Hatf. MSS., 228/32.

[3] Hatf. MSS., 228/32 : ". . . of which (*i.e.* spending time viciously) I thank God those that love you and me worst, cannot accuse you " (Salisbury to Cranborne).

[4] Hatf. Bills, 1610, Bundle 49.

[5] H.M. C. Rep., Hothfield MSS., p. 89.

[6] I infer this from the fact that Frances was thought a suitable match both for a son of Northumberland's (Hatf. MSS., 126/168–9) and for Buckhurst (S. P. Dom., Jas. 1., 37/53) and from her being able to dance (S. P. Dom., Jas. 1., 57/2).

friend the misshapen child. " Because," he writes, " I know the fashion of the Court and London is to laugh at all deformities . . . I would be exceeding glad that somewhat was done to cover the poor girl's infirmity before such ladies and others as here will find her out, should see her in such ill-case as she is."[1] Lady Sturton undertook the charge ; but we hear no more, and Salisbury's language[2] suggests that no perfect cure was possible. All that is certain is that Catherine was still alive when her father died in 1612, and that he questioned his chaplain tenderly about her religion on his death-bed.[3]

If we pass outside the range of his immediate family we find similar traces of warm affection. For the pleasure of visiting his nieces, Lady Derby and Lady Norris, he undertook what must have been a rather troublesome journey into Lancashire in the summer of 1608.[4] Out of a gift which, after the manner of well-educated uncles, he had presented to the former there was made a fine story. The article in question was a locket enclosing a miniature of himself. The Queen catching sight of it, Lady Derby shyly or slyly tried to hide it away. But Elizabeth snatched it, set it on her shoe, then on her arm. Salisbury, getting wind of what was done, wrote an ode detailing the affair and had it put to music. The Queen insisted upon hearing the verses sung. And the world, taking note of the matter long after the event, concluded, without too close inquiry, that Salisbury had been something of a lively gallant.[5]

To Exeter's son, Sir Edward Cecil, his uncle paid the best of all compliments in desiring to see him the constant companion of his own son.[6] And

---

[1] Add. MSS. (Br. Mus.), 29,974/7.   [2] Add. MSS., 29,973.
[3] Peck, *Desid. Cur.*, p. 208.   [4] S. P. Dom. Jas. I., 35/22.
[5] See the article on Cecil in the *D. N. B.* Miss Strickland tells the story in *The Lives of the Queens of England.*
[6] Birch, *Court and Times of James I.*, p. 142.

with Exeter himself Salisbury enjoyed an intercourse of singular felicity, if we take into consideration all the dividing influences of age, of ability, and of disposition. Much, no doubt, was due to Exeter's exceptional character. In all the voluminous collection of letters addressed to Salisbury there is none more full of grace and charm than that which the elder brother sends to the younger in reply to a charge of waning affection :—

"But we be brothers," Exeter concludes, "and to contest one with another in unkindness is but to blow away the ashes that the fire may be the warmer. And let this letter be kept as a witness against me if you shall not find in me towards you a love void of envy, of mistrust, and as glad of your honour and merit as a dear brother ought to be. For I am not partial, but confess that God hath bestowed rarer gifts of mind upon you than upon me.[1] I know you have deserved far greater merit both of his Majesty and of your country, and, if it lay in me in power as it doth in wish, there is no honour that can be laid upon you whereof I would not participate of your joy and contentment with you."[2]

Salisbury, surely, must have been a little lovable to be loved so well. And, indeed, to those who knew him best he seemed worthy of love. Dorset, in leaving to him some trinkets as a remembrance of their long association together, has left to us the fragrant memory of what he had been to an intimate friend :—

"I give, will, and bequeath," he wrote, "unto my singular good Lord, my most special and dearest friend, the Earl of Salisbury one chain of gold of open Spanish work (and so forth) desiring his Lordship to wear them and keep them as faithful memories of my most hearty love unto him ; being most assured that his Lordship, according to the nobleness of his own nature and the sincere merit of my true heart towards him, will not behold the value of the gift unto him, which both himself and myself may esteem as a mere trifle, but rather the value of the giver's heart towards him, which always hath been . . . and

---

[1] In the original, ' unto you than of me.'
[2] Hatf. MSS., 100/94.

ever will be so long as life endureth as firmly and as tenderly
devoted and knit unto him as is possible for one friend to be
unto another. With which faithful bond the heavenly God
doth know I have felt my heart these many years fast tied unto
him, not only in respect of those private particular benefits and
favours which he so often and so amply hath showed both towards me and mine . . . but also and most chiefly even in
regard of his public merit both towards his Majesty and this
Commonwealth. Wherein when I behold the heavy weight of
so many grave and great affairs which the special duty of his
place as principal secretary doth daily and necessarily cast upon
him, and do note withal what infinite cares, crosses, labours, and
travails both of body and mind he doth thereby continually
sustain and undergo ; and, lastly, do see with how great dexterity, sincerity, and judgment he doth accomplish, and perform
the painful service of that place, these divine virtues of his so
incessantly exercised and employed for the good of the public . . .
have made me long since so greatly to love, honour, and esteem
him . . . that I do daily and heartily pray unto Almighty God
to continue all strength and ability both of body and mind in
him that he sink not under the weight of so heavy a burden. . . .
Thus I have faithfully set down in some sort the noble parts
of this honourable Earl who, besides such his worthiness and
sufficiency for the public service of his sovereign and country, is
also framed of so sweet a nature, so full of mildness, courtesy,
honest mirth, bounty, kindness, gratitude, and good discourse,
so easily reconciled to his foe and enemies, so true unto his
friends, that [1] I may justly say it were one of the choicest felicities
that in this world we can possess to live, converse, and spend
our whole life in mutual love and friendship with such an one.
Of whose excellent virtues and sweet conditions so well known
to me in respect of so long communication by so many years in
most true love and friendship together, I am desirous to leave
some faithful remembrance with my last will and testament,
that since the living speech of my tongue when I am gone from
here then ceases and speaks no more, that yet the living speech
of my pen which never dieth, may herein thus for ever truly
testify and declare the same." [2]

Nor were the meaning and claims of friendship
realities of which Salisbury only became conscious
when the world had turned to vanity. The same
delicate hand, which was at such pains to raise a
lasting memorial to his fidelity, had so early as 1595

[1] 'As.'   [2] The will is at Somerset House.

had occasion to acknowledge his worth in the fullest and most affectionate terms.[1] It was not merely that he gave of his abundance, and that his manner was courteous and obliging. These things we should expect to find in one towards whom Fortune had been so lavish. But it was that, as Fulke Greville put it, " your kindness to your friends is a living kindness and works diligently upon itself for their good."[2] We are made sensible of that in his letters to Gray[3] and Carew[4]; by casual shreds of correspondence, such as the grateful thanks he receives for a letter of condolence to one who had not looked for it;[5] or again, in the bold defence which, if Weldon (for once his friend) can be trusted, he made before King James on behalf of Sir Robert Mansell. That last affair deserves something more than a passing allusion. Northampton had accused an admirable public servant of embezzling £14,000, of which considerable misappropriation all that could be proved against him, after seven years' search, was the receipt by his servant of one pair of silk stockings for a New Year's gift. James was apparently resolved in his own mind that so great a smoke could not have been kindled by so small a fire, and persisted in believing the accusation. Then " the Earl of Salisbury kneeled down and said, ' Sir, if you will suffer malice so far to prevail as to have your honest servants traduced to satisfy the humours of any, I beseech you take my staff, for were myself and the Earl of Worcester here present put in the balance against Sir Robert Mansell, we should prove too light. I am in a great place and cannot say but by myself, or servants, I may fail ; yet not with our wills ; therefore, Sir, if you will

---

[1] Hatf. Cal., v. p. 312.
[2] *Ibid.*, vii. p. 217. Cp. Hatf. MSS., 100/151.
[3] Hatf. MSS., 187/30 and 99/149.
[4] *Letters of Cecil to Carew*, Camden Soc., pp. 10, 88.
[5] S. P. Dom. Eliz., Add., 33/86.

suffer such inquisitions there will be no serving your
Majesty in such place as I hold, by your Majesty's
favour.' " [1] Salisbury did even more for Coke than
he did for Mansell. When James was literally clench-
ing his fists with rage at the Chief Justice's assertion
of the Common Law, and that dignitary was literally
crouching ' flat on all fours ' before his Sovereign,
he had the courage to draw the blast of the King's
anger upon himself.[2] And if Majesty were not
august one might wish that so prodigious a scene
had found a painter.

Friendship has its problems ; and these are never
more insistent than when a man has come to great
place. Salisbury states, with perfect frankness, the
canon by which he himself was guided in the distribution of patronage. " The true rule is," he writes to
the Prince of Wales, " to prefer friends, except in
cases where just cause appeareth to the contrary." [3]
There can be little doubt that, provided our critical
faculty is not lulled to sleep by affection, this is the true
rule. The more intimately we know a man the more
deeply are we acquainted with his qualities and
defects. And Salisbury, so far as can be learned,
applied his precept with all discretion. " I have had
the honour, my Lord, to know you long," Lord Grey
wrote to him, " and while I was in place, I studied
you more than man that lived, yet never found you
forward to blow your friends with unseasonable
hopes, nor faint in prosecution of your own en-
couragements." [4]

For the rest, no claims of friendship were permitted to set aside the claims of justice. One of his
servants, who gave him pleasure by virtue of a talent
for music, had abducted a young ' gentlewoman ' ;

[1] *Secret Hist. of the Court of James I.*, i. p. 334.
[2] Hatf. MSS., 125/36, February 1609. Boswell to Milborne.
[3] Birch, *Life of Henry, Prince of Wales*, p. 129.
[4] Hatf. MSS., 106/119, 120.

and Hicks apparently invited him to interfere in the
man's favour. " Sir," he replied, " I hate the fact
so much to steal away any man's child that [1] I am
sorry it is not death by the law, seeing he that cuts
my purse with fourteen pence shall be hanged. I
am a Master of Wards, I am a Counsellor of State, and
in my private conscience opposite to all fraud. If
now I favour him, it will both confirm in the world
(as it doth in me) that he would not have offered it,
but in hope of my protection to bear him out ; in
which I will deceive whosoever shall most believe it,
and for mine own part mean to be no broker in their
bawderies. To yourself I say no more than I have
said to greater persons." [2]

Outside the sphere of personal intimacy there were
many who yet had cause to call him friend. One
significant letter, acknowledging some unknown
kindness, preserves perhaps the memory of many
silent charities :—" My Lord, I beseech you accept of
the poor widow's mite from her that desires to do you
services. I have had many good words from sundry
great persons, only deeds from your Lordship." [3]

Towards those who were poor in a more literal
sense than the writer of the letter, Salisbury displayed
the kind of thoughtfulness that his position required.
We hear of what the Bishop of Lincoln calls ' a truly
Christian provision ' [4] for the poor of Hatfield to be
instructed in the art of weaving and kindred employ-
ments ; [5] of a foundation in the parish of Cheston for
teaching pin-making to forty poor boys ; [6] and of
an almshouse for ten poor soldiers at Hoddesdon.[7]
Gifts to the poor, though certainly of no extravagant amount, figure in his return of expenditure ;
and we learn from more than one source that in his

---

[1] In the original, ' as.'   [2] Lansdowne MSS., 90/69.
[3] Hatf. MSS., 106/45.   From Lady Mary Wingfield.
[4] S. P. Dom., Jas. I., 44/84.   [5] Ibid., 38/71, 72, 73.
[6] Hatf. MSS., 115/31.   [7] Ibid., 192/81.

public capacity he took steps to enable the poor to
buy food cheap in time of dearth.[1] According to the
ideas and facilities of the time, this may have seemed,
and have been, a full discharge of his duty towards less
fortunate persons than himself. But at the end—at
Bath and in his will—there is the suggestion of a
stronger regard for these, the best friends a man can
have as he approaches the eternal habitations.

Yet it would be over-bold to affirm that he enjoyed any particular popularity with his poorer neighbours ; and the enclosure of Hatfield Wood, though
it appears to have been effected quite regularly with
the consent of the cottagers concerned,[2] was not calculated to raise him in local esteem. The distich—

> " Not Robin Goodfellow, nor Robin Hood,
>   But Robin the encloser of Hatfield Wood."

quite possibly preserves the general feeling about him
in the adjacent part of the county.

It was fortunate, indeed, for him that he lived in an
age when a man might rise to great place without ever
having to expose himself on a platform. No one was
ever worse fitted than he to please or impress the mob.
His figure was not merely deformed—the result of a
fall from his nurse's arms [3]—but very short, being,
according to one not contemporary account, no more
than five feet three inches in height ; [4] and even in the
height of his power he had to submit, as he did very
good-naturedly, to be ridiculed on his diminutive
size. When he was seated, however, this superficial

---

[1] See Harl. MSS., 36, p. 394, Wm. Turneur's Character of Salis-
bury. He was, however, repaid £385, 4s. 7d. in 1608-9 by the
Exchequer " for meal and corn sold to the poor at an under-rate "
(Hatf. MSS., Accts., 160/1).

[2] S. P. Dom., Jas. I., 63/88.

[3] Mayerne's diagnosis. See Ellis, *Letters on Engl. Hist.*, ser. ii.
vol. iii. p. 246.

[4] Hatf. House Catalogue of Pictures (compiled by Lawrence
Holland). I have, I think, seen the contemporary authority for this
statement.

impression would pass away and disclose that ' sweet
and grave presence ' about which one chronicler
makes the quaint suggestion that it was "as if Nature,
understanding how good a counsellor he would make,
gave him no more lovely of person anywhere else of
purpose, because it should not remove him into
action." [1] It was then that the observer had an
opportunity of realising his rare power of expression—
' that dexterity of cleverness ' which made his words
at once ' sweet to a curious ear and easy to a common.' [1]
His touch, so far as one can guess, was far lighter and
more whimsical than Burghley's. And we know that
the matter of his conversation did not fall behind
the manner. " He was sufficiently learned for his
calling, and learning appeared the more in himself
because he loved it in another man." [2] There is
evidence of a fertile curiosity in the résumé which,
Strype [3] tells us, he made of Dr. Dee's criticism of the
prevailing Julian Calendar on lines even more severely
correct than those which had prompted the introduction of the Gregorian, and again in Timothe
Bright's selection of him, when quite young, as the
most promising patron for that remarkable man's new
invention of shorthand. [4] Naunton's description of
him as " our great Mæcenas " [5] suffers, it is true,
from the fact that Ben Jonson—the only great man
of letters, [6] with the obvious exceptions of Bacon and
Ralegh, whom we know for certain that he ever came
across—complained of being insulted whilst dining at
his table. The hot-tempered dramatist's blunt retort,
on being taxed with showing a sad countenance—
" My Lord, you promised I should dine with you, but

[1] Turneur's Character of Salisbury, Harl. MSS., 36, p. 394.
[2] Ibid.
[3] Strype, Ann. (ed. 1824), ii. p. 527.
[4] W. J. Carlton, Timothe Bright, pp. 64–8. The date of the
appeal to Cecil was 1586 or 1587.
[5] Hatf. MSS., 133/144.
[6] I am not reckoning Lyly or Hakluyt as such.

ROBERT, FIRST EARL OF SALISBURY

(Painted by Marc Gheeraedts the Younger. Hatfield House)

[*To face p.* 380

Salisbury's tenure of the Chancellorship of Cambridge University, inadequate for the work as he felt his leisure to be,[1] really promoted the advance of learning. What we know for certain is that he became the referee of sundry disputes amongst learned men, which it would be as unprofitable as it would be tedious to recount.[2] For the rest he took a survey of religious opinion in the University, which disclosed so large a preponderance of Anglicans over Puritans as to excite Bishop Montagu to wish him on the Episcopal-Bench so as to bring about a like conformity in the Church of England.[3]

But his work at Cambridge, whatever its merit or demerit, has left no notable traces. Historians, on the other hand, are bound to him by a lasting and visible obligation. He it was who consolidated the shadowy institution of the State-Paper Office, established in 1578, into a living collection of national records located in the Palace of Whitehall and placed under the direction of two of our passing acquaintance —Levinus Munck and Thomas Wilson.[4]

Outside his official despatches, Salisbury wrote little, and that little contained nothing of much consequence. His little treatise on " The State and Dignity of a Secretary's Place " does not seem to the present writer to contain anything worthy of citation. There is attributed to him, besides, an essay " On the State of the Scottish Commonwealth "[5] and a " Dia-

---

[1] S. P. Dom., Eliz. and Jas. I., Add., 34/51. Salisbury was High Steward of the University for nine years before he became Chancellor in 1601.

[2] There were disputes at Caius College. References to it will be found in Hatf. MSS., 121/165 and 136/159, 163, 183; and at Bennett College (Hatf. MSS., 136/167, 168).

[3] Hatf. MSS., 103/130, 131.   [4] Introd. to vol. i. of the Hatf. Cal.

[5] This was (H.M. C. Rep., i. App.) in the Hatton Collection. Since that Report was issued the collection has been divided, and part of it is now in the British Museum, part in the possession of Lord Winchilsea and Nottingham. I am unable to find the MS. in the British Museum; and Lord Winchilsea writes to me to say that he would gladly place it at my disposal, but that he cannot at present identify it.

I do not ! " [1]—still bears awful witness against him,
after three hundred years, for a breach of tact or
manners probably too common even to have occupied his attention.   For host and guest were in
fact being served from separate dishes.   But to like
letters and to like men of letters are in fact very
different things.   And Salisbury, though he probably
regarded literature rather as a means to an end than
as an end in itself, was certainly not indifferent to
its study.   His particular additions to the family
library, now at Hatfield, are not, indeed, as numerous
or as recondite as those of Burghley, but they show a
sufficient disposition towards solid reading.   Natalis'
Adnotationes et Meditationes in Evangelia, a *Trésor des
Morales de Plutarch*, Rosières' *Stemmatum Lotharin-
giæ ac Barri Ducum*, Setonus' *Dialectica*, Strigelius'
Ethica, Ubaldino's *Lo Stato delle Tre Corti*, Vigenère's
Traicte des Chiffres — some of them perhaps books
he had been educated upon—do not suggest a leisure
devoted, at any rate, to idle tales.   From a
letter to his son [2] we know that he regarded Latin,
French, and Logic as the prime elements in a gentleman's education.   Of these he places the last first,
though he is free from any subservience to formal
logic, the end in view being ' not to speak of logic,
but to speak logically.' [2]   French we know that he
talked well enough ; [3] and his letters and speeches show
that the phrases and wisdom of the Latins mingled
easily with his criticism of passing events.   From
Oxford there came an echo of Naunton's praise—an
assurance that the Muses of the Isis had been fed also
from the abundance of their sisters on the Granta.[4]
We may hope that this was no academic dream ; that

[1] *Notes on Ben Jonson's Conversations with Drummond of Haw-
thornden.*
[2] Hatf. MSS., 228/28.
[3] Barozzi and Berchet, *Relazioni, Inghilterra*, i. p. 60.
[4] Hatf. MSS., 120/39.

logue between Two Friends, Servants to His Majesty,"
which turns upon the differences between himself
and Carr, but is plainly by another hand.[1] He also
wrote an ' elegant ' Latin treatise, no longer extant,
against traitors (" Adversus Perduelles ") ; [2] persons
about whom there cannot have been much left to say
at a time when Coke had fully exhausted the vitu-
perative, and Shakespeare was rapidly exhausting
the imaginative aspect of the subject.

Study, then, was, in all probability, the principal
resource of Salisbury's leisure. He esteemed books,
so he told a correspondent, ' more than gold.' [3]
But he had other tastes—a love of music, of which
there is more than one proof ; [4] a desire for ' ancient
masterpieces of painting ' ; [5] and an effective desire
for precious stones.[6] These are, however, the seden-
tary affections of a delicate man. There had been
a time when his pulses had beaten more quickly.
In 1595, on a September evening, he went hawking
with Queen Elizabeth and bagged three partridges ; [7]
in 1600 he is charged £3, 10s. for a crossbow,[8] which
was doubtless directed against certain ' flying tame
fowl ' supplied expressly for him to be able to take
his pleasures in the winter of 1602 ; [9] and in 1603
he expresses him willing to pay a long price for a river-
hawk that will fly high.[10] This, however, exhausts
the list of his athletic exercises, unless, indeed, we make

---

[1] H.M. C. Rep., i. Harvey MSS., Ickwellbury. I have seen and
read the original.

[2] *Secret Hist. of the Court of Jas. I.*, p. 148, and Lloyd's *Worthies : Sir
R. Cecil.*

[3] Hatf. Cal., ix. p. 8.

[4] Lansdowne MSS., 90/69. Hatf. MSS., 125/111. Hatf. Cal., vi.
p. 68.

[5] S. P. Dom., Jas. i., 61/33.   [6] *Ibid.*, 26/27.   Hatf. MSS., 121/64.

[7] H.M. C. Rep., vii. Molyneux MSS., p. 654. Cp. Hatf. Cal., vii.
p. 150.

[8] Hatf. Estate Papers, Accts., 6/12.

[9] Hatf. Cal., xii. p. 221.

[10] Lodge, *Illustr. of Brit. Hist.*, iii. p 39.

him into something of a swordsman on the strength
of a curious story, told by Donne,[1] to the effect that
about 1605, after a petty squabble, he sent Hertford
a challenge, and was actually on his way to the encounter when he was stopped by the King's orders.
But his office and Hertford's age, the absence of any
contemporary allusion to a quarrel which would have
set all tongues wagging, and the known good relations
between the two families implicated, both before and
after the alleged event, to say nothing of Salisbury's
generally unaggressive demeanour, reduce the affair
to a legend, which one is bound to mention and at
liberty to reject.

Communications with the animal world can be
kept open by other means than that of slaughter and
by other methods than that of physical exercise.
Salisbury bred horses,[2] and stocked his park with
deer,[3] and manifested a really vigorous interest in the
matrimonial and maternal affairs of the lioness at the
Tower.[4] But when all has been said, all does not
come to very much ; and it is a nice point to decide
whether Burghley or his younger son was the more
deficient in all those branches of human energy which
we assemble together under the broad title of a love
of sport—the former addicted as he was to ambling
round his garden on a mule, the latter apparently
more reliant on his legs, yet exciting anxious fears
in Lord Shrewsbury's mind that he might thereby
have contracted ' an aching of the heels.'[5] It is
some little consolation to remember that in the time
in which he lived such matters were still no more
than ' toys.'

---

[1] Donne's *Letters* (ed. 1651), pp. 214, 215. Jessopp makes this letter
1609. I do not know why. The allusion to Hertford's Embassy
would make it 1605.

[2] Hatf. Cal., x. p. 148.   [3] Lansdowne MSS., 87/66.

[4] Hatf. MSS., 111/146, 157. The lioness, we are told, would bite
the lion if he remained away longer than she liked.

[5] S. P. Dom., Jas. I., 57/56.

He might, perhaps, have taken more physical exercise if he had enjoyed better health. Or we may turn the argument round, and say that he would have enjoyed better health if he had taken more physical exercise. But at best he was clearly a man of low vitality. Mayerne's elaborate diagnosis [1] discloses certain bodily infirmities which not a few of his descendants would read of with sympathetic understanding if it were proper to translate them out of the Latin tongue. For the rest his appetite, the physician noted, was better than his digestion. He liked fruit, especially early cherries and grapes ; the latter, so Mayerne declares, always injurious. Wine he neither cared for nor commonly drank ; excepting a mouthful of Spanish wine taken as a stomachic. Ale he took between meals, with something of the same idea. Fish he did not touch ; but he was fond of salted beef, though not generally of edibles seasoned with salt or pepper. There we may take leave of these trivialities. They serve to round off the picture, and are, besides, of some natural interest to beings who take such grave and frequent counsel about diet as ourselves.

.   .   .   .

Such a man, then, was Robert Cecil in his relations with God, and with his friends and his family, and with the poor ; in his abilities and disabilities, in his temperament and in his tastes ; in those things whereby men are tried and wherein they make manifest their dispositions—so far, that is, as one of his descendants has been able to disinter the memorials of him from among a mass of manuscripts and at a distance of three hundred years. Biography at such a disadvantage is as a piece of crystal-gazing. We peer into obscurity, wondering what we shall see, or if we

[1] A convenient Latin abstract may be seen in Ellis' *Original Letters*, ser. ii. vol. iii. p. 246. I do not advise the reader who is not a physician to grapple with the diagnosis in Mayerne's *Opera Medica*.

shall be able to see anything at all. Gradually the haze parts. A figure forms upon the surface of the crystal and grows into ever sharper outline as we look. We tell others what we perceive, asking them to accept our impressions as their own. But at the end, when the cloud has closed down again, we ask ourselves in what relation the vision stood to reality, whether it has been baseless fabric or eternal truth, whether that which we thought we saw conveys that which we desired to learn ; or whether, after all, the mind has been the dupe of the imagination, or the dupe of things less pleasing than the imagination—of idle tales, of fond fancies, of the incredible absurdities that men believe of one another, or of the equally incredible hypocrisies that they sometimes practise upon one another with success. When all is said and done, we have to admit that we have been in an alchemist's chamber, seeking to learn secrets which we cannot really come at. A man's character, we say in our wiser moments, is known only to himself and to God.

The character of Robert Cecil, as it has been drawn in the preceding pages, is, on the whole, of a more favourable complexion than the estimates of him that are commonly given. He has not indeed been presented as a saint or as a sage ; but it has been argued on his behalf that he was, doubtless with more qualifications than we are aware of, both a good and a wise man. Such a view, whether it is or is not the true one, is at least no mere piece of historical idealisation. There were men like Buckhurst and Cope, who, with a knowledge of the facts to which we cannot now pretend, would have approved and endorsed it. And if there are any charities in history, we may hardly reject favourable contemporary opinion, unless the facts force us to an opposite conclusion.

At whatever loss the historical biographer may be in determining a man's character, he possesses at least every possible advantage in estimating a man's

career. There ought to be no difficulty at all in fixing
Salisbury's place in history, with a great gulf of three
hundred years already fixed between his day and
ours. Perspective has come. Prejudice and passion
have almost wholly passed away. Issues, even
though with new faces they present themselves
again and again at the bar of opinion, have changed
out of easy recognition. New statesmen have established new standards of policy and service. We can,
if we will, see the statesmanship of the seventeenth
century steadily and see it whole.

It is clear at a glance that Salisbury does not
take rank amongst the greatest rulers—with Henry v.,
for example, or Elizabeth, or Chatham ; with those
few who have had the will and the presence and the
inspiration to weld men together and spur them on
to do the actions that become as household words.
Such things were quite beyond his reach. He
achieved his ends diplomatically, by a skilful calculation and nice handling of the common forces that
move mankind. Lacking any kind of inspiration,
he not unnaturally lacked also—and this was, perhaps,
the most serious of all his defects—the capacity to
attract and make use of other men's labour. Perhaps he distrusted mankind too much ; perhaps his
natural reserve presented an insurmountable barrier ;
perhaps he had to the full that fatal dislike of seeing
things done rather differently or rather worse than he
would have done them himself. At any rate, he en-
grossed more and more the whole burden of government until he had incensed others and exhausted himself. But the greatness that is from above neither
excites envy, nor fears assistance, nor spends itself
idly upon detail.

He falls, then, into the second class of statesmen,
amongst those of whom Walpole might be taken for
the type, amongst men of good sense, efficiency, and
talent falling somewhat short of genius. There are

some who will think that this is still to place him too
high. They will urge, and urge with perfect truth,
that he was never proved in the fires of adversity ; that
he was born, so to say, in the purple ; that his great
position was rather a legacy he had inherited than a
fortune he had made. But, though this is the case,
the fact that he held his post for fourteen years,
unsheltered by his father's shadow, and unsupported,
as Somerset was and as Buckingham was, by the
capricious predilections of the King, is a sufficient
proof of his fitness to occupy it. He never fell, and in
all likelihood he never would have fallen, because, as
Naunton quaintly observes, " his little crooked person
. . . carried . . . a headpiece of a vast content."
He was as wise a man as could be looked for, and
probably as wise a man as could be found to accomplish the particular work he had to do. Like Walpole
and like William III., he was required to establish a
dynasty, and like them he did his business with an
unassuming but unfaltering perseverance. It was no
fault of his that the dynasty which he introduced
proved the most undesirable that the country has ever
known. He had, in 1602, not to call up the spirits
of the past to read the riddles of the future, but to
consider how he might avoid a war of succession, such
as in his own day devastated France and such as was
to devastate Spain a hundred years later. He did
avoid it. There was not even the ghost of a pretender,
as had been the case at Queen Mary's accession just
fifty years before and, as many people thought, there
must be again. And, if Prince Henry had chanced
to live, the world might even now be blessing the skill
and wisdom which established the Stuarts.

It is of a piece with the idea that Salisbury was
nothing but his father's nominee to regard him as the
slave of his father's policy. He stood, no doubt, for
much the same principles as had guided Burghley's
statesmanship, but they are principles with which it

is hard to quarrel. His diplomacy, like his predecessor's, was directed towards a peace resting upon
the old alliance of England with the Low Countries,
and stands out, as Burghley's did, in contrast to the
martial but premature imperialism of Essex and
Ralegh. National liberty had but just been vindicated, at the cost of a long and exhausting struggle.
We can hardly blame him for want of originality,
because he did not plunge the country into a policy
of rapid expansion ; and all the less since, as it
chanced, the first fruitful seeds of Empire were sown
by Smith and watered by De la Warr during the very
time that he was piloting the ship of State.

Again, at home he held, no doubt, by the theory of
the Constitution that he had received. He believed
in monarchy ; he believed in English gentlemen ;
he believed in the doctrines of degree and order and
obedience which breathe in the then recent Church
Catechism and still more recent " Ecclesiastical Polity."
" I have no fear of men of worth," he told the Star
Chamber in 1599. " When has England felt any harm
by soldiers or gentlemen or men of worth ? The
State has ever found them truest. Some Jack Cade,
or Jack Straw, and such rascals are those that have
endangered the kingdom." [1]   " I shall never forget,"
says Lloyd, " his or his father's discourse with Claud
Grollart, premier president of Rouen, about the
troubles in France, wherein he advised him to stick
to the King though he saw difficulties ; for it was his
maxim that ' kings are like the sun, and usurpers
like falling stars.' For the sun, though it be obfus-
cated and eclipsed with mists and clouds, at length
they are dispersed, where the others are but the
figures of stars in the eyes of view and prove no more
but exhalations which suddenly dissolve and fall to
the earth where they are consumed." [2]

[1] S. P. Dom., Eliz., 273/37.
[2] Lloyd, *State Worthies, Observ. on the Life of Sir Robert Cecil.*

Such opinions, even now that Rousseau has been at work a hundred years and more, are not unknown, or undefended, or incapable of defence. In Salisbury's time they were the natural convictions of every astute and experienced student of human nature :—

> "Degree being visarded
> The unworthiest shows as fairly in the mask.
> The heavens themselves, the planets and this centre
> Observe degree, priority and place
> Insisture, course, proportion, season, form,
> Office and custom, in all line of order.
> And therefore is the glorious planet, Sol,
> In noble eminence enthron'd and spher'd
> Amidst the other. . . ."

We need not pause to amplify that famous text, or to discuss its merits. All that we need to remember is that the conservatism with which it rings had not as yet become a matter of serious debate ; and consequently that to make originality the touchstone of the men of the seventeenth century is to put them to a test by which they cannot with any propriety be tried. They had, for better or worse, no golden visions of the future ; and legislation was therefore an incident rather than the principal of their work, dependent in the main, as we see in the most important of Salisbury's measures—the repressive laws directed against the Catholics—upon the practical exigencies of administration. Their care was to carry on the King's Government with efficiency, with security, without agitation. Continuity, not ' progress,' thus became dominant among political virtues ; and Salisbury would probably have supposed that he had earned the highest praise in accomplishing his father's policy. For men can only yield an active and fruitful obedience when government is conducted on consistent and well-understood lines. " Depuis longtemps," said Frederick the Great,[1] crystallising that thought

[1] Edgcumbe, *Lady Shelley's Diary*, vol. ii.

into an audacious paradox, " je suis convaincu qu'un mal qui reste vaut mieux qu'un bien qui change."

Such a general similarity, then, as is to be found between the policy of Burghley and his successor was engendered rather by the problems and conceptions of the age than by any particular similarity in their own characters. Their aims and methods were such as would have been adopted and approved by the moderate men of all centuries. And, if we fail to find there the dramatic strokes and civic visions which constitute the statesmanship of public fancy and public applause, we may console ourselves with the dictum of an acute observer that " what was not done, easily escapes notice ; and yet the masterpieces of the statesman's art are for the most part not acts but abstinence from action."[1] We know, at least, that Salisbury sought to give his country ' peace with honour,' since the phrase, which has become permanently associated with the policy of his descendant, was, in fact, his own.[2] And history tells of no loftier, no more comprehensive ideal.

It is an observation of Brewer's that Burghley and his successor had, perhaps, more grave and knotty problems to resolve than any in history.[3] Whether or not we regard this as a piece of affectionate exaggeration it is at least certain that the two men found their way through a remarkably tangled skein of difficulties. Salisbury did not, it is true, settle the financial issue between King and Parliament, which was to rage for half a century and to open all the flood-gates of the Constitution. But he came so near to effecting a working agreement, and he exhibited so markedly throughout the negotiations that quality of patience which Pitt was presently to declare the most valuable of all qualities to the

---

[1] Seeley, *Growth of British Policy*, ii. p. 324.
[2] Birch, *View of the Negotiations*, p. 121.
[3] *English Studies*, p. 127.

statesman, that his failure lies upon the borderland
of success. Another attempt under another king and,
for all we can say, he might have succeeded.

It is a last tempting speculation to inquire whether
the father or the son was really the abler man of the
two. Tempting, but also idle! For they did kindred
work under essentially different conditions. We shall
never know exactly what was of Elizabeth and what
was of Burghley in the fruits of that wonderful combination ; we can never say what either might have
been without the counsel of the other. All that we
have to go upon is Burghley's own statement that the
Queen saw further than any of her ministers. With
Salisbury it is different. From the time of his father's
death up to the very end he stands alone. Elizabeth
was aging when he came into power ; James was a
fool, and an idle fool to boot. Whatever credit there
is to be given is almost certainly his to have. And
here lies the answer to that half-contemptuous judgment of Bacon's which has been taken for a just
measure of his abilities. " I do think," his cousin told
the King, " he was no fit counsellor to make your
affairs better ; but yet he was fit to have kept them
from getting worse." [1] James himself knew better
than that. Early in his reign he had told Hume that
of all the men he had ever known Salisbury was the
best fitted to be a counsellor in all matters of State.[2]
Bacon's epigram was a half-truth, and as damaging
as most half-truths are. Salisbury certainly could do
little to mend his master's fortunes. No more could
anyone else. For James himself was the root of
the evil. If we seek the true measure of Salisbury's
abilities we shall find it in the later passages of James's
reign, when national finance fell into increasing confusion, and British foreign-policy became a laughing-
stock, and Parliament passed altogether out of hand.

[1] Spedding, *Letters and Life of Francis Bacon*, iv. p. 278, note.
[2] Hatf. Papers, 108/115.

We might even go further and say that of all the ministers of the Stuarts, with the possible exception of Clarendon, he was the only one who secured to the English people their proper place in the counsels and the consideration of Western Europe. So volatile and elusive a thing is that which we call national prestige !

Sagacious and pacific and patient, the pilot of his country through one of the great crises of her history, Robert Cecil deserves, then, some modest remembrance amongst English statesmen. He was great, as his father was great, not with the shining splendour which sets all the fires of the imagination aflame, but with that tenacious wisdom which also accomplishes great things, and of which also, in our more sober moods, we do well to take account. To his countrymen he has left the example of an untiring industry subduing the languors of a frail and feeble body. But to his family he transmitted, undimmed and unimpaired, a more intimate tradition of public service. For over two centuries that priceless inheritance scarcely seemed to stir the sluggish motions of the blood. Then, beneath another Queen and in an England changed out of all recognition, it woke to new and pregnant life once more.

BIBLIOGRAPHY

THERE is no large work devoted to Salisbury. The following account of the printed matter directly relating to him contains as complete a list as I have been able to accumulate.

Courtenay's essay upon him, among the lives of " Eminent British Statesmen " in Lardner's *Cabinet Cyclopædia*, though written in 1838, and in some points, of course, completely out of date, is still easily the best and most readable account of him. Next, perhaps, comes Jessopp's slightly inaccurate and not very well-informed sketch in the *Dictionary of National Biography*. Then there are some chapters devoted to him in Mr. Ravenscroft Dennis' *House of Cecil*, published in 1914 ; and two articles by James Emilius Viscount Cranborne (d. 1865), included amongst that author's historical essays. An American, named Victor G. A. Tressler, has written in German, under the title of *Sir Robert Cecil*, a most industrious but not very illuminating account of Salisbury's career between 1563 and 1598 (Leipzig, 1901). Besides these there is the old sketch in Collins' *Peerage* and the older one among Lloyd's *State Worthies*. Naunton's little notice of him in the *Fragmenta Regalia* is, of course, by a contemporary, as is the anonymous *Remembrance of the Honours due to the Life and Death of Robert, Earl of Salisbury* (1612). The " Character of Salisbury," attributed to Wotton by Pearsall Smith (*Life and Letters of Sir H. Wotton*, vol. ii. App. 4, p. 13) is not, in fact, by Wotton but by one Turneur, and is to be found among the Harl.

MSS. It may, however, be regarded as a contemporary authority.

Some mention, though the article is upon Hatfield House and not upon Salisbury, ought also to be made of Brewer's sketch in the *Quarterly Review* (vol. cxli. No. 281).

I need scarcely add that the reader will find numerous other authorities of an indirect character cited in the footnotes.

The general history of the period may be read in Pollard, *Political History of England*, 1547–1603; Trevelyan's *England under the Stuarts*; Gardiner's *History of England*, vols. i. and ii. ; and in Cheyney's as yet incomplete *History of England from the Defeat of the Armada to the Death of Elizabeth.*

INDEX

[Salisbury's contemporaries in the peerage are noticed under the titles they had in the year of his death (1612). The same rule applies to their eldest sons, bearing courtesy titles.]